Issues in Human Rights

Edited by

Azizur Rahman Chowdhury
Md. Jahid Hossain Bhuiyan
Shawkat Alam

ATLANTIC
PUBLISHERS & DISTRIBUTORS (P) LTD

Published by
ATLANTIC
PUBLISHERS & DISTRIBUTORS (P) LTD
7/22, Ansari Road, Darya Ganj,
New Delhi-110002
Phones : +91-11-40775252, 23273880, 23275880, 23280451
Fax : +91-11-23285873
Web : www.atlanticbooks.com
E-mail : info@atlanticbooks.com
Branch Office
5, Nallathambi Street, Wallajah Road,
Chennai-600002
Phones : +91-44-64611085, 32413319
E-mail : chennai@atlanticbooks.com

ISBN 978-81-269-1333-6

Printed in India at Glorious Printers, A-13, D.S.I.D.C, Jhilmil Industrial Area, Delhi-110095

Acknowledgements

We are profoundly grateful to the following for their valuable suggestions and assistance: Dr. Sarkar Ali Akkas, Associate Professor, Department of Law and Justice, Rajshahi University, Bangladesh (now Head, Department of Law, Daffodil International University, Bangladesh); Prof. Dr. M. Shah Alam, Department of Law, Chittagong University, Bangladesh; Prof. Dr. M. Badaruddin, Ex-Dean, Faculty of Law and Justice, Rajshahi University, Bangladesh (now Chairman, Department of Law, Premier University, Bangladesh); Dr. Nirmal Kanti Chakrabarti, Reader and Former Head of the Department of Law, Calcutta University, India; Prof. Dr. Muhammad Faiz-ud-Din, Department of Law and Justice, Rajshahi University, Bangladesh; Dr. Abdullah Al Faruque, Associate Professor and Chairman, Department of Law, Chittagong University, Bangladesh; Dr. M. Abdul Hannan, Associate Professor, Department of Law and Justice, Rajshahi University, Bangladesh; Professor Dr. M. Rabiul Hossain, Chairman, Department of Law and Justice, Rajshahi University, Bangladesh; Prof. Dr. J.L. Kaul, Faculty of Law, University of Delhi, India; Dr. Md. Abdul Karim Khan, Associate Professor, Department of Law and Muslim Jurisprudence, Islamic University, Bangladesh; Prof. Dr. M. Habibur Rahman, Department of Law and Justice, Rajshahi University, Bangladesh; Prof. Dr. Begum Asma Siddiqua, Dean,

Faculty of Law, Rajshahi University, Bangladesh; and Prof. Dr. Ranbir Singh, Vice-Chancellor, NALSAR University of Law, India.

We are deeply indebted to Dr. V. Seshaiah Shastri, Associate Professor and Acting Dean, Faculty of Law, National Law University, India. He is an inspirational friend who lends us a hand whenever we need help.

Azizur Rahman Chowdhury
Md. Jahid Hossain Bhuiyan
Shawkat Alam

Preface

Ever since the adoption of Universal Declaration of Human Rights on 10 December 1948, the world community has passed through a long journey towards the fulfilment of the objectives of the Declaration. Human Rights which had once been a myth in the ancient world, are no longer so, mainly because of the infinite urge of mankind to create an awareness for the global protection of Human Rights. The caravan is still on its way and glitterings of the rays of hope and peace for mankind are reflecting ahead. In context of the present world situation, the nucleus of peace, solidarity and better governance is embodied in the widespread dissemination, practice and protection of Human Rights in the states of the world. So far the developed states have made great strides in the development of Human Rights through laudable enactments and ratification of the international conventions, declarations, covenants and treaties. To a modern man, Human Rights gossip of the past is a reality now. The states in utter violation of Human Rights can hardly make any progress towards establishment of a democratic world. True that there are violations of Human Rights in many spheres in the international arena, and that Human Rights have been denied in the face of protest, nevertheless the eternal message of Human Rights cannot be paralyzed for ever, nor can the unflinching faith of mankind be effaced because of these violations.

With this end in view we have ventured to publish this anthology of Human Rights issues in order to accentuate the knowledge and development of Human Rights activities throughout the world as a panacea for the protection and enforcement of Human Rights against all violations. We hope the anthology will find support of teachers, students, lawyers, judges, scholars, Human Rights activists, philanthropists and common people from all walks of life.

We express our heartfelt gratitude to the scholars who have contributed their scholarly papers to this book. We extend our sincere thanks to Atlantic Publishers and Distributors (P) Ltd for extending their valuable help in making this project a success.

Azizur Rahman Chowdhury
Md. Jahid Hossain Bhuiyan
Shawkat Alam

Contents

1

Promotion, Protection and Enforcement of Human Rights: An Introduction to the Issues

Azizur Rahman Chowdhury,
Md. Jahid Hossain Bhuiyan and *Shawkat Alam*

Writing an introduction to a collection of essays—thoroughly researched and intricately articulated—is an extremely challenging endeavor. When the range of themes is spread across a variety of contemporary issues, and importantly, when each of the writers enjoys great academic repute and authority, the task becomes even more daunting. These essays will certainly leave a lasting impression on the emerging trends in the position and protection of Human Rights of various groups of personnel of concern and provide invaluable and most expedient directions for the progressive development of the Human Rights protection regime. Being beholden to the task of writing an introductory note to the academically enriching attempts so as to weave the garland of thought-provoking writings we seize this opportunity to be a part of the academic elite and in the realm of their Human Rights concerns.

Developments in the international Human Rights regime and mechanisms of protection have been a matter of periodical review and the subject matter of frequent debates across the world and particularly in Asia. Developments—both at the regional and international fronts—continue to influence and shape the establishment of new regimes of rights and duties, while new mechanisms of supervision, monitoring and enforcement emerge to promote and augment the effective implementation of these rights and duties. Progressive legislative, executive and judicial responses in relation to the continuing concerns of modern generations and the underlying principles of traditional systems and mechanisms require a meticulous analysis.

The Human Rights discourse, which ought to have found its central focus in every branch of jurisprudence, still remains alienated from the mainstream and finds its place only in the occasional efforts of scholars. Besides making attempts to push a Human Rights discourse to the central current of national responses, efforts have been made to bring in an interface amongst a vast variety of senior academicians and a brand new generation of young and promising researchers and scholars into the fold of expressional endeavor with a common concern to serve the cause of Human Rights education. This is especially true when, across Asia, the concerns being expressed are not limited only to the emergence of new rights but more importantly, the effective implementation of the existing Human Rights. This collection of essays will certainly fill the gap in the scholarly materials of reference in Human Rights studies, for, it introduces a reader to an invaluable experience of interfacing philosophical notions with ground realities and provides a treat of stimulation.

The present anthology, *Issues in Human Rights* comprises twenty academic writings covering issues ranging from general concern of Human Rights to administration and implementation of Human Rights, and the role of various institutions in promotion and protection of Human Rights. In addition, the articles also study the Human Rights of specific vulnerable groups, and the emerging trends of their protection.

In the writing entitled "The Significance of Fair Trial under Human Rights Law in Matters of Criminal Justice: A Case Study of the Trial of Former Iraqi Leader, Mr. Saddam Hussein" the author addresses the scope and significance of the notion of the fair trial and its importance in the context of

Human Rights connotations with the help of the much acclaimed trial of the former Iraqi President Saddam Hussein. The effort assumes special significance in light of the contemporary focus of the anthology. The author rightly says that fairness of a criminal trial is a *sine qua non* to the canons of the fundamental and jurisprudential notions of judicial administration. By keeping the vast variety of legal instruments in the background, the author advances a detailed inquiry in the present work as to the antecedents of the Iraqi war which raises questions of political expediency and non-justiciability in the trial of Saddam Hussein. Notwithstanding the trial was conducted within the corners and parameters of municipal context, the author outlines the scope of fair trial and examines the political compulsions that resulted in new dimensions of victimization of alleged criminals and puts forth a formidable question like whether it was Saddam Hussein alone who deserved to be singled out for his allegedly shocking crimes. Outlining the fundamental notions of fair trial, namely impartial and independent tribunal; competent, qualified, unbiased and neutral authorities of adjudication; and respect to the recognized and time-tested rights and notions of justice administration, the author attempts to raise a serious self-enquiry as to how the conducive environment, that otherwise determines the very character and credibility of a criminal trial, can become a casualty of compelling coalition compulsions. Arguing upon the illegitimacy of the very constitution of the special tribunal in itself, the venue set out for the trial, the indictment made out, witnesses presented and importantly, the hasty and shady manner in which the entire trial had been concluded in a record span of condensed time, the author points out a variety of slips and shortfalls of the trial. Thus, the author through a thorough and meticulous articulation of concerns and apprehensions, reminds not only the general reader but also the world at large, as to the dangerous implications of hastily concluded national trials and calls for a fresh debate as to why, despite the limitations, the age-old legal maxim that justice hurried is justice buried is too important to be ignored in the context of Human Rights jurisprudence.

In the article "The International Covenant on Civil and Political Rights and the International Covenant on Economic Social, and Cultural Rights: Their Implementation and Progress" the author refers to an important set of international legal instruments in the realm of Human Rights and advances a critical evaluation in the special context of the responses and implementation progress on the part of the States Parties often acclaimed to the instruments of codification of first and second generation Human Rights—a nomenclature as controversial as the very dichotomy itself. For this precisely, the author stakes the claim to address and attempts to resolve the so-called contrasts between the two sets of rights, which otherwise are believed to be two sides of the same coin. Banking upon the structural constructs of the two instruments, the author advances a prologue to the debate by stating that the distinct mechanisms of the two instruments are one amongst, if not the exclusive reason for different levels of implementation. In the initial phases of the analysis the author refers as to how in the wake of unwillingness of States to accept any greater obligations, keeping in mind their nationalistic and sovereignty-centred arguments, the United Nations General Assembly continued its steadfast efforts to progress from the initially but noteworthy degree of acceptances of States. Basing the argument of contrasts of the two sets of rights in the light of the researched findings from noted jurists, the author draws an inference that the alleged distinction is more ideological than of any other structural significance. To reiterate in the words of the author, what makes a State comply with these two categories of rights is not the nature of rights involved but more importantly, the availability of a system before which such violations are challenged or questioned. Thus, seeking the attention of a reader towards a fresh appreciation of the petition system contemplated under these instruments, the author poses a question to deeply ponder over by reiterating the need to understand the importance of the mechanisms on a holistic perspective.

In the article "Ecological Perspective of Right to Information: Need for Participatory Approach to Governance" the author while emphasizing the importance of right to information as an integral part of Article 19(1)(a) of the Constitution of India in implicit terms, advances the argument that courts in India, over a period of time, have ruled in favor of the need to reiterate the right in more express terms. Thus, the author brings to the forefront the background under which a whole lot of public campaign had been advanced in the Indian scenario so as to give the right to information a distinct shape, bringing the same out of the domain and influence of State administration. Keeping the background of the significance of right to information in the context of public governance, the author outlines the importance of the right in the context of public governance so as to strengthen the argument that the exchange of information must address not only the immediate concerns of State and functionaries but also the concerns of the inhabitants and persons around. Outlining the importance of exchange of information as an extremely significant aspect, the author vividly interlaces its importance from the perspective of maintaining an effective and overall ecological balance amongst various components of the environment. After reviewing a plethora of international instruments, the author draws the inference that there is a distinctly emerging trend in the international relations amongst States wherein the States are seeking more and more relevant scientific, technological, technical, socio-economic and legal information in relation to the climate system and climate changes. Referring to the interface amongst the right to information, prior informed consent and right to know, the author advances the reason as to why the relationship needs a holistic perspective. Arguing for this need from the point of view of effective public participation in the meaningful and effective environmental decision-making, the author reiterates that the governance process cannot sideline or ignore this important priority. Taking the responsibility of institutions of governance to the next important benchmark of emphasis and transparency, the author raises concerns in the mind of the reader as to how often the governments tend to collude with the interested parties and seek protection under the guise of official secrecies and that this defeats their larger social responsibility. To this extent, the author relies on a series of judicial decisions on one side and the gradually advanced efforts that have culminated in the ultimate realization of right to information, and calls for effective appreciation of its importance and for due implementation. Thus, in conclusion, drawing a parallel with the extent to which the resort to the usage of right to information was made in the United Kingdom, in the context of creation of environmental awareness, the author calls for greater and effective implementation in the Indian scenario.

In the article "Right to Education in Global Economy: Indian Perspective", the author tries to draw attention to a contemporary debate as to whether the ongoing process of globalization is in tune with the recognized norms of the international Human Rights. Reiterating the age-old and emphatic underlying notations of the Human Rights philosophy such as their inalienability and universality, the author advances an argument that in the choice of *modus operandi* to further their effective implementation and meaningful realization, one can neither lose sight of cultural relativism nor can its importance be sidelined or ignored. Advancing an argument that entitlement of basic socio-economic rights is a condition *sine qua non* for stable and democratic societies, the author raises a debate on the very efficacy of the increasing trend of commercialization of education, its short-term and long-term implications. Cautioning on the inclination towards the apparent short-term gains, the author advances the need for caution as to why systematic and step-by-step approaches are the important building blocks in leading towards the realization of the constitutional mandates. At the same time the author also seeks how education can be utilized as an important means in fine tuning the national development and reap the fruit of the very globalization, thus making the reader ponder over how and what kind of changes are important in the current system of education prevailing in India.

In the article "Human Rights and the WTO: A Critique on Compatibility" the authors not only provide a bird's eye view of the nature and scope of Human Rights but, with a critical analysis of various juristic opinions, attempt to bring out an interface of the relationship and the inherent conflict between international trade and international Human Rights regimes. The authors stress that in order to strike a balance between these two frameworks formulation of systematic mechanisms and evaluation of the normative conflicts are highly essential. With a detailed examination of the provisions of the GATT followed by those under the WTO Agreements, the authors pose the query for the reader as to why and to what extent it is important on the part of the States Parties to incorporate and weave Human Rights norms in their WTO obligations in the fulfilment of their international commitments.

In the writing titled "Human Rights of Children: A Study of the Implementation of CRC in India", the author begins with the benign benedictions on the part of Government of India in deciding to ratify the International Convention on Rights of Child, 1989. Outlining the most important dimensions thereunder, namely right to survival, right to protection, right to development and right to participation, the author reiterates the mapping process of the rights under the convention and relevant provisions under the Indian legislative scenario so as to find out to what extent the constitutional makers had cast a similar agenda for accomplishment before the institutions of governance in Indian scenario. Taking the view that a nationalist regime in the context of protection of the child is already *a priori*, the author advances a critique on a holistic note of the degree of success and limitations in the implementation process by the Government of India and its various national agencies. While the author sums up by calling for a multi-pronged plan of action on the part of the governmental and non-governmental agencies, the efforts of the author raise new questions of concern for a reader amongst which the notables being judicially recognized protections against exploitation and subjecting of children to hazardous works, the inadequacy of State monitoring processes; progressive interpretation of protective judiciary towards the plight of juveniles in the light of series of legislative advancements. The author in the concluding moments provokes the reader to ponder over the challenges of industrialization and urbanization and importantly negative discrimination and the needful larger course of action in the interests of the children.

In the next article of continuing relevance in the context of protection of children titled "The Administration of Criminal Justice System in India: Many Miles to Go, Many Goals to Achieve and Many Children to Protect", the author critically examines and evaluates the historical and legislative background of the juvenile justice system in India. Examining the reasons that influenced a paradigm shift in the approach towards the protection and safeguarding of the rights of children, the author thoroughly examines the developments advanced and amendments incorporated in the legislative frameworks in India. Taking a critical stand as to why the categorization of children into children in conflict with law and children in need of protection requires a review, the author highlights the challenges of the children and advances a series of suggestions for the effective implementation of the juvenile justice system that would lead towards the better protection and real development of a child. Thus, by posing intricate philosophical concerns, the author seeks to find solutions to pertinent questions.

The article "Role of United Nations in Protection and Promotion of Human Rights" through an emphasis on the developments of the 20th century relating to the Human Rights protection regime, examines how the United Nations as an important international institution attempted to codify the framework of rights and obligations of the international community. Referring to various forms of legal instruments through which the United Nations has attempted to further its mandate and objectives, the author takes an exceptional critique on the State practices that continue to result in unabated incidents of Human Rights violations. Thus, the author recalls the background scenario in which international criminal law has come to stay and criminal tribunalization found its formidable presence in the efforts for implementation and enforcement for the persistent abuses and violations. The author thus demonstrates a painstaking effort in outlining and providing an overview of various progressive efforts being rigorously pursued by and under the auspices of the United Nations.

In the next writing in this series entitled "Role of Non-Governmental Organizations in the Promotion of Human Rights" the authors attempt to demonstrate a historical and biographical approach to the very role and significance of non-governmental organizations (NGOs) in the promotion of Human Rights. Realizing their importance and agreeing with the predominantly persuasive role played by these institutions and requiring them to play a much more aggressive and assertive role—both at the international and national levels—the authors assert their ability to build positive as well as adverse public opinion on the States Parties so as to change their policies, adopt new and better standards for the effective safeguarding and promotion of Human Rights. Taking a perspective broader than that of a single nation, the authors scan through the efforts being advanced by various national and international Human Rights NGOs at the Asian level in the context of both civil and political rights as well as social, cultural and economic rights and most importantly, on what are being visualized in recent times as third generation or community development rights. Besides analyzing the influential role of these NGOs in facilitating societal and judicial processes, the authors outline the steps and interventions necessary to be taken for a more concerted approach on their part in fulfilling the larger international mandate. Interestingly, the vivid analysis of their role and contribution and at the same time the caution being sounded on the part of the authors make the reader appreciate the role of the NGOs in terms of the circumscribed limits of their contextual relevance.

The article "Promoting and Protecting Human Rights Education" analyzes the protection and safeguarding of the Human Rights of various cross sections of the civil society in the context of Human Rights education. Here the authors outline the inalienable interface between Human Rights education and human dignity. Reiterating that in giving a facelift as well as attributing a sense of value to the concept of human dignity, education and creation of awareness go a long way, the authors embark upon the task of outlining the contours of this challenge. Providing a broad spectrum to the scope of Human Rights education, the authors emphasize that through formal and non-formal means along with efforts to train professional workers to ensure regular dissemination, societal attitudes can be influenced towards progressive directions. Summing up the mission of Human Rights education as preparing the forthcoming generations towards a pluralistic society, the authors call for an exploration of a variety of means and methods in the full realization of Human Rights.

In the writing entitled "Humanizing the Criminal Justice System: The Victim Perspective" the author brings to the forefront an issue of concern which hitherto did not find its appropriate place in the administration of criminal justice in India, i.e., the protection of victims. Starting the argument from a basic premise of the criminal justice system focusing on the protection of the rights of individuals as against anyone who violates the same, the author highlights the deplorable position which a victim is relegated to. Narrowing down from a victim in general to a victim of rape in particular, the author through a critical review of the existing legal position and the series of judicial pronouncements rendered, highlights the distinct *lacunae* between the precepts and practices in the Indian scenario. Tracing out in clear terms the plight of a rape victim from the beginning of the violation of her personal dignity, the author examines how unsatisfactory the long drawn legal process is. Attributing due recognition and credit to the sensitivity demonstrated, the author takes the attention of a reader through a series of case laws analyzed, in the context of recognition of right to compensation and the guidelines to deal with the plight of the victims of child sexual abuse. Reiterating the latest international standards incumbent on the States Parties in this specific regard, the author forwards an argument before the reader to ponder over, as to why from the Indian perspective, legislative changes are the imminently needful measures. At the end, the author further poses a series of alternatives for the consideration of the reader, which mainly include legislative recognition to the right to compensation of rape victim, institutional care and treatment, humane treatment and importantly, participation of a victim in the conduct of the criminal trial.

In the thought-provoking article entitled "Revisiting Award of Compensation for Violation of Fundamental Rights: An Analysis of Indian Supreme Court Decisions", the authors reiterate that violation of Fundamental Rights cannot merely be resolved via monetary remedies but that sound alternate practices alone can remedy the otherwise grim scenario. The authors examine the progressive role advanced by the Indian Supreme Court, the institution of ultimate say in the constitutional consolidation of the resolution of conflicting interests in India. Referring to the efforts of the Supreme Court of India in the exercise of the discretionary jurisdiction and in evolving a regime of compensation as one of the most progressive contributions, the authors outline its importance as essentially construed in the context of public law domain. Reflecting upon the inherent limitations in this regard, namely the discretionary nature of the award from case to case and non-establishment of sound principles for such award, the authors pose before the reader a question of future concern. Clearly enunciating that an alternative approach of this sort cannot be a replacement to a mainstream constitutional obligation, the authors emphasize that the ultimate solution lies in the legislative portals until which the benign endeavors of the Supreme Court shall continue as stop-gap arrangements to bridge the gap between the violation and remedy.

In the article "The Presumption of Innocence and Fair Trial", the author begins with an evolutionary approach, by attempting to trace out the origin of this highly acclaimed right of an accused and puts forth a vehement view as to why this is the most indispensable human right in the criminal justice administration. Highlighting its present position under various international legal instruments, the author draws the attention of the reader to the recent trend of creating more exceptions to this very inherent right. Referring to the judicious caution often sounded by courts as to why this right needs to be seen in the holistic context of the criminal justice system and the trend of legislations in various countries recognizing exceptions, the author poses before the reader, a dilemma as to whether this is a sound, acceptable and acknowledgeable trend in the interests of the accused as well as the society as a whole. Basing the arguments on the premises of the recommendations of Justice Malimath's Committee Report on Criminal Justice Reforms in India, 2003, the author draws the attention of the reader as to why this issue requires larger degree of debate and dialogue.

Through a thought-provoking article "Terrorism and Human Rights: A Saga of Opposites?" the author opens the debate on the ongoing conflict of interests between the rebel groups and regular forces. Taking a top-down approach starting from the responses of the international community to combat the impunity of terrorism, the author poses the question in light of the recognized principle of non-derogation of basic Human Rights as incorporated under various international Human Rights instruments and particularly the International Covenant on Civil and Political Rights, 1966, and whether the nationalist responses of States Parties such as counter-terrorism measures which include target hardening, pre-emptive neutralization and domestic intelligence and surveillance, notwithstanding their emergent compulsive reflections, fall short of standards minimum to be complied with, even towards the repression of reprehensible conduct and thus are becoming new issues of fresh concern. Thus, spreading the analysis and evaluation wide across the reflections of various international Human Rights bodies within and beyond the United Nations, the author vividly examines the contents and contours of the United Nations General Assembly and Security Council resolutions to assert that never in the history of human civilization countenance of combat is posed with intriguing challenges as much as the acts of repression resulting in new concerns in themselves. Bringing a debate on whether even the most abhorred terrorist groups are entitled for any basic and minimum humanitarian standards or that their acts of shocking human conscience deprive and deny them even the basic minimum protections of law, the author warns about the dangers of any authoritarian approaches. Pondering whether the principle of proportionality will in any way have brought a balance of arguments, the author calls for the counter-terrorism measures not only to be Human Rights centric, but the means through which they are being resorted to must be adopted through legitimate means and are not outlawed by the very purpose for which they are brought in.

In the writing entitled "Indigenous People's Rights and Protection Mechanisms: An Overview" the author emphasizes the impositions over these cross sections of society for generations together and the deprivations justified in the name of economic and industrial developments. Taking a stand as to why the existing mechanisms cannot provide adequate safeguards for these highly marginalized cross sections of people, the author renders an exhaustive evaluation of the strengths and limitations of these mechanisms. Describing at length the definitional endeavors—both nationally and internationally—the author traces out the very conceptualization of indigenous people during the early part of 20th century and the subsequent efforts to widen and elaborate the scope and protection. Taking the stand further as to why these groups of people need to be appreciated from an individualized point of view, the author argues at length and puts forth a legitimate demand for a restorative paradigm. Canvassing the extended application of a vast variety of Human Rights—including self-determination, land and livelihood, legal and international personality, cultural integrity, compensation and participation in decision-making processes, the author injects fresh life into the arguments as to why and how Human Rights—both philosophically and functionally—are universal in their nature and character and reiterates that the barriers at various levels need a critical appreciation. In brief, the effort highlights how and why the collective recognition of the international community of these long time ignored cross sections of civil society is the need of the hour.

In the writing titled "Rights of Women under International Law" the author attempts to provide an overview of international community's holistic responses in this regard. Beginning with the Universal Declaration of Human Rights, 1948, as the first instrument of expression of aspirations, the author examines in a holistic sense how, over a phase of time, various specific instruments were incorporated and thereby States Parties were obligated to accept and evolve national standards, and under necessary circumstances re-align the domestic law so as to upgrade and fine-tune the same with the spirit of equal enjoyment of rights without any gender discrimination. To a greater extent, the author devotes time attention to analyze the important international legal instruments like the Convention on Elimination of all Forms of Discrimination against Women, 1979 and its Optional Protocol 2000, Beijing World Conference and Platform for Action, Independent Assertions under the Vienna Conference on Human Rights, 1993 wherein the rights of women are recognized as Human Rights. In addition, the author also outlines the importance of various Human Rights of women which predominantly include right to maternity benefits, right to protection against HIV and AIDS, right to education, employment, right to protection against violence and outlines in conclusion as to why and how the concerted actions of States alone will further these aspirations into concrete reality.

The article "Legal Control of Domestic Violence in India in Perspective of International Human Rights Instruments" provides specific reference to the rights of women and the concomitant legal responses from a country specific response, namely India. In this article, the author specifically undertakes an examination of the scope of violence against women as an infraction of life, liberty and dignity of a woman and how in response various international legal instruments have been concluded over a period of time. In this context, the author presents a detailed analysis of each of the instruments keeping in mind the right-duty perspective. Further, referring to India's efforts in the direction of enacting a national legislative framework as a laudable endeavor, the author notes with satisfaction that the definition rendered under the national legislation is sufficiently wide to encompass a vast variety of situations. Thus, the author leaves to the reader a broad and undefined spectrum to examine and arrive at one's own conclusions.

In the article "Cataclysmic Indian Dialectics of Collective Rights", which stands unique for its content and contours, the author looks at the challenges and opportunities on the part of the Union of India in evolving what the author views as Human Rights and standards and norm-setting processes. Referring to the circumstances under which the National Human Rights Commission in the Indian scenario has come to be established and in the light of its painstaking contribution, the author demonstrates how it played a supporting role along with the Indian judiciary in the progressive realization of the constitutional aspirations. In context of the emergence of third generation Human Rights or group and collective rights, as an important phenomenon of late 20th century, the author poses a challenge before the reader as to why, in recent times, these rights have assumed special significance and within the framework of the national sovereignty claims these rights of specific cross sections of society need a fresh interpretation.

In the article "Protecting Human Rights in European Union: The Charter of Fundamental Rights Perspective" the author attempts to draw the attention of the reader as to how the age-old European Convention on Human Rights and Fundamental Freedoms had successfully governed the frame of relations amongst the Member States of the Council of Europe for over half a century. Against this backdrop, the author projects the drafting of a Charter of Fundamental Rights for European Union as a milestone in the European Union context. Acknowledging that, at the time of the conclusion of the negotiations process for the most important regional Human Rights instrument, and in substantiating the importance of the contours and contents of the new legal instruments in the light of the earlier instrument, the author advances a valiant effort to substantiate with national judicial decisions. In characterizing this document as a bill of rights in the context of the European Union, the author heavily relies upon a series of juristic and scholarly writings in building the interface and linkage. Certain important aspects that raise the attention and curiosity of a comparative reader are the background of the Charter, its legal status, and the complementary character between the two regional Human Rights instruments. Thus, the author provides a contemporary approach for a reader to examine the European Union responses in the light of the rest of the contributions in this collection which essentially provide a distinct perspective of Asian concerns and reflections.

This endeavor provides a multi-dimensional effort to bring to the forefront the latest challenges and ramifications would not have been a distinct reality without the humane assistance and support of a number of colleagues and well wishers whose efforts of contribution cannot be left unnoticed or unacknowledged. Hence, with all sublimity, we express our deep sense of gratitude and sincere thanks to all those, who have, in a number of ways, rendered their assistance in making this effort a distinct reality. We are highly indebted to all the contributors from various corners of Asia, who, in spite of their contemporary academic commitments and pressures on their time, resources and energies, have conceded to our request and contributed their scholarly essays for the present effort. Personally as well as professionally, we hold each of them in high esteem.

2

The Significance of Fair Trial under Human Rights Law in Matters of Criminal Justice: A Case Study of the Trial of Former Iraqi Leader, Mr. Saddam Hussein

K.V.K. Santhy

When public men indulge themselves in abuse, when they deny others a fair trial, when they resort to innuendo and insinuation, to libel, scandal, and suspicion, then our democratic society is outraged, and democracy is baffled.

—J. William Fulbright

A fox should not be on the jury at a goose's trial.

—Thomas Fuller

One of the fundamental requisites of criminal justice is fairness in a criminal trial. This has the meaning that while the person is being prosecuted and punished by the tribunal, it should observe the fundamental principles of criminal justice. This is one of the basic Human Rights recognized by Universal Declaration of Human Rights. If these principles are not observed then the trial is vitiated and is tantamount to denial of justice. The right to an impartial trial is found under Article 14(1) of the International Covenant on Civil and Political Rights,[1] Article 10 of the Universal Declaration of Human

Rights,[2] Article 6(1) of the European Convention on Human Rights[3] and Article 7(1) of African Charter of Human and People's Rights.[4]

The concept of fairness in matters of criminal justice has very wide implications and needs to be observed at every stage of criminal process. In view of this it is absolutely necessary to know what a fair procedure is and whether it has been observed in any criminal trial.

The Iraq War which lasted for four years has raised several questions as to the justness of the war, the role of the international organizations in such a situation, the responsibility of the occupying powers, and above all the question of whether it was proper for the new Government in Iraq to try the former Head of State, Mr. Saddam Hussein, on certain charges and conduct the trial the way it was conducted. A lot of criticism has been leveled against the handling of the situation in Iraq by all those who are involved in the Iraq War and one of the important questions is whether the trial of Mr. Saddam Hussein was in accordance with the fundamental principles of criminal justice, nay whether it was a fair trial or not.

This article has the object of highlighting the elements of 'fair trial' as enunciated in legal literature and international instruments, and examining the question of whether the trial was just, fair and reasonable. If the issues concerning this trial are not examined now it is possible that many more trials may be conducted in the same manner and claims of criminal justice defeated by the powers that be. The significance of this lies in the fact that if one set of principles of fair procedure are laid down in the international instruments and some others are followed in violation of those principles then there is no sense in having the concept of fair procedure in criminal jurisprudence.

I. The Object of the Trial of Saddam Hussein

What is the reason for the criminal trial of Saddam Hussein, indeed, for the criminal law generally? What are goals set out before the start of the trial?[5] Because one cannot start looking for solutions until the goals are identified. Let us look into few important goals of any punishment.

1. Is it retribution: "An eye for an eye?" Because Saddam Hussein tortured a group of people (allegedly people belonging to Shia group) he should have also been hanged in their presence.

2. Deterrence of the actor: What were the chances the Iraqis would have elected or selected Hussein for a leadership position again?

3. Deterrence of others: Who are the other leaders going to be deterred by this trial? Is it George W. Bush? Vladimir Putin? Fidel Castro? The Chinese Leaders? What are the chances that any of them will be deterred by a trial of Hussein?

4. To stake out a moral leadership position for the captors: Moral as judged by whom? Is our perception of what is moral binding on Iraqis; Is their's binding on us?

5. Closure for the villain's victims: Are they informed of the capture? What of the villain's supporters? This seems to be the most significant of the reasons for Hussein's trial, but is it sufficient?

6. To avoid reciprocal atrocities: Is there any evidence that Hussein's supported plan them or will be deterred by the trial of Hussein? One can expect an attitude of reciprocity more than one of deterrence.

Assuming the first goal of the Interim Government was to bring justice for the victims of genocide and other war crimes committed since 1968 when Saddam Hussein assumed the leadership. In that case, the list should also include victims of Iran and Iraq war because they were thousands in number. But interestingly, he was not prosecuted for those crimes and the Tribunal confined itself only to the crimes committed inside Iraq. The ostensible reason may be when Saddam Hussein was committing those atrocities against Iranians and Kurds, the United States was a close ally of Saddam and his regime. The Reagan administration perceived the *ayatollahs*' Iran to be the over-riding threat to US national interests, and it adopted Saddam as the best available counter-balance. The United

States began to supply Baghdad with military assistance, including detailed satellite information about Iranian troops deployments.[6] It was American intelligence through satellites that provided the raw information about Iranian positions and let Saddam drench them with poison gas and it was the Reagan administration that convinced the US Senate not to condemn Saddam of the bombings and encourage American suppliers and NATO allies to provide Iraq with chemical weapons. This relationship of tacit support continued despite the growing catalogue of atrocities associated with Saddam's Iraq. In the 1980s, believing that Iraqi Kurds in the north of the country were in league with Iran, Saddam forcibly removed hundreds of thousands from their land and razed their villages. In 1988, he used chemical weapons, killing 5,000 Kurds at the village of Halabja.[7] Kurdish leaders turned to the West for help. Saddam's former friend, Dr Mahmoud Osman, went to Washington and found no one wanted to listen. Thus the US did not wish any atrocities connected with the Iran war to come up during the trial for the reason whatsoever. Being the ostensible supervisors of the trial, they have ensured this will not happen.[8]

A second goal may be to bring acknowledgment to the victims. The families of the victims want a Court trial not to tell them what happened, they know the fact, perhaps they want an official and public acknowledgement through a fair trial.

Whatever may be the goal, it cannot be achieved unless the trial is both in fact and in perception scrupulously fair. In a criminal trial the following are the hallmark issues to conduct a fair trial.

1. Impartial and independent Tribunal or Court.

2. Competent and unbiased judges.

3. Qualified prosecutors and defense lawyers.

4. Giving due recognition to the rights of the accused like right to consult the legal counsel, right to cross examination, right to know the charges leveled, right to silence, right to go for an appeal.

5. Certain basic and fundamental standards set at the international level in the criminal justice process are to be observed like *Nullum peona sine lege, Nullum crimen sine lege*, the standard of proof should be proof beyond reasonable doubt.

6. There shall not be any political interference, and the trial must be conducted in a conducive environment.

After having discussed the basic issues, the next issue which is to be discussed is the procedure adopted by the Tribunal in trying Saddam Hussein in light of the principles of fair procedure.

II. Legitimacy of the Establishment of the Iraqi Special Tribunal (IST)

An independent and impartial Court is a fundamental prerequisite for meeting international standards of fairness in a trial. In the case of Saddam a special Court was constituted by name Iraqi Special Tribunal (IST) which was a domestic Iraqi Court that exists within the Iraqi judicial system under the authority of the Iraqi Government. The IST is a special tribunal in that it is not part of the ordinary system of justice. Its special nature is evidenced by its temporary existence and for the exercise of jurisdiction over only certain crimes committed within a defined period of time and only by certain persons. Article 1 of the Statute limits the IST's temporal jurisdiction to crimes committed in Iraq or elsewhere between the Ba'athists' assumption of power on July 17, 1968, and their deposition on May 1, 2003. It specifically incorporates liability for crimes committed during the wars with Iran and Kuwait and for crimes committed against Iraqi ethnic or religious groups, whether during armed conflict or not. The IST has adjudicatory power only over people, not on parties or corporate entities.[9]

The Court which conducts the trial must be the competent one and must also be able to deliver justice without fear or favor. Important questions regarding the legitimacy of the Tribunal are: did the Tribunal established by the Interim Government have power to try Saddam Hussein? And the second question is how far it was correct to conduct a trial in Baghdad itself amidst pressures.

Actually there were four options open for the Interim Government of Iraq and US to ensure fair trial. The first was a wholly domestic trial in Baghdad before Iraqi Judges. That could even be conducted outside Iraq in consequence of a treaty or under universal jurisdiction.[10] This option has its own range of difficulties starting from the competency of the judges to prosecutors and lack of amicable environment. The second option was a hybrid international/domestic court of the form that is operating in Sierra Leone.[11] It is a domestic Court with international involvement through an agreement between Sierra Leone and United Nations. The third option was a treaty based multinational Court in the lines of Nuremberg War Crimes Tribunal. The fourth option was an *ad hoc* tribunal established by the Security Council under Chapter VII of the United Nations Charter,[12] on the lines of the International Criminal Tribunals for the former Yugoslavia and Rwanda. The International Criminal Court is not an option as it does not have jurisdiction in respect of offences committed prior to July 1, 2002.[13] Moreover, neither Iraq nor any other relevant country has ratified the Rome Statute establishing the Court.

Clearly the most sensible route for the United States and the Interim Government was that they would have selected any one amongst second, third or fourth options and the US could request the Security Council itself to select the judges and prosecutors instead of leaving the discretion to the head of the Interim Government. This arrangement would have the appearance and fact of being independent because of the involvement of international community and it would necessarily reflect impartiality in the attitude of judges, transparency in the process and procedure of the trial and commitment to principles of international criminal law. Saddam Hussein was in the custody of US and they did not hand him over for a trial that was just and fair. If the United States had been really interested in maintaining the rule of law and following the due process they should have not handed him over to any Court which does not meet the international standards in conducting the trial. But none of the above options were exercised by the Iraq and US led interim regime and a special tribunal was established by the Prime Minister of the Iraq with few international observers.

The exceptional nature of the IST, which contradicts International Human Rights norms is reflected in the characteristics described below:[14]

1. The establishment of the IST by an occupying power violates the Geneva Conventions and customary international humanitarian law applicable to conflicts of an international character.
2. The specific naming of the Tribunal as a "special" judicial body violates the International Covenant on Civil and Political Rights.
3. The assignment of English as the Tribunal's controlling language is in violation of Iraqi law, which requires Arabic to be the official language of the State.
4. The appointment of sitting judges, investigative judges, and the prosecutors by a temporary political authority, the GC, whose authority was derived from the occupying power, affects judicial independence and the impartiality of the Tribunal.
5. The Statute's provision on appointing foreign judges may be in violation of Iraqi law.
6. The appointment of foreign experts and observers as monitors, and the conduct of criminal investigations by foreign experts not under the control of the investigative judges, is in violation of Iraqi law.
7. The Statute confuses the roles of investigative judges and prosecutors, which results in violations of Iraqi procedural law, possibly to the detriment of the defense's rights.
8. The determination of compensation of the sitting judges, investigative judges, and prosecutors by a temporary political authority, the GC, appointed by an occupying power, effaces judicial independence

and the impartiality of the Tribunal, and thus constitutes a violation of international Human Rights law.

9. The exclusion of sitting judges, investigative judges, and prosecutors solely on grounds of membership in the Ba'ath party, infringes upon the principle of impartiality.
10. The failure to allow for challenges of judges and investigative judges on the basis of conflict of interest or partiality violates the principle of judicial impartiality established in international Human Rights law.
11. The definition of crimes in the Statute that are not contained in Iraqi law are in violation of the principles of legality recognized in Iraqi law and international Human Rights law.

The IST's subject matter jurisdiction is limited. It can undertake prosecutions only for Genocide, War crimes, Crimes against Humanity as defined largely by international law, and a small set of domestic Iraqi violations, including invading other Arab countries, wasting natural resources, abusing power, squandering public funds and assets, and attempting to manipulate the judiciary. Judges are appointed by the Iraqi Government to trial chambers and a nine-members appellate body, which may include non-Iraqi nationals at the Government's discretion.[15] Provision is also made for creation of a twenty member body of permanent "investigative judges", who will issue subpoenas, arrest warrants, and indictments, as well as collect and evaluate evidence, essentially building up the cases for the Court.[16]

Each investigative judge is a separate organ and independent from the tribunal judges. Interestingly, the chief investigative judge is required to appoint non-Iraqi foreign advisors to act in an assistant or observer capacity while also monitoring the work of the Iraqi investigative judges, to ensure that general due process standards are observed. Similarly, up to twenty prosecutors will be appointed by the Government and be accompanied by international advisors who will monitor their work.[17] However appointment of professional staff from the new International Criminal Court or other truly international bodies would have given greater legitimacy to the IST.

The laws applied at Nuremberg have now become customary international law. They were unanimously approved and adopted by the General Assembly in 1948.[18] The recognition of Crimes against Humanity has led to the development of universal jurisdiction in domestic and international Courts. For huge War Crimes for Genocide, for grave breach provisions of the Geneva Conventions,[19] for violations of the Torture Conventions,[20] and contraventions dealing with terrorism, there is universal jurisdiction conferred upon domestic courts.[21] The same law could have been applied to try Saddam Hussein also, instead of following the Iraqi criminal procedure.

Violating all norms recognized by international law President Bush announced that Saddam would be tried by his own Court and his own people and according to his own law. The paradox is the accused was tried for International Crimes or Crimes against Humanity in a domestic Court by applying Iraqi Code of Criminal Procedure. The law is neither wholly domestic nor international. What principles were to be applied in the trial process was confusion. The Statute says the system of criminal procedure is a conglomeration of both adversarial and inquisitorial systems, which leads to a lot of problems in deciding the standard of proof, weight to be given to the outcome of the investigation and the role of judges.

III. The Venue for the Trial

Counsels of the legal team[22] defending Saddam and his associates were killed and injured, resulting in the resignation and reassignment of the work to other lawyers. The first Chief Judge Rizgar Mohammed Amin resigned because of political interference (an offence and violation under both the Iraqi Constitution and the Statutes of the Iraqi Special Tribunal, now the Iraqi High Tribunal), the second Chief Judge Sayeed al-Hamashi was dismissed because of an alleged involvement in the Ba'ath party and the third judge was appointed simply to carry out the political wishes of the Iraqi Government. Raouf Abdel-Rahman, a Kurdish was appointed as a succeeding Chief Judge finally who sentenced Saddam to death.

It is quite obvious that there can be no fair trial without providing security for witnesses, judges and defense lawyers on an equal footing with the prosecution. This precarious situation raises many pertinent questions like, is it right to conduct the Trial in Baghdad amidst Bombings without any security to the defense counsels and witnesses? Can the judges deliver the judgment without fear and favor? And how impartial the judgment delivered in those circumstances would be?

There can be no question that criminal trials should ideally be held where the crimes were committed. It is very important for Courts, especially criminal Courts to be accessible to the victimized so that the victims can feel part of the process. But that is not always possible. The Yugoslavia Tribunal was put in the Hague, a long way from the places where the crimes were committed. In the case of Rwanda, it was a little closer, Arusha in Northern Tanzania, a neighboring country not too far from the place of the commission of the offence. Therefore the trial could have been conducted outside Baghdad, but closer to it to ensure safety and security to the defense counsel and also to judges.

IV. Standard of Proof

The standard of proof in any criminal trial is "Proof Beyond Reasonable Doubt". All international Statutes prescribe the same standard like the International Criminal Statute,[23] the International Criminal Tribunal for Rwanda,[24] International Criminal Tribunal for the Former Yugoslavia.[25] Proof beyond reasonable doubt has also been read into fair trial requirements under the International Covenant on Civil and Political Rights, to which Iraq is a party.[26]

Fundamentally, the rules of procedure applicable to trials by the Iraqi Special Tribunal do not require that guilt be proven beyond reasonable doubt as is required international

Human Rights law.[27] Rule 79(1) states that the Tribunal shall apply the rules of evidence set out in the Tribunal Rules and in the Iraqi Code of Criminal Procedure,[28] which has a lower standard of proof.

Existing Iraqi law, that supplements the Statute and rules, requires that the Tribunal be satisfied of the guilt by the evidence presented to the satisfaction of the Judge. Lower burden of proof is especially troubling as the Tribunal has the power to impose the death penalty. International Human Rights groups have expressed concern about a legal process where guilt does not have to be proven "beyond a reasonable doubt", as in international trials. Instead, the Iraqi Tribunal has only to be "satisfied" of guilt. This standard of proof is insufficient to assure a fair trial, particularly given the large evidentiary base and multifaceted elements of the crime that must be proved in trials for Genocide.

V. Presumption of Innocence

The right to presumption of innocence requires that an individual must not be pre-judged. It is a direction to officials how they are to proceed while dealing with the accused.[29] In *Allenet de Ribemont v. France*,[30] it was held that this right requires all public officials of the State prosecuting an individual must not make statements expressly stating or implying that the guilt of a person who has yet not been convicted. In *Minnelli v. Switzerland,*[31] it was reiterated that this is a fundamental principle which protects everybody against being treated by public officials as if they were guilty of an offence even before such guilty is established by a competent Court. In this case all through the trial seems to be proceeded on the presumption of guilt. The outcome of the trial was very much predicted by the Interim Government and U.S. Mr. Jalal Talibani (Iraqi interim President)[32] stated in an interview with Reuters that "there is no doubt that Saddam deserves more than just execution.... I am among those who are going to file a complaint for killing 64 members of my family. For these crimes alone he deserves 64 executions."[33] Similarly, the Iraqi Prime Minister Nouri Al-Maliki said that "if Saddam Hussein was not executed, a Presidential Council would carry out the mission".[34] Repeated statements by the Iraqi Government and the occupying powers undermined the fairness of the trial and violated the valuable right of the accused.[35] It gives an impression that the trial started with a preconceived notion and continued all through with a determined goal, i.e. execution of the accused which is fair neither to the accused nor to the trial procedure.

VI. Principle of *Nullum Poena Sine Lege and Nullum Crimen Sine Lege*

The right reflected in these maxims prohibits punishment or imprisonment of an individual for acts that were not deemed crimes under the law of the country concerned at the time of their commission. It also precludes the prosecution of an individual before special Courts that were created to prosecute specific individual for acts made crimes long after the acts constituting the alleged crimes were committed.[36] These rights are non-derogable as enshrined under Article 4[37] of the ICCPR, Article 11(2), UDHR,[38] Article 22 of the Statute of the International Criminal Court,[39] Article 9 of the American Convention on Human Rights,[40] Article 70 of the Fourth Geneva Convention.[41]

In *Veeber v. Estonia*[42] it was held that from these principles, it follows that an offence must be clearly defined in law. With regards to special courts, it was stated in *Castillo Petruzzi v. Peru*[43] and was held that tribunals that do not use duly established procedures of legal process.... To displace the jurisdiction belonging to the ordinary courts or judicial tribunals, amounts to a violation of Human Rights of the accused.

The IST Statute was created on 10th December, 2003 long after the alleged crimes were committed by the accused. Moreover, when the alleged acts were committed ordinary courts existed in Iraqi law, hence the accused could not have reasonable knowledge that he may be made subject to the jurisdiction of a special tribunal.

The Iraqi Penal Code did not contain references to crimes against humanity at the time of the commission of the offence.

Furthermore, these crimes as applicable to non-international armed conflicts came into existence only recently with the creation of the two *ad hoc* tribunals in Rwanda and Yugoslavia, as was observed in *Prosecutor v. Dusko Tadic.*[44] Therefore Saddam Hussein was not to be tried by the new law which came very much latter which is against the general principles of Criminal Law.

VII. The Trial Process and Violation of Principles of Fairness during the Trial

Any trial procedure presupposes few fundamental principles to be observed such as giving fair opportunity to the accused to defend his case and in order to sufficiently exercise that right making available the other rights such as right to legal counsel, right to be informed of grounds of arrest, right to be informed of charges, right to free access to the legal counsel, right to be present when the prosecution witnesses are examined, right to have enough time to prepare defense argument, Saddam's defense counsel filed a series of motions addressing issues such as the impartiality of the judges and access to witnesses and documents. One of the most glaring shortcomings of the Court was its failure to articulate a response to these motions until the final Trial Chamber opinion was issued at the end of the Dujail trial. The Court's silence significantly weakened its transparency and undermined the credibility of the judicial process. This part of the article examines as to where the procedure failed to achieve the goal.

(i) *Charges leveled against Saddam Hussein*

The charges leveled against Saddam Hussein include War Crimes, Crimes against Humanity, Aggression and Genocide. The seven acts substantiating Hussein's indictment are:[45]

1. Anfal campaign against Kurds in the late 1980's;
2. Gassing Kurds in Halabja in 1988;
3. Invasion of Kuwait in 1990;
4. Crushing Kurdish and Shia's rebellions after the 1991 Gulf war;
5. Killing political activists over thirty years;

6. Massacring members of Kurdish Barzani tribe in the 1980's;
7. Killing religious leaders in 1974. The rationale for the selection of the offences committed by the accused is not known to anybody. It is done to the convenience of the interested parties. The list is a conglomeration of municipal offences and international crimes.

(ii) *Delay in informing the accused of the charges leveled against him*

The specific charges leveled against Saddam Hussein were informed to him on 15th May, 2006 approximately two and a half years after his arrest, and about seven and a half months after the commencement of the trial.

The right to a prompt hearing is enshrined in International Customary law as is reflected by Article 14(3)(a) of the ICCPR,[46] Article 67(1)(a) of the statute of the International Criminal Court,[47] Article 8(2)[48] of the American Conventions on Human Rights and Article 6(3)(a) of the European Convention on Human Rights.[49] It was held in *Annette Pagnoulle v. Cameroon*,[50] the inter American Court of Human Rights observed that the Principle of Reasonable time is to prevent accused persons from remaining in that situation for a protracted period and to ensure that the charge is promptly disposed of.

(iii) *Trial must be conducted in the presence of the accused*

The criminal trial must be conducted in the presence of the accused. He should know the version of the opposite party to prepare his arguments effectively. But Rule 56 of Rules of Procedure and Evidence of Iraq allows for trials *in absentia* for defendants who have not been arrested and those who have been arrested but then escaped. Though trials *in absentia* are not strictly prohibited under international criminal law as in the case when defendant refuses to appear before Tribunal, however, they comprise various rights of the defendants like the right to adequately prepare a defense, right to communicate with a counsel of choice and right to examine witnesses, available to him within the fabric of fair trial proceedings.[51]

Article 63 of the Rome Statute,[52] Article 21(4)(d) of the ICTY Statute[53] and Article 20(4)(d) of the ICTR Statute[54] strictly prohibit trials *in absentia.*

(iv) *Right to defend the case impaired and Right to access to Counsel undermined*

The defense suffered from spate of handicaps. Few important issues are discussed here under:

(1) The accused was not allowed to meet his counsel freely all through the trial. This right was completely abrogated at the investigation phase. The presence of the solicitor at the police interview is a particularly important safeguard. In *Averill v. United Kingdom*[55] the European Court of Human Rights holds that in the circumstance where the suspect is confronted by a 'fundamental dilemma' of remaining silent and drawing an adverse inference or speaking up and prejudicing a possible defense, the fairness inherent in 6(1) and 6(3)(C) demands that the suspect be given immediate access to legal assistance. Similarly in *Condron v. United Kingdom*[56] and in *Magee v. United Kingdom*[57] place considerable emphasis on the suspect's right to legal advice. The US military holds in custody on behalf of the SICT more than 90 so-called "High Value Detainees", comprising most of the senior leadership of the former government. The SICT, although established by law in December 2003, did not become functional until December 2004, and consequently the detainees did not have access to counsel until that time. Yet in July 2004, twelve of the detainees were brought before a judge of the Central Criminal Court of Iraq and notified of possible charges punishable under the Penal Code.[58] Reports submitted to the U.S. Congress by the U.S. Department of State record that, between June and December 2004, U.S. investigators from the RCLO reviewed seized government documents held in Qatar in order to question detainees, and questioned thirty of the detainees.[59] *Prima facie*, it would appear that this questioning occurred before any of these detainees had access to legal counsel, and it is impossible to determine whether they were properly informed of their right to counsel and freely waived that right.

This is a violation of Miranda's rights which has become the *jus cogens* of international law.

(2) During the trial Iraqi lawyers for several accused including Saddam alleged that they faced difficulties in gaining regular access to their clients. The first problem faced by them was not getting the registration done by the SICT, in spite of which the defense lawyers could not access to the accused and therefore unable to defend them.

(3) All applications filed by foreign lawyers were rejected by the Tribunal.

(4) The defense counsel could meet his client only before the Investigative Judge will question him. Ramsay Clark, one of the defense counsels for Saddam Hussein reiterated repeatedly that none of the meetings with the accused were confidential. For instance, it has been stated that on 3rd April 2006, in addition to American soldiers, even an Iraqi translator was made party to the meetings between the counsels and the client. Moreover, it has been alleged that all secret documentation of the counsels were checked by the security guards and no documents could be passed to the accused without the prior approval of the authorities. It has been further alleged that on 4th April 2006, the authorities cancelled one of the scheduled meetings between the accused and his counsel without any prior notice to the counsel. Moreover, on 5th April, 2006, it was announced that the verification of the authenticity of the documents and signatures would be done by an officer of the Minister of Interior. Objections raised as to the impartiality of such verification were never heard.

(5) No access to documents or evidence was given and transcripts of judicial questioning were not made available during the course of investigation which seriously impairs the defense counsel in preparing their arguments. Saddam's defense council repeatedly argued for a delay in the proceedings, insisting that it had not been given evidence secured by the prosecution, had not been given sufficient time to review any prosecution documents, but so far these submissions have received no response from the Court.

(6) The defense lawyers were not present during the taking of other witnesses' statements or the collection of evidence by the Investigative Judge.

(7) The Court did not provide any reasoned decision on the following motions submitted by the defense counsel.

(i) *19th October, 2005*: A motion indicating that notice of evidence and witnesses was not provided to the defense in a timely manner.

(ii) *19th October, 2005*: A motion calling for the adjournment of the proceedings due to insecurity.

(iii) *8th December, 2005*: A preliminary motion challenging the legality of the IST and its failure to ensure respect for Human Rights.

(iv) *1st February, 2006*: A supplementary motion challenging the legality of the IST.

(v) *20th February, 2006*: A preliminary motion requesting the disqualification of Chief Judge Abdel-Rahman on the grounds of bias.

(vi) *15th March, 2006*: 17 point request, including respect for some basic elements of fair trial.

(vii) *13th June, 2006*: A request to prevent Mr. William Wiley who alleged to work for the IST from interfering with defense witnesses and from contact with defense lawyers who he has threatening.

(8) On 19th June, 2006, the Court directed the prosecution to present its closing remarks.[60] It is important to note that till this point the Court had heard about 50 prosecution witnesses and less than 20 defense witness[61] with the prosecution's case having commenced eight months prior, and the defense given formal charges only two and a half months previously. Also, when the defense counsel boycotted the trial, the trial was not suspended but the IST appointed lawyers without consultation with the accused or the defense.

(v) *Right against self-incrimination not available to the accused*

The defendant's right to silence is universally recognized in common statutory and constitutional law as one of the defining characteristics of the accusatorial-adversarial system of criminal justice. The silence principle of the 21st century has been redesigned and widened into immunity against the answering of pre-trial interrogatory questions and into a right not to give evidence at trial. In the United States, the constitutional silence principle has been construed to include an absolute prohibition against the drawing of adverse inferences.[62] At the trial the accused's failure to testify cannot be used to draw a direct inference of guilt. To draw a direct inference of guilt would result in the accused being compelled to give evidence.[63] The European Court of Human Rights judgment in *Murray v. United Kingdom*[64] holds that the right to silence, during police interrogation and at trial is a generally recognized international standard drawn from fairness principle entrenched within 6(1) of the European Convention.

The SICT Statute duly provides that an accused has a right to silence and cannot be compelled to testify, and that silence cannot be a consideration in the determination of guilt or innocence.[65] However, the Iraqi Code of Criminal Procedure permits the judges to ask questions directly to a defendant, regardless of whether the defendant is willing to testify or has chosen to give an unsworn statement to the Court. Where the defendant refuses to answer a question posed by the Court, "it *will* be considered as evidence against the defendant."[66] In June 2003 the CPA issued a regulation ("Memorandum 3") that suspended the requirement that a refusal to answer be considered as evidence against the defendant.[67] It is uncertain whether the judges will consider themselves bound by CPA Memorandum 3, because it is not mentioned as part of the procedural law applied by the SICT.[68]

Rule 46[69] of the Iraqi Special Tribunal limit the right to a counsel and to be informed of the right to remain silent only upon investigation before an Investigative Judge. This leaves the accused vulnerable to be interrogated without due regard to these rights prior to questioning by an Investigative Judge. Till the legal custody of the detainees in the present case the accused was transferred from the United States to the Iraqi Interim Government, and till their production before an Investigative Judge, they were susceptible to be interrogated without a counsel or without a right to remain silent. The Court must accordingly, examine the evidence produced from investigation during this stage. Pre-trial silence in the face of authoritative questioning has no probative value.[70] And it is not known how much weight was attached to the statements made during the investigation.

(vi) *Legality of death sentence*

(a) **Principle of *Ex Posto Application* not applied to Death Penalty:** Iraqi law did not impose the death penalty for the crimes that were committed, as the same did not exist in Iraqi law at the time of their commission. Moreover, death penalty was suspended vide section 3(i) of the CPA Order No. 7.[71]

Section 2(2) of the Iraqi Penal Code[72] to which Section 17(a)(ii) and Section 24 of the IST Statute make reference, clearly states that if there are changes in a law after a certain date then the most favorable and not the latest law should apply. This means that the death penalty having been one suspended cannot be re-invoked with retrospective action as the most favorable law must apply in the intervening period.[73]

The retrospective application of death penalty violates the Iraqi Penal Code, which states in Article 1 that no act or omission shall be penalized except in accordance with a legislative provision under which the said act or omission is regarded as a criminal offence at the time of its occurrence. The same also violates of Article 6, paragraph 2 of the ICCPR.[74]

The death penalty has also been abolished by the statutes of the International Criminal Court, International Criminal Tribunal for the former Yugoslavia and for Rwanda, the Special Court for Sierra Leone, the Special Panels for East Timor, the Special Panels in Kosovo and the Extraordinary Chambers in Cambodia.

Saddam should not have been executed because other charges/trials are still continuing and they could not be conducted in his absence, his presence is very much required. In addition, the defendants may face other charges relating, for instance, to the suppression of the 1991 Shia and Kurdish uprisings or the wars with Iran and Kuwait.

(b) No death penalty can be imposed after an unfair Trial: According to safeguard 4 of the Authoritative UN Safeguards Guaranteeing the Rights of those Facing the Death Penalty, it may be applied only pursuant to the final judgment rendered by a competent Court after legal process which gives all possible safeguards to ensure a fair trial, tallest equal to those contained in Article 14 of ICCPR. Moreover, execution after an unfair trial would violate the non-derogable right not to be arbitrarily deprived of life guaranteed under Article 6 of the ICCPR.

The Prime Minister of Iraq yet again interfered with the judicial process in the Saddam Hussein case stated that Saddam would have been executed by the end of the year. This was a presumption, or perhaps an order to the appeal Court to dismiss the appeal that is automatic end of right. Chief Judge of the Revolutionary Court Awad Hamad al-Bandar was in fact convicted with Saddam Hussein and sentenced to death simply because he was a judge who, the prosecution stated, carried out the orders of the Saddam Hussein Government. Mr. Ramsey Clark, the ex-US Attorney General, in the disgraceful way he was ejected from the Court by Judge Rahman on the day of the verdict.

(vii) *Right to appeal*

The right to appeal at least, once is nearly universal.[75] The right is a protection against error, prejudice, and human failings in general...Justice and good law are needed for little cases as well as for big ones, and even frivolousness is a matter of opinion.[76] This statement suggests that appeal of right furthers the substantive goal of a correct decision in every case. The right of appeal is a fundamental element of procedural fairness.[77] The appeal of right is also rooted in process values; that is to say that we are committed to arriving at decisions correctly in a manner that assures that litigants are, and feel they are, treated fairly.[78]

Article 25(a) of the Tribunal Statute provides only three grounds for an appeal by either the prosecutor or by the convicted person: an error on a question of law invalidating a decision; a procedural error; or an error of material fact that has occasioned a miscarriage of justice. Article 81 of the Rome Statute of the ICC, by contrast, allows a convicted person to appeal a conviction or sentence on four grounds: (i) procedural error, (ii) error of fact, (iii) error of law, and (iv) any other ground that affects the fairness or reliability of the proceedings or decision. Additionally, Article 14(5) of the ICCPR requires that: "[e]veryone convicted of a crime shall have the right to his conviction and sentence being reviewed by a higher tribunal according to law." Article 25(b) of the Tribunal Statute states that: "[t]he Appeals Chamber may affirm, reverse or revise the decisions taken by the Trial Chambers." While the Tribunal Statute guarantees the right to appeal, though in a limited way, it is not clear from this if appeal is for both conviction and sentence.

Saddam Hussein appealed against his conviction but Iraq's Appeals Court upheld the verdict and sentence on 26th December. Under Iraqi law, sentence must be carried out within 30 days of the result of the appeal. Commenting on the appeal procedure Ramsay Clark, the defense counsel for Saddam said "[t]he sudden decision of the so-called appeals court in Iraq, which did not take the time to examine the trial record and defense briefs, has set the stage for the imminent execution of Saddam Hussein, two other defendants and the surrender of four other defendants to the Iraqi government, exposing them to summary executions, torture and cruel, inhumane and degrading punishment—all in violation of U.S. and international law".

VIII. Conclusion

At the minimum we insist that the process be fair in form; that the parties be afforded an adequate opportunity to present their cases and to respond to their adversaries; that tribunals be competent and unbiased; and that appropriate rules of decision be followed. Related to this concern with formal fairness is a desire that the legal process provide appropriate satisfactions to the parties caught up in it. The underlying assumption is that the way in which parties experience a process may be as important as its outcome.[79] For the injured party, the opportunity to participate meaningfully in the vindication of her rights (or, less loftily, the chance to see the other side squirm) may be a far greater and even more socially useful reward than monetary damages. For the injuring party, the realization that she has been treated fairly and has had a full opportunity to put matters in the best possible light arguably promotes an acceptance of outcome and a belief in the legitimacy of the system that is essential to the success of both private ordering and official compulsion.[80]

In the case of Saddam Hussein starting from the very first step of the trial, i.e. from arrest, to the execution at every step and every stage fairness and transparency was the biggest casualty. Undoubtedly, one can say that Saddam was denied a fair trial. If the accused was not fair to the victim it doesn't mean that the justice process also can behave with him in the same way.

All through the trial, the American high handedness was writ large. One cannot bring justice to victims unless they believe that the process has been a fair one. A fair trial in turn cannot be held unless there is adequate security for the judges, the defendants, the witnesses, and counsel, both prosecution and defense. A fair trial cannot be held if the judges are not independent and competent. It would be a great shame if anger or haste or politics is allowed to dictate the decisions. Given the situation in Iraq to put on a trial in Baghdad is just beyond any thought. How can they have a trial with bombs going off daily? People being attacked daily? How any one can expect a Court to sit in Baghdad and be able to operate and have a fair trial? Moreover, there have been no independent courts sitting in Iraq since 1968. For thirty-five years there have been no regular courts sitting. There have been few judges who were judges before 1968. It is left to the imagination of every reasonable person how competent they would be? Then there have been no independent prosecutors in Iraq for thirty-five years. One has got to have courts sitting in judgment over Saddam Hussein that will have the respect and confidence of all the people of Iraq and not appealing to one sector, either for Saddam Hussein or against Saddam Hussein. It is still doubtful how the local Iraqi Judges operated in a fair and just manner in the absence of an independent and democratic Government. There cannot be a fair trial without the international involvement by all means by Iraqi Judges. This was not the sort of trial that is going to achieve any of the goals of a fair trial. A universal law relating to the establishment of the Court, the procedure to be followed must be developed and applied in a uniform way to all the accused.

The international community now has a unique opportunity to ensure justice for past violations. Genocide, Crimes against Humanity and War Crimes are crimes under international law. The investigation and prosecution of these crimes and the provision of reparations to victims and their families are not solely the responsibility of authorities of the victim State. These are international responsibilities and the international community must provide the Tribunal with all the necessary expertise at its disposal and ensure that the Tribunal's proceedings are closely monitored. Otherwise it would be shameful if the trials of this category are left open to the criticism of being victor's justice.

Notes

1. All persons shall be equal before the courts and tribunals. In the determination of any criminal charge against him, or of his rights and obligations in a suit at law, everyone shall be entitled to a fair and public hearing by a competent, independent and impartial tribunal established by law. The press and the public may be excluded from all or part of a trial for reasons of morals, public order or national security in a democratic society, or when the interest of the private lives of the parties so requires, or to the extent strictly necessary in the opinion of the Court in special circumstances where publicity would prejudice the interests of justice; but any judgment rendered in a criminal case or in a suit at law shall be made public except where the interest of juvenile persons otherwise requires or the proceedings concern matrimonial disputes or the guardianship of children.

2. Article 10: Everyone is entitled in full equality to a fair and public hearing by an independent and impartial tribunal, in the determination of his rights and obligations and of any criminal charge against him.
3. Article 6: In the determination of his civil rights and obligations or of any criminal charge against him, everyone is entitled to a fair and public hearing within a reasonable time by an independent and impartial tribunal established by law. Judgment shall be pronounced publicly by the press and public may be excluded from all or part of the trial in the interest of morals, public order or national security in a democratic society, where the interests of juveniles or the protection of the private life of the parties so require, or the extent strictly necessary in the opinion of the Court in special circumstances where publicity would prejudice the interests of justice.
4. Article 7: 1. Every individual shall have the right to have his cause heard. This comprises: (a) the right to an appeal to competent national organs against acts of violating his Fundamental Rights as recognized and guaranteed by Conventions, laws, regulations and customs in force; (b) the right to be presumed innocent until proved guilty by a competent Court or tribunal; (c) the right to defense, including the right to be defended by counsel of his choice; (d) the right to be tried within a reasonable time by an impartial Court or tribunal. 2. No one may be condemned for an act or omission which did not constitute a legally punishable offence at the time it was committed. No penalty may be inflicted for an offence for which no provision was made at the time it was committed. Punishment is personal and can be imposed only on the offender.
5. Alfred P. Rubin, "Milosevic and Hussein on Trial", 38 Cornell Int'l L.J. 1013, 2005.
6. *Allan Little is a former BBC correspondent in Baghdad* http://www.timesonline.co.uk/tol/news/world/middle_east/article1265315.ece, retrieved from website on 12-16-2007.
7. *Ibid.*
8. In 1983 Reagan even sent a personal envoy to meet Saddam face to face. His name was Donald Rumsfeld.
9. Statute of the Iraqi Special Tribunal, Dec. 10, 2003, 43 I.L.M. 231.
10. Justice Richard Goldstone, "The Trial of Saddam Hussein: What kind of Court should prosecute Saddam Hussein and others for Human Rights Abuses", 27 Fordham Int'l L.J. 1490, 2003-04.

11. *Ibid.* Agreement between the United States and the Government of Sierra Leone on the establishment of a Special Court for Sierra Leone, Aug., 2000, US-Sierra Leone.
12. UN Charter Article 39, para 1.
13. Rome Statute of the International Criminal Court, July, 1998, Article XI.
14. M. Cheriff Bassiouni, "Post-Conflict Justice in Iraq: An Appraisal of the Iraq Special Tribunal", 38 Cornell Int'l L.J. 327, 2005.
15. Michael J. Kelly, "The Tricky Nature of Proving Genocide against Saddam Hussein before the Iraqi Special Tribunal", 38 Cornell Int'l L.J. 983, 2005.
16. *Ibid.*
17. *Ibid.*
18. G.A. Res. 95(1), U.N. Doc. A/64/Add. 1, at 188, 1946.
19. Geneva Convention for the Amelioration of the Condition of the Wounded and Sick Armed Forces in the Field, Aug. 12, 1949, Article XLIX; Geneva Convention for the Amelioration of the Wounded, Sick and Shipwrecked Members of Armed Forces at Sea, Aug. 12, 1949, Article L; Geneva Convention relative to the Treatment of Prisoners of War, Aug. 12, 1949, Article CXXIX; Geneva Conventions relative to the Protection of Civilian Persons in Time of War, Aug. 12, 1949, Article CXLVI.
20. Convention against Torture and other Cruel, Inhuman or Degrading Treatment or Punishment, Feb. 4, 1984, Article VII.
21. Convention on offences and certain other acts committed on Board Aircraft, Sept. 14, 1963, Article III; Convention for the suppression of unlawful Seizure of Aircraft, Dec. 16, 1970, Article IV; International Convention for the Suppression of Terrorist Bombings, Jan. 12, 1998, Article VI; International Convention for the Suppression of the Financing of Terrorism, Jan. 10, 2000, Article X.
22. On October 20, 2005, attorney Saadoun Sughaiyer al-Janabi, charged with the defense of Awad Hamed al-Bandar, was abducted from his office by gunmen, and found shot dead near his office a few hours later. On November 8, 2005, attorney Adel al-Zubeidi, who had been representing Vice President Taha Yassin Ramadan and Abdullah Kazim Ruwayyid, was killed by three gunmen in Baghdad. Barazan Ibrahim's lawyer Thamer Hamoud al-Khuzaie was also wounded in the attack. On June 21, 2006, Saddam's chief defense lawyer, Khamis al-Obeidi, was assassinated in Baghdad. http://english.people.com.cn/200511/09/eng20051109_220110.html, last visited on 15th March, 2007.
23. Article 66(3) of the Rome Statute.

24. ICTR Rules of Procedure and Evidence, Rule 87(a).
25. ICTY Rules of Procedure and Evidence, Rule 87(a).
26. Human Rights Committee, General Comment 13 (on Article 14) ("[b]y reason of the presumption of innocence... [n]o guilt can be presumed until the charge has been proven beyond reasonable doubt.").
27. Human Rights View "(2006)". Briefing Paper: *The Iraqi Special Tribunal*. Available at <http://www.hrw.org>, last visited on 14th March, 2007.
28. Article 182 of the Iraqi Code of Criminal Procedure states that: "if the trial has been conducted in accordance with the law, and the Court is satisfied that the defendant has committed the offence, it issues the verdict of guilt and rules on the penalty to be applied. If, however, it becomes clear to the Court that there is not sufficient evidence to condemn him, the charges are dropped and he is released."
29. Herbert L. Packer, "Two Models of Criminal Process", *University of Pennsylvania Law Review*, Vol. 113, No. 1, pp. 1-68: (Nov. 1964).
30. ECHR, Ser. A. No. 308, at p. 16, Para 35.
31. ECHR, Appl. No. 8860/79.
32. On 5th October, 2005.
33. Interview with Jalal Talibani, Radio Free Europe 5th October, 2005.
34. Arab Times (Kuwait), "Execution of Saddam Soon", 6th July, 2006.
35. Article 14(2) of the ICCPR, Article 11 of the Universal Declaration of Human Rights , Principle 36(1) of the Body of Principles for the protection of all persons under any form of Detention or Imprisonment.
36. Jerome Hall, General Principles of Criminal Law, p. 27.
37. 1. In time of public emergency which threatens the life of the nation and the existence of which is officially proclaimed, the States Parties to the present Covenant may take measures derogating from their obligations under the present Covenant to the extent strictly required by the exigencies of the situation, provided that such measures are not inconsistent with their other obligations under international law and do not involve discrimination solely on the ground of race, colour, sex, language, religion or social origin.

    2. No derogation from Articles 6, 7, 8 (paragraphs 1 and 2), 11, 15, 16 and 18 may be made under this provision.

3. Any State Party to the present Covenant availing itself of the right of derogation shall immediately inform the other States Parties to the present Covenant, through the intermediary of the Secretary-General of the United Nations, of the provisions from which it has derogated and of the reasons by which it was actuated. A further communication shall be made, through the same intermediary, on the date on which it terminates such derogation.

38. No one shall be held guilty of any penal offence on account of any act or omission which did not constitute a penal offence, under national or international law, at the time when it was committed. Nor shall a heavier penalty be imposed than the one that was applicable at the time the penal offence was committed.

39. Article 22: *Nullum Crimen Sine Lege*: 1. A person shall not be criminally responsible under this Statute unless the conduct in question constitutes, at the time it takes place, a crime within the jurisdiction of the Court. 2. The definition of a crime shall be strictly construed and shall not be extended by analogy. In case of ambiguity, the definition shall be interpreted in favour of the person being investigated, prosecuted or convicted. 3. This Article shall not affect the characterization of any conduct as criminal under international law independently of this Statute.

40. Article 9. *Freedom from Ex Post Facto Laws*: No one shall be convicted of any act or omission that did not constitute a criminal offense, under the applicable law, at the time it was committed. A heavier penalty shall not be imposed than the one that was applicable at the time the criminal offense was committed. If subsequent to the commission of the offense the law provides for the imposition of a lighter punishment, the guilty person shall benefit therefrom.

41. Article 70: Protected persons shall not be arrested, prosecuted or convicted by the Occupying Power for acts committed or for opinions expressed before the occupation, or during a temporary interruption thereof, with the exception of breaches of the laws and customs of war.

    Nationals of the Occupying Power who, before the outbreak of hostilities, have sought refuge in the territory of the occupied State, shall not be arrested, prosecuted, convicted or deported from the occupied territory, except for offences committed after the outbreak of hostilities, or for offences under common law committed before the outbreak of hostilities which, according to the law of the occupied State, would have justified extradition in time of peace.

42. Appl. No. 45571/99 at para 31, 21st January, 2003.

43. Ser. C. No. 52, Inter-American Court of Human Rights at para 129, 30th May, 1999.
44. ICTY Case No. IT 94 I (2nd October, 1995).
45. http://edition.cnn.com/2004/WORLD/meast/07/01/iraq.saddam/.
46. "(a) To be informed promptly and in detail in a language which he understands of the nature and cause of the charge against him."
47. "(a) To be informed promptly and in detail of the nature, cause and content of the charge, in a language which the accused fully understands and speaks."
48. Prior notification in detail to the accused of the charges against him.
49. Everyone charged with a criminal offence has the following minimum rights: (a) To be informed promptly, in a language which he understands and in detail, of the nature and cause of the accusation against him.
50. ACHPR Comm. No. 39/90 (2000).
51. Article 14 of the International Covenant on Civil and Political Rights.
52. Article 63: *Trial in the Presence of the Accused*: The accused shall be present during the trial. If the accused, being present before the Court, continues to disrupt the trial, the Trial Chamber may remove the accused and shall make provision for him or her to observe the trial and instruct counsel from outside the courtroom, through the use of communications technology, if required. Such measures shall be taken only in exceptional circumstances after other reasonable alternatives have proved inadequate, and only for such duration as is strictly required.
53. In the determination of any charge against the accused pursuant to the present statute the accused shall be entitled to the following minimum guarantees, in full equality: to be tried in his presence, and to defend himself in person or through legal assistance of his own choosing; to be informed, if he does not have legal assistance, of this right; and to have legal assistance assigned to him, in any case where the interests of justice so require, and without payment by him in any such case if he does not have sufficient means to pay for it.
54. Article 20: *Rights of the Accused*: To be tried in his or her presence, and to defend himself or herself in person or through legal assistance of his or her own choosing; to be informed, if he or she does not have legal assistance, of this right; and to have legal assistance assigned to him or her, in any case where the interest of justice so require, and without payment by him or her in any such case if he or she does not have sufficient means to pay for it.

55. [2000] Crim. LR 683 at para 47.
56. [2000] Crim. LR 679.
57. [2000] Crim. LR 681.
58. Robert Worth, "Saddam Hussein Sees Lawyer for First Time Since Capture," *New York Times*, December 17, 2004.
59. Department of State, Quarterly Update to Congress: Section 2207 Report on Iraq Relief and Reconstruction (October 2004), I-28; Department of State, Quarterly Update to Congress: Section 2207 Report on Iraq Relief and Reconstruction (December 2004), I-41.
60. The defense were asked to present their closing remarks on 10th July, 2006.
61. The Court had in fact refused to hear any more defense witnesses on 13th June, 2006.
62. *Griffin v. California* 380 US 609 at 614 (1965), *Miranda v. Arizona* 384 US 436 at 468 (1966). *Fisher v. United States* 425 US 391 at 400 (1976).
63. C. Theophilopoulos, "The evidentiary value if adverse inferences from the accused's right to sielence", 15 S. Afr. J. Crim. Just. 321, 2002.
64. (1993) 16 EHRR 297 at 325.
65. SICT Statute, Article 22(4)(f).
66. Code of Criminal Procedure, Para. 179, emphasis added.
67. CPA Memorandum 3, s. 4(g), CPA/MEM/27 June 1994/03.
68. http://www.hrw.org/english/docs/2003/12/19/iraq6770.htm: retrieved on 02-02-2007.
69. Rule 46: *Rights of Suspects during Questioning by an Investigative Judge*:

    A. Suspect who is questioned by an Investigative Judge shall have the following rights of which he shall be informed by the Investigative Judge prior to questioning in a language he speaks and understands:

    (i) The right to legal assistance of his own choosing, including the right to have legal assistance provided by the Defense Office if he does not have sufficient means to pay for it;

    (ii) The right to have the free assistance of an interpreter if he cannot understand or speak the language to be used for questioning; and

    (iii) The right to remain silent. In this regard, the suspect or accused shall be cautioned that any statement he makes may be recorded and may be used in evidence;

B. An accused may voluntarily waive his right to have legal assistance during questioning if the Investigative Judge determines that the waiver is voluntarily and intelligently made.

C. If an accused has exercised his right to legal assistance, questioning by an Investigative Judge of a suspect shall not proceed without the presence of counsel, in a case of the waiver, then the accused expresses his will to have legal assistance, accordingly the questioning should be stopped and never resume until the defense be present.

70. S.V. Maritz 1974(1) SA 266 (NC).

71. Section 3: *Penalties*:

(1) Capital punishment is suspended. In each case where the death penalty is the only available penalty prescribed for an offense, the Court may substitute the lesser penalty of life imprisonment, or such other lesser penalty as, provided for in the Penal Code.

(2) Torture and cruel, degrading or inhuman treatment or punishment is prohibited.

(3) No person will be prosecuted for aiding, assisting, associating with, or working for Coalition Forces or the CPA.

72. The occurrence and consequences of an determined in accordance with the law in force at the time of its commission and the time of commission is determined by reference to the time at which the criminal act occurs and not by reference to the time when the consequence of the offence is realized.

73. The principle of *lex mitior*.

74. Article 6 para 2: In countries which have not abolished the death penalty, sentence of death may be imposed only for the most serious crimes in accordance with the law in force at the time of the commission of the crime and not contrary to the provisions of the present Covenant and to the Convention on the Prevention and Punishment of the Crime of Genocide. This penalty can only be carried out pursuant to a final judgment rendered by a competent Court.

75. Harlon Leigh Dalton, "Taking the Right to Appeal (more or less) Seriously", 95 Yale L.J. 62, 1985-86 at p. 62.

76. R. Leflar, Internal Operating Procedures of Appellate Courts 4, 9-10 (1976).

77. ABA Comm. on Standards of Judicial Administration: Standards relating to Appellate Courts, Commentary at 12 (1977).

78. Michelman, "The Supreme Court and Litigation Access Fees: The Right to Protect One's Rights—Part-1", 1973, Duke L.J. 1153, 1172-75.

79. *Ibid.*, at 1172-75.

80. Indeed, quite apart from any such instrumental benefits, it has been argued that securing the satisfaction of the parties and derivatively, of society should be viewed-as the primary purpose of the judicial system. See C. Curtis, it's your law 21 (1954). For Curtis, the decision whether to retain appeal of right presumably would turn on the question of whether appeal on demand maximizes party satisfaction. For a more complete description of satisfaction theory, see Golding, on the "Advisory System and Justice", in *Philosophical Law*, 112-16 (R. Bronough ed. 1978).

3

The International Covenant on Civil and Political Rights and the International Covenant on Economic, Social and Cultural Rights: Their Implementation and Progress

M. Abdul Hannan

1. Introduction

The International Covenant on Civil and Political Rights[1] and the International Covenant on Economic, Social and Cultural Rights[2] have been described as "the bedrock of the international normative regime in relation to human rights".[3] They together with the Universal Declaration of Human Rights[4] constitute the "International Bill of Rights".[5] Although the Covenants were literally delivered as twins and came into force in the same year,[6] any student of international Human Rights law will not hesitate to submit that the ICCPR has so far made more progress, and the rights in it more enjoyed and protected than the ICESCR.[7] Up till 1986, as Craven rightly observes, the ICESCR "existed only as a textual reference point".[8] This has been due to many factors, the most apparent of which are:

(i) the inherent differences between the two groups of rights covered by the Covenants and

(ii) the different implementation procedures for each Covenant.

2. The Background

After the Second World War, the United Nations (UN) declared the protection and promotion of Human Rights and fundamental freedoms as one of its purposes.[9] A Commission on Human Rights[10] was created in 1947 with the mandate, *inter alia,* to draft an "International Bill of Rights" consisting of a general Declaration on Human Rights, a binding Covenant and an implementation procedure.

The UDHR was drafted and was adopted in 1948 containing general provisions on both civil and political rights (C&P Rights) and economic, social and cultural rights (ESC Rights.) An early disparity, however, exists in terms of an imbalance between the provisions on the C&P Rights against the ESC Rights in the UDHR. Szabo, observes that the ESC Rights "are referred to only in passing" and "are not examined in a manner comparable to that of other rights."[11] He further identifies that there are only five[12] Articles on the ESC Rights out of the thirty Articles of the UDHR. The two groups of rights therefore seem to have been handled differently right from the beginning. Robertson opines that this was due to the different evolution of each group of rights, that while "civil and political rights have grown through centuries of struggle and legal evolution" many of the economic, social and cultural rights "were first established in international law".[13] This seems to find support in the classification of C&P Rights as "first generation" rights and the, ESC Rights as "second generation" rights. Eide and Rosas however, reject this notion of "generations" and assert that "economic and social rights found acceptance at the international level before civil and political rights".[14]

Between 1948 and 1951 the Commission continued its mandate on the "International Bill of Rights". There arose divisions, with the Eastern Bloc States requesting the inclusion of the ESC Rights in the draft Covenant and the Western States asserting the priority of the C&P Rights and opposing the inclusion of ESC Rights. The UN General Assembly intervened, requesting that ESC Rights be included "in a manner which relates them to the civil and political freedoms proclaimed by the draft Covenant"[15] and also emphasized that "the enjoyment of civil and political freedoms and that of economic, social and cultural rights are interdependent".[16] The Commission then prepared a single draft Covenant of seventy-three Articles grouped into six parts covering both C&P Rights and ESC Rights.[17]

Some Western States, however, indicated their unwillingness to be parties to a Covenant, which will commit them to provisions on ESC Rights.[18] The General Assembly was forced to reverse its earlier decision and allowed for two separate Covenants, "one to contain civil and political rights and the other to contain economic, social and cultural rights, in order that the General Assembly may approve the two Covenants simultaneously and open them at the same time for signature, the two Covenants to contain, in order to emphasize the unity of the aim in view and to ensure respect for and obedience of human rights, as many similar provisions as possible."[19]

The separation succeeded in putting the ESC Rights outside the main stream of Human Rights for a long time due to the ineffective implementation measures subsequently formulated for the ICESCR. McGoldrick rightly observes that while the separation proved beneficial to the ICCPR in terms of implementation, "the implementation procedure and practices established under the ICESCR has been somewhat disappointing."[20] That might as well have been the desire, at that time, of the States that called for the separation.

3. The Inherent Differences between the Two Groups of Rights

The two groups of rights differ in nature, origin and significance and were emphasized during the drafting by those States that advocated for their separation. The main differences canvassed were that:

(a) While C&P Rights were enforceable, justiciable and of an absolute nature, the ESC Rights were not;

(b) While C&P Rights were generally rights of individuals against unlawful and unjust action of the State (i.e. negative rights) the ESC Rights were rights which the State would have to take positive action to promote (i.e. positive rights);

(c) While C&P Rights were immediately applicable, the ESC rights were to be progressively implemented;

(d) While C&P Rights were "legal rights" the ESC Rights were "programme rights".

The eventual separation was, therefore, generally seen as a confirmation of the "hierarchical ascendance of the civil and political rights" and has "since been used as evidence of the inherent opposition of the two categories of rights."[21] Authors such as Vierdag[22] and Bossuyt[23] have expressed strong views re-enforcing the superiority of the C&P Rights over the ESC Rights on the basis of their inherent differences and consequent relegation of the ESC Rights are only results of the ideological rivalry between the East and the West during the drafting period.[24] Shue in particular concedes no general difference, either in respect of importance or scope, between the two groups of rights and argues that the ESC Rights are quite as important as the C&P Rights.[25]

It is an over-simplification to contend that no difference exists between the two groups of rights at all. Going back to the differences, the first two points touch specifically on the nature of the rights while the second and third refer to the implementation or realization of the rights. The contended "negative" *contra* "positive" nature of the respective group of rights is a strong factor that may not be ignored.

Since most of the C&P Rights are "protection rights" or rights of non-interference against some inherent qualities and dignity of the human being, people tend to react promptly against any negative act by the State in violation of those rights. This is further assisted by the justiciable status conferred on the C&P Rights and the petition system available for individuals to challenge such violations. On the other hand, most of the ESC Rights are "provision rights" against which only few will react to its non-fulfilment by the State. This is, conversely, further aggravated by the non-justiciable status conferred on the ESC Rights and the non-availability of a petition system for individuals to question the non-fulfilment of the rights by the State.

The question of resources is also a very important one. Although it has been argued rightly that some of the C&P Rights also require resources to achieve,[26] it is a fact that the ESC Rights generally required greater resources to achieve. This is evidenced by Article 2 of the ICESCR which obligates each State Party to devote "The maximum of its available resources with a view to achieving progressively the full realization" of those rights. The developed nations have not committed the maximum international assistance and co-operation towards the realization of the ESC Rights. They have rather been more interested in the C&P Rights. This, I submit, relates more to ideological and political leanings that to the inherent differences of the two groups of rights. The changing attitude towards the ESC Rights after the period of the Cold War is an evidence of this fact.

Another point usually raised is the lack of conceptual clarity and the vagueness of many of the norms reflected in the ICESCR. Alston rightly identifies that this is not peculiar to the ICESCR but that the difference was the extent of elaboration enjoyed by the ICCPR in the clarification of concepts.[27] This has been examined below.

3.1. *The effect of the differences on the progress of the rights*

While it is unrealistic to deny that some significant differences exist between the two groups of rights, it is also true that these differences are mostly overstated to an extent detrimental to the ICESCR. This has been due principally to ideological reasons.

The United States of America (USA) for instance, for a long time categorically denied the recognition of ESC Rights. The Reagan administration deleted the sections dealing with ESC Rights from the State Department's annual *Country Reports on Human Rights Practices* submitted to the US Congress in 1982.[28] In defense of this, the then Assistant Secretary of State argued to the effect of the Covenants "the rights that no government can violate are the C&P Rights which should not be watered down to the status of rights and governments should do their best to secure the ESC Rights".[29]

It is hereby submitted that it is not the nature of the C&P Rights that keeps States away from violating them (because they actually do violate them) but rather the availability of a system of implementation allowing individuals to challenge such violations and the possibility of bringing violating States into disrepute through such avenues.

The oversimplification of the non-justiciable classification of the ESC Rights also makes some national courts to give rarely effect to the ESC Rights.[30] I find it difficult to assimilate that the ESC Rights are inherently non-justiciable unlike the C&P Rights. It is an artificial and assumed difference rather than an inherent one.[31] The main effect of the differences is that they were exploited in an excessive manner to obtain a separation and to formulate different implementation procedures for each group of rights which in turn has been a greater factor for the different degrees of progress achieved by the Covenants as has been shown below.

4. The Implementation Procedures of the Covenants

On the basis that the C&P Rights were rights immediately applicable and also "legal rights" while the ESC Rights were rights to be progressively implemented and also "programme rights",[32] different implementation procedures were designed for each Covenant by the Commission in fulfilment of the last part of the International Bill of Rights.

4.1. *Implementing bodies*

There is no doubt that a Human Rights guarantee is as good as its system of implementation and supervision.[33] The measures of implementation are at the heart of any Covenant without which the Covenant has little practical value.[34] While the Commission approved the establishment of a permanent and independent body, the Human Rights Committee[35] with clear functions, for the implementation of the ICCPR,[36] the debates produced quite an obscure method of implementation for the ICESCR.[37] Article 17(1) of the ICESCR subjected the supervision and implementation of the ESC Rights to a clumsy system involving different bodies.[38] Craven rightly identifies that the system outlined in the ICESCR was "unclear as to the nature, purpose or degree of supervision to be given and as to the extent to which the bodies mentioned should involve themselves."[39]

That the Session Working Group initially created by the Economic and Social Council (ECOSOC) to assist with implementation of the ICESCR was ineffective, is evidenced by a survey report of the International Commission of Jurists on the work of the Group.[40] Therefore, while the ICCPR had a competent supervisory body right from the beginning, the ICESCR suffered a false start with an abortive supervision system and remained merely as a "textual reference point" until after 1986 when the Committee on Economic, Social and Cultural Rights was created by ECOSOC with functions similar to that of the HRC to supervise the implementation of the ICESCR.[41] This functionally, had placed the implementation of the ICESCR ten years behind the ICCPR.

4.2. *Methods of implementation*

Both the ICCPR and the ICESCR provide for the reporting system by which State Parties undertake to submit reports on measures adopted and the progress made in respect of the rights.[42] The modes of reporting however differ.

The ICCPR provides that State Parties should submit reports:

(a) within one year of the entry into force of the Covenant for the State Party concerned; and

(b) thereafter whenever the HRC so requests. The HRC on this basis developed the initial, supplementary and periodic reporting under the ICCPR.[43] The supplementary and periodic reports serve as follow ups to the initial report, which must be submitted by

States within one year of the entry into force of the Covenant for them.

Under the ICESCR State Parties undertake to submit reports in stages, in accordance with a programme to be established by ECOSOC. ECOSOC created a three stage biennial reporting system with a cycle of six years for the ICESCR.[44] The first report to cover Articles 6 to 9, the second on Articles 10 to 12 and the third on Articles 13 to 15. Time has since proved this mode as less effective. A new mode following the pattern of reporting under the ICCPR whereby an initial single report will be submitted within two years of the entry into force of the Covenant for the State Party and thereafter at five yearly intervals was therefore adopted by ECOSOC in 1988 on the recommendation of the Committee. Another indicator of an initial ineffective implementation mode for the ICESCR.

4.3. *The petition system*

The petition system is generally considered as a very effective method of protecting Human Rights. In 1950 the UN General Assembly had requested ECOSOC to request the Commission to consider provisions "to be inserted into the draft Covenant or in separate Protocols, for the receipt and examination of petitions from individuals and organizations with respect to alleged violations of the Covenant."[45] The petition system was adopted in a separate Protocol in 1966 with a preamble which says: "in order further to achieve the purposes of the ICCPR and the implementation of its provisions it would be appropriate to enable the HRC...to receive and consider...communications from individuals claiming violations of any rights set forth in the Covenant."[46] The OP1 has contributed to further achieve the purposes of the ICCPR as envisaged in its preamble. The HRC has through it developed a wide jurisprudence and clarified many concepts on the rights contained in the ICCPR. Although compliance with State Parties with the views of the HRC under the OP1 has been described elsewhere as disappointing,[47] the system has no doubt assisted in the progress achieved so far in the protection of the rights contained in the ICCPR.

The petition system is not applicable to the rights contained in the ICESCR. Proposals for it to be were rejected during the drafting. However, time has proved that the petition system is an advantage which contributes to the progress of the C&P Rights above the ESC Rights. In confirmation of this, the Committee which was created in 1986 at its seventh session observed that:

> The Committee believes that there are strong reasons for adopting a complaints procedure in respect of the economic and social rights recognised in the Covenant. ...They would be similar in nature to those applying under the First Optional Protocol to the International Covenant on Civil and Political Rights.[48]

The Committee, therefore, at its ninth session requested Professor Alston to prepare a Draft Optional Protocol for consideration in this respect. This was another move towards the adoption of similar implementation procedures of the ICCPR for the ICESCR in an attempt to invigorate the enjoyment and protection of the ESC Rights.

4.4. *The General Comments of the HRC*

Another important implementation aid in respect of the C&P Rights is the General Comments of the HRC on the Articles of the ICCPR. It provides clear guidelines for State Parties and also goes a long way in clarifying or defining any vague concepts that exist in the ICCPR. They had been described as being very purposeful and progressive with respect to the implementation of the Covenant.

This system was also not available in the implementation procedure of the ICESCR before the creation of the Committee in 1986. The Committee, realizing the importance of the General Comments of the HRC decided "to begin, as from its third session, the preparation of General Comments based on the various Articles and provisions of the ICESCR with a view to assisting the State Parties in fulfilling their reporting obligations."[49]

One can therefore observe that for a period of ten years (1976-86) while the HRC utilized different effective modes of implementation to ensure the progress of the C&P Rights under the ICCPR, the ICESCR was static due to the ineffective implementation procedure and lack of an appropriate supervisory organ to monitor whatever implementation procedure available.

This has been the factor, more than any other, which has crippled the progress of the ICESCR in comparison with the ICCPR.

5. Conclusions

While conceding that there exist some inherent differences between the C&P Rights and the ESC Rights, the differences cannot be considered as the major factor responsible for the different degrees of progress between the two groups of rights. The differences were only exploited and used during the drafting stage to divide the rights for ideological and political reasons and to create different methods of implementation which has in turn been beneficial to one group of rights and crippled the other.

The implementation organs and procedures set up for the achievement of the C&P Rights worked better in all ramifications than those of the ICESCR. Even with the reporting system which applied to both groups of rights, the HRC proved more dynamic. The European Social Charter (ESC) which is a regional counterpart of the ICESCR shows that an effective implementation procedure could have also enhanced the progress of the ICESCR. Professor Harris observed that the ESC's success in establishing itself during the first years of its life was as a result of the effectiveness of the Committee of Independent Experts charged with its implementation.[50] The efforts undertaken since 1986 to remedy the implementation procedure of the ICESCR along the lines of the ICCPR with the creation of the Committee on Economic, Social and Cultural Rights are therefore commendable.[51] With the elimination of the East-West confrontation and a change of attitude by the Western States towards the ESC Rights, it is hoped that the implementation of the ICESCR will be pursued, *bona fide,* and in the spirit of the interdependence of each group of rights as expressed by the UN General Assembly in

1951 and restated in the preamble of the American Protocol of San Salvador adopted in 1988.[52]

The Committee should place more importance on the use of the General Comments to create a framework of outlining the general scope and content of the rights upon which the intended petition system may develop when eventually adopted. This will go a long way to develop a broad understanding of the norms within the ICESCR. Practices also seem to demonstrate that the idea of ESC Rights being wholly non-justiciable is no longer accurate.[53] This therefore calls for the adoption of the Optional Protocol establishing the petition system for the ICESCR "in order to further achieve the purposes of the Covenant and implementation of its provisions."[54]

With an effective implementation and supervisory procedure, it is submitted that the ICESCR will overcome the sterile and artificial antithesis between the two groups of rights.

Notes

1. (1976) 999 UNTS 171 (*hereinafter referred to as* the ICCPR).
2. (1976) 993 UNTS 3 (*hereinafter referred to as* the ICESCR; the ICCPR and ICESCR will be referred to together as the Covenant).
3. Steiner, H.J., and Alston, P., *International Human Rights in Context: Law, Politics and Morals (1996), 256.*
4. *Hereinafter referred to as* the UDHR.
5. *See* Harris, D., "The International Covenant on Civil and Political Rights and the United Kingdom Law: An Introduction", in Harris, D. J., and Joseph, S., (Eds.), *The International Covenant on Civil and Political Rights and United Kingdom Law* (1995), p. 1 *and also* Part 1 A (2), "The Limburg Principles on the Implementation of the ICCPR", UN Doc. EC/CN. 4/1987/17 Annex (1987), *9 HRQ*, 122.
6. Both entered into force in 1976. The ICESCR on 3 January 1976 and the ICCPR on 23 March 1976.
7. *See* Harris, *Supra,* p. 2 and Eide, A. and Rosas, A., "Economic, Social and Cultural Rights: A Universal Challenge", in Eide, A., et al (Eds.) *Economic, Social and Cultural Rights: A Textbook* (1995), p. 15.

8. *See* Craven, M., *The International Covenant on Economic, Social and Cultural Rights: A Perspective on its Development* (1995), p. 1.
9. *UN Charter*, Article 1(3). *See also* Szabo, I., *Historical Foundations of Human Rights and Subsequent Developments* in Vasak, K., (Ed.), The International Dimensions of Human Rights (1982) Vol. 1, pp. 20-23. (For a brief but rich account of the emergence of Human Rights at the international level).
10. *Hereinafter referred to as* the Commission.
11. Szabo, *Supra,* p. 25. *See also* Craven, *Supra,* p. 17.
12. These are probably Articles 22-26 of the UDHR., Article 27 also refers to ESC rights.
13. Robertson, R.E., *Measuring State Compliance with the Obligation to Devote the "Maximum Available Resources" to Realizing Economic, Social and Cultural Rights* (1994), 16 HRQ 693.
14. *See* Eide and Rosas, *Supra*, note 6, p. 27.
15. GA Res. 421 (V) 4 Dec. 1950, 5 UN GAOR. Supp. 20 (A/1775) pp. 42-43.
16. *See* Annotations on the text of the *Draft International Covenants on Human Rights* by the Secretary General, UN Doc. A/29, July 1, 1955, GAOR Annexes (X) hereinafter A/2929, p. 7, para 7.
17. *See* Commission on Human Rights, Report of the 7th Session, 13 UN ESCOR, Supp. 9 (E/1992) 24 May 1951, pp. 20-26.
18. *See generally* Sohn, L.B. "United Nations and Human Rights A Short History of United Nations Documents on Human Rights," in 18th Report of the Commission to Study the Organisation of Peace (1968) Hereinafter UN & HUMAN RIGHTS), p. 38 at 105-06
19. GA Res. 543 (VI) 5 Feb. 1952, 6 UN GAOR, Res. Supp. (No. 20) (1952), 36.
20. McGoldrick, D., *The Human Rights Committee: Its Role in the Development of the International Covenant on Civil and Political Rights* (1991), p. 11.
21. *See* Craven, *Supra,* p. 9. *See also* Viljanen, V., "Abstention or Involvement? The Nature of State Obligation under Different Categories of Rights" in Drzewicki., K., et al. (Eds.) *Social Rights, As Human Rights, A European Challenge* (1994), p. 43.
22. *See* Vierdag, E.W., *The Legal Nature of the Rights Granted by the International Covenant on Economic, Social and Cultural Rights* (1978), 9NYBIL 69.

23. *See* Bossuyt, M., *La Distinction juridique entree les droits civils et politiques et les droits economiques, sociaux et culterels* (1975), 8HRLJ 783.
24. *See* generally Craven, *Supra, pp. 8-16, see also* Vincent, R.J., *Human Rights and International Relations* (1988), *pp. 11-13* and Donnelly, J., *Universal Human Rights In Theory and Practice* (1989), pp. 28-45.
25. Shue, H., *Basic Rights: Sustenance, Affluence and US Foreign Policy* (1980), p. 7.
26. *See* e.g. Craven, *Supra*, p. 15.
27. *See* Alston, P., "The Committee on Economic, Social and Cultural Rights", in P. Alston (Ed.) *The United Nations And Human Rights: A Critical Appraisal* (1992), p. 490.
28. *See* Alston, P., "US Ratification of the Covenant on Economic, Social and Cultural Rights: the need for an entirely new strategy (1990)", 48 AJIL 365 at 367 and 372-75. It is important to note that an Additional Protocol to the American Convention on Human Rights (The Protocol of San Salvador) was adopted in 1988 adding guarantees regarding certain economic, social and cultural rights to the American Convention. It is however not in force yet. Also the US has not ratified it.
29. *Ibid.* p. 373.
30. *See* Craven, M., *The Domestic Application of the International Covenant on Economic, Social and Cultural Rights* (1993), 40 NILR 367.
31. *See* Addo, M.K., "Justiciablity Re-examined", in Beddard, R. and Hill, D.M. (Eds.) *Economic, Social and Cultural Rights: Progress and Achievements* (1992), 93.
32. *See* Point (c) and (d) on differences between the rights above.
33. *See* Harris, D.J., *The European Social Charter* (1984), p. 261.
34. *See* A/2929, *Supra*, para. 37.
35. *Hereinafter referred to as* the HRC.
36. *See* McGoldrick. D., *The Human Rights Committee: Its Role in the Development of the International Covenant on Civil and Political Rights* (1991), p. 6 and Chapter 2, *See also* Part IV. Articles 28-30 of the ICCPR.
37. *See* Craven, *Supra*, pp. 35, 38.
38. *See* Articles 17-25 *of the* ICESCR.
39. *See* Craven, *Supra*, p. 38.
40. *See* commentary: "Implementation of the ICESCR: ECOSOC Working Group (1981)", 27 ICJ Review 26. *See also* Simma, B., "The Implementation of the International Covenant on Economic,

Social and Cultural Rights", in Matscher, F., (Ed.) *The Implementation of the Economic, Social and Cultural Rights: National, International and Comparative Aspects* (1991), 75 at 82 where the author describes the Session Working Group as "a mockery of a monitoring system".

41. For a rich exposition on the evolution of the Committee *see* Alston, P., *Out of the Abyss: The Challenges Confronting the New UN Committee on Economic, Social and Cultural Rights* (1987), 9HRQ 332 at 340-49.
42. *See* Article 40 ICCPR *and* Article 16 ICESCR.
43. *See* McGoldrick, *Supra,* p. 63.
44. *See* UN Doc. E/5464 p. 5 para. 24 (1976) 60 UN ESCOR, Annexes (Ag. Item). (The periods of the 2nd and subsequent reports was extended by ECOSOC to 9 years in 1985 by ECOSOC Res. 1985/ 132 UN ESCOR, Supp. (No. 1), p. 42.
45. GA Res. 421 (V) See A/2929 *Supra*, para 22.
46. *See* First Optional to the ICCPR (hereinafter OPI).
47. *See* MacGoldrick, *Supra*, p. 202.
48. *See* Alston, P.C., "Draft Optional Protocol" in Coomans and Van Hoof (Eds.), *The Right to Complain and Economic, Social and Cultural Rights* (1995), 179-80.
49. *See IHRR*, Vol. 1. (1994), p. 1, (The Committee has so far issued six General Comments).
50. *See* Harris, *Supra*, note 33, p. xiv.
51. *See* Craven, M., "Towards an Unofficial Petition Procedure: A Review on the Role of the UN Committee of Economic, Social and Cultural Rights" in Drzewicki. K., et.al. *Supra*, note 21, pp. 91-110 for an appraisal of the Committee's bold steps towards effective implementation of the Covenant.
52. *See Supra* note 22.
53. *See* Craven, p. 106 and footnote 62 thereof.
54. *See* "The 3rd Preambular paragraph to Draft Optional Protocol for the ICESCR" in Alston *Supra*, note 48 p. 183.

4

Ecological Perspective of Right to Information: Need for Participatory Approach to Governance

Sairam Bhat

Improving the availability of information on the state of the environment and on activities which have adverse or damaging effects are well established objectives of international environmental law. Information is recognized as a prerequisite to effective national and international environmental management, protection and co-operation. The availability of, and access to, information allows preventative and mitigation measures to be taken, ensures the participation of citizens in national decision-making processes, and can influence consumer behavior. Information also allows the international community to determine whether States are complying with their legal obligations.

Environmental Impact Assessment is one important technique for acquiring environmental information. International agreements and practice have developed other techniques for ensuring that States and other members of the international community are provided with information on the environmental consequences of certain activities.[1]

No fewer than four of the Rio Declaration's twenty-seven Principles are concerned with improving the provision of, and access to, environmental information. The Rio Declaration calls for exchange of knowledge [information]; individual access to environmental information; public awareness; notification of emergencies; and prior and timely notification on certain potentially hazardous activities. Chapter 40 of Agenda 21, entitled 'Information for decision-making', recognizes that the need for information arises at all levels, from senior decision-makers at international levels to the grassroots and individual level, and to that end calls for the development of two programme areas: to bridge the 'data gap' and to improve information availability.[2]

Information Exchange

The general obligation to exchange information is found, in one form or another, in virtually every international environmental agreement. 'Information exchange' can be characterized as a general obligation of one State to provide general information on one or more matters on an *ad hoc* basis to another State, especially in relation to scientific and technical information. 'Information exchange' may be distinguished from specific obligations to provide regular or periodic information on specified matters to a specified body [reporting] or to provide detailed information on the occurrence of a particular event or set of events, such as an accident or emergency or proposed activity. 'Information exchange' of a general nature is endorsed by Principle 20 of the Stockholm Declaration and by Principle 9 of the Rio Declaration, which supports exchange of scientific and technical knowledge as a means of strengthening 'endogenous capacity-building for sustainable development by improving scientific understanding'.

Under environmental treaties, the obligation of exchange information can be a requirement between States, between States and international organizations, and between international organizations and non-governmental actors.[3]

Information exchange can be required in respect of general and undefined matters or in relation to specific matters. Examples of the former include the obligation to exchange information: on general scientific, research and technical matters; on helping 'align or co-ordinate' national policies;[4] on research results and plans for science programmes;[5] on appropriate technologies;[6] on relevant national records;[7] on national legislation; on implementation;[8] on relevant national authorities and bodies; and even on the availability of professors and teachers.[9] Examples of more specific requirements include information exchange on: aspects of pests of pest and plant diseases;[10] the conservation of species of wild flora and fauna;[11] and the conservation and sustainable use of biological diversity.[12]

In recent years, several conventions have established more detailed rules on the type of information to be exchanged. The 1982 UNCLOS requires exchange of scientific information and other data relevant to conservation of fish stocks, on marine scientific research, and on marine pollution.[13] Article 8 of the 1979 LRTAP Convention requires the exchange of 'available information', through an Executive Body and bilaterally on emission data at periods of time to be agreed upon of certain air pollutants; major changes in national policies and general industrial development; control technologies for reducing air pollution; the projected cost of the emission control; meteorological and physic-chemical data relating to processes and effects; and national sub-regional and regional policies. Article 4 of the 1985 Vienna Convention requires the exchange of 'scientific, technical, socio-economic, commercial and legal information', as further elaborated in Annex II to that Convention, as well as information on alternative technologies. The 1987 Montreal Protocol calls for information exchange on best technologies possible alternatives to controlled substances and products and costs and benefits of relevant control strategies.[14]

A widespread concern about the limited effectiveness of the traditional language on information exchange is evident from the language adopted in more recent conventions. Increasingly, parties are being called upon to provide inventories or statistics of their natural and cultural resources[15] and to report on their emissions and discharges and their consequences. The 1992 Climate Change Convention, for expel, calls on parties to promote and co-operate in 'the full, open and prompt exchange of relevant scientific, technological, technical, socio-economic and legal information related to the climate system and climate change and to the economic and social consequences of various response strategies'.[16]

The 1992 Climate Change Convention illustrates the extent to which reporting requirements have become increasingly onerous. Reporting, which is described as 'the communication of information related to implementation', is a central technique for ensuring implementation of the Convention. All parties must publish and make available to the conference of the parties 'national inventories of anthropogenic emissions by sources and removals by sinks of all greenhouse gases not controlled by the 'Montreal Protocol', and communicate to the conference of the parties 'information related to implementation'.[17] These reports must include a general description of steps taken or envisaged to implement the Convention and 'other information the party considers relevant to the achievement of the objective of the convention and suitable for inclusion in its communication, including, if feasible, material relevant for calculations of global emission trends'.[18]

Prior Informed Consent

The obligation to consult is closely linked to the principle of 'prior informed consent'.[19]

Prior informed consent is the principle that international shipment of a chemical that is banned or severely restricted in order to protect human health or the environment should not proceed without the agreement, where such agreement exists, or contrary to the decision, of the designated national authority in the importing country.

The prior informed consent procedure, which requires the formal obtaining and disseminating of the decisions of importing countries on whether they wish to receive further shipments of chemicals which have been banned or severely restricted, has been used in UNEP[20] and FAO[21] not binding instruments and integrated into the legal binding arrangements for international trade in hazardous waste established by, for example, the 1989 Basel Convention,[22] the 1991 Bamako Convention,[23] and the 1993 EC Regulation.

The body of international rules on improving the availability of environmental information is now extensive, and information is now rightly a central technique for the implementation of environmental standards set by treaties and other international agreements. Citizen's access to environmental information will have to be developed in practice and further guidelines developed to ensure that natural resources and equitable managed.

National Perspective of Right to Know

'In India secrecy is the normal rule, openness an exception.' This is more strictly followed by government authorities responsible for pollution control and 'development' issues. Lack of information and the extremely uncooperative attitude of the concerned government authorities is the stumbling block in environment cases. Groups, especially those fighting major projects and development areas are faced with extremely hostile government authorities.

Public participation in environmental decision-making can be meaningful and effective only if people have right to know.

This is imperative in environmental matters because, for example, government decisions to site dams and large projects may displace thousands of people and deprive them of their lifestyles and livelihood. It has been stressed by the Court in the *Doon Valley* case that the question involving issues relating to environment and ecological balance brings into sharp focus the conflict between development and conservation and serves to emphasize the need for reconciling the two in larger interest of the people residing within the area and the country.[24] The reconciliation of conflict between development and conservation can be served better if the facts, basis and reasons for decision that affect health, life, liberty and livelihood of people are known to those whose interest and rights are affected. This becomes all the more important because in a developing society large segments of the populations are illiterate or unaware of their legal rights. The massive development projects leading to socio-economic transformation result in depletion of vast resources including wild flora and fauna, which are linked with the questions of life, liberty and livelihood of people. Therefore, desirability or otherwise of accelerated development can be decided only in the context of its socio-economic impacts particularly those concerning local people. Right to know becomes important from this perspective.

In pollution cases, the problem is more of collusion of the government authorities with the polluters. Under the prevailing special environmental enactments the concerned citizens or activists have no right to information. Even when the government authorities undertake investigation on a complaint by the concerned citizen or activist the said activist or citizen does not have the right to the investigation reports. There is more disabling legislation in this regard. Government authorities have used Section 5 of the Official Secrets Act to declare documents and even areas[25] as 'secret' and therefore inaccessible. In addition to this, the government claims immunity from producing documents in Court under Section 123 of the Evidence Act.

The right to information is considered a fundamental right in many countries. Special Acts have also been enacted to facilitate right to information.[26] The Air Act 1981[27] and the Water Act 1974[28] were amended to allow private citizen access to information on polluting industries, if they were complaining about them.[29] As usual, they also had a proviso allowing withholding of the information of the officials thought the interest of the public would not be served.[30] In India the right to information has been read into the Fundamental Rights to free speech and expression. This has been done in cases that raised wide constitutional problems. As early as in 1975 in the case of *State of Uttar Pradesh v Raj Narain*[31], the apex Court derived the right to information from freedom of speech. They said that the accountability of the Government could be safeguarded with information as a check against corruption.

Later in *S.P. Gupta v Union of India,*[32] popularly known as Judges case, Justice Bhagwati recognized the right to know to be implicit in the right to free speech and expression.

The first observation of any Court regarding right to information in environment cases is found in *L.K. Koolwal v State of Rajasthan,*[33] wherein the decision is based on tenuous legal logic and right to information is merely an observation in the *ratio decidendi*. In this case, PIL was filed for the issue of *Mandamus* against Jaipur City Municipal Corporation to provide better sanitation facilities.[34] The Court opined that the citizen has a right to know about the activities of the State. The privilege of secrecy does not survive now to a great extent. Under Article 19(1)(a) the right to freedom of speech is based on the foundation of the right to know. But this right is limited, particularly in the matter of sanitation. Every citizen has a right to know how the State is functioning in such matters because maintenance of health preservation of the sanitation and environment falls within the purview of Article 21 of the Constitution as it adversely affects the life of the citizen and it amounts to slow poisoning, if not checked.[35]

In *Bombay Environmental Action Group,*[36] the Court upheld the right of a citizen's group to inspect documents of a government agency, the Poona Cantonment Board; which was habitually suppressing information regarding illegal structures. The Court categorically held that it was not any Tom Dick or Harry that was asking for information but a group acting in public interest that required information and thus should have full access to it.

However, the right to information in both these cases was read into fundamental right to free speech and expression and both these decisions pertain to the times prior to the Court's observation that the right to clean air and water and wholesome environment is part of Article 21. It would be useful to advocate the argument that right to clean air, water and environment also includes the right to information that is absolutely necessary to exercise this right. Thus, it can be argued that the State cannot suppress information which is vital to the exercise of a fundamental right. The argument has not been used in any environment case, but is a promising one. It—the right to information—is achieved in this manner it will facilitate the exercise of right to life in all its aspects, including the right to a clean environment.

In *M.C. Mehta v Union of India*,[37] Mehta filed this application in the public interest, asking the Supreme Court to: (1) issue direction to cinema halls that they show slides with information on the environment; (2) issue direction for the spread of information relating to the environment to All India Radio; and (3) issue direction that the study of the environment become a compulsory subject in schools and colleges. Petitioner made this application on the grounds that Article 51A(g) of the Constitution requires every citizen to protect and improve the natural environment, including forests, lakes, rivers and wildlife, and to have compassion for living creatures. To fulfil these obligations to the environment, the Petitioner argued that people needed to be better educated about the environment.

India is a democratic country. Political democracy empowers its citizens to demand that its need to be fulfilled by the elected Government. Democracy allows demonstration, campaigns and *gherao* to achieve these demands. Courts may not be the proper forum for directing the executive to comply with the law.[38] Judicial action would be subverting the political democratic process, which is more effective.

The Freedom of Information Bill 2000 was introduced in the Lok Sabha in July 25, 2001. The Bill aims to provide for freedom to every citizen to secure access to information under the control of public authorities, consistent with public interest in order to promote openness, transparency and accountability in administration.[39] This definition is missing the dynamisms of the right which must include the right of the citizen to demand all information pertaining to any of the State's actions, and the right to participate in a question decision etc. It does not include the right of the citizen to demand proactive, *suo moto* and mandatory disclosure from Government and its agencies and others under its control and supervision.

Further, most of the provisions are very generally framed, which leaves much room for confusion. Likewise, it leaves too much room for administrative discretion, defying its very purpose. While the Bill gives a time consuming and tiring process for requesting information and appealing its refusal, there is no system for holding anyone responsible for unreasonable delays or unwarranted refusals. The Bill does not initiate systems, for easy information retrieval or for simplification of procedures and official language, which are the main hurdles between information and the public as seen in the case of Bangalore-Mysore Infrastructure Project.

Participation Means Cooperation

The Citizenry are the ultimate beneficiaries [or victims] of policy. Thus their cooperation is vital to the success of any policy. Unfortunately, the hierarchical structure of our society, coupled with the inadequate information, has alienated the common man from the Government. In order to secure their cooperation it is imperative to seek it first. The common man must be instructed on his role in environmental conservation. India lives in her villages and conservation must take place at the microcosmic level. Only if the common man feels relevant will be assisted. To feel relevant he must be convinced that the policy will not be inimical to his interests. More importantly, he must be convinced that the myopic, immediate interest must be subordinated to the long term interest. This is sustainable development, which includes in its ambit pollution control.[40]

Right to know strengthens participatory democracy also as armed with information on government programmes, citizens may influence decision-making through representation, lobbying and public debate.[41] Public access to government information enables citizens to exercise their political options purposefully. A government that conceals its actions and policies from the people who are affected by such actions and policies cannot be judged by the people and cannot be held accountable for its misdeeds. Moreover, governments in modern welfare states exercise vast powers that affect economic interests and impinge on citizen's liberty. These powers are susceptible to misuse by the executive for private gains. Thus, the right to be informed of public acts can help check the abuse of executive power. Likewise, access to government records, can better equip a public spirited litigant, particularly environmental groups to fight cases of environmental degradation and clearly establish where does public interest lie.[42]

Lack of proper appreciation of environmental information may often lead to decisions going against the interest of the general public. Consequently, priority is given to developmental activities aimed at short term benefits over conservation oriented actions with a long term perspective of sustainable benefits.[43]

Comparative Analysis

As regards the origins of right to environmental information in the UK, there is Environmental Information Regulation of 1992 and the Freedom of Information Act, 2000. Both of them heavily rely on European Union Information Directive and the provision of the Aarhus Convention[44] which was finally drafted[45] in 1998.[46] The peculiarity of the right to information in the English contest is that it completely hands over this issue to be determined by the Regulation of 1992 and the Freedom of Information Act plays only a very cursory role in endorsing this freedom. The Regulation itself is a detailed instrument on promoting the existence of the right to environmental information but nevertheless seems to be tinged with culture of secrecy that had existed with respect to official documents in UK and other Commonwealth countries. The UK is attempting modification of its Information Act with the Aarhus Convention[47] which speaks of the right to information, providing opportunity for public participation and lastly making way for a system where there is a smooth access to justice. The UK Freedom of Information Act 2000[48] specifically through Section 39 shifts over the burden of providing information to the Regulation of 1992 and gives the Regulation overriding powers. Section 39 is also supported by Section 74 which says that the Regulation shall be made by the Secretary of State keeping in mind the principles of the Aarhus Convention[49] and that the 'obligations imposed by the regulation in relation to disclosure of information is to have effect notwithstanding any enactment or rule of law'.

Under the 1992 Regulations in UK information on the environment can be got from a wide range of persons extending from the executive category [Ministers of the Crown] to bureaucrats at all levels and even those who undertake administrative work outside the public administrative system.[50] In India, on the other hand, only the Pollution Control Board are required to give information and no other body.

Information that relates to the environment is very widely interpreted in UK to include the dead state of flora and fauna. This, therefore, is a rather unique extension of right to information because it makes it easier to get information relating to 'human conditions in the aftermath of a disaster'. The existing Regulation of 1992 works under the assumption that it intends to cover information not accessible otherwise through specific statutory provisions [Regulation 2(c)(i)]. This provision in the Regulation is not to restrict the applicability of the Regulation but on the other hand seems to be an indication that it is expected of specific legislations that they will allow for a procedure of accessing information.

Environmental information in the UK is usually recorded in registers by respective agencies and departments.[51] In India, PCB have no statutory duty to maintain registers and whatever reports they maintain from inspections they undertake are meant purely for the benefit of legal proceeding if any are initiated.

Information can be kept confidential, if they are record of internal communication or within the process of completion.[52]

However, in spite of how much everyone may provide for the right to information not every person in society will know what information is available and accessible. In light to this problem, it has been expressed that there is a need to compile the list of routinely used environmental information and the places/sources from which the same can be obtained. The final dimension of securing information should be in an understandable form.[53]

Notes

1. Principle 2 of the Stockholm Declaration called for the 'free flow of up-to-date scientific information and transfer of experience'. The 1982 World Charter for Nature broadened the scope and extent of obligations relating to information, calling for the dissemination of knowledge of research, the monitoring of natural processes and ecosystem, and the participation of all persons in the formulation of decisions of direct concern to the environment.
2. Agenda 21, para. 40.1.
3. The 1993 London Convention requires information exchange on the adoption of certain implementation measures, including import and export [Articles 8(6), 9 and 12(1)].
4. 1982 Benelux Conservation Convention, Article 2(2).
5. 1959 Antarctic Treaty, Article III (1)(a) and (c); 1973 Polar Bears Agreement, Article VII.
6. Under Agenda 21, UNEP is to facilitate 'information exchange on environmentally sound technologies' including legal aspects'. Para 38.22 (j).
7. 1952 North Pacific Fisheries Convention Article VIII.
8. 1958 Danube Convention, Article 12(3); Cartagena Oil Spills Protocol, Article 4.
9. 1959 Plant Protection Agreement, Article IV(3).
10. 1951 European Plant Protection Convention, Article V(a)(5).
11. 1979 Berne Convention, Article 3(3).
12. 1992 Biodiversity Convention, Article 17(1). Article 17(2) provides that information exchange shall include 'specialised knowledge and indigenous and traditional knowledge' and shall also, where feasible, include repatriation of information.
13. Articles 61, 143, 200 and 244.
14. Article 4(1)(h).
15. 1972 World Heritage Convention, Article 11(2) [property forming part of the cultural and natural heritage]; 1979 Bonn Convention, Article VI(2) [migratory species of wild animals]; 1983 ITTA, Article 27(1) and (2) [tropical timber]; 1992 Biodiversity Convention, Article 7(a) and (b), 1992 Climate Change Convention, Article 4(1)(a).
16. Article 4(I)(h). It remains to be seen whether this form of language can influence the willingness of States, and the private sector, to

improve flows of information. It will always be difficult to gauge the effectiveness of general obligations to exchange information.

17. Article 4(1)(a) and (j).
18. Article 12(1)(b) and (c).
19. In 1983 the General Assembly adopted a resolution which provided the basis for the principle of 'prior informed consent', declaring that: 'products that have been banned from domestic consumption and/or sale because they have been judged to endanger, health and the environment should be sold abroad by companies, corporations or individuals only when a request for such products is received from an importing country or when the consumption of such products of officially permitted in the importing country....'
20. UNEP London Guidelines 1989.
21. 1985 FAO Pesticides Guidelines.
22. Chapter 12, 504-06.
23. Chapter 12, 507-08.
24. G.S. Tiwari; "Conservation of Biodiversity and Techniques of People's Activism" Journal of the Indian Law Institute, April-June 2001, Vol. 43, No. 2, p. 215.
25. Eg: The Submergence zones of the Narmada Dam was initially put under the 'secret clause' and later due to public outcry was made available to the citizens.
26. United States; The Freedom of Information Act.
27. Sec. 16 of the Act provides for the functions of the Central Board among which collection and dissemination of information in respect of matters relating to air pollution is one. But the Section fails to specify to whom this information and what is the nature of this information; is to be disseminated.
28. Sec. 25(6) provides for inspection of the register maintained by the State Board.
29. Sec. 3(2)(xii) of the EPA provides the Central Government with powers to take measures for collection and dissemination of information relating to environmental pollution. It appears that the Central Government has forgotten about this power.
30. *See* Sec. 25 of the Air Act 1981.
31. AIR 1975 SC 865, 884.
32. AIR 1982 SC 149; also see *Dinesh Trivedi v Union of India*, 1997 (4) SCC 306.
33. AIR 1988 Rajasthan 2. This case was a PIL seeking directions to the Municipal Corporation of Jaipur to improve the sanitation of the city and remove filth, garbage and dirt from the city.

34. Jaipur had bad sanitation facility. This caused inconvenience to the citizens and environmental hazard due to accumulation of filth, rubbish, night soil, odor etc.
35. Under Chapter 6 of the Rajasthan Municipalities Act, 1959, the Municipality is under a duty to maintain the city clean. Chapter 6 deals with three duties of the municipality namely primary, secondary and special duty. Cleaning public streets, places, sewers and all such spaces, and removing off rubbish, filth is the primary duty of the municipality. It is for the municipality to see how to perform the primary duties and how to raise resources for the performance of that duty. In the performance of primary duty no excuse can be taken and can be directed also as it is primary, mandatory and obligatory duty to perform the same.
36. *Bombay Environment Action Group v Poona Cantonment Board.*
37. Writ Petition (Civil) No. 860 of 1991.
38. *Almitra H. Patel v Union of India*, 2000 2 SCC 679.
39. Not only does the Bill restrict itself to information from public authorities, it also defines the 'freedom of information' narrowly. It restricts the right to the mere right of access to documents.
40. Public participation is a very important part of the 1990 U.S. Clean Air Act. Throughout the Act, the public is given opportunities to take part in determining how the law will be carried out. For instance, you can take part in hearings on the State and local plans for cleaning up air pollution. You can sue the government or a source's owner or operator to get action when EPA or your State has not enforced the Act. You can request for action by the State or EPA against violators. The reports required by the Act are public documents. A great deal of information will be collected on just how much pollution is being released; these monitoring (measuring) data will be available to the public. The 1990 Clean Air Act ordered EPA to set up clearing-houses to collect and give out technical information.

    Typically, these clearing-houses will serve the public as well as State and other air pollution control agencies. See the list at the end of this summary for organizations to contact for additional information about air pollution and the Clean Air Act.
41. *State of U.P. Raj Narain*, AIR 1975 SC, 865.
42. Tiwari Journal of ILN April-June 200, p. 216.
43. Prasad, 'Silent Valley Case: An Ecological Assessment', 8 Cochin University Law Review 128 [1984].
44. 'Convention on Access to Information, Public Participation in Decision-Making and Access to Justice in Environmental Matters' was adopted on 25 June 1998 in the Danish city of Aarhus (Århus)

at the Fourth Ministerial Conference in the "Environment for Europe" process.

45. In December 1997, the Government issued a White Paper entitled "*Your Right to Know*" (Cm 3818) on its proposals for a Freedom of Information Act. It sought views by 28 February 1998. More than 550 responses to the White Paper were submitted. Copies were placed in the Library of both Houses of Parliament and published on the Internet.
46. Just a few months before the signing of the international Aarhus Convention on access to information in 1998, Kai Barlund, Director of the United Nations Economic Commissions for Europe, argued that "industry and government agencies collect environmental data, but they either do not report them to the public or report them when they're out of date". http://www.rec.org/REC/Bulletin/Bull91/ InfoSoc.html
47. The Convention calls right to information as an essential green right.
48. Section 1 confers a general right of access to information held by public authorities. An applicant has a right to be told whether the information requested is held by that authority (the duty to confirm or deny whether it holds information) and, if it is held, to have it communicated to him.
49. The Aarhus Convention lays down the basic rules to promote citizens' involvement in environmental matters and enforcement of environmental law. The Aarhus Convention consists of three pillars, each of which grants different rights: the first pillar gives the public the right of access to environmental information; the second pillar gives the public the right to participate in decision-making processes and; the third pillar ensures access to justice for the public.
50. Gisele Bakkenist, *Environmental Information*; London: Cameron May Ltd., 1994, p. 8.
51. Regulation 2(4).
52. These two grounds have been severely criticized.
53. Though under the EIA process, the Executive Summary of the EIA report shall be made available to the general public for scrutiny, the complicated and detailed scientific report is hardly understandable by an expert, leave alone the common man.

5

Right to Education in Global Economy: Indian Perspective

Swarupama Chaturvedi

I. Introduction

The relationship between education, economy and society is interactive. Education has always been influenced by changes in the economy and society. It is the key to participation in the global economy of the 21st century.[1] There is a big change going in the way people see the world; the change in the concept of development and in the way people live together. But for this change to bear fruit, we need education on a global scale. Humankind will not uplift without education.[2] In this new era the aim of education goes far beyond literacy. Now it means learning to live together, learning to know and learning to do.[3] Education broadly serves two purposes; first, it equips people with knowledge and skills of analysis and realize freedom to enjoy life. Second, it prepares them to become economically independent. That is why nowadays education is being considered as an important socio-economic right. The orientation of global development strategies towards eradicating poverty offers a powerful opportunity to education as human right because there is close relation between poverty and education.

In this paper the effect of liberalization and globalization on the education system has been examined. The aim of this paper is to examine the aim of education in the era of Human

Rights and global economy. The million-dollar question is whether it is getting concretized as a right in the real sense of the term or it is being converted into a traded service. In this regard, the role of government and judiciary will also be examined.

II. Education as Human Right and Economic Development

Human Rights are what we understand necessary for us to live life with human dignity however, this understanding is not a fixed one. Human Rights, therefore, will change over time, as human values will change, and as people reach new understanding of what being human really means.[4] They will also be understood differently in different national contexts, and just because Human Rights are universal it does not mean that they will be defined or realized in the same way in all countries. The universal right to education does not mean that children of every country should go to the same standard of school, or learn the same thing in the same way in every country. Universality of Human Rights does not mean uniformity. The method of realization of rights can be different in different countries but it should be uniform in the same country. The same fact is true with right to education, as educational needs are susceptible to variation according to the level of economic development of every nation so it can be varied with countries.[5] It can be achieved in different countries by different means due to socio-economic diversities. Education is a universal right but it can be realized in different ways.[6]

There are two ways to think about global education. One way is import of western schooling, technology and science without thinking of the cultural as well as social diversities of the country concerned. The second way to think about global education is to think in accordance with future plans, which are suitable to the socio-economic conditions of a country.[7] The educational system, which would meet the needs of the present and future economy, should be adopted. Adoption of the educational model of another country without understanding of one's own needs and resources can result in injustice to the people.

Education as an economic right necessitates the adoption of schooling to facilitate subsequent economic self-sufficiency through employment or self-employment. Integrating economic, social, cultural and political facets of education is facilitated by the indivisibility and inter-relations of Human Rights.[8] Competitiveness-driven reforms of education systems imposed by globalization are critical for long-term economic growth and hence sustainable poverty reduction.[9] Right to education can be helpful to achieve goals of poverty eradication, gender inequality, or the prevention of terrorism and violence.[10]

No country can be said, as yet, to have achieved full compliance with all international Human Rights obligations in education.[11] The current progress in terms of access to and quality of education is not satisfactory. The expansion of this sector must be carefully planned and monitored.[12] Due to resource constraint, partnership with the private sector needs to be fostered. But the role of the State as a regulator and organizer of the framework for the expansion is critical.[13] It is vitally important that Human Rights, of which right to education is an important facet, must be recognized and protected by government, especially taking into account legislative changes around the world. Greater autonomy in developing education systems, as a free traded service must be balanced against individual's rights, particularly, each child's right to entitlement to free and compulsory education.[14]

The goal of education to participate in the global economy is not bad but it should be balanced with individual's right to education. The higher standards that we set for our education system will make our country stronger. The students of today are leaders of the economy and representatives of the society tomorrow.[15] The rationale behind global Human Rights standards is to assist with their incorporation in national educational strategies, because education has a multiplying effect: where the right to education is effectively guaranteed, it enhances the enjoyment of all Human Rights and freedoms. The human right to education is inextricably linked to other fundamental Human Rights—rights that are universal, indivisible, interconnected and interdependent including: the human right to equality between men and women and to equal partnership in the family and society; the human right to work and receive wages that contribute to an adequate standard of living; the human right to freedom of thought, conscience, religion and belief; the human right to an adequate standard of living; and the human right to participate in shaping decisions and policies affecting one's community, at the local, national and international levels.[16] When right to education is denied, it precludes the enjoyment of many, if not all, other Human Rights.[17] Amartya Sen[18] also explored the importance of basic education in economic development. According to him, without compulsory education, no economic development is possible. Neglect of basic education sustains social disparities. And we all know social disparities give rise to human right violations. Realization of Human Rights will come when the world becomes educated about global values and humanity.

III. Global Education

Global education is knowledge, which opens people's eyes to the realities of the world, and awakes them to bring about a world of greater justice, equity and Human Rights for all.[19] Global education is understood to encompass developmental education, Human Rights education, education for sustainability, education for peace and conflict prevention and intercultural education.

The use of the term global education is an attempt to bring together all countries that work on different types of education for change at the global level. It is also called education for democratic citizenship or learning for sustainability, peace education or Human Rights education, co-operative exchange of ideas, networking on local, national and international level and it benefit all of us. It would be possible only through accessibility of education to all. Education is not accessible to a number of people in different developing countries. Children who are privileged enough to attend school learn that education is life insurance. Over 115 million children between the ages of 6 and 11 have no access to education at global level. Of these children, 38% live in Asia and 39% live in sub-Saharan Africa, where 40% of children are not in school. In over 45 countries, less than 25% of girls are enrolled in secondary school. Over 60% of our world's adults live in Bangladesh, China, India, and Pakistan.[20]

The idea to make an individual a global citizen is only fruitful through global education.[21] The global citizen is the person who looks at problems in a global context, work co-operatively and responsibly. He is able to accept cultural differences and solves conflicts non-violently. If we want a large number of global citizens from India, we must ensure free and compulsory education to each child. Without the achievement of the target of education accessible to all, we cannot achieve other targets of development.

IV. Impact of Globalization on Right to Education

Education is necessary to build a society that is fair and just for all its citizens, that respects universal values of democracy and Human Rights and whose development social as well as economic will be equitable and sustainable.[22] Extremes of wealth and poverty within and among countries are greater than ever. In every country the global economy questions the right to education.

At a time when fundamental changes in economy and society are visible, there are great new challenges for education also, such as:

(i) achieving education for all;

(ii) reaffirming the values of education in relation to personal development.

However, there are also threats to right to education arising out of global economy:

(i) Commercialization of education, and subsequent risks of inequality and discrimination;

(ii) Changes in the role of State, with more emphasis on liberalization and less on guarantee of equity and nondiscrimination;

(iii) Huge public funds are released to encourage the development of on-line education, and the promise of education via new technologies is being used as an excuse to deny legitimate claims regarding maintenance of schools and recruitment of teachers.[23]

The urgency to reaffirm the right to education has been heightened by resumed negotiations on liberalizing trade in education services. Exporters of education services have set the tone, slanting education towards an internationally traded service, and it is therefore important to define the nature and scope of that part of education that should remain exempt and continue as free to the public. The question is: are we headed towards realizing of "education as a right" or towards a view of "education as commodity"?[24] International Human Rights law defines free and compulsory education as a government obligation, thus implying that it should be a free public service. Article 26 of the Universal Declaration of Human Rights, 1948;[25] Articles 13 and 14 of International Covenant on Economic, Social and Cultural Rights, 1966;[26] Article 28 of Convention on the Rights of the Child, 1989;[27] World Conference on Education for All at Jomtien in 1990[28] and adoption of World Declaration on Education for all at the same Conference and its assessment at Dakar in 2000 have well established the importance of education in the social, economic and political development of the Nation.[29]

V. Right to Education in India

In India, Constitution makers realized the importance of universal elementary education and directed the Government to ensure free and compulsory education within ten years from the commencement of the Constitution.[30] Nothing could be done in this regard until 1992. Movement in this direction was started when judiciary declared education as a fundamental right[31] under Article 21[32] and rejected the 'economic capacity' argument of the Government.[33]

After a lot of pressure on national and international level an amendment was incorporated in the text of the Constitution. It is Constitution (86th Amendment) Act, 2002 that makes education a fundamental right for those between the ages of 6-14 years. The Act incorporated three separate changes in the Constitution.

(i) The insertion of Article 21-A, which provides that the State shall provide free and compulsory education to all children between the ages of 6-14 in such a manner as the State may by law determine.

(ii) An amendment to Article 45, that is provision for early childhood care and education to children below the age of 6 years; the State shall endeavor to provide early childhood care and education for all children up to the age of 6 years.

(iii) In Article 51-A, after clause (j) the following clause (k) has been inserted, which says that a parent or guardian shall provide opportunities for education to his children or ward between the ages of 6-14 years.

However, the Act ignored the period from 3-6 years for children, which are crucial. Children of this age group have not been given any fundamental right to education. They have been left at the mercy of the State.[34] It is the important age group for mental as well as physical growth. The provision of Article 21-A is directory in nature. There is a Bill pending in the Parliament to give effect to this Amendment.[35]

From the Constitutional provisions it is clear that free and compulsory education is a governmental obligation.[36] But the draft Free and Compulsory Education Bill, 2005 is not in favor of people at large.[37] The Bill seeks to provide education through a combination of government schools, aided schools and unaided (private) schools.[38] State schools and fully aided schools shall provide free education to all admitted children.[39] Partly aided schools shall provide free education to at least such proportion of admitted children to the extent that government funds its annual expenses, subject to a minimum of 25%.[40] Unaided schools and special category schools shall provide free education to at least 25% of students;[41] the government shall reimburse the school to the extent of the per child expenditure in government schools or the school fee, whichever is lower.[42] Exemption of unaided schools from responsibility to provide free and compulsory education is unjustified.[43] It promotes autonomy of private educational institutions.[44] The Bill does not address the problem of inadequacy of the government educational institutions, which gives the scope to the private schools to come in name of filling the gap.[45] The Bill exempts the private unaided schools from regulation of the Government.[46] It can promote the exploitation of people in different forms. First, by charging high fees; second, by bad infrastructure and poor education; and third, exploitation of teachers by payment of low salary. In this way three classes of society may be affected. If this Bill gets passed in its present form, private educational institutions may be converted into places where infringement rather than realization of Human Rights will be in practice.

The State's intervention in education has been decreasing and it is alarming that the private bodies have entered the field of education in a big way.[47] The sufferers are the masses of poor people for whom education is becoming more and more inaccessible.[48] It was hoped in this context that the Supreme Court would focus more on how to make education available to poor. It should be ensured that private educational institutions are regulated sufficiently so that the poor have access to education.[49] One would expect that the judiciary would spend some time ensuring that large masses of the people are given access to education. One would have thought that the Court would be ensuring the spread of free and subsidized education. Instead in the last few years, the Supreme Court has spent months justifying the freedom to charge high fees and doing away with reservations in unaided private educational institutions. Now, right to education has become the shocking failure of the Supreme Court in the last few years. It should be remembered that the same Court once ensured right to education as an integral part of the right to life and ensured it as one of the Fundamental Rights.[50]

Right to education got attention by the Supreme Court in *Mohini Jain's case*.[51] The Court held that the right to education is infringed by charging high fees by private educational institutions. The State is under a constitutional mandate to provide educational institutions to enable the citizens to enjoy their fundamental right to education. The State may discharge their obligation through State owned or State recognized educational institutions. Charging high capitation fees in consideration of admission to educational institutions is a denial of citizens' right to education. Capitation fees make the availability of education beyond the reach of the poor. The opportunity to acquire education cannot be confined to the richer sections of the society. It brings to the fore a 'clear class bias'. It enables the rich to take admission whereas the poor have to withdraw due to financial inability.[52]

However, this rule could not stand for more than a year. In *Unnikrishnan's case,*[53] management of private educational institutions went to the Court for reconsideration of the decision of *Mohini Jain.*[54] In this case the Court welcomed the decision of *Mohini Jain's case*, which said right to education is a fundamental right under Article 21[55] but this right is limited only up to fourteen years of age as per *Unnikrishnan's case.* After fourteen years the right would depend on whether the State has financial resource or not.

The decision of *Unnikrishnan's case* concerning fees was overruled by the Supreme Court in *T.M.A. Pai Foundation v State of Karnataka.*[56] The Court observed that private educational institutions should not only have freedom to charge fees which enable them to recover the cost of education but fix fees in a manner that sufficient surplus is generated for future expansion of educational activities. So the students will not only pay for their own expenses but also for the future generation.[57] The Court also observed that governmental domination in the educational field must be resisted.

This was a shocking departure from the earlier view, which regarded education as a Sovereign function and looked at private intervention only as a supplemental effort. If private schools are exempted from necessary regulation it may become a barrier to achieve the objects which we plan to achieve through education.[58] In this decision Court is very insensitive about the people of India who live below poverty line.[59] The largest part of Indian population is far away from life with human dignity, who struggle for their basic needs. Any law or policy which ignores them cannot be justified.

T.M.A. Pai Foundation's case[60] came up for interpretation in two subsequent judgments of the Supreme Court. *In Islamic Academy of Education*,[61] it was discussed that whether educational institutions were entitled to fix their own fee structure. The Court directed every state government to appoint a committee to fix fee structures especially for professional colleges. It is submitted that this kind of committee should be appointed to fix fee structure in unaided private schools also. Because in the country where right to free and compulsory education is a fundamental right, no one should be permitted to infringe this right in any covert manner.[62]

Again *T.M.A. Pai Foundation*[63] came up for further interpretation in *P.A. Inamdar v State of Maharashtra*.[64] The Supreme Court held that any reservation especially for backward classes in unaided private professional colleges is not permitted. On the other hand, Court advocated reservation for non-resident Indians at 15 per cent. The Court also held that the decision in *Islamic Academy's case*[65] in so far as it sets up two committees, one for fee structure and the other for admission is valid.

It is difficult to understand what happened to the wisdom and understanding of the judiciary. The judiciary is known as the protector of justice. Is it justice to the people of India for whom the Constitution guaranteed the right to education? Is it the symptom of the realization of right to education? Privatization is a good thing because government alone is unable to fulfill the desired fund for education suggested by different commissions[66] but it must be regulated in favor of the fundamental right to education. Privatization agenda hurt average citizen more than it helped them.

VI. Conclusion and Suggestions

It is submitted that economic development and citizens' rights must proceed hand in hand. Economic development that does not take account of citizens' rights lead to inequality, social division and the few profiting at the expense of many. On the other hand, citizens' rights in absence of economic development are of only limited value. Indeed, many[67] have argued that to benefit from economic development is itself a human right, which should not be denied to anyone. It is only when economic developments take place in the context of the rights of the citizen that social equity and progress can result. Thus, the nations that have successfully achieved economic development and stability have done this ensuring at the same time that the rights of the citizens are respected. To concentrate on economic prosperity without due concern for the rights of the individual would ultimately lead to an unbalanced development for which the nation would have to pay much. Education is one of the Human and Fundamental Rights; it is government's obligation to ensure it.

The process of privatization is increasingly creating two parallel education systems, with two corresponding tiers of quality; one is for the 'rich' another is 'poor education for poor'. The option of free education for many is not free in the real sense.[68] Huge amounts are being charged by private educational institutions making children's education dependent on the purchasing power of their family, which is in direct conflict with international Human Rights law which requires government to ensure equal access to education for each child and Indian constitutional law which ensures right to education as a fundamental right of the children between 6-14 years. It is possible only by regulating fee structure of private educational institutes.[69] This is the obligation of the State because State is responsible for ensuring a quality education that is available to all. Right to education is essential for global economy. Education and the rise of global economy relate to the fact that both lie hand in hand.

It is now widely recognized and accepted that a society that denies basic social and economic rights cannot be stable and democratic. In this way global trade should be promoted with protection of economic, social and cultural rights of individuals.[70] There is no difference of opinion that commercialization of education will infringe the right to education of vulnerable sections of the society.[71] In bird's eye view it seems that autonomy of private educational institutions is helpful in human resource development but if one looks in depth it is not good for a developing country like India.[72] It is against basic constitutional mandates. If we want to improve human resources and global economy we should not think about short-term profit, we must go systematic and step wise and the first step towards this is to achieve education for all. In present socio-economic conditions, *Unnikrishnan's decision* is appropriate at least up to achievement of desired literacy. One does not assert that nothing has been done towards realization of right to education but much more is still required to be done. The arrival of the Right to Education Bill is an appropriate step but this Bill has lack of clarity. The only positive aspect of the Right to Education Bill, 2005 is the formation of School Management Committees for State and aided schools.[73] Three-fourth of the members will be parents, which will give them genuine power in the committees. But again this provision is applied to State school and aided schools only. The rest of private schools are not included in the jurisdiction of this provision.[74] Rethinking the provisions of the Bill is necessary in view of the present state of affairs prevailing in the area of educational rights of citizens especially of those who are not economically well off.

Notes

1. "Educating in a Global Economy: Education International Policy Resolution" available at http://www.ei-i.e.org/worldcongress/docs/wc03Res-GlobalizationEconomy-e.pdf (last visited 06 March, 2006 at 10 pm).
2. Nobel Peace laureate Rigoberta Menchu Tum, "A Plea for Global Education", available at http://www.global-vision.org/interview/menchu.html (last visited 23 June, 2007 at 10 am).
3. Gerard Lommerse, "About Sustainable Development and Education for Democratic Citizenship", available at http://sbf.admin.ch/edc/ html/dc/html/refereat-2-e.pdf (last visited 02 March, 2006 at 11.30 pm).
4. Prof. Jim Ife; Head, School of Social Work and Social Policy, Curtin University of Technology, "Challenges for Human Rights in the New Global Order", CHOGM Conference, University of Queensland, October 2001, available at http:/www.humanities.curtin.edu.au/pdf/hre/challengesForHumanRights.pdf (last visited 28 Feb, 2006 at 01.30 am).

5. Cecile Fabre, *Social Rights under the Constitution: Government and the Decent Life* (Clarendon Press, Oxford, 2000) 36.
6. Prof. Jim Ife, *Supra* note 4.
7. Carol R. Choy, "Education and Globalization", available at http://www.gse.harvard.edu/news/features/ mso04012004.html (last visited 07 March, 2006 at 02 am).
8. Annual report of the Special Rapporteur on the right to education, Katerina Tomasevski, submitted pursuant to Commission on Human Rights resolution 2001/29; Commission on Human Rights Fifty-eight session Item 10 of the provisional agenda Economic, Social and Cultural Rights at p. 58, available at right-to-education.org (last visited 06 March 2006 at 11 pm).
9. Olivier Dupriez, September 2003, Adopting Education to the Global Economy, ERD Policy Brief Series No. 22, available at http://www.adb.org/Economics (last visited 09 March 2005 at 02 pm).
10. Katerina Tomasevski, above note 9.
11. Katerina Tomasevski, "Manual on Right-Based Education: Global Human Right Requirements Made Simple", Bangkok: UNESCO Bangkok, 2004, available at http:/www.right-to-education.org (last visited 03 April, 2005 at 11 am).
12. Remarks given by Chairman Alan Greenspan, The critical role of education in the nation's economy. At the Greater Omaha Chamber of Commerce 2004 Annual Meeting, Omaha, Nebraska, February 20, 2004. He said "We need to be forward looking in order to adapt our educational system to the evolving needs of the economy and the realities of our changing society. Those efforts will require the collaboration of policy-makers, education experts, and importantly our citizens." This remark proved the importance of education even in developed countries and participation of citizens in policy-making. It is the real democracy which we achieve only through education. This remark could be read in detail at http:/www.federalreserve.gov/BOARDDOCS/SPEECHES/ 2004/200402202/default.htm (last visited 04 March, 2006 at 11.30 pm)
13. Gerard Lommerse, above note 3; Katerina Tomasveski also expressed the same opinion when she visited to China for the study of the condition of free and compulsory education in China. She felt that privatization is a hurdle to achieve education to all in China. Special Rapporteur Katerina Tomasevski meticulously demolished every myth about China's upholding of the right to education. The country was spending only two per cent of its gross domestic product on education as against the six per cent recommended by the United Nations. This opinion is shared in

"Right to Education: China Fails to make a Grade", Human Right Features, 08 October, 2003; details are available at http://www.countercurrents.org/hr-hrf081003.htm (last visited March 12, 2006 at 6 pm). Her opinion is equally relevant in Indian condition.

14. Katerina Tomasveski; *Supra* note 8.
15. Prof. Govinda, National Institute of Education Planning and Administration (NIEPA) give his opinion on Right to Education Bill, 2005. His comments are available on http://southasia.oneworld.net/Article/view/122392/1/ (last visited March 22, 2006 at 10.30 pm). He said that the government should cut its expenditure on the other heads if necessary and increase allocation for the education sector. He also mentioned that if we neglect our education today we all have to face problem in the future so there is great urgency to implement the Right to Education Bill.
16. Detail discussions on this issue are available at http://www.hri.ca/hrdevelopment/chapter4/education/index.html (last visited 03 Feb, 2006, at 04 pm).
17. Katerina Tomasevski; *Supra* note 8.
18. PUCL Bulletin, December 1998, Amartya Sen's on the role of basic education; available at http://www.pucl.org/from-archives/Academia/basic-education.htm (last visited 09 March, 2006 at 01 am).
19. Gerard Lommerse, *Supra* note 3.
20. "Global Education: Education As A Human Right", provides statistics of education at global level, available on http://www.elca.org /education/global.html (last visited March 24, 2005 at 12.30 pm).
21. Gerard Lommerse, *Supra* note 4.
22. Mr. Arjun Sengupta, "Right to Development, Independent Expert, Commission on Human Rights". His report available on http://www.hri.ca/fortherecord2003/documentation/commossion/e-cn42003-wg18-2htm (last visited 01 March, 2006 at 10 am). He said in his report that (a) the fact that the opportunities provided by globalization and integration into the world economy to developing countries have not resulted in an improved enjoyment of the right to development; (b) the fact that they have failed to do so because appropriate polices for realizing the right to development have rarely been adopted; (c) the need, in the design and implementation of appropriate policies, to set as their objective the realization of rights-based development; (d) the need of states, the international community and others to fulfil their obligations to carry out appropriate development policies; and (e) the need to base a development policy on a coordinated

programme of different policies to realize the individual rights (to food, health, education, work, social security, etc.) with policies to realize sustainable and participatory economic growth with equity.

23. *Supra* note 1.
24. Katerina Tomasevski, *Supra* note 8.
25. The Universal Declaration of Human Rights, adopted by the United Nations General Assembly in 1948, is the foundation of modern international Human Rights defense and promotion. The concept of the right to education as part of international Human Rights law appears for the first time in 1948, details are available at http:/ www.eip-cifedhop.org (last visited 27 Feb, 2006 at 7 pm). The Declaration is built on the principle that Human Rights come from the "inherent dignity" of every person. This dignity, and the rights to freedom and equality which derive therefrom are inalienable. It is discussed in "How the International Monetary Fund and the World Bank Undermine Democracy and Erode Human Rights: Five Case Studies" which is published by Global exchange in September 2001 and available at http:/ www.globalexchange.org/campaigns/wbimf (last visited 03 March, 2006 at 09 pm).
26. It was 18 years after the adoption of the *UDHR* that the content on the right to education was detailed in Article 13 of the *International Covenant on Economic, Social and Cultural Rights*. This Covenant was adopted and opened to signature, ratification and adherence by the UN General Assembly by Resolution 2200 A (XXI) on December 16, 1966.
27. *The Convention on the Rights of the Child*, which entered into force on September 2, 1990, stipulates in Article 28 that the States Parties recognize the specific right of children to education.
28. The Jomtien Conference (1990) was full of hope when it affirmed the desire for education for all by the year 2000. This commitment has not been respected. The deadline was moved to 2015, and nothing today leads us to believe that the objective will be met by that deadline.
29. Paul Hunt, member of the Committee on Economic, Social and Cultural Rights, summarizes the situation in his *General Observations* concerning Article 13 of the Covenant: "The Committee is very aware that for millions of people throughout the world, exercising the right to education remains a far away objective that keeps moving further away. In addition, the Committee is conscious of the fact that there are enormous structural obstacles amongst others that inhibit the full application of Article 13." This comment is available at http:/www.eip-

cifedhop.org/english/publications/dossierspeda2.html (last visited 25 Feb, 2006 at 05 pm).

30. Original Article 45 was the Provision for free and compulsory education for children. This Article said that the State shall endeavor to provide within a period of ten years from the commencement of this Constitution, for free and compulsory education for all children until they complete the age of fourteen years.
31. *Mohini Jain v State of Karnataka*, AIR 1992 SC 1858.
32. Article 21 provides protection of life and personal liberty. According to this Article no person shall be deprived of his life or personal liberty except according to procedure established by law.
33. *Unnikrishnan J.P. v State of Andhra Pradesh*, AIR 1993 SC 2178.
34. *See* amended Article 45 of the Constitution of India, which gives direction to the State governments for early childhood care and education below 6 years of children.
35. The Bill has objective that every child between the age of 6 and 14 years has the right to elementary education that is (a) free, (b) compulsory, (c) of equitable quality, and (d) available in his or her neighborhood. This education will be available between Grade I and VIII, and provided at a recognized school satisfying specified norms.
36. Shripad S. Bolashetty and Girija L.L., "Fundamental Human Right to Free and Compulsory Elementary Education in India: Origin, Progress and Present Status", *Indian Bar Review,* Vol. XXX (2 & 3) 2003, p. 359.
37. Draft Bill of Free and Compulsory Education, 2005 is available at http:/www.pratham.org/documents/RightToEducationBill2005.pdf (last visited 12 Jan., 2006 at 02 pm).
38. Heading of the Section 14 of the Right to Education Bill, 2005 are 'responsibility of schools to provide free and compulsory education' reflects that the responsibility is shared between government and private educational institutions.
39. Sec. 14(1)(i) of the Right to Education Bill, 2005.
40. Sec. 14(1)(ii) of the Right to Education Bill, 2005.
41. Sec. 14(1)(iii) of the Right to Education Bill, 2005.
42. Sec. 14(2) of the Right to Education Bill, 2005.
43. If one interprets this provision in the light of the decision of the Supreme Court in *P.A. Inamdar v State of Maharashtra*, AIR 2006 SC 3226, there is scope of charging high fees. Though it is held by Court that fees should be fixed by an independent committee but it is also upheld that private educational institutions should not only have freedom to charge fees which enables them to recover the

cost of education but fix fees in a manner that sufficient surplus is generated for future expansion of educational activities.

44. Some educationists believe that the 'common school system' should have been adopted instead of the 25% quota in private schools. That is, all children from all strata of society in a locality should go to the same set of schools in that locality and receive free education. They believe that this will (a) improve the overall standards in government schools as the influential upper strata of society pushes for higher standards, (b) reduce the disparity of opportunity among children, and (c) lead to a better society as children from different sections mingle from an early age. Comments on Right to Education, Bill 2005 are available on http://www.indiatogether.org/2005/dec/edulbrighted.htm (last visited March 27, 2006 at 11.30 pm).
45. Private schools are establishing business of education in the name of necessity. In the decision of *Unnikrishnan J.P. v State of Andhra Pradesh*, AIR 1993 SC 2178, it is clearly said that the term education is not included in the definition of trade or business for the purpose of Article 19(1)(g) of the Constitution which provides the freedom to practise any profession, or to carry on any occupation, trade or business.
46. How right is the Right to Education Bill, 2005? Dr. Nilay Ranjan, One World South Asia, 17 Nov, 2005. The campaign aims at making available to the poorest children quality education that has so far been out of their reach. The government has been running and managing schools for more than 50 years and the results are not very positive. One of the points which is most debated is the immunity offered by the Bill to private and unaided schools in the country. "Why does the regulation in the Bill cover only Government and aided schools?" Mr. Madhav Chavan, Director programs, Pratham, an NGO working on education asked in a discussion forum organized by "New Delhi: Centre for Civil Society" on "Right to Education Bill 2005" at India International Centre, New Delhi, on 16th November. Details are available at http://southasia.oneworld.net/article/view/ 122392/1 (last visited March 16, 2006 at 4 pm).
47. Prof. Govinda, National Institute of Education Planning and Administration (NIEPA) gives his comment on Right to Education Bill, 2005. His comment is available on http://southasia. oneworld.net/ article/ view/122392/1/ (last visited March 22, 2006 at 10.30 pm). He said that the government should not talk about financial implications. Education is an important issue for everyone and it is the responsibility of the government to provide quality education for each and every child.

48. Under the human right to education every person is entitled to: free and compulsory elementary education.
49. Katerina Tomasveski, The Special Rapporteur on the right to education in her 2004 report prioritized the financial obstacles in the realization of the right to education. She has repeatedly brought the dual legal status of education, as entitlement and traded service. She has recently carried out a global review of the charging of school fees in primary education around the world to find out that not even primary education is free in 91 countries. For details visit www.rightto-education.org
50. *Supra* note 31.
51. *Ibid.*
52. Everyone has right to education, this education should be accessible to every children but the decision of the Delhi High Court in *Tushar Welfare Society v Central Board of Secondary Education* (AIR 2006 Del 28) held that "It would be progressive step if educational institutions maintain themselves and regulate their affairs without draw in upon the State funds for which there invariably are many other supplants where the parents of students are unable to afford the fees of private institutions, State schools should be available. No further regulation of education are called for". This statement is very ignorant about the right to education of children. It is clearly class bias. These kinds of decisions are not appreciated in Indian social and economical conditions.
53. *Supra* note 33.
54. *Supra* note 31.
55. *Supra* note 32.
56. AIR 2003 SC 355.
57. *See generally* Dr. Chidananda Reddy S. Patil, "Judicial Endeavor to End Commercialisation of Education : An analysis", *Indian Bar Review*, Vol. XXX (4), 2003 at p. 645.
58. Preamble of the Right to Education Bill, 2005 runs as the objectives of democracy, social justice and equality can be achieved only through the provision of elementary education of equitable quality to all.
59. Katerina Tomasveski, "Right to Education: China Fails to Make a Grade, Human Right Features", 08 October, 2003; details are available at http://www.countercurrents.org/hr-hrf081003.htm (last visited March 12, 2006 at 6 pm). Katerina Tomasveski said that the budgetary funds for education in China have been inadequate, with the result that public schools charge fees to make up for the deficit. The World Bank has confirmed that the main

reason for drop-outs or non-enrolment is known to be "the high out-of-pocket costs of education". The same fact is true in India.

60. *T.M.A. Pai Foundation v State of Karnataka*, AIR 2003 SC 355.
61. *Islamic Academy of Education v State of Karnataka* 2003 6 SCC 697.
62. Private unaided educational institutes used to get many benefits from Government from land allotment to other facilities. They can earn more than State aid from parents and students. So it is not justified to give full autonomy to these institutes. As stated in *Unnikrishnan J.P. v State of Andhra Pradesh*, AIR 1993 SC 2178, high fees are against the realization of the right to education. So government must take care of fee structure. In *Mohini Jain v State of Karnataka*, AIR 1992 SC 1858 Court held that the capitation fee is nothing but a price for selling education. The concept of 'teaching shops' is contrary to the constitutional scheme and it is totally against Indian culture and heritage. These judicial pronouncements established that nothing is permitted at the cost of poor people.
63. *Supra* note 60.
64. 2005 6 SCC 537.
65. *Supra* note 61.
66. Education Commission, which is commonly known as Kothari Commission, suggested in 1966 that the 6% of GDP should be used for education. In 2004, Central Advisory Board of Education (CABE) also suggested that 6% is urgently required for elementary education.
67. Prof. Jim Ife; *Supra* note 4.
68. Katerina Tomasveski, *Supra* note 59. She said that the history of the right to education has shown that education cannot be made compulsory unless it is free. However, budgetary funds for education in China have been inadequate, with the result that public schools charge fees to make up for the deficit.
69. "Education in India: Past, Present and Future" available at http:/www.prayatna.tyofpepad.com/education (last visited 03 March, 2006). Despite the legal position, this Court cannot shut its eyes to the hard realities of commercialization of education and evil practices being adopted by many institutions to earn large amounts for their private or selfish ends. If capitation fee and profiteering is to be checked, the method of admission has to be regulated so that the admissions are based on merit and transparency and the students are not exploited. It is permissible to regulate admission and fee structure for achieving the purpose just stated.

70. By Robert Howse and Makau Mutua, "Protecting Human Rights in a Global Economy: Challenges for the World Trade Organization" available at http://www.ichrdd.ca/english/commdoc/publications/ globalization/wtoRightsGlob.html (last visited Feb 27, 2006 at 3 pm).
71. In *Unnikrishnan J.P. v State of Andhra Pradesh*, AIR 1993 SC 2178, another important aspect that was considered by Supreme Court was necessity of private educational institutions. In this regard Court said that the private educational institutions are absolutely necessary but the commercialization of education is not permitted. The Court balanced the individual's right and duty of State that cannot fulfill due to lack of resources.
72. In *Mohini Jain v State of Karnataka*, AIR 1992 SC 1858, Court held that when the State government grants recognition to the private educational institutions, it creates an agency to fulfill its obligation under Constitution. Why the principal cannot regulate the activities of their agent.
73. Sec 22 of the Right to Education Bill, 2005 is completely devoted to the School Management Committee.
74. The basic shortcoming of this Bill is that it exempted private educational institutes even at elementary level from control of the government. If the object of the Bill is to enforce 86th Amendment Act, which ensures free and compulsory education, all educational institutions imparting elementary education should be covered under this Act except the institutions covered under Articles 29 and 30.

6

Human Rights and the World Trade Organization: A Critique on Compatibility

V.P. Tiwari and *Rajarshi Sen**

INTRODUCTION

Human Rights and International Trade: The Nature of the Debate

The question as to whether there exists a relationship between International Trade and Human Rights (and if so, what this relationship may be) is an issue of increasing significance in this present era of globalization.[1] As this discussion progresses, national economies grow increasingly global,[2] while the respect for Human Rights advances in many States,[3] thus necessitating the present debate.

Scholars have argued both for,[4] and against,[5] the notion that Human Rights can be and/or are integrally related to

* The Authors wish to thank Professor Dr. A.K. Koul (Vice-Chancellor, National Law University, Jodhpur, India) and Mr. Bipin Kumar (Lecturer, National Law University, Jodhpur, India) for their assistance and guidance during the writing of this article. The Authors are especially indebted to Mr. Adarsh Ramanujan (4th year student, B.Sc. LLB (IPR Hons) National Law University, Jodhpur, India for the stimulating exchange of ideas, which forms the basis of this present article.

international trade, so the linkage of Human Rights with international trade remains highly controversial.[6]

This article argues that there can be, and in fact, is, a "direct and appropriate involvement by international trade in the protection of Human Rights", as others have argued before us.[7]

Within this context, however, this article limits itself to the possibility of such an "involvement" only within the narrow perspective of the feasibility and justifiability of trade-related Human Rights measures under the General Agreement on Tariffs and Trade, as it could not possibly hope to address the same question of "involvement" as regards each and every one of the World Trade Organization agreements, or of the several decisions and Declarations of the Ministerial Conferences, as it could conceivably be argued that almost all of the agreements, decisions and Declarations may, could, would, or should have some possible involvement, interaction or relationship with Human Rights.

PART I: DEFINITIONAL UNDERPINNINGS OF THE DEBATE

In this part, we attempt to derive a definitional or classificatory understanding of the term "Human Rights" as a necessary precondition to engaging in this present debate. Using the concept of Human Rights "generations", we attempt to determine the nature, scope and content of the Human Rights under discussion in this present article, before beginning the analytical critique regarding their compatibility with the WTO regime.

Human Rights: Definitional Underpinnings

Although the definition of "Human Rights" seems the logical place to begin this article; propounding this has been problematic.[8] Makau Wa Mutua finds it interesting to note that despite almost universal reliance on the language of Human Rights, there has been a failure to create agreement on the scope, content, and philosophical bases of the Human Rights corpus.[9] Rather, he states, intellectual and policy battles have focused on its cultural relevance, ideological and political orientation, and thematic incompleteness.[10]

Professor Rebecca M.M. Wallace writes:

> Human rights are difficult to define. Generally speaking, they are regarded as those fundamental and inalienable rights which are essential for life as a human being. There is, however, no consensus as to what these rights should be.
>
> What human rights may be interpreted as being differs according to the particular economic, social and cultural society in which they are being defined. Human rights have, therefore, escaped a universally acceptable definition, presenting a problem to international regulation.[11]

Professor Malcolm Shaw had a slightly different perception of problems:

> While there is widespread acceptance of the importance of human rights in the international structure, there is considerable confusion as to their precise nature and role in international law. The question of what is meant by a 'right' is itself controversial and the subject of intense jurisprudential debate. Some 'rights', for example, are intended as immediately enforceable binding commitments, others merely as specifying a possible future pattern of behaviour.[12]

Other scholars seem to be saying that international Human Rights are an important element of international law, deserving a unique niche. Professor W. Michael Reisman noted that Human Rights "...is more than a piecemeal addition to the traditional corpus of international law, more than another chapter sandwiched into traditional textbooks of international law."[13]

His Excellency Judge Thomas Buergenthal of the International Court of Justice provides one of the most concise, workable definitions: "...the international law of human rights is defined as the law that deals with the protection of individuals and groups against violations by governments of their internationally guaranteed rights, and with the promotion of these rights. This branch of law is sometimes also referred to as international protection of human rights or international human rights law."[14]

Any modern approach to Human Rights must be coherent. It must start from the full range of Human Rights and from the axiom of indivisibility. This has become increasingly clear in recent discussions on the conceptual development of economic, social and cultural rights.[15]

Keeping in mind these definitional underpinnings, for the purposes of this article, the authors would not wish to attempt to provide a narrow definition of Human Rights in determining their compatibility with the WTO regime, but would, as far as possible, prefer to attempt such a compatibility critique *in extenso*, absent any restrictions on the nature, scope or content of the Human Rights being considered. If the necessity arises for determining the same, the authors would hope that such an attempt at such a determination would be made only at that stage, allowing, we hope, for the preliminary analysis of the compatibility of Human Rights and the WTO regime to be as broad as possible. Regrettably, however, even for the purposes of this article, there does need to be some determination of what the term "Human Rights" would denote, as the authors would, at least within a limited context, be required to identify which International Human Rights they are discussing.

Defining and Identifying International Human Rights

An international Human Right may be thought of as one which "all States have the same duty to respect" as they do their own municipal legislation.[16] Nevertheless, no single precise definition of an international human right exists as a universally accepted standard, prompting one writer to State that "a claim is an international Human Right if the United Nations General Assembly says it is."[17] There is some truth in this assertion, given that Human Rights Covenants, adopted by the General Assembly and subsequently ratified by States, are the primary source of binding international Human Rights law.[18] It is thus apparent that recognized international Human Rights are the result of pragmatic and political decisions rather than purely theoretical considerations.[19]

Louis Henkin points out that the United Nations Charter,[20] and the Universal Declaration of Human Rights (hereinafter "Universal Declaration"),[21] assume the existence of fundamental Human Rights and delineate their content on the basis of practical considerations; as a result, no extensive theoretical justification is required.[22] In efforts to formulate concepts and language that would appeal and apply to "diverse political systems governing diverse peoples, [the General Assembly]...eschewed philosophical exploration."[23] In fact, the United Nations has not articulated a specific justification for the Human Rights it has adopted and denoted as fundamental; rather, the General Assembly has merely agreed upon them. Nonetheless, by defining international Human Rights, assuming their incumbent obligations, and subjecting themselves to international scrutiny, the members of the United Nations implicitly and explicitly accepted Human Rights norms and demonstrated an international moral consensus.[24]

"New" Human Rights come into existence not by fulfilling theoretical guidelines, but as a result of recognition and agreement by the United Nations. The United Nations can respond to changing world circumstances and reach agreements regarding newly proposed Human Rights. As world conditions change, the advocacy or protection of Human Rights which previously had been "for economic or technological reasons...impossible or perhaps too difficult, too costly, to justify imposing them as duties" becomes possible.[25] Another force in the recognition of new Human Rights emerges "because people have become sensitive to certain needs of all humans to which [they] were hitherto oblivious."[26]

THE CURRENT INTERNATIONAL HUMAN RIGHTS FRAMEWORK

Generations of Human Rights

The term "generation" distinguishes the various conceptual groups of Human Rights currently recognized in international law.[27] Professor Wallace describes it this way:

> ...under contemporary international law, human rights are increasingly subdivided into three classifications,

"first, second, and third generation" rights. Civil and political rights constitute "first generation" rights; economic, social and cultural rights, the "second generation"; whilst group rights are characterized as "third generation" rights.[28]

Use of this term does not imply a hierarchical division of Human Rights, nor does it imply that succeeding generations preempt or gain primacy over earlier generations;[29] rather, it recognizes that the Human Rights regime is essentially dynamic and that additional Human Rights may be proclaimed as changing human needs are recognized and addressed. Maintaining an effective Human Rights regime presents the challenge of "balanc[ing] between the need to maintain the integrity and credibility of the human rights tradition, and the need to adopt a dynamic approach that fully reflects changing needs and perspectives and responds to the emergence of new threats to human dignity and well-being."[30]

First Generation Human Rights

Human Rights, as they emerged in the eighteenth century, generally consisted of those rights which could be invoked against the State,[31] and lend themselves to...immediate implementation.[32] "First-generation" rights are, as one scholar points out, "the traditional liberties and privileges of citizenship, covered by the first twenty Articles of the (Universal Declaration of Human Rights): free speech, religious liberty, the right not to be tortured, the right to a fair trial, the right to vote, and so forth."[33] These rights largely occupy the focus of Human Rights practitioners and advocates.[34] These rights are understood as promoting equal treatment among individuals, and include prohibitions against State interference.[35] Sometimes these rights are thought of as "negative rights".[36] Examples of first-generation rights are the rights to life, movement, thought, expression, association, religion, and political participation as well as the freedoms from torture, arbitrary arrest, and interference in private communication and the right to due process of law.[37]

The United Nations Charter was the first manifestation of this concern for individual Human Rights, and the Universal

Declaration later enumerated specific Human Rights which were agreed upon by the international community of nations. Finally, certain of these Human Rights obligations were made explicitly binding under international law through the ICCPR, which was adopted in 1966. These documents represent consensus among the signatories that the rights they describe are significant and deserving of deference.[38]

Under international law, the Universal Declaration, adopted in 1948 by the General Assembly of the United Nations, has become the keystone of the existing Human Rights regime.[39] It exists alongside the United Nations Charter as the principle authoritative source on Human Rights worldwide.[40]

Arguments that the United Nations Charter and the Universal Declaration create binding international law take two forms. First, the Universal Declaration and subsequent Covenants created binding obligations which gave detail to the general Human Rights objectives of the United Nations Charter, and solidified the commitments to create positive law initiated in the Charter.[41] Second, the United Nations Charter and the Universal Declaration, along with their progeny, established a customary international law of Human Rights.[42] Customary international law is established by the consistent general practice of States over time, and the acceptance of such action as binding law upon the States; such "collective practices should...reflect widely held opinions and represent a broad consensus" in order to be regarded as customary law.[43]

Second Generation Human Rights

Although the first generation rights as proclaimed in these documents were said to inhere in all individuals as human beings,[44] for many individuals, however, the adoption of binding agreements guaranteeing first generation rights made little substantive difference in their lives as deleterious social conditions such as hunger, poverty, inadequate health care, the lack of educational opportunity, and hazardous workplaces inhibit the individual realization and enjoyment of first generation rights and freedoms.[45]

The development of second-generation rights, known as "economic, social and cultural rights",[46] which are traditionally the province of development agencies, understood as providing equal opportunity, and often thought of as "positive rights",[47] was in order to enhance the protection of first generation rights.[48] Second-generation rights generally focus on standards of living, including issues such as the availability of housing and education,[49] and also include the rights to work and a decent workplace, health, education, and social insurance.[50] Some of these additional rights were enacted through the International Covenant on Economic, Social, and Cultural Rights (ICESCR), which was adopted in 1966.

First and second generation rights exist in a paradoxical yet symbiotic relationship. Guarantees of economic, social, and cultural rights require State intervention, and yet are necessary to secure effective enjoyment of the first generation rights which protect individuals against State intervention.[51] While such active government participation may appear antithetical to the freedoms articulated in the ICCPR, the second generation of Human Rights is, in fact, necessary for the enjoyment of the first generation of Human Rights by most of the world's population. In short, for the illiterate and impoverished, the fruits of a free society simply are not accessible without the guarantees of the second generation Human Rights.[52]

The acceptance of the first two generations of Human Rights into international law occurred through two mechanisms. The first, mentioned above, was the gradual increase in deference and authority accorded the Universal Declaration until the rights it enumerated became part of the customary international law of Human Rights.[53] The second mechanism was the adoption of the ICCPR and the ICESCR by the United Nations General Assembly, the subsequent ratification of the Covenants, and their entry into force.[54] Unlike Declarations, the ratification of a Covenant creates an explicit binding obligation on States to guarantee the rights therein to all their citizens and to formulate their municipal law to incorporate the necessary Human Rights protections.[55]

Both Covenants are now binding international law for the parties acceding to them.[56]

First and Second Generation Human Rights: Equal Legitimacy

It must be understood, of course, that such mere classification into "generations" of Human Rights is not an attempt at ranking or prioritization.[57] Hence, the first and second generations of Human Rights should be approached more as a unity than as a duality, with equal respect and gravity despite the nomenclature.[58]

Third Generation Human Rights

Many of the world's people, however, continue to live under conditions which impede or prohibit their exercise of basic Human Rights. A third generation of Human Rights, therefore, was proposed to facilitate fuller exercise and enjoyment of those Human Rights currently embodied in international law,[59] and to incorporate the critique of prevailing Human Rights theory from the communitarian perspective,[60] as well as the critique from cultural relativism.[61]

Karel Vasak, Legal Adviser to the United Nations Educational, Scientific, and Cultural Organization (UNESCO) and former director of the UNESCO Division of Human Rights and Peace, first used the term "third generation Human Rights" to describe a group of policy goals achievable through concerted international action.[62] Since then a debate has ensued over whether this group of proposals, also termed solidarity rights,[63] are in fact Human Rights.[64] Some theorists take the position that Human Rights are static in number; any additional Human Rights must be inferred from existing rights rather than created or recognized outright.[65] Other critics have voiced concern that additional third generation rights will diminish the authority of existing Human Rights.[66] Theorists who favor a third generation of Human Rights argue for a dynamic view of Human Rights that considers and accommodates changing international situations and the increasing international capacity to cope with impediments to the enjoyment of freedoms and life by many of the world's people.[67]

A third generation may be characterized as the logical extension of a dynamic international Human Rights process. Vasak equates each of the three generations of Human Rights to a corresponding principle in the triumvirate of the French Revolution: *liberté*, *égalité*, and *fraternité*.[68] The first generation of political and civil rights, embodied in the Universal Declaration and the ICCPR, are freedoms from State intrusion: *liberté*.[69] The second generation furthers realization of the first generation by guaranteeing minimum standards, demandable upon the State, of education and health, a liveable wage, decent working conditions, and social insurance for all persons: *égalité*.[70] Finally, the third generation consists of rights which may be invoked against and demanded of the State.[71] These rights require all the organs of society—individual, State, regional, and international—to cooperate in order for the rights to be realized: *fraternité*.[72] Third generation rights cannot be realized without shared objectives and commitment to concerted group action.[73] For this reason, Vasak termed third generation rights solidarity rights.[74]

The debate over the validity of third generation rights often focuses on the alleged "collective" quality of such rights.[75] Critics assert that third generation rights are illegitimate because they are collective, whereas first and second generation rights are held by individuals.[76] Advocates claim that distinctions between individual and group rights are spurious and inaccurate.[77] They claim third generation rights should be understood as individual Human Rights,[78] not meaningfully different from first and second generation rights, and that in all three generations the individual remains the cardinal subject of the Human Rights.[79] Notably, the first provision of each of the Covenants, which set forth the first and second generations of rights, contains the "collective" right to self-determination,[80] despite the fact that this right is usually considered a third generation right.[81] Louis Sohn explains that although certain Human Rights, such as self-determination, may devolve directly upon groups, "because collective rights are always ultimately destined for individuals, they are *ipso facto...* individual rights".[82] Thus, each generation of rights has both individual and collective elements.[83]

The debate over third generation rights also reveals confusion and imprecision as to the constituents of a third generation.[84] Despite a mistaken tendency to view the many proposed third generation rights as homogenous, they are, in most cases, very different from and not obviously related to each other.[85] Effective consideration of third generation rights requires that each proposed right be considered independently because each differs fundamentally.

THE DEFINITIONAL UNDERPINNINGS OF HUMAN RIGHTS: CONCLUSION

It is in this background that the authors propose to attempt their determination of the compatibility of Human Rights with the WTO regime. The authors will be attempting such a critique within the restriction that the Human Rights values under discussion be either almost universally accepted as *jus cogens*, or as moral standards, or as necessary for the protection of human life and health (as will be seen *infra* in Part-II). Therefore, it is highly probable that while most (if not all) first and second generation Human Rights will fulfil the above criteria, almost none of the proposed third generation rights will be able to do so, given the almost universal acceptance of first and second generation Human Rights and the debate over the validity and content of third generation Human Rights (as detailed above). Therefore, while the determination of the compatibility of the normative values of Human Rights with those of the WTO regime is not necessarily exclusive of third generation Human Rights, such "collective" rights would definitely be more difficult to justify within the current framework of the GATT-WTO.

PART II: THE NORMATIVE FRAMEWORK OF THE DEBATE

In this part, we examine the controversial connection and potential conflict between International Trade and Human Rights by way of an examination of the opinion of several jurists for and against the issue, concluding that the incorporation of Human Rights and International Trade values requires some systemic mechanism for the formulation and evaluation of normative conflicts.

Human Rights and Market Globalization: New Challenges?

Frank J. Garcia argues that while market globalization may represent in some aspects a unique opportunity for Human Rights law, the globalization of the market economy may also pose a threat to the continued effectiveness of Human Rights law, just as the rise of the market economy itself has been blamed for leading to conditions requiring the formal development of Human Rights law.[86]

He goes on to argue that the regulatory framework which international economic law provides for globalization operates according to a view of human nature, human values and moral decision-making fundamentally at odds with the view of human nature, human values and moral decision-making which underlies international Human Rights law. The Human Rights movement could thus find in market globalization the ultimate victory of a regulatory system that, by nature and operation, cannot properly take into account what the Human Rights movement holds most dear: that underlying positive Human Rights laws are moral entitlements that ground moral, political, and legal claims of special force, claims which must be morally and legally prior to society and the State.[87]

Human Rights and WTO: Hierarchy or Co-ordination?

Thus, the normative relationship of trade rules and Human Rights is of paramount importance. Is it possible to establish that Human Rights norms are of a higher moral and legal rank than trade rules?

Human Rights standards emerged as key indicators and standards of contemporary and widely shared standards of justice.[88] It is well established that Human Rights have become the benchmarks for the good and the bad.[89] Does it follow that Human Rights therefore trump trade rules?

Some of the Human Rights, as will be shown later,[90] are of a peremptory nature (*jus cogens*) and trump other norms of international law. But most Human Rights, under current international law, are not of a higher rank than other sources of treaty or customary law. They do not inherently prevail.[91] Moreover, fundamental principles of trade law, in particular non-discrimination, are of equal and paramount importance in their own way and right. For trade regulations, they reflect equally important basic standards of justice, going beyond economic efficiency.[92] Therefore, conflicts between Human Rights standards and basic principles of trade law thus cannot be solved by giving *a priori* preference to Human Rights, except for *jus cogens*.[93] To some extent, there is room to grant exceptions under special provisions of trade agreements.[94] But as in constitutional law, conflicting rights need co-ordination and concordance to the utmost extent possible. It is difficult to say which in the abstract should prevail as a matter of principle. It is rather a matter of a mutual dialogue and of interaction of what should enjoy equal status in its own right, taking into account strengths and weaknesses alike.[95]

Equal Legitimacy

The power and legitimacy of Human Rights relies upon different grounds: ethical foundations, expression and aspiration of justice, the rule of law and functional importance for open and democratic society and peace at large.[96] There are different traditions in founding Human Rights: natural law, positivism, legal experience, and theory of justice.[97] There is no single theory. The respect of human dignity is at the core of law, of the idea of law and the very purpose of a homocentric legal system in terms of "generational" rights.[98] It enjoys a high level of support in public opinion and by civil society actors and the judiciary, while governments often remain ambiguous beyond rhetoric as they remain the principal targets of Human Rights claims and seek to defend non-intervention into domestic affairs.[99] Its main weakness relies upon high aspirations combined with relatively weak enforcement and compliance with the international system in the real world.[100]

The power and legitimacy of the multilateral trade system essentially relies upon the same underlying values as Human Rights.[101] Yet, it is justified differently. Legitimacy is mainly drawn from economic theory and experience ("comparative advantage")[102] and remains essentially utilitarian, that is, looking at benefits for a majority without conceptualizing trade regulation in terms of individual rights.[103] It has a powerful record of bringing about welfare and growth and a high level of implementation, supported by powerful economic interests.[104] Its weakness relies upon one-sided emphasis of economic efficiency, difficulties with fully taking into account non-economic interests and policies, and in its limitation to an intergovernmental system that faces difficulties in coping with the challenge of democratic governance.[105]

It is in this background that the authors propose to attempt their determination of the compatibility of Human Rights with the WTO regime.

International Trade and Human Rights

As a matter of justice, Frank J. Garcia argues, our society is committed to both markets and rights. Therefore, it is inevitable that there will be some level of conflict between the rationality of markets and the rationality of rights. In many respects, the challenge facing the global community is akin to the challenge facing any society based on both markets and rights—how to carve out the respective spheres for rights and for free market choices, and how to regulate or limit the range of market choices when they threaten Fundamental Rights. This comes down to institutional decisions, of both a norm-creating and adjudicative nature. In other words, how do we incorporate both trade values and Human Rights values in comprehensive policies respecting both markets and rights, and what rules do we apply when these values, and the laws incorporating these values, conflict?[106]

Perhaps obviously, developing countries, free trade economists, and many private enterprises in developed countries are the primary opponents to the establishment of any linkage between International Trade and Human Rights.[107] Arguments for the exclusion of Human Rights linkages in free trade—whether by expansive interpretation or by amendment of treaty language—insist that trade liberalization rightly remains the WTO-GATT's sole preoccupation.[108] They argue that conditioning free trade on Human Rights is detrimental to the promotion of welfare-enhancing free trade.[109] Moreover, this linkage harms the economy of developing countries because it limits their ability to increase export trade, one of the best methods of economic improvement. They reason that connecting trade with Human Rights would deprive the South of its key comparative advantage,[110] namely the ability to use cheap labour.[111] They further argue that the same would invade their sovereignty.[112] It is instead simply a guise for protectionism.[113] This seems to find some support in the WTO 1996 Singapore Declaration,[114] which does appear to establish some kind of limit to the sort of trade measures that WTO Members deem consistent with the WTO legal framework.[115] The Declaration states: "We reject the use of labour standards for protectionist purposes, and agree that the comparative advantage of countries, particularly low-wage developing countries, must in no way be put into question."[116]

Advocates of a link between Human Rights and free trade, on the other hand, state that the export of products produced under low standards results in unfair competition that negatively affects working conditions in countries with higher labor standards. This disparity results in a "race to the bottom",[117] and weakens the working conditions in previously "high standard" countries.[118]

Other supporters argue that all countries engaged in international trade should respect Human Rights. These authors deny that such a link would increase protectionism. In contrast they believe that a linkage would eliminate one of the main justifications for trade restrictions.[119] A common standard, supporters note, would prevent States from restricting trade on the basis of domestic standards.[120]

The authors agree with Frank J. Garcia inasmuch as they believe that the resolution of globalization/Human Rights conflicts in a manner which enhances the effectiveness of Human Rights law is going to require a mechanism for the recognition within international economic law of the priority, which at least certain fundamental Human Rights must enjoy. In other words, there must be some mechanism for a constitutional level of deference within international economic law toward at least certain elements of the International Bill of Human Rights, such as the core rights involving life, freedom, security and bodily integrity, and the recognition within international economic law of rights-enforcement techniques such as trade sanctions, which make such rights effective, and which cannot be balanced or traded off in international economic law dispute resolution decisions. Where some sort of trade-off is inevitable, there must be clear recognition of the priority which Human Rights claim must have in any value conflict.[121]

This article, in the next part, analyzes whether, such a mechanism, in fact, exists within the GATT-WTO framework and, if so, how that may be used in effecting trade-related (perhaps trade-restrictive) Human Rights-based measures.

PART III: RESOLVING THE DEBATE: A CRITIQUE ON COMPATIBILITY

In this part, we discuss the relation between International Trade and Human Rights by way of an examination of the scope of the General Agreement on Tariffs and Trade (GATT), as incorporated in the World Trade Organization Agreement (WTO). In this regard, particular attention will be paid to Article XX, the General Exceptions clause, to determine whether any linkage can be established between the enumerated exceptions and trade-related Human Rights measures. Such a discussion would centre firstly on the Article's *chapeau* or introductory phrase and then detail clauses (a), (b), and (d) of Article XX, which constitute the most relevant sections concerning the controversial linkage of Human Rights and GATT provisions. Further, in this part, the authors will discuss the requirements or application of the paragraphs (as provided for in the *chapeau*), related controversial issues, and the possible inclusion of Human Rights within the Article's scope. Finally, this article argues that through careful application of these paragraphs, the GATT can be used to protect Human Rights.

GATT General Exceptions and Human Rights

I. *GATT General Exceptions*: Since the GATT does recognize to a certain extent certain important social policy concerns based in values other than trade,[122] one must analyze, whether, in fact, the same allows contracting parties to address Human Rights issues through trade-related measures. This part of the article proposes to do just that; firstly, by analyzing GATT requirements from such policy based trade-restrictive measures in general, and then, upon identifying the particular provisions that may be of use in this context, analyzing their requirements in determining whether, in fact, trade-restrictive measures may be justified as a Human Rights based policy consideration within the GATT framework.

1. *GATT General Exceptions:* Article XX: Recognizing that the non-discrimination norm[123] may not in all cases be an adequate dividing line between legitimate public policies and trade liberalization commitments, the GATT text provides explicit exceptions for policies that may even entail elements of discrimination, provided that they are justified in terms of certain non-protectionist goals and that their application does not entail unjustified or arbitrary discrimination.[124] Article XX, entitled "General Exceptions", primarily addresses the general exceptions available under the GATT for purposes of public policy. It lists protection of public morals [Article XX(a)], the protection of human, animal or plant life or health [Article XX (b)], and measures securing compliance with GATT-consistent laws [Article XX (d)], among the public policy related exceptions. This provision authorizes governments to apply otherwise illegal measures when such measures are necessary to deal with the listed social or economic policy problems, relieving the contracting parties from the obligations imposed by the GATT.

2. *Requirements of the General Exceptions*: Basics: In order to use Article XX to justify a trade measure designed to enhance or protect Human Rights, a party must meet several conditions.[125] First, a nation must show that the policy meets the standards in the introductory phrase, which requires non-discriminatory trade policies.[126] Second, a nation must show

that the adopted measure falls within one of the policy areas recognized in the General Exceptions.[127] Finally, the nation must show the connection between the social or economic policy justification and the trade sanctions and that the policy is needed in order to reach the stated end.[128] A GATT panel confirmed this limited interpretation of the character of Article XX,[129] stating "Article XX is a limited and conditional exception from obligations under other provisions of the General Agreement, and not a positive rule establishing obligations in itself. Therefore, the practice of panels has been to interpret Article XX narrowly."[130]

3. *Requirements of the General Exceptions*: Not "a disguised restriction on international trade": In one of the earliest cases concerning the requirement of being "undisguised", the Tuna I Panel noted that a publicly announced trade measure could not be considered disguised.[131] The Panel also emphasized the importance of the publication of the trade measure in question in its decision regarding U.S. restrictions on the importation of certain automotive parts.[132]

However, it is warned that an overemphasis on publication can be abused and serve to disguise protectionist measures. This emphasis risks possible misuse of Article XX, where blatantly protectionist measures might pass the disguised regulation test precisely because of their blatancy.[133] Jan Klabbers, considering the interpretation of disguised restriction, harshly critiques the "publication" interpretation, calling it manifestly absurd.[134]

4. *Requirements of the General Exceptions*: "necessary": The Section 337 Panel found that a party could not invoke Article XX as necessary when a reasonable alternative measure existed and when that measure was not inconsistent with "other GATT provisions available to it." In cases where a reasonable alternative does not exist, a party must adopt the measure "which entails the least degree of inconsistency with other GATT provisions",[135] inasmuch as it must be determined whether there were other measures that could have achieved the same policy goals but interfered with trade to a lesser degree.[136] Under this standard, it is the individual measure in

question that must meet the "necessary" criterion and not the various social policies listed under Article XX.[137]

However, the "least restrictive" test must be interpreted and deployed with substantial deference to member's regulatory choices.[138] Thus, the responding party must demonstrate that the measure falls somewhere between "indispensable to" and "making a contribution to" the policy interest being pursued by it. In making this determination, the measure should be significantly closer to the former—indispensable—than the latter—making a contribution to the interest pursued by it.[139]

In recent case law, the Appellate Body has taken a flexible view of the level of scrutiny appropriate under those exceptions in Article XX of the GATT where the word "necessary" does appear. Thus, in the recent Korea-Beef[140] and EC-Asbestos[141] cases, the Appellate Body has suggested that a measure may be found to be "necessary" even if it is not indispensable for achieving a particular goal, provided that the measure is proportional to the objective, and it has also held that where values such as human life are at stake the margin of appreciation for domestic regulators should be particularly wide. In construing Article XX exceptions, the WTO has characterized the necessity requirement as involving the balancing of a number of factors. These include the relative importance of the values being protected, the effectiveness of the measure (or "the extent to which the measure contributes to the realization of the end pursued"), and the degree of burden imposed on international trade.[142]

5. *Requirements of the General Exceptions*: Not "arbitrary or unjustifiable discrimination": In the Shrimp/Turtle case, the Appellate Body understood the first of these criteria as related to the even-handedness with which the measures are applied, taking into account different conditions that may exist in different countries.[143] "Arbitrary discrimination", again as understood in the Shrimp/Turtle case, will occur when the sanctions are applied in a manner that does not respect due process and transparency requirements.[144]

It has been suggested that such measures must be "transparent and performance oriented",[145] inasmuch as the terms of the measure must be duly publicized and negotiated, or, at least, discussed,[146] and that the measure should be expressed in terms of the objectives it seeks to accomplish rather than merely stating the production process that regulated industries must or must not employ.[147] Further requirements would include that the measures be supported by some level of objective evidence,[148] such as scientific studies.[149]

6. *Extraterritoriality*: The WTO in Shrimp/Turtle I construed Article XX to allow some theoretical authority for States to target conduct abroad.[150] In Shrimp/Turtle, the Appellate Body came to the conclusion that the conservation exception in Article XX(g) of the GATT could, in principle, provide a legal basis for unilateral trade measures to protect the global environment, in this case endangered species of sea turtles, even where directed against other countries' policies. It opined:

> It is not necessary to assume that requiring from exporting countries compliance with, or adoption of, certain policies (although covered in principle by one or another of the exceptions) prescribed by the importing country, renders a measure a priori incapable of justification under Article XX. Such an interpretation renders most, if not all, of the specific exceptions of Article XX inutile, a result abhorrent to the principles of interpretation we are bound to apply.[151]

Further, the very existence of international Human Rights, international labor rights law, and the institutions developed to deal with these areas suggest that the international community accepts that a State's legitimate concern about the morality of the treatment of individuals is not limited to its own nationals.[152] Rather, Human Rights reflect a full universe of human life and of the condition humane.[153]

Having established how the requirements of the General Exceptions *chapeau* may be met in case of certain *bona fide* Human Rights-based, trade-restrictive measures, the authors would move on to establishing what provisions of the GATT

General Exceptions may, in fact, be utilized in justifying these measures at a substantive level. The authors would now consider the three provisions, namely clauses (a), (b) and (d) in establishing their claim that the GATT General Exceptions may allow nations to justify certain *bona fide* Human Rights-based, trade-restrictive measures, in certain circumstances.

II. Article XX(a): *Protection of Public Morals*: Article XX(a), which allows for the suspension of GATT obligations when the same is necessary to protect public morals, is the first provision considered with regard to establishing a possible Human Rights related exception in Article XX so as to allow for the suspension of GATT obligations based on violations of trade related Human Rights. Because neither GATT nor WTO bodies have interpreted or evaluated Article XX(a), its interpretation remains difficult and uncertain.[154] In order to successfully use Article XX(a) to defend an adopted policy, a party must first establish all of the above *chapeau*-based considerations to be satisfied, and then must go on to prove that the substance of the policy of the measure, for which the provision was invoked, is protection of public morals. Because a definition of Article XX(a) is essential for its use, the purpose of this section is to define "public moral."

1. *Inhumane Treatment and the Human Rights Exception*: Australia's position in the Tuna-Dolphin case resulted in one useful definition of "public morals", wherein Australia argued that "Article XX(a)...could justify measures regarding inhumane treatment of animals, if such measures applied equally to domestic and foreign animal products."[155] If its view on inhumane treatment of animals is accepted, however, there is no reason why the same should not be valid for the treatment of human beings. Under this interpretation, Article XX(a) could justify trade actions concerning the inhumane treatment of human beings.[156]

2. *Moral Standards and the Human Rights Exception*: Another way to include Human Rights in Article XX(a) is to consider certain Human Rights as "moral standards", arguing that main international Covenants on Human Rights are moral standards that few countries would contest and that most have

accepted by virtue of membership.[157] In *United States—Gambling and betting services*, the Panel stated that "public morals" denoted "standards of right and wrong conduct maintained by or on behalf of a community or nation", which could vary in time and space, depending on prevailing social, cultural, ethical and religious values, and that WTO members "should be given some scope to define and apply for themselves [these concepts] in their respective territories according to their own systems and scales of values".[158] The recent review of the decision by the Appellate Body appears to uphold the Panel's interpretations.[159]

Most literature admits that "It is well established that human rights have become the benchmarks for the good and the bad." inasmuch as "violations of human rights equals morally bad conduct",[160] since Human Rights is the "only political-moral idea that has received universal acceptance",[161] thus conforming to the "ordinary meaning" interpretation required under Article 31 of the Vienna Convention on the Law of Treaties.[162] This is especially true considering that the exception appears to have been adopted in part to address international concerns such as trade in slaves, opium, and firearms, and foreign use of forced or compulsory labor.[163] The obligation to take into account "applicable rules of international law between the parties" has been adopted by the Appellate Body, which, in the *United States—Gasoline* case, held that WTO law cannot be read in "clinical isolation from public international law".[164]

3. *Historical usage of the Human Rights Exception*: In fact, unilateral trade sanctions designed to promote Human Rights abroad have long been an established practice and authors are reasonably certain that the GATT text can reasonably be read to accommodate certain Human Rights sanctions including those targeting Human Rights and labor violations that occur in production of goods for export, GSP measures, restrictions on military technology, and general trade measures targeting *jus cogens* violations such as genocide.[165]

For example: The Jackson-Vanik Amendment of the Trade Act of 1974[166] had allowed the United States to withhold "most-favored-nation" (MFN) benefits from communist governments such as China that denied their citizens the freedom to emigrate and other Human Rights, and its recent lifting of its longstanding annual review of China's Human Rights practices paved the way for China's entry into the World Trade Organization.[167] Similarly, in 1978, in response to the state-sponsored murder of civilians in Idi Amin's Uganda, the United States barred all imports and exports between Uganda and the United States until the President certified that Uganda was "no longer committing a consistent pattern of gross violations of Human Rights".[168] Similarly, the United States withheld MFN trading status from Poland in 1982 following the suppression of the Solidarity labor union movement.[169] Poland's MFN status was restored in 1987[170] and in the 1980s, the US barred the importation of sugar and other sweeteners from Panama until the President certified that "freedom of the press and other constitutional guarantees, including due process of law, have been restored to the Panamanian people".[171] Similarly, in 2001, the US House of Representatives approved legislation that would deny the importation of diamonds used to fund violent conflicts overseas.[172] Similarly, in 1983, the European Commission barred the importation of skins of certain seal pups because of public outrage at the killing of baby seals by Canadians.[173] Similarly, the European Commission has forbidden the importation of animal pelts unless the country of origin has banned leghold traps or unless the trapping methods used for the species meet "internationally agreed humane trapping standards."[174] Restricting imports is not the only way to exert moral or humanitarian influence on other countries. Exports can also be controlled. For example, in 1985, the United States banned the export of computer technology to certain entities of the South African Government.[175] Similarly, the United Nations Security Council had called for voluntary sanctions against South Africa.[176]

III. Article XX(b): ***Protection of Life or Health*****:** Article XX(b) validates measures which may be otherwise trade restrictive and might have otherwise violated the general principles of the GATT, if these measures were taken for the protection of human or animal life, or health. Since no contracting party has ever invoked Article XX(b) for Human Rights issues, in determining whether the said provision may indeed be relied on in case of measures restricting trade so as to protect Human Rights, reliance for its interpretation must be placed on earlier dispute settlement reports on somewhat tangential matters.

1. *Methods of Production and Practice*: There is some controversy over the scope of the application of this provision, however, inasmuch as we must determine whether it may be applied only to the manufactured product or to the methods of production and practice ("MPP") utilized in manufacturing the product.[177] If the interpretation of this provision did, in fact, apply to the MPP of the final product, Article XX(b) could serve as a basis for the defense of a much broader variety of trade related Human Rights.

Taking MPP into account, however, remains highly disputed and no GATT or WTO panel has ever approved their consideration in this regard. However, Panel decisions regarding MPP, interpreting other provisions of the GATT, involve situations sufficiently analogous to those in Article XX(b) cases to extend their analysis. For example, the Tuna-Dolphin Panel, in its decision, stated that the United States' protection measures concerning the production methods of tuna violated the GATT,[178] holding that Article XX(b) did not legitimize this violation,[179] on three major grounds: namely, Article XX(b)'s limitation to trade measures (inasmuch as the application of Article XX(b) refers only to trade measures violating GATT obligations and not other, broader life or health regulations established by the Contracting Parties); the non-extraterritorial application of Article XX(b) exceptions (finding against unilaterally determined life or health protection policies on the ground that it eroded the multilateral framework); and the necessity of the trade measure in question.[180]

It may be noted, however, that the Panel's rejection of extraterritorial application of unilaterally determined standards was not repeated in the Shrimp/Turtle case, wherein the

Appellate Body held that the same would, in fact, render the very object of the provision "inutile".[181] Further, since, as has already been established, the trade-related Human Rights considered in this article refer to standards that few countries would contest,[182] it has been observed that unilateral action with respect to their observance should not be confused with the unilateral acts to which the Tuna-Dolphin Panel referred.[183] The goal of achieving these rights has, in fact, been endorsed by the international community by including the same in the Preamble of the GATT, which states that contracting parties recognize that "their relations in the field of trade and economic endeavor should be conducted with a view to raising standards of living."

The Shrimp-Turtle Appellate Body Report noted the importance of the Preamble within the context of environmental issues.[184] The Vienna Convention on the Law of Treaties, by way of Article 31(2) further confirms that, for the interpretation of a treaty its preamble must be taken into account.[185]

The Preamble's reference to raising standards of living is, therefore, highly significant inasmuch as trade-related Human Rights would undoubtedly contribute to living standards.[186] As more countries guarantee these rights, living standards will rise. By implementing policies aimed towards these ends, the countries do not unilaterally determine the health or protection policies, but comply with the text of the Preamble and arguably with obligations agreed upon in a multilateral framework.

Finally, an exclusion of MPP non-trade concerns from the analysis of Article XX would have contradictory effects on other Article XX norms. Robert Howse, an internationally recognized expert on trade regulation and labor rights, explains this conflict:

> Even if one thinks that Article XX(a) is somehow limited to matters such as the regulation of pornography, imposing a limitation on its scope to measures on "products" would prevent a country from banning imports of pornographic films made with children or

involving (but not necessarily depicting) involuntary acts of sex and other illegal violence. One has only to think of this example to see how unduly and irrationally restrictive of the ability of members to protect public morals Article XX(a) would be if it excluded PPM [MPP] based measures. Indeed, unless independently harmful, any product manufactured in the context of racketeering or organized crime would have to be given the full protection of GATT![187]

Furthermore, Article XX(b) allows a contracting party's health interests to prevail over the trade interests of other contracting parties.[188]

The drafters of the GATT did not specifically designate the Article XX measures that relate to MPP, but an examination of Article XX(e) shows that it should be applied to measures concerning the MPP of imported goods. Although the clause does not contain any specific provision to this effect, one can deduce this from its structure because a ban on products made by prison labor refers to the conditions under which the product was produced. Thus, Article XX(e) takes into account the MPP under which the final product is produced. It is unlikely that the drafters of the GATT had another interpretation in mind.[189] The same is applicable to the other paragraphs of Article XX, namely paragraphs (a), (b), and (d).[190] If the drafters had not wanted the latter paragraphs to be interpreted in the same way as paragraph (e) with regard to the MPP, they would have made such an intention explicit.[191] Since the wording of the paragraphs (a), (b), and (d) does not contain any statement excluding Article XX measures based on MPP, it follows that these concerns can also be taken into account.

IV. Article XX(d): ***Necessary to Secure Compliance with Laws or Regulations not Inconsistent with GATT***: The Panels that have dealt with the meaning of the phrase "laws or regulations" have agreed that the "'laws or regulations' to be examined under sub-paragraph (d) are the laws or regulations the contracting party invoking Article XX(d) claims to secure compliance with."[192] Subsequent panels have maintained the domestic nature of the laws or regulations, noting that, "Article XX(d) [authorizes] a contracting party to secure compliance with its national laws or regulations...."[193]

Had the drafters of GATT contemplated such a restrictive understanding, however, it is suggested that they would have chosen wording that indicates such intent.[194] The addition of the terms "internal" or "domestic" to the laws or regulations would have been enough to justify such an interpretation. However, the drafters did not add these terms and, therefore, it is very unlikely that the panels' limited interpretation of the laws or regulations corresponds with the drafters' intent. Accordingly, the panels' restrictive view with regard to the domestic or international character of the laws or regulations is incorrect.[195]

As a general rule, any application of Article XX(d) measures must be necessary to secure compliance with laws or regulations that are not inconsistent with GATT provisions. Because the GATT is devoted exclusively to free trade issues, it does not embody any Human Rights. In fact, they embody different normative underpinnings.[196] Therefore, any invocation of Human Rights is inconsistent with the provisions of the GATT.[197]

However, the above analysis of Human Rights does not include *jus cogens* norms because of the peremptory nature of *jus cogens* norms. Therefore, no internationally binding treaty can violate *jus cogens* norms.[198]

The concept of *erga omnes* obligations is similar to norms of *jus cogens*. The International Court of Justice defined *erga omnes* obligations as "obligations of a State towards the international community as a whole."[199] Because *erga omnes* obligations are by their nature concerns of all nations, "all States can be held to have a legal interest in their protection."[200] Because "all States...have a legal interest" in the outlawing of activities violating *erga omnes* obligations, any nation could take legal action to end such activity. Thus, the Human Rights examples concerning *erga omnes* obligations provided by the International Court of Justice can surely be regarded as *jus cogens* rules.[201]

While Article XX(d) generally bars laws or regulations concerning Human Rights that are inconsistent with the GATT, the foregoing discussion demonstrates that the GATT conflict with *jus cogens* norms. It follows, then, that laws or regulations regarding *jus cogens* norms are "not inconsistent" with GATT provisions. Therefore, if it can be demonstrated that Human Rights that are regarded as *jus cogens* norms, laws or regulations concerning these standards would be consistent with the provisions of the GATT.

Whether Human Rights should be considered as *jus cogens* norms is, however, a controversial issue, as there is considerable confusion as to their precise nature and role in international law, despite the widespread acceptance of the importance of Human Rights in the international structure.[202] However, certain Human Rights may now be regarded as having entered into the category of "Customary International Law",[203] in light of "State Practice",[204] such as the principle of non-discrimination and the prohibition of genocide; slavery or slave trade; the murder or causing the disappearance of individuals; torture or other cruel, inhuman, or degrading treatment or punishment; prolonged arbitrary detention; systematic racial discrimination; and a consistent pattern of gross violations of internationally recognized Human Rights.[205] Customary Human Rights laws "are based on principles of concern to all States and protect interests which are not limited to a particular State or group of States."[206] Therefore, they are very similar to *jus cogens* norms. However, despite their similarity, no authoritative body has used them synonymously.

The standing of the UDHR, for example, in the international legal framework is a special one;[207] it is, at the very least, a principle of customary international law, binding on parties *erga omnes*,[208] if not a peremptory norm (*jus cogens*) of international law.[209] The Prohibition of Torture is internationally recognized as *jus cogens*.[210]

PART IV: ALTERNATIVE STRATEGIES

In previous section, the authors demonstrated, how, to a limited level, as circumscribed by the provisions of the GATT

General Exceptions, Human Rights concerns could, in fact, be made the basis of certain trade-restrictive measures. However, other solutions also present themselves, and it is these that the authors propose to analyze in this part of this article. In substance, the authors wish to adopt Frank J. Garcia's excellent critique in this regard in particular.[211]

Include Human Rights Rules in Trade Agreements

It has been suggested that one approach would be the incorporation of certain Human Rights norms into the WTO agreements.[212] This approach could add to that foundation laid in the previous part by modifying the WTO agreements to add a core list of recognized Human Rights,[213] and creating a specialized Human Rights body within the structural framework of the WTO, with authority to hear Human Rights related complaints and to impose trade sanctions.[214]

This approach has the benefit of reversing the current trend of institutional specialization which complicates the trade-Human Rights and other trade linkage issues. However, it is precisely for this reason that such an approach is unlikely to succeed, in that there does not appear to be the requisite degree of political support that such a sweeping overhaul would require.[215] In fact, the trend seems in the opposite direction, as the majority of the world's trading nations have decided that the WTO is not the appropriate institution to articulate Human Rights norms, leaving that to other specialized agencies such as the ILO.[216]

Limit Trade Jurisdiction over Human Rights Measures

Alternatively, the jurisdiction of the WTO could be limited such that the legitimacy of any Human Rights-related trade actions would not be adjudicated in the WTO.[217] The broadest across-the-board restriction on the WTO's jurisdiction over Human Rights measures would be a general exception added to either the GATT, the WTO Charter or the WTO Dispute Settlement Understanding, excluding national measures taken in response to violations of treaty-based or customary Human Rights from WTO review.[218] However, contrary to existing Article XX exceptions, which incorporate some form of trade-off mechanism presupposing panel review, such an exception would have to be drafted more along the lines of the national security exception in Article XXI, vesting in the sanctioning State some form of unilateral discretion in the face of Human Rights violations. Otherwise, Human Rights-based measures are not really excluded from WTO review, but privileged according to some form of trade off mechanism.[219]

An alternative approach, more limited in scope, would only apply to Human Rights treaties involving products which themselves embody or are the fruits of Human Rights violations, such as pornography and the products of indentured child labor; or to any Human Rights treaties negotiated in the future to expressly provide for the use of economic sanctions in response to Human Rights violations.[220] In such cases, the WTO could be required to recognize the legitimacy of sanctions imposed within the constraints of such a treaty, and such measures should not have to undergo the necessity test as applied through the Article XX exceptions.[221] Such recognition could take the form of a pure hierarchy of norms provision, ensuring that in the event of a conflict between a trade measure and a measure taken pursuant to an obligation under such an enumerated treaty, the obligations of that treaty should prevail.[222]

There are several benefits to adopting either of these variants. First, this approach would represent the decision by the international community at the political or legislative level[223] that trade-related Human Rights measures are appropriate despite their potentially adverse trade effects. Second, either amendment eliminates the interpretive problems attendant to including Human Rights measures within the scope of existing exceptions.[224] Third, in its Article XXI-like form, such an exception could grant the broadest possible scope for State action, including both economic measures taken pursuant to a Human Rights treaty authorizing sanction, and economic measures taken unilaterally by a State in response to violations of rights which, while they are the subject of binding international custom or treaty law, are not expressly contained within instruments authorizing economic sanctions. In its narrower, hierarchy-of-norms form, such an amendment would still grant a very high level of deference to at least treaty-based Human Rights measures.

In granting to Human Rights measures an automatic exclusion from review according to trade values and trade principles, such a general exception would be quite congenial to the philosophic approach of the Human Rights movement, which seeks recognition of the priority of Human Rights claims.[225] However, the very breadth of such an approach, coupled with its preference for Human Rights over trade values, would make such an amendment difficult to enact in the face of concerted opposition from WTO Member States committed to a higher priority for trade values. Moreover, an Article XXI approach, or a pure hierarchy of norms, would be unpopular for its very non-justiciability, already a concern with the existing Article XXI exception. This non-justiciability would be resisted on formal grounds, in view of the strong preference in the WTO for rule-based adjudicative dispute resolution, and by Member States reluctant to open themselves to such broad unreviewable use of economic sanctions. Finally, such an approach would raise quite legitimate concerns over the invitation to protectionist abuse that such a blanket exception would invite.[226]

CONCLUSION

Ultimately, therefore, at the end of this determination of the compatibility of Human Rights and the World Trade Organization, the authors find that it would be possible, even within the current framework of the WTO-GATT to address certain Human Rights-based concerns through trade-restrictive means, even finding positive support for trade-based sanctions as a response to violation of Human Rights obligations. Attempts by nations to balance both trade and Human Rights concerns, could, and should, therefore, find active assistance in Article XX considerations, within the circumscribed requirements thereof, by way of the "Public Morals", "Protection of Human Life or Health" and "Securing Compliance with GATT consistent Laws & Regulations" exception (in this regard, to the extent only of *jus cogens* (and perhaps *erga omnes*) obligations). Since the authors believe that certain of the alternative methods suggested for addressing this determination, that is, the incorporation of certain Human Rights values in trade documents and/or certain trade values in Human Rights documents, deserve some support inasmuch as they would, hopefully, provide some consistency, constancy and clarity to this ambiguous determination, the authors doubt whether the same would find much support at the international stage, given that it is already possible to address both trade and Human Rights concerns within the current framework.

Notes

1. Salman Bal, "International Free Trade Agreements and Human Rights: Reinterpreting Article XX of the GATT", 10 *Minn. J. Global Trade* 62 at 62 (hereinafter Bal); Frank J. Garcia, "The Global Market and Human Rights: Trading away the Human Rights Principle" (Symposium: "The Universal Declaration of Human Rights at 50 and the Challenge of Global Markets: The Global Market as Friend or Foe of Human Rights") 25 *Brook. J. Int'l L.* 51 (hereinafter Garcia).
2. In this regard, see extensively, Garcia. See also Alfred C. Aman, Jr., 'Introduction', 1 *Ind. J. Global Legal Stud.* 1, 1 (1993). In our view, '*globalization*' refers to complex, dynamic legal and social processes.

   ...Today, the line between domestic and international is largely illusory."); Rudolph Dolzer, 'Global Environmental Issues: The Genuine Area of Globalization', 7 *J. Transnat'l L. & Pol'y* 157, 157 (1998); S. Tamer Cavusgil, 'Globalization of Markets and its Impact on Domestic Institutions', 1 *Ind. J. Global Legal Stud.* 83, 84 (1993); Jost Delbrück, 'Globalization of Law, Politics, and Markets—Implications for Domestic Law—A European Perspective', 1 *Ind. J. Global Legal Stud.* 9, 9-10 (1993); Miguel de la Madrid H., 'National Sovereignty and Globalization', 19 *Hous. J. Int'l L.* 553, 555-60 (1997); Alberto Tita, 'Globalization: A New Political and Economic Space Requiring Supranational Governance', 32 *J. World Trade* 47 (1998); Alex Y. Seita, 'Globalization and the Convergence of Values', 30 *Cornell Int'l L.J.* 429 (1997) ("Globalization...is a multifaceted concept encompassing a wide range of seemingly disparate processes, activities, and conditions...connected together by one common theme: what is geographically meaningful now transcends national boundaries and is expanding to cover the entire planet.

Globalization has led to an awareness that international issues, not just domestic ones, matter.") (hereinafter Seita).

3. See Malcolm N. Shaw, *International Law*, 252-53 (2005) (hereinafter Shaw). See generally T. Meron, *Human Rights Law Making in the United Nations* (1986); A.H. Robertson and J. Merrills, *Human Rights In The World* (1996); P. Alston and J. Crawford (eds.), *The Future of UN Human Rights Treaty Monitoring* (2000); H. Steiner and P. Alston, *International Human Rights In Context* (2000); P. Sand and P. Klein (eds.), *Bowett's Law Of International Institutions* (2001); J. Rehman, *International Human Rights Law* (2002). See generally Oona A. Hathaway, 'Do Human Rights Treaties Make A Difference?', 111 *Yale L.J.* 1935; John King Gamble, Teresa A. Bailey, Jared S. Hawk, Erin E. McCurdy, 'Human Rights Treaties: A Suggested Typology, An Historical Perspective', 7 *Buff. Hum. Rts. L. Rev.* 33 (hereinafter Gamble); Natsu Taylor Saito, 'Beyond Civil Rights: Considering "Third Generation" International Human Rights Law in the United States', 28 *U. Miami Inter-Am. L. Rev.* 387 (hereinafter Saito); Joy Gordon, 'The Concept Of Human Rights: The History And Meaning Of Its Politicization', 23 *Brook. J. Int'l L.* 689 (hereinafter Gordon); Makau Wa Mutua, 'The Ideology Of Human Rights' 36 *Va. J. Int'l L.* 589 (hereinafter Mutua).
4. Professor Doctor Ernst-Ulrich Petersmann, 'Theories Of Justice, Human Rights, and the Constitution of International Markets', 37 *Loy. L.A.L. Rev.* 407; Ernst-Ulrich Petersmann, "Human Rights and International Economic Law in the 21st Century", 4 *Journal of International Economic Law* (2001) 3-39; Ernst-Ulrich Petersmann, 'Time for a United Nations 'Global Compact' for Integrating Human Rights into the Law of Worldwide Organizations: Lessons from European Integration', 13 *Eur. J. Int'l L.* 621; Ernst-Ulrich Petersmann, 'Taking Human Dignity, Poverty and Empowerment of Individuals More Seriously: Rejoinder to Alston', 13 *Eur. J. Int'l L.* 845, Thomas Cottier, 'Trade and Human Rights: A Relationship to Discover: Part I: The State of International Economic Law', 5 *J. Int'l Econ. L.* 111 (hereinafter Cottier); Philip M. Nichols, 'Trade Without Values', 90 *Nw. U.L. Rev.* 658 (hereinafter Nichols).
5. Philip Alston, *Resisting* 'The Merger and Acquisition of Human Rights By Trade Law: A Reply to Petersmann', 13 *Eur. J. Int'l L.* 815; Claude Barfield, *Free Trade, Sovereignty, Democracy: The Future of the World Trade Organization* (2001); Robert Howse, 'Human Rights in the WTO: Whose Rights, What Humanity? Comment on Petersmann', 13 *Eur. J. Int'l L.* 651.

6. Bal, at 62; Lance A. Compa & Stephen F. Diamond (eds.), 'Human Rights, Labor Rights, and International Trade (1996). Andrew T.F. Lang, Re-Thinking Trade and Human Rights', 15 *Tul. J. Int'l & Comp. L.* 335; Adelle Blackett, 'Whither Social Clause? Human Rights, Trade Theory and Treaty Interpretation', 31 *Colum. Hum. Rts. L. Rev.* 1 (hereinafter Blackett); Tarek F. Maassarani, 'WTO/GATT, Economic Growth, and the Human Rights Trade-off', 28 SPG *Environs. Envtl. L. & Pol'y J.* 269. Perhaps as a forerunner to this debate, Keynes, for example, claimed that the prescription of free or freer trade was contingent and contextual, and might well have to yield to the demands of justice in given social and economic circumstances. See José E. Alvarez and Robert Howse, 'From Politics To Technocracy—And Back Again: The Fate of the Multilateral Trading Regime', 96 *Am. J. Int'l L.* 94 at 100 (hereinafter Alvarez-Howse); John Maynard Keynes, "Mitigation by Tariff", in *Essays in Persuasion* 271 (1991); Douglas A. Irwin, *Against the Tide: An Intellectual History of Free Trade* (1996).
7. Bal, at 63. See also, generally *Supra* n. 4.
8. See Burns H. Weston, 'Human Rights', *Human Rights Quarterly*, Vol. 6, No. 3. (Aug., 1984), pp. 257-83, at 262-64 (hereinafter Weston). Some of the most basic questions have yet to receive conclusive answers. Whether Human Rights are to be viewed as divine, moral, or legal entitlements; whether they are to be validated by intuition, custom, social contract theory, principles of distributive justice, or as prerequisites for happiness; whether they are to be understood as irrevocable or partially revocable; whether they are to be broad or limited in number and content—these and kindred issues are matters of ongoing debate and likely will remain so as long as there exist contending approaches to public order and scarcities among resources. Despite this lack of consensus, however, a number of widely accepted and interrelated postulates may be seen to assist, if not to complete, the task of defining Human Rights. Five in particular stand out, although it is to be noted that not even these are without controversy. First, regardless of their ultimate origin or justification, Human Rights are understood to represent individual and group demands for the shaping and sharing of power, wealth, enlightenment, and other cherished values in community process, most fundamentally the value of respect and its constituent elements of reciprocal tolerance and mutual forbearance in the pursuit of all other values. Consequently, they imply claims against persons and institutions who impede realization and standards for judging the legitimacy of laws and traditions. At bottom, Human Rights limit State power. Second, reflecting varying environmental circumstances, differing

worldviews, and inescapable interdependencies within and between value processes, Human Rights refer to a wide continuum of value claims ranging from the most justiciable to the most aspirational. Human Rights partake of both the legal and the moral orders, sometimes indistinguishably. They are expressive of both the "is" and the "ought" in human affairs. Third, if a right is determined to be a human right it is quintessentially general or universal in character, in some sense equally possessed by all human beings everywhere, including in certain instances even the unborn. In stark contrast to "the divine right of kings" and other such conceptions of privilege, Human Rights extend, in theory, to every person on earth without discriminations irrelevant to merit. Fourth, most assertions of Human Rights—arguably not all—are qualified by the limitation that the rights of any particular individual or group in any particular instance are restricted as much as is necessary to secure the comparable rights of others and the aggregate common interest. Given this interdependency, Human Rights are sometimes designated prima facie rights, and it makes little or no sense to think or talk of them in absolutist terms. Fifth and finally, Human Rights are commonly assumed to refer, in some vague sense, to "fundamental" as distinct from "nonessential" claims or "goods." In fact, some theorists go so far as to limit Human Rights to a single core right or two—for example, the right to life or the right to equal freedom of opportunity. The tendency, in short, is to de-emphasize or rule out "mere wants". In several critical respects, however, this last postulate raises more questions than it answers. What does it mean to say that a Right is Fundamental? Does it entail some bare minimum only, or, more plausibly, does it admit to something greater? If the latter, how much greater and subject to what conditions, if any? In other words, however accurate, this last postulate is fraught with ambiguity about the content and legitimate scope of Human Rights and about the priorities, if any, among them. Except for the issue of the origin and justification of Human Rights, no cluster of preliminary Human Rights considerations is more controversial. See also Gamble, at 34.

9. Mutua, at 590.
10. *Ibid.* For discussions of different and conflicting cultural, historical, and intellectual bases and traditions in Human Rights, see Josiah A.M. Cobbah, 'African Values and the Human Rights Debate: An African Perspective', 9 *Hum. Rts. Q.* 309 (1987); Jack Donnelly, 'Cultural Relativism and Universal Human Rights', 6 *Hum. Rts. Q.* 400 (1984); Bilahari Kausikan, 'Asia's Different Standard', 92 *Foreign Pol'y* 24 (1993) (advancing the view that Asia has its own distinctive historical and cultural values which

may differ or should not be easily analogized with the "universal" Human Rights norms promoted by the West); Makau wa Mutua, 'The Banjul Charter and the African Cultural Fingerprint: An Evaluation of the Language of Duties', 35 *Va. J. Int'l L.* 339 (1995); Raimundo Pannikar, 'Is the Notion of Human Rights A Western Concept?', 120 *Diogenes* 75 (1982). For discussions on the hierarchy and "importance" of some rights over others, see Philip Alston & Gerard Quinn, 'The Nature and Scope of States Parties' Obligations under the International Covenant on Economic, Social and Cultural Rights', 9 *Hum. Rts. Q.* 156 (1987) (arguing against a prejudiced hierarchy of rights which subordinates economic, social, and cultural rights to civil and political rights); Theodor Meron, 'On a Hierarchy of International Human Rights', 80 *Am. J. Int'l L.* 1 (1986). For discussions on the inclusion or exclusion and enforcement of women's rights as Human Rights, see Sandra Coliver, "United Nations Machineries on Women's Rights: How Might They Better Help Women Whose Rights are Being Violated?", in Ellen L. Lutz *et al.* (eds.), New Directions In Human Rights 25 (1989); Margaret E. Galey, 'International Enforcement of Women's Rights, 6 *Hum. Rts. Q.* 463 (1984).

11. Rebecca M.M. Wallace, *International Law* 195 (1992) (hereinafter Wallace).
12. Shaw, at 247.
13. W. Michael Reisman, 'Sovereignty and Human Rights in Contemporary International Law', 84 *Am. J. Int'l L.* 866, 872 (1990).
14. Thomas Buergenthal, *International Human Rights* 1 (1995).
15. Rolf Künnemann, 'A Coherent Approach to Human Rights', 17 *Hum Rts. Q.* 323 (1995) (hereinafter Künnemann); Gamble, at 36.
16. Imre Szabo, "Historical Foundations of Human Rights and Subsequent Developments", in 1 Karel Vasak & Philip Alston (eds.), *The International Dimensions Of Human Rights 11*, 20 (1982) (hereinafter Szabo).
17. Richard B. Bilder, 'Rethinking International Human Rights: Some Basic Questions', 2 *Hum. Rts. J. 557, 559* (1969). See also Jack Donnelly, *Universal Human Rights In Theory and Practice* at 12-15 (1989), (discussing that while the concept can be explained, it is very difficult to refine to a single definition) (hereinafter Donnelly).
18. Albert P. Blaustein *et al.*, *Human Rights Sourcebook* 4 (1987) (stating that treaties and Covenants evince international law when ratified and establish rules "expressly recognized" by the parties ratifying the Covenant). See also Statute of the International Court

of Justice, June 26, 1945, Article 38(1), 59 Stat. 1031, 1060 (instructing the Court to apply international Covenants).

19. Donnelly, at 9-27 (1989), (setting out an analytic theory of universal Human Rights).
20. Charter of the United Nations, June 26, 1945, 59 Stat. 1031, T.S. 993, 3 Bevans 1153, entered into force Oct. 24, 1945. The Charter of the United Nations (also known as the UN Charter) was signed at San Francisco, June 26, 1945 and entered into force October 24, 1945. The Charter is the cornerstone of the United Nations Organization, affirming faith in fundamental Human Rights, justice and peace. In the Human Rights context, the Charter also provides the basis for Charter-based (such as the Commission on Human Rights) and Treaty-based (such as the Human Rights Committee) Human Rights bodies. The Charter is both an international treaty and the constitution of the United Nations organization. It established the six major organs of the UN and their functions: General Assembly, Security Council, Economic and Social Council, Trusteeship Council, International Court of Justice, and Secretariat. The Charter delineates the principles on which the UN is based, such as sovereign equality of States, and the limitations on the organization such as nonintervention in domestic affairs of States. It sets out the purposes of the UN which encompass maintenance of international peace and security, promotion of economic and social co-operation, and protection of Human Rights. Member States, which now include virtually every country in the world, agree by signing the Charter to the principles of non-use of force and peaceful settlement of disputes. Louis B. Sohn is unstinting in his praise, when he refers to the UN Charter as the "constitution of the world, the highest instrument in the intertwined hierarchy of international and domestic documents, [which] prevails expressly over all other treaties, and implicitly over all laws, anywhere in the world." See Louis B. Sohn, 'The New International Law: Protection of the Rights of Individuals rather than States', 32 *Am. U.L. Rev.* 1, at 13 (1982) (hereinafter Sohn).
21. Universal Declaration of Human Rights, G.A. Res. 217A(III), U.N. GAOR, 3d Sess., at 71, U.N. Doc. A/810 (1948) (hereinafter Universal Declaration). The Universal Declaration is said to be the "spiritual parent of and inspiration for many Human Rights treaties". See Henry J. Steiner, 'Political Participation as a Human Right', 1 *Harv. Hum. Rts. Y.B.* 77, at 79 (1988). See also Mutua, at 605.

22. Louis Henkin, "International Human Rights as 'Rights'", in J. Roland Pennock and John W. Chapman (eds.), *Human Rights* 257, 264-65 (1981).
23. *Ibid*, at 264.
24. *Ibid.*
25. J. Roland Pennock, "Rights, Natural Rights, and Human Rights—A General View", in J. Roland Pennock and John W. Chapman (eds.), *Human Rights* 1, 7 (hereinafter Pennock). See also David D. Raphael, "The Rights of Man and the Rights of the Citizen", in David D. Raphael (ed.), *Political Theory and the Rights of Man* 101, 11718 (1967).
26. Pennock, at 7.
27. See Weston, at 264; Saito, at 389. The generational terminology was first articulated by French scholar Karel Vasak in Karel Vasak, "Pour une Triosième Génération des Droits de L'homme", in Christophe Swinarski (ed.), *Studies And Essays On International Humanitarian Law And Red Cross Principles In Honour Of Jean Pictet* (1984) (hereinafter Vasak). See Kevin T. Johnson, *Charting Global Responsibilities: Legal Philosophy And Human Rights* 16 (1994). This is the general understanding. In fact, Ruti Teitel suggests that Rights "generation" be considered in at least three different senses ("First, the language represents rights creation as a natural process. The rhetoric of "genesis" at once evokes the language of science and of nature. Scientific rhetoric imbues international Human Rights theory with legitimacy by implying that the theory follows the natural laws of the universe—as if Human Rights are just out there, existing as an autonomous and objective reality. Second, generation also conveys rights in a genetic sense. Put this way, rights generation casts the Human Rights story in terms of the broader human condition—of scientific, historical, and political generations. Third, the rhetoric of genesis and generation propounds the international Human Rights movement's distinctive account of natural rights made positive.") See Ruti Teitel, *Human Rights Genealogy*, 66 Fordham L. Rev. 301, at 304 (1997) (hereinafter Teitel); Louis Henkin, 'A New Birth of Constitutionalism: Genetic Influences and Genetic Defects', 14 *Cardozo L. Rev.* 533, 538-45 (1993).
28. Wallace, at 195; Gamble, at 37-38.
29. See United Nations Educational, Scientific and Cultural Organization, Working Group of the Standing Committee of International Non-Governmental Organizations, Symposium on the Study of New Human Rights: The "Rights Of Solidarity", *The Rights Of Solidarity: An Attempt At Conceptual Analysis*, at 2, U.N. Doc. SS-80/Conf.806/ 6 (1980) (hereinafter The "Rights Of

Solidarity"). See also, Sohn, at 62 ("The very terminology used, especially the word 'generation,' has created some problems. To many persons, the word connotes a succeeding generation replacing on older one, rather than generations existing convivially together. Some of the hostility to the economic, social, and cultural rights can be traced to insistence by several proponents that these new rights should have precedence over the old ones, that they were more important than the old rights they supposedly replaced, and that the old rights would have to wait in line until the basic needs represented by the new rights had been satisfied properly. Much time passed before the two categories—civil and political rights on the one hand, and economic, social, and cultural rights on the other hand—were considered to be interdependent and complementary: achievement of the rights in either category can be accomplished only with the help of the rights in the other category, and, similarly, failure in one area is likely to bring deterioration in the other"). But see Donnelly, at 144 (1989), (suggesting that "generation" is a disturbing metaphor because it "*fl[ies] in the face*" of the idea of the interdependence of Human Rights by implying that newly proposed rights are either dependent upon, or replace, already established Human Rights).

30. Philip Alston, 'Conjuring Up New Human Rights: A Proposal for Quality Control', 78 *Am. J. Int'l L.* 607, 609 (1984).
31. Paul Sieghart, *The Lawful Right Of Mankind* 26-29 (1985) (hereinafter Sieghart). See also Teitel, at 302-04; Saito, at 392; William Andrew Shutkin, 'International Human Rights Law and The Earth: The Protection of Indigenous Peoples and the Environment', 31 *Va. J. Int'l L.* 479, at 487 (1991) (hereinafter Shutkin).
32. Theodor Meron, 'Norm Making and Supervision in International Human Rights: Reflections on Institutional Order', 76 *Am. J. Int'l L.* 754, 757 (1982) (hereinafter Meron); Gamble, at 38.
33. Jeremy Waldron, *Liberal Rights* 5 (1993); Gordon, at n. 7.
34. Michael Ashley Stein, 'Disability Human Rights', 95 *Cal. L. Rev.* 75, at 77.
35. Weston, at 264 (stating that it favors the abstention rather than the intervention of government in the quest for human dignity, as epitomized by the statement attributed to H. L. Mencken that "... all government is, of course, against liberty.").
36. Isaiah Berlin, "Two Concepts of Liberty", in Isaiah Berlin, *Four Essays on Liberty,* 118, 122 (1958) (declaiming that authentic liberty is simply the absence of "the deliberate interference of other human beings within the area in which I could otherwise act")

(hereinafter Berlin). See also Weston, at 264; Shutkin, at 487; Saito, at 392.

37. See, e.g., International Covenant on Civil and Political Rights, G.A. Res. 2200A (XXI), Article 6, para. 1, U.N. GAOR, Supp. No. 16, U.N. Doc. A/6316 (Dec. 16, 1966) ("Every human being has the inherent right to life.") (hereinafter ICCPR); ICCPR, Article 9, para. 1 ("Everyone has the right to liberty and security of person."); ICCPR, Article 12, para. 1 ("Everyone lawfully within the territory of a State shall, within that territory, have the right to liberty of movement and freedom to choose his residence."); ICCPR, Article 18, para. 1 ("Everyone shall have the right to freedom of thought, conscience and religion.").
38. Jennifer A. Downs, "A Healthy and Ecologically Balanced Environment: An Argument for a Third Generation Right", 3 Duke J. Comp. & Int'l L. 351, at 358 (1993) (hereinafter Downs).
39. Lung-Chu Chen, *An Introduction To Contemporary International Law* 207-09 (1989) (hereinafter Chen); Szabo, at 23.
40. Chen, at 209. The Universal Declaration has been said to be "almost...legally binding", although this is not technically accurate. Szabo, at 33. The Universal Declaration is no more than a statement of United Nations thinking and is not binding on States. States may express their adherence and devotion to the principles of the Universal Declaration by including it in their own constitutions; however, this does not make the Universal Declaration itself binding on those States.
41. Louis Henkin *et al.*, *International Law* 985 (2nd edn., 1987).
42. *Ibid.*
43. Theodore van Boven, "Survey of the Positive International Law of Human Rights", in 1 Karel Vasak & Philip Alston (eds.), *The International Dimensions Of Human Rights* 87, 106 (1982) (hereinafter van Boven). See also Peter Malanczuk, *Akehurst's Modern Introduction To International Law* 37-39 (7th edn., 2000) citing the *Nicaragua case* (*Nicaragua* v. *United States of America*) ICJ Rep 1986 14 and the *Continental Shelf case* (*Libya* v. *Malta*) ICJ Rep 1985 29. See also *Advisory Opinion on the Legality of the Threat of use of Nuclear Weapons* 35 ILM 809 (1996). See generally Anthony D'Amato, *The Concept Of Custom In International Law* (1971); Anthony D'Amato, 'Wanted: A Comprehensive Theory of Custom in International Law', 4 *Tex. Int'l L. Forum* 28, (1968); Jo Lynn Slama, '*Opinio Juris* in Customary International Law', 15 *Okla. City ULR* 603.
44. See U.N. Charter, Article 55; ICCPR, Preamble, Universal Declaration, Preamble.

45. Saito, at 395; Meron, at 757 (discussing the divide between Third and First World States including the fact the former must achieve a "level of economic development that enables them to implement social rights, and that those States must therefore give priority to social rights and to economic and social development in order to facilitate the realization of civil and political rights."); Gamble, at 38. See generally International Covenant on Economic, Social, and Cultural Rights, G.A. Res. 2200, U.N. GAOR, 21st Session, Supp. No. 16, at 49, Preamble, U.N.Doc. A/6316 (1966) ("[T]he ideal of free human beings enjoying freedom from fear and want can only be achieved if conditions are created whereby everyone may enjoy his economic, social and cultural rights, as well as his civil and political rights."). The 1968 Declaration of the Teheran International Conference on Human Rights Stated that "[s]ince Human Rights and fundamental freedoms are indivisible, the full realization of civil and political rights without the enjoyment of economic, social and cultural rights, is impossible." 23 U.N. GAOR Supp. (No. 41) at 1, U.N. Doc. A/Conf. 32/41, paragraph 13 (1968), cited in Sohn, at 18, n. 63.
46. See Weston, at 265. See extensively, in Sohn, at 32-48. See also Dianne Otto, 'Rethinking The "Universality" Of Human Rights Law', 29 *Colum. Hum. Rts. L. Rev.* 1 at 6 (1997) (hereinafter Otto); Shutkin, at 487.
47. See Weston, at 265; Berlin, at 123 (defining positive liberty as the result of self-reliance and the ability to direct one's own agency). See also Shutkin, at 487. See, for example, International Covenant on Economic, Social and Cultural Rights, G.A. Res. 2200A (XXI), Article 11, para. 1, U.N. GAOR, Supp. No. 16, U.N. Doc. A/6316, 993 U.N.T.S. 3 (Dec. 16, 1966) ("States parties... recognize the right of everyone to an adequate standard of living") (hereinafter ICESCR).
48. Downs, at 360; Shutkin, at 487.
49. It is significant that development agencies have only more recently embraced first-generation rights. Human Rights scholars have long criticized these entities for neglecting Human Rights to focus exclusively on subsistence issues, meaning food and clean water. See, e.g., Philip Alston, "The Fortieth Anniversary of the Universal Declaration of Human Rights", in J. Berting *et al.* (eds.), *Human Rights in a Pluralist World* 1, 11-12 (1990). See also Mutua, at 617-620 (detailing how certain international non-governmental organization generally assumed an unsympathetic, and at times, hostile posture towards calls for the expansion of their mandates to include economic and social rights). In this regard, see also See Aryeh Neier, "Human Rights", in Joel Krieger *et al.* (eds.), *The*

Oxford Companion to Politics of the World 401, at 403 (1993); "Human Rights Watch", *Indivisible Rights: The Relationship of Political and Civil Rights to Survival, Subsistence and Poverty* (1992). In 1993, Aryeh Neier, the former executive director of HRW, expressed his opposition to the deployment of rights rhetoric to economic and social concerns: "When it comes to the question of what are called economic rights, I'm on the side of the spectrum which feels that the attempt to describe economic concerns as rights is misguided. I think that when one expresses this opinion, it is often thought that one is denigrating the significance of economic misery and inequities. I would like not to be accused of that. I regard economic equity and economic misery as matters of enormous significance. I just don't think that it's useful to define them in terms of rights." See Aryeh Neier, "Remarks to East Asian Legal Studies & Human Rights Program Symposium" (Harvard Law School) (May 8, 1993), in *Human Rights and Foreign Policy: A Symposium* 16 (1994). For a critique of NGOs and their restrictive mandates, see James Gathii & Celestine Nyamu, 'Note, Reflections on United States-based Human Rights NGOs' Work on Africa,' 9 *Harv. Hum. Rts. J.* 285, 291 (1996).

50. *Ibid.* See also, generally, Chen, at 211.
51. Donnelly, at 143-44.
52. Downs, at 360-61.
53. See, for example, Szabo, at 24 ("[T]he [Universal] Declaration has gradually come to command increasing authority throughout the world....."); Donnelly, at 33 ("[T]he Universal Declaration has acquired a moral authority such that it has almost become legally binding...[although it may have] a value no greater than that of custom.").
54. Each Covenant required thirty-five ratifications to enter into force. ICCPR, Article 49; ICESCR, Article 27. See United Nations, *Multilateral Treaties Deposited With The Secretary-General* 122, 133 (1992).
55. Szabo, at 33.
56. Sieghart, at 25-26, Szabo, at 33-34.
57. Shutkin, at 487, citing Sieghart, *Economic Development, Human Rights and the Omelette Thesis* (Book Review), 1 *Dev. Pol'y Rev.* *1*, 8 (1983).
58. See Gamble, at 38. See also Künnemann, at 325-26. As a matter of political theory, the dialectic between individualistic, or classical liberal, conceptions of human society and communitarian notions is a sophisticated and protracted one. See, e.g., R. Dworkin, *Law's Empire* (1986); A. MacIntyre, *After Virtue* (1981); J. Rawls,

A Theory of Justice (1971); R. Rorty, *Contingency*, *Irony*, and *Solidarity* (1989); R. Unger, *Knowledge and Politics* (1975). Nevertheless, it is well understood in the context of Human Rights that individual and group rights are deeply entwined, if not one and the same. See, e.g., I. Brownlie, "The Rights of Peoples in Modern International Law", in J. Crawford (ed), *The Rights of Peoples* 2 (1988).

59. Otto, at 6.
60. Teitel, at 312; Will Kymlicka (ed.), *The Rights of Minority Cultures* (1995).
61. Teitel, at 312; Michael J. Perry, *Are Human Rights Universal? The Relativist Challenge and Related Matters*, 19 Hum. Rts. Q. 461 (1997).
62. Vasak, at 837, 839; Weston, at 264.
63. The "Rights Of Solidarity", paragraph 8; Weston, at 265.
64. Donnelly, at 144-45. Solidarity rights, rather than necessarily being vested in groups or peoples, may be expressed and understood as individual rights exercised by individuals as group members. The "Rights Of Solidarity", paragraph 8. See, e.g., Berta Esperanza Hernández-Truyol, *Report of the Conference Rapporteur*, 44 Am. U.L. Rev. 1389, 1407 (1995) (Final Report to the Conference on the International Protection of Reproductive Rights, referring to "first (civil and political rights), second (social and economic rights) and third (solidarity) generation Human Rights."); Kathleen Mahoney, 'Theoretical Perspectives on Women's Human Rights and Strategies for their Implementation', 21 *Brook. J. Int'l L.* 799, 837-38 (1996) (noting that third generation "group or peoples' rights are of greatest interest to developing countries."); Stephen P. Marks, 'Emerging Human Rights: A New Generation for the 1980s?', 33 *Rutgers L. Rev.* 435, 441 (1981) (observing that Karel Vasak has distinguished the third generation of Human Rights as being "predicated on brotherhood (fraternité), in the sense of solidarity" as opposed to rights predicated on *liberté* (first generation rights) or *égalité* (second generation rights)); Feisal Hussain Naqvi, 'People's Rights or Victim's Rights: Reexamining the Conceptualization of Indigenous Rights in International Law', 71 *Ind. L.J.* 673, 713 (1996) (understanding third generation rights, such as the right to "cultural integrity" and "the right to development" as "expand(ing) the economic entitlements of individuals."); Barbara Stark, 'Conceptions of International Peace and Environmental Rights: "The Remains of the Day",' 59 *Tenn. L. Rev.* 651, 654 (1992).
65. See *Infra* nn. 76-83 and accompanying text.

66. Richard B. Bilder, "An Overview of International Human Rights Law", in Hurst Hannum (ed.), *Guide To International Human Rights Practice* 1, 16 (1984) (hereinafter Bilder).
67. See Donnelly, at 26. See also Bilder, at 561-62 ("[T]here seems nothing inherently wrong in either changing concepts or expanding the list of Human Rights. As our societies, technology, problems, attitudes, and expectations change, there is bound to be a corresponding change in the claims we view as basic, in the order of importance in which we rank these claims, and in the things we expect governments to do or not to do. Moreover, there is perhaps something to be said for an increase alone in the number and types of broadly humanitarian claims we are prepared to call Human Rights, since this will hopefully increase the pressures for their practical achievement."). See also Organization Of American States, "*Annual Report Of The Inter-American Commission On Human Rights*: 1980-1981", at 54, OEA. Ser. L/V/II.54, Doc. 9, rev. 1 (1981) (Dissent of Dr. Luis Demetrio Tinoco Castro on Resolution No. 23/81) "[T]he international community...may, and on certain occasions should, revise the rules of international law in force at the moment, including the...ones for the international protection of Human Rights, for the purpose of establishing new precepts that will correspond to the advances of science, to the teaching of experience, to the changing realities of social and international life, to the needs determined by the inevitable changes that new epochs create in the course of the years, and the aspirations that arise as generation follows generation. The international community...could not refuse to accept innovations that have a logical and just basis, because doing so would imply stopping the progress of the law and repudiating the principle contained in the [Universal Declaration] that the system of protection of the rights of man should be strengthened more and more in the international field as social and legal circumstances become more propitious.".
68. Vasak, at 839; Weston, at 264.
69. *Ibid* (stating that such rights liberated mankind from the political constraints of the old federal order). See also Donnelly, at 143.
70. Vasak, at 839 (stating that people need equal access to economic, social, and cultural opportunities). See also Donnelly, at 143-44.
71. Vasak, at 839.
72. Vasak, at 839. See also Donnelly, at 144 (noting that new forms of international cooperation are required).
73. Vasak, at 839.
74. *Ibid.*
75. Sohn, at 61.

76. See Donnelly, at 143-49 (setting out the major arguments against third generation rights based on their allegedly collective nature).
77. See van Boven, at 53-54 (suggesting that delineating too strictly between individual and collective rights is artificial and that most currently accepted rights and proposed third generation rights have both collective and individual aspects).
78. See Donnelly, at 150.
79. See The "Rights Of Solidarity", paragraphs 10, 12 (stating that third generation rights [solidarity rights] would give effect to "the creative development of every nation, every community, and every individual"); Richard N. Kiwanuka, 'The Meaning of "People" in the African Charter on Human and Peoples' Rights', 82 *Am. J. Int'l. Law* 80, 84 (1988).
80. ICCPR, Article 1; ICESCR, Article 1. See also van Boven, at 56 (explaining that "the very first Article of both the International Covenants on Human Rights sets out a collective right").
81. Self-determination is generally recognized as a third generation human right, even though its origins can be traced to the beginning of international law. See extensively, Sohn, at 48-52; Russel Lawrence Barsh, 'Indigenous Peoples in the 1990s: From Object to Subject of International Law?', 7 *Harv. Hum. Rts. J.* 33, 38-39 (1994). See generally Antonio Cassese, *Self-determination of Peoples: A Legal Reappraisal* (1995). See also Saito, at 395-98; Teitel, at 312; Sara E. Allgood, 'United Nations Human Rights "Entitlements": The Right to Development Analyzed within the Application of the Right of Self-Determination', 31 *Ga. J. Int'l & Comp. L.* 321, at 326.
82. Sohn, at 48 "[T]he effective exercise of collective rights is a precondition to the exercise of other rights, political or economic or both."
83. See Sieghart, at 125.
84. See James Crawford, "The Rights of Peoples: 'Peoples' or 'Governments'?", in James Crawford, *The Rights of Peoples* 67 (ed.), (1988) (asking for "more orthodox terminology" in analysis, after discussing the six varieties of "collective rights" enumerated by Sieghart in Paul Sieghart, *The International Law of Human Rights* 367-78 (1983)). See The "Rights Of Solidarity", paragraphs 5, 23, 34, 46, 52, 62, 71 (including as potential third generations rights the rights to development, peace, the common heritage of mankind, communication, environment, and international humanitarian assistance); Consultative Assembly, Council of Europe, *Parliamentary Conference On Human Rights* 24 (1972) (determining that there should be new rights to a healthy and clean environment, to social security, and to self-

determination); Sieghart, at 368-78 (discussing self-determination, liberation, international peace and security, use of natural wealth and resources, development, and the protection of minority group rights); Vasak, at 840 (listing rights to development, peace, environment, communication, and the common heritage of mankind). See also Weston, at 266 (also recognizing six "collective rights").

85. For example, compare the right to communication (involving, *inter alia*, the right to publish, to reply to mass media reports, and to have access to information sources) with the right to international humanitarian assistance and the right to peace. See generally the "Rights Of Solidarity", paragraphs 34-45, 51-61, 70-78.
86. See extensively, Garcia. See also Donnelly, at 64 (1989) ("Modern markets also created a whole new range of threats to human dignity and thus were one of the principal sources of the need and demand for Human Rights." It may be, for example, that the globalization of markets erodes the social and normative preconditions for Human Rights protection, as well as for the market itself. Daniel M. Hausman & Michael S. McPherson, 'Taking Ethics Seriously: Economics and Contemporary Moral Philosophy', 31 *J. Econ. Literature* 671 (1993) (arguing that core trade and economic values such as economic efficiency depend upon ethical values which paradoxically may be undermined by market economies. Hausman & McPherson list honesty, trust and goodwill as three values critical to the efficient function of markets, which may in fact be undermined by appeals to rational self-interest, at least in certain forms).
87. Donnelly, at 9 (1989). See also, Garcia.
88. See *Supra* nn. 8-14.
89. See *Infra* nn. 153, 157-59
90. See *Infra* nn. 191-94 and accompanying text.
91. Cottier, at 114.
92. See *Infra* n. 124.
93. See *Infra* nn. 190-94, and accompanying text.
94. See *Infra* Part-II.
95. Cottier, at 114-15.
96. Cottier, at 114-15; Saito; Mutua; Gordon.
97. Gamble; Mutua.
98. Saito; Gamble; Carl Wellman, 'Solidarity, the Individual and Human Rights', 23 *Hum. Rts. Q.* 639 (2000); Meron, at 757. The generational terminology was first articulated by French scholar Karel Vasak. See also Kevin T. Johnson, *Charting Global Responsibilities: Legal Philosophy and Human Rights* 16 (1994).

See also James Crawford (ed.), *The Rights of Peoples* 44 (1988); Wallace, at 195.

99. Richard Falk, *Human Rights and State Sovereignty* (1981). See also Charles E. Ritterband, *Universeller Menschenrechisschutz and völkerrechtliches Interventionsverbot* (1982).

100. Cottier, at 114-15.

101. Cottier, at 115-19. Friedl Weiss, Erik Denters and Paul de Waart (eds.), *International Economic Law With A Human Face* (1998).

102. See *Infra* n. 111.

103. See *Infra* nn. 105, 109-14.

104. See generally John H. Jackson, *The Jurisprudence of GATT and the WTO: Insights on Treaty Law and Economic Relations* (2000); John H. Jackson, William Davey and Alan O. Sykes, *Legal Problems of International Economic Relations* (1995); John H. Jackson, *World Trade and the Law of GATT* (1969); Edmond McGovern, international trade regulation (1995); Mitsuo Matsushita, Thomas J. Schoenbaum & Petros C. Mavroidis, *The WTO–Law, Practice and Policy* (2003); Jagdish Bhagwati, *Writings on International Economics* (1997); Raj Bhalla and Kevin Kennedy, *World Trade Law* (1998); Raj Bhalla, *Modern GATT Law: A Treatise on GATT* (2005) ; David Palmeter & Petros C. Mavroidis, *Dispute Settlement in the World Trade Organisation–Practice and Procedure*, (2004) Autar Krishen Koul, *The World Trade Organisation: Law, Economics and Politics* (2005).

105. Cottier, at 114-15.

106. See Garcia (Garcia argues that the importance of mechanisms to balance the conflicts which can occur between fundamental normative elements of a globalized liberalism, such as the conflict between free markets and Human Rights, is recognized as one of the central challenges of globalization). See also Seita, at 484-85.

107. Bal, at 64.

108. Jagdish Bhagwati, "Trade Linkage and Human Rights", in Jagdish N. Bhagwati & Mathias Hirsch (eds.), *The Uruguay Round and Beyond* 241(1998); Tarek F. Maassarani, 'WTO-GATT, Economic Growth, and the Human Rights Trade-Off', 28-SPG *Environs Envtl. L. & Pol'y J.* 269, at 271.

109. *Ibid.* See also Michael J. Trebilcock et al., *Trade and Transitions: A Comparative Analysis of Adjustment Policies* 45 (1990). See also Robert E. Baldwin, 'The Ineffectiveness of Trade Policy in Promoting Social Goals', 8 *World Econ.* 109 (1985); Robert Howse, 'The World Trade Organization And The Protection Of Workers' Rights', 3 *J. Small & Emerging Bus. L.* 131, 158.

110. Robert Howse, 'The World Trade Organization and the Protection of Workers' Rights', 3 *J. Small & Emerging Bus. L.* 131, 133; William K. Wilcox, 'GATT-Based Protectionism and the Definition of a Subsidy', 16 *B.U. Int'l L.J.* 129, 161 (1998); Tarek F. Maassarani, 'WTO-GATT, Economic Growth, And The Human Rights Trade-Off', 28-SPG *Environs Envtl. L. & Pol'y J.* 269, at 273-277. In this regard, see also David Ricardo, *On the Principles of Political Economy and Taxation* (1821). See also Ralph E. Gomory & William J. Baumol, *Globalization: Prospects, Promise, and Problems* (Georgetown U.L. Center Sloan Interdisciplinary Workshop, Discussion Paper No. 5, April 23, 2004); Joel R. Paul, 'Do International Trade Institutions Contribute to Economic Growth and Development?', 44 *Va. J. Int'l L.* 285, 291 (2003).
111. Robert Howse & Makau Mutua, *Protecting Human Rights in a Global Economy*, Rights & Democracy, at http://www.ichrdd. ca/ 111/english/commdoc/publications/globalization/ wtoRights Glob.html; Bal, at 64; Clyde Summers, 'The Battle In Seattle: Free Trade, Labor Rights, And Societal Values', 22 *U. Pa. J. Int'l Econ. L.* 61; Lance Compa,' Labor Rights and Labor Standards in International Trade', 25 *Law & Pol'y Int'l Bus.* 165, 167 (1993); Jagdish Bhagwati, "Policy Perspectives and Future Directions: A View from Academia", in (*Symposium: U.S. Department of Labor, International Labor Standards and Global Economic Integration?*) 57, 58 (1994); Blackett, at 50.
112. Clyde Summers, 'The Battle In Seattle: Free Trade, Labor Rights, And Societal Values', 22 *U. Pa. J. Int'l Econ. L.* 61; See generally Lance Compa, 'International Labor Rights and the Sovereignty Question: NAFTA and Guatemala, Two Case Studies', 9 *Am. U. J. Int'l L. & Pol'y* 117 (1993) (discussing the issue of sovereignty in light of two case studies).
113. Benjamin James Stevenson, 'Pursuing an End to Foreign Child Labor Through U.S. Trade Law: WTO Challenges And Doctrinal Solutions', 7 *UCLA J. Int'l L. & Foreign Aff.* 129, 139. See Steven Charnovitz, *The World Trade Organization and Social Issues*, 28 J. World Trade 17, 32 (1994) (quoting then-GATT Director General, Peter Sutherland: "Simplistic demands for drastic trade remedies against so-called eco-dumping or social dumping sometimes bear a striking similarity to more Conventional forms of protectionist rhetoric...."). See generally Steven Charnovitz, 'The Influence of International Labour Standards on the World Trading Regime: A Historical Overview', 126 *Int'l Lab. Rev.* 565 (1987).

114. WTO Singapore Ministerial Declaration, WT/MIN(96)/DEC/W (Dec. 13, 1996), available at http://www.wto.org/english/thewto_e/minist_e/ min96_ e/wtodec_e.htm

115. Robert Howse, 'The World Trade Organization And The Protection Of Workers' Rights,' 3 *J. Small & Emerging Bus. L.* 131, 148; William K. Wilcox, 'GATT-Based Protectionism and the Definition of a Subsidy', 16 *B.U. Int'l L.J.* 129, 161 (1998).

116. *Ibid* at para 4.

117. In the international context, a "race to the bottom" is a continuing reduction in regulatory standards accelerated by international competition. See, e.g., Frederick M. Abbott, 'International Trade and Social Welfare: The New Agenda', 17 *Comp. Lab. L.J.* 338, 368 (1996) (noting race-to-the-bottom pressures that exist in developing countries); Daniel C. Esty, 'Toward Optimal Environmental Governance', 74 *N.Y.U.L. Rev.* 1495, 1558-59 (1999) (discussing the need for international environmental governance structures to prevent races to the bottom); Eyal Benvenisti, 'Exit and Voice in the Age of Globalization', 98 *Mich. L. Rev.* 167, 168 (1999) (describing the lower levels of consumer protection that can result from lowered regulatory standards); Richard L. Revesz, 'Rehabilitating Interstate Competition: Rethinking the "Race-to-the-Bottom" Rationale for Federal Environmental Regulation', 67 *N.Y.U. L. Rev.* 1210, 121319 (1992) (discussing races to the bottom in the context of domestic environmental regulation). Politicians have made similar points. See John F. Kerry, 'Trade and the Environment: Charting a New Course', 27 *Cornell Int'l L.J.* 447, 452, 551-52 (1994). See also John O. McGinnis and Mark L. Movsesian, 'The World Trade Constitution', 114 *Harv. L. Rev.*, 511 at 517; Alvin K. Klevorick, 'The Race To The Bottom In A Federal System: Lessons From The World Of Trade Policy', 14 *Yale J. on Reg.* 177.

118. See J.M. Servais, 'The Social Clause in Trade Agreements: Wishful Thinking or an Instrument of Social Progress?', 128 *Int'l Lab. Rev.* 423 (1989) (noting that, if a country allows its workers to be employed under conditions of work that are miserable, it can export its products at lower prices and thus acquire an unfair advantage over its competitors). According to this theory, because other countries are not willing to lose their exports, they will react by lowering their standards as well. Thus, the "race to the bottom" would be unavoidable.

119. See generally Steven Charnovitz, 'The Influence of International Labour Standards on the World Trading Regime: A Historical Overview', 126 *Int'l Lab. Rev.* 565 (1987).

120. See generally Blackett, at 48-55 (considering linkage between ILO labor regulations and trade, and discussing role of GATT in protecting rights); Paul de Waart, "Minimum Labor Standards in International Trade from a Legal Perspective", in Pitou van Dijck & Gerit Faber (eds.), *Challenges to the New WTO* 245, 256-61 (1996) (arguing for greater trade regulation to protect worker rights); Michael R. Gadbaw & Michael T. Medwig, "Multinational Enterprises and International Labour Standards: Which Way for Development and Jobs?", in Lance A. Compa & Stephen F. Diamond (eds.), *Human Rights, Labor Rights and International Trade* 141, 143-46 (1996) (highlighting legal and economic issues in the linkage debate); Brian A. Langille, "Labour Standards in the Globalized Economy and the Free Trade/Fair Trade Debate", in Werner Sengenberger & Duncan Campbell (eds.), *International Labour Standards and Economic Interdependence* 329 (1994) (emphasizing how the free/fair trade debate is central to the debate on labor standards in the new economy); Virginia A. Leary, "Workers' Rights and International Trade", in Jagdish Bhagwati & Robert E. Hudec (eds.), *Fair Trade and Harmonization: Legal Analysis*, Vol. 2, p.177 (1996) (discussing opposition to and support of linkage between trade and rights); Alejandro Portes, "By-Passing the Rules: The Dialectic of Labour Standards and Economic Interdependence", in Werner Sengenberger & Duncan Campbell (eds.), *International Labor Standards and Economic Interdependence* 159, 160 (1994) (explaining the relationship between labor standards and economic strategies of less developed countries, and presenting proposals for an alternative labor regime); see Garcia, analyzing effect of globalization on Human Rights law; Robert Howse, 'The World Trade Organization and the Protection of Workers' Rights', 3 *J. Small & Emerging Bus. L.* 131 (1999) (advocating for the adoption of labor rights-based trade related measures); Ray Marshall, 'Trade Linked Labor Standards', 37 *Acad. Pol. Sci.* 67-78 (1990) (encouraging the United States to use international trade to grow world economies and to protect rights); Gijsbert Van Liemt, 'Minimum Labor Standards and International Trade: Would a Social Clause Work?', 128 *Int'l Lab. Rev.* 433-34 (1989) (supporting adoption of a social clause for international trade in order to institutionalize labor protection). See also Jagdish Bhagwati & T. N. Srinivasan, "Trade and the Environment: Does Environmental Diversity Detract from the Case for Free Trade?", in Jagdish Bhagwati & Robert E. Hudec (eds.), *Fair Trade and Harmonization: Economic Analysis*, Vol. 1, 160 (1996) (providing an economic analysis of linkages generally); Herbert Feis, "International Labor Legislation in the Lights of Economic

Theory", in Werner Sengenberger & Duncan Campbell (eds.), *International Labor Standards and Economic Interdependence* 29, 47 (1994) (discussing whether international action should be aimed at uniform standards).

121. See Garcia.
122. See Garcia; Steven Charnovitz, 'The World Trade Organization and Social Issues', 28 *J. World Trade* 17, 23-24 (1994).
123. See generally Mitsuo Matsushita, Thomas J. Schoenbaum & Petros C. Mavroidis, *The WTO–Law, Practice and Policy* 143 *et. Seq.* (2003); Raj Bhalla and Kevin Kennedy, *World Trade Law* 59 (1998), ("...any advantage, favour, privilege or immunity granted by any contracting party to any product originating in or destined for any other country shall be accorded immediately and unconditionally to the like product originating in or destined for the territories of all other contracting parties."). See also Gary Clyde Hufbauer *et. al.*, 'The GATT Codes and the Unconditional Most-Favoured-Nation Principle', 12 *Law & Pol'y Int'l Bus*, 59 (1980); Henrik Horn and Petros C. Mavroidos, 'Still Hazy After All These Years: The Interpretation of National Treatment in GATT/WTO Case Law On Tax Discrimination', 15 *EJIL* 39 (2004); Ernst-Ulrich Petersmann, *Economic, Legal and Political Functions of the Principle of Non-Discrimination*, (1986) The World Economy 113. See also, generally, Report of the Panel, *Canada—Certain Measures Affecting Automobile Industry*, WT/DS139/R, WT/DS142/R of 11 Feb 2000; Report of the Panel, *Spain—Tariff Treatment of Unroasted Coffee*, 11 June 1981, GATT BISD (28th Supp.) 1982; Appellate Body Report, *Canada—Certain Measures Affecting Automobile Industry*, WTO Doc. WT/DS139/AB/R, WT/DS142/AB/R, para. 69; Appellate Body Report, *EC—Regime for the Importation, Sale and Distribution of Bananas*, WT/DS27/AB/R of 9 Sept 1997, para. 191 ("the essence of the nondiscrimination obligations is that like products should be treated equally, irrespective of their origin").
124. Alvarez-Howse, at 97.
125. See GATT Dispute Panel Report on *United States: Standards for Reformulated and Conventional Gasoline*, Jan. 26, 1996, 35 I.L.M. 274 (1996) (hereinafter Gasoline Panel). See also GATT Dispute Panel Report on *United States: Section 337 of the Tariff Act of 1930*, Nov. 7, 1989, GATT B.I.S.D. (36th Supp.) (1989) 345 at 392 (hereinafter Section 337 Panel).
126. The introductory phrase, sometime called the "chapeau", applies once a contracting party invokes Article XX. Compliance with its substantive requirements is the precondition for application of one or more of the exceptions listed in Article XX. The chapeau reads

as follows: "Subject to the requirement that such measures are not applied in a manner which would constitute a means of arbitrary or unjustifiable discrimination between countries where the same conditions prevail, or a disguised restriction on international trade, nothing in this Agreement shall be construed to prevent the adoption or enforcement by any contracting party of measures." The introductory phrase contains two requirements for all measures falling within the scope of Article XX: "arbitrary or unjustifiable discrimination" and "disguised restriction on international trade." See Section 337 Panel, at 392. The conditions enunciated in the introductory phrase must be satisfied for any measure enacted on the basis of any of the exceptions listed in Article XX. The fulfillment of the conditions mentioned in paragraphs (a) through (j) of the Article is not sufficient; all measures must also be neither arbitrary, discriminatory, nor a disguised restriction on trade. See also GATT Dispute Panel Report on *United States: Imports of Certain Automotive Spring Assemblies*, May 26, 1983, GATT B.I.S.D. (30th Supp.) at 107, 125 (1983) (hereinafter Spring Assemblies Panel) (noting that "the Preamble of Article XX made it clear that it was the application of the measure and not the measure itself that needed to be examined") and indicating that, in order for a contracting party to undertake a legal measure on the basis of Article XX, the measure must also satisfy the conditions of the introductory phrase.

127. See John H. Mathis, 'Trade Related Environmental Measures in the GATT', 2 *Leg. Issues Eur. Integration* 47 (1991) (arguing that this narrow interpretation "illustrates the GATT preference to permit trade flows"); Bal, at 70.
128. Bal, at 69.
129. See GATT Dispute Panel Report on *United States: Restrictions on Imports of Tuna*, Aug. 16, 1991, GATT B.I.S.D. (39th Supp.) at 155, 204 (1993) (hereinafter Tuna-Dolphin Panel).
130. *Ibid* at 197. See also Section 337 Panel at 345, 392-96.
131. See GATT Panel Report on *United States: Prohibition of Imports of Tuna and Tuna Products from Canada*, February 22, 1982, GATT B.I.S.D. (29th Supp.) at 108 (1982) (hereinafter Tuna I Panel) (involving complaint by Canada alleging a U.S. restraint on Canadian imports violated the GATT) explaining that "the United States action should not be considered to be a disguised restriction on international trade, noting that the United States prohibition of imports of tuna and tuna products from Canada had been taken as a trade measure and publicly announced as such".
132. See also Spring Assemblies Panel, at 125 (noting that, because the exclusion order was published in the Federal Register and based

on a valid patent whose infringement had been clearly established, no disguised trade restriction could be identified).

133. Steve Charnovitz, 'Exploring the Environmental Exceptions in GATT Article XX', 25 *J. World Trade* 37, 47 at 48 (1991); Bal, at 75.

134. Jan Klabbers, 'Jurisprudence in International Trade Law: Article XX of GATT', 26 *J. World Trade* 63 at 91 (1992).

135. See also Michael J. Trebilcock & Robert Howse, 'Trade Liberalization and Regulatory Diversity: Reconciling Competitive Markets with Competitive Politics', 6 *Eur. J.L. & Econ.* 5, 33 (1998); Robert Howse, 'The World Trade Organization And The Protection Of Workers' Rights', 3 *J. Small & Emerging Bus. L.* 131, 144.

136. Kevin C. Kennedy, *The GATT-WTO System at Fifty*, 16 Wis. Int'l L.J., 421 at 458-59 (1998); Maury D. Shenk, 'WTO Dispute Settlement Body—Article XX Environmental Exceptions to GATT—National Treatment—Consistency with GATT of US Rules Regarding Imports of Reformulated Gasoline', 90 *Am. J. Int'l L.* 669, 672-74 (1996); John O. McGinnis and Mark L. Movsesian, 'The World Trade Constitution', 114 *Harv. L. Rev.*, 512 at 579.

137. Section 337 Panel, at 392-93.

138. Kevin C. Kennedy, 'The GATT-WTO System at Fifty', 16 *Wis. Int'l L. J.*, 421 at 459 (1998); Alan O. Sykes, 'Regulatory Protectionism and the Law of International Trade', 66 *U. Chi. L. Rev.* 1, at 21-22 (1999); John O. McGinnis and Mark L. Movsesian, 'The World Trade Constitution', 114 *Harv. L. Rev.*, 512 at 579.

139. Report of the Appellate Body, *Korea—Measures Affecting Imports of Fresh, Chilled and Frozen Beef*, WT/DS161, 169/AB/R, 11 December 2000 (adopted 10 January 2001) (hereinafter Korea-Beef), at para 161.

140. Korea-Beef, paras 161-64.

141. Report of the Appellate Body, *European Communities—Measures Affecting Asbestos and Asbestos-Containing Products*, WT/DS135/AB/R, 12 March 2001 (adopted 5 April 2001) (hereinafter EC-Asbestos). For a detailed analysis of these aspects of the Korea-Beef and EC-Asbestos cases, see Howse and Tuerk, 'The WTO Impact on Internal Regulations: A Case Study of the Canada—EC-Asbestos Dispute', in G. de Búrca and J. Scott (eds), *The EU and the WTO: Legal and Constitutional Issues* (2001), pp. 324-27.

142. Korea-Beef, paras 162-64. See also EC-Asbestos, para 172.

143. Appellate Body Report, 'United States—Import Prohibition of Certain Shrimp and Shrimp Products,' WTO Doc. WT/DS58/AB/R (Oct. 12, 1998) paras. 161-76 (hereinafter Shrimp/Turtle Appellate Body Report); Robert Howse, 'The World Trade Organization and the Protection of Workers' Rights', 3 *J. Small & Emerging Bus. L.* 131, 145.
144. Robert Howse, 'The World Trade Organization and the Protection of Workers' Rights', 3 J. Small & Emerging Bus. L. 131, 145.
145. John O. McGinnis and Mark L. Movsesian, 'The World Trade Constitution', 114 Harv. L. Rev., 512 at 573.
146. Catherine Curtiss and Kathryn Cameron Atkinson, 'United States-Latin American Trade Laws' *21 N.C.J. Int'l L. & Com. Reg.* 111, 117-18 (1995); Mark J. Spaulding, 'Transparency of Environmental Regulations and Public Participation in the Resolution of International Environmental Disputes', 35 *Santa Clara L. Rev.* 1127, 1142 (1995); Jonathan T. Fried, 'Two Paradigms for the Rule of International Trade Law', 20 *Can.-U.S. L.J.* 39, 49 (1994); John O. McGinnis and Mark L. Movsesian, *The World Trade Constitution*, 114 Harv. L. Rev., 512 at 573.
147. Patti Goldman, 'The Legal Effect of Trade Agreements on Domestic Health and Environmental Regulation', 7 *J. Envt'l L. & Litig.* 11, 13-14 (1991); John O. McGinnis and Mark L. Movsesian, *The World Trade Constitution*, 114 Harv. L. Rev., 512 at 573.
148. Daniel C. Esty, 'Greening The GATT: Trade, Environment And The Future' (1994) at 117-21, 235; John O. McGinnis and Mark L. Movsesian, *The World Trade Constitution*, 114 *Harv. L. Rev.*, 512 at 577.
149. Alan O. Sykes, 'Regulatory Protectionism and the Law of International Trade', 66 *U. Chi. L. Rev.* 1, at 17 (1999); Kevin C. Kennedy, 'The GATT-WTO System at Fifty', 16 *Wis. Int'l L. J.*, 421 at 456 (1998); Vern R. Walker, 'Keeping the WTO from Becoming the "World Trans-Science Organization: Scientific Uncertainty, Science Policy and Fact-finding in the Growth Hormones Dispute', 31 *Cornell Int'l L.J.* 251 at 262-63 (1998); John O. McGinnis and Mark L. Movsesian, *The World Trade Constitution*, 114 Harv. L. Rev., 512 at 577.
150. Robert Howse, 'Back To Court After Shrimp/Turtle? Almost But Not Quite Yet: India's Short Lived Challenge To Labor And Environmental Exceptions In The European Union's Generalized System Of Preferences', 18 Am. U. Int'l L. Rev. 1333 at 1367; Sarah H. Cleveland, 'Human Rights Sanctions and International Trade: A Theory of Compatibility', *5 J. Int'l Econ. L.* 133 at 159.
151. Shrimp/Turtle Appellate Body Report, para. 121.

152. Robert Howse, 'Back To Court After Shrimp/Turtle? Almost But Not Quite Yet: India's Short Lived Challenge To Labor And Environmental Exceptions In The European Union's Generalized System Of Preferences', 18 *Am. U. Int'l L. Rev.* 1333 at 1369.

153. Cottier, at 111-12.

154. Robert Howse, 'Back To Court After Shrimp/Turtle? Almost But Not Quite Yet: India's Short Lived Challenge To Labor And Environmental Exceptions In The European Union's Generalized System Of Preferences', 18 *Am. U. Int'l L. Rev.* 1333 at 1367-68. See also See C.T. Feddersen, "Der Ordre Public in der WTO: Auslegung und Bedeutung des Article XX lit. a) GATT" in Duncker & Humblot (eds.), *Rahmen der WTO-Streitbeilegung* (2002) (examining Article XX(a) in depth).

155. Tuna-Dolphin Panel, at 181.

156. Bal, at 76-77. In order to practically use the inhumane treatment standard, a working definition is needed. The European Commission of Human Rights provides one possible definition, whereby, according to the Greek Case, inhumane treatment involves, "at least such treatment as deliberately causes severe suffering, mental or physical, which in the particular situation, is unjustifiable." (See Greek Case, 1969 Y.B. Eur. Conv. On H.R. 12 at 104 (Eur. Ct. H.R.). After the *coup d' état* in 1967 the Greek military government proclaimed a State of emergency and announced a series of derogations under Article 15 of the European Convention for the Protection of Human Rights and Fundamental Freedoms. Denmark, the Netherlands, Norway and Sweden referred this to European Commission in order to clarify whether there was an "emergency threatening the life of the nation" (within the criteria set in Article 15), and if so, whether the actions undertaken by the military government were "strictly required by the exigencies of the situation." The prohibition against torture and other Articles of the Convention were allegedly violated.) The use of the term "deliberately" is apparently "aimed at specifying intentional rather than merely negligent ill-treatment and is presumably designed to shield those who might unwittingly cause suffering."156 The word "unjustifiable" exempts certain treatment; first, suffering that must be for no other reason than the benefit of the recipient; and second, situations where the recipient freely gives consent. [Nigel S. Rodley, *The Treatment of Prisoners Under International Law*, 74 (1987).]

157. Virginia A. Leary, "Workers' Rights and International Trade", in Jagdish Bhagwati & Robert E. Hudec (eds.), *Fair Trade and Harmonization: Legal Analysis*, Vol. 2, 177 at 221 (1996) (discussing opposition to and support of linkage between trade

and rights,). See also Blackett, at 34 (1999); Robert Howse, "Back To Court After Shrimp/Turtle? Almost But Not Quite Yet: India's Short Lived Challenge To Labor And Environmental Exceptions In The European Union's Generalized System Of Preferences", 18 *Am. U. Int'l L. Rev.* 1333 at 1368 (arguing that the very idea of public morality has become inseparable from the concern for human personhood, dignity, and capacity reflected in Fundamental Rights). Some describe Human Rights as the central moral issue in international relations today—as the "currency of international moral discourse", as in Martin Shupack, 'The Churches and Human Rights: Catholic and Protestant Human Rights Views as Reflected in Church Statements', 6 *Harv. Hum. Rts.* J. 127, 127 (1993); Gordon, at n. 2; or as the "modern tool of revolution" in *the struggle for...human dignity in our time*, as in Irwin Cotler, "Human Rights as the Modern Tool of Revolution", in Kathleen E. Mahoney & Paul Mahoney (eds.), *Human Rights in the Twenty-first Century* 7, 7 (1993);. Gordon, at n. 3.

158. Report of the Panel, *United States—Gambling and betting services*, WTO Doc. WT/DS285/R, paras. 6.465–6.468 and 6.461 (10 November 2004); Office of the High Commissioner for Human Rights, *Human Rights and World Trade Agreements: Using General Exceptions Clauses to Protect Human Rights*, Document No. HR/Pub/05/5 (New York and Geneva, 2005).
159. Appellate Body Report, *United States—Gambling and betting services*, WTO Doc. WT/DS285/AB/R, paras. 293 f. (7 April 2005).
160. Cottier, at 114.
161. Louis Henkin, *The Age Of Rights ix* (1990).
162. Vienna Convention on the Law of Treaties, opened for signature May 23, 1969, 1155 U.N.T.S. 331 (hereinafter Vienna Convention). On this, see Steve Charnovitz, 'The Moral Exception in Trade Policy', 38 *Va J Int'l L* 689 (1998) at 699-710, 716-18; Christoph T. Feddersen, 'Focusing on Substantive Law in International Economic Relations: The Public Morals of GATT's Article XX(A) and "Conventional" Rules of Interpretation', 7 *Minn. J. Global Trade* 75. On this, see especially, Joost Pauwelyn, *Conflict of Norms In Public International Law: How WTO Law Relates to Other Rules Of International Law* (Cambridge University Press, London, 2003); Piet Eeckhout, Book Review: *8 J. Int'l Econ. L.* 583; Symposium *Diversity or Cacophony?: New Sources of Norms in International Law* Article Joost Pauwelyn, 'Bridging Fragmentation and Unity: International Law as a Universe of Inter-Connected Islands', 25 *Mich. J. Int'l L.* 903 (Summer 2004).

163. Sarah H. Cleveland, 'Human Rights Sanctions and International Trade: A Theory of Compatibility', 5 *J. Int'l Econ. L.* 133 at 158. See also Steve Charnovitz, 'The Moral Exception in Trade Policy', 38 *Va J Int'l L* 689 (1998) at 705-16.

164. Appellate Body Report, *United States–Standards for Reformulated and Conventional Gasoline*, WTO Doc. WT/DS2/AB/R (29 April 1996). In this regard, see also Joost Pauwelyn, *Conflict of Norms in Public International Law: How WTO Law Relates to Other Rules of International Law* (2003); Joost Pauwelyn, 'The Role of Public International Law in the WTO: How Far Can We Go?', 95 *AJIL* (2001) 535; Alvarez-Howse, at 110; Weiler, 'The Rule of Lawyers and the Ethos of Diplomats: Reflections on the Internal and External Legitimacy of WTO Dispute Settlement', 35 *J. World Trade* (2001) 191, at 197; Mavroidis, 'Remedies in the WTO Legal System: Between a Rock and a Hard Place', 11 *EJIL* (2000) 763; International Law Commission, M. Koskenniemi, 'Study on the Function and Scope of the "Lex Specialis" Rule and the Question of "Self-Contained Regimes"', Preliminary Report by the Chairman of the Study Group submitted for consideration during the 2004 session of the International Law Commission, Doc. ILC(LVI)SG/FIL/CRD.1 and Add. 1, available from the Codification Division of the UN Office of Legal Affairs. See generally Bruno Simma and Dirk Pulkowski, 'Of Planets and the Universe: Self-Contained Regimes in International Law', 17 *Eur. J. Int'l L.* 483.

165. Patricia Stirling, 'The Use of Trade Sanctions as an Enforcement Mechanism for Basic Human Rights: A Proposal for Addition to the World Trade Organization', 11 *Am. U. J. Int'l L. & Pol'y* 1; Sarah H. Cleveland, 'Human Rights Sanctions and International Trade: A Theory of Compatibility', 5 *J. Int'l Econ. L.* 133.

166. 19 USC § 2432(a)(1994)

167. People's Republic of China—Trade Relations, Pub. L. No. 106-286 § 302, 114 Stat. 880 (2000).

168. An Act to Amend the Bretton Woods Agreement Act, Pub L No 95435, § 5(c), 92 Stat 1051, 1052 (1978), repealed by Pub L No 96-67, § 2(a), 93 Stat 415 (1979).

169. 47 Fed. Reg. 49,005 (1982).

170. 52 Fed Reg 5,425 (1987).

171. Pub L No 100-202, § 562, 101 Stat 1329-175 (1987); *see also* Pub L No 101-167, § 562(a), 103 Stat 1241 (1989) (both codified at 7 USC § 3602 note (1994)).

172. Clean Diamond Trade Act, H.R. 2722, 107th Cong (2001).

173. In this regard, see Ludwig Krämer, 'Environmental Protection and Trade—The Contribution of the European Union', in Rüdiger Wolfrum (ed.), *Enforcing Environmental Standards: Economic Mechanisms as Viable Means*? 413, 439-40 (1996); Boris Johnson & Greg Neale, "EC to lift ban on seal skin imports—Now culling will resume, warn animal activists", *Sunday Telegraph*, Nov. 21, 1993, at 2; Steve Charnovitz, 'The Moral Exception in Trade Policy', 38 *Va J Int'l L* 689 (1998) at 697.

174. Council Decision 97/602, 1997 O.J. (L 242); Commission Regulation 3254/91, Article 3, 1991 O.J. (L 308)). See generally Gillian Dale, 'Comment, The European Union's Steel Leghold Trap Ban: Animal Cruelty Legislation in Conflict with International Trade,' 7 *Colo. J. Int'l Envtl. L. & Pol'y* 441 (1996) (providing background on the import ban). For further discussion, see Richard B. Lillich and Hurst Hannum, *International Human Rights, Problems of Law, Policy, and Practice* (Little, Brown & Co., Boston, 3rd edn, 1995) 74-75. See also Gary C. Hufbauer and Jeffrey J. Schott, *Economic Sanctions Reconsidered* (Institute for Int'l Economics, Washington, DC, 1985) 455-60

175. Prohibiting Trade and Certain Other Transactions Involving South Africa, Exec. Order No. 12532, 50 Fed. Reg. 36,861 (1985)

176. Gen. Ass. Res. 1899 (SVIII), U.N. GFN. ASS. OFF. REC. 18th Sess., Supp. No. 15, at 46 (A/5515) (1963); and Security Council Res., U.N. SECURITYC OL~CIOLF F. REC. 18th year, Supp. Oct.-Dec. 1963, (S/5471) (1963). See 11 U.N. REV. 21 (1964; 11 U.N. REV. 14 (1964). See World Law: Comment, *International Recognition and Protection of Fundamental Human Rights*, 4 Duke Law Journal 846, (Autumn, 1964); Gary Clyde Hufbauer *et al.*, *Economic Sanctions Reconsidered* 223 (2nd ed. 1990).

177. Christoph T. Feddersen, 'Focusing on Substantive Law in International Economic Relations: The Public Morals of GATT's Article XX(a) And "Conventional" Rules of Interpretation', 7 *Minn. J. Global Trade* 75, at 109 ("...the language of Article XX(b) mentions nothing about its application to methods of production. Based on the wording of this section, however, one could assume that measures taken with regard to certain production methods could be justifiable.").

178. Tuna-Dolphin Panel, at 195.

179. Tuna-Dolphin Panel, at 200.

180. Tuna-Dolphin Panel, at 199

181. Shrimp/Turtle Appellate Body Report, para. 121.

182. *Supra* n154, 158-60.

183. Bal, at 83.

184. Shrimp-Turtle Appellate Body Report, at 162.

185. See also Manfred Nowak, *U.N. Covenant on Civil and Political Rights: CCPR Commentary* 2 (1993) (stating that the legal significance of the preamble is generally recognized under international law).

186. GATT Dispute Panel Report on *Thailand: Restrictions on Importation of and Internal Taxes on Cigarettes*, 30 I.L.M. 1122 (Nov. 7, 1990) (hereinafter Thai Cigarettes Panel) at 1129 (noting Thailand's reference to the Preamble as it sought to prove that smoking among other things lowered the standard of living; unfortunately, the Panel did not deliberate this interesting point).

187. Robert Howse, 'The World Trade Organization and the Protection of Workers' Rights', 3 *J. Small & Emerging Bus. L.* 131 at 143-44 (1999).

188. See Frieder Roessler, 'Diverging Domestic Policies and Multilateral Trade Integration', in Jagdish Bhagwati & Robert E. Hudec (eds.), *Fair Trade and Harmonization: Legal Analysis*, Vol. 2, pp. 34-35 (1996). See also Shrimp-Turtle Appellate Body Report, at 843 ("Article XX can accommodate a broad range of measures aiming at the conservation and preservation of the environment").

189. See Christoph T. Feddersen, 'Focusing on Substantive Law in International Economic Relations: The Public Morals of GATT's Article XX(A) And "Conventional" Rules of Interpretation', 7 *Minn. J. Global Trade* 75, at 109. *See* also See Charnovitz, 'The Law of Environmental "PPMs" in the World Trade Organization', 27 *Yale Journal of International Law* (2002) 59; Gabrielle Marceau, *WTO Dispute Settlement and Human Rights*, 13 Eur. J. Int'l L. 753, at 807.

190. This line of reasoning is supported by statutory canons of interpretation: (1) the "presumption of consistent usage" and (2) a breed of in "pari material", which normally dictates that provision should be construed together when their scope and aim are similar, or, as is true in regards to Article XX, the legal framework embraces similar purposes or policies. On the "presumption of consistent usage", see Jonathan Marx, *How To Construe A Hybrid Statute*, 93 Va. L. Rev. 235, at 252, 265, 266-76 ("[when] the text under consideration is not merely a duplicate appearing somewhere else in the statute, but is the original phrase in the original setting...the same statutory language must receive only one construction"); William N. Eskridge, Jr. and Philip P. Frickey, *Legislation: Statutes and the Creation of Public Policy* 645 (1995); Paul Champ and Amir Attaran, 'Patent Rights and Local Working under the WTO TRIPS Agreement: An Analysis of the U.S.-Brazil Patent Dispute', 27 *Yale J. Int'l L.* 365, at 388 (using the same to

interpret Articles 8 and 31 of TRIPS); Caleb Nelson, *Statutory Interpretation and Decision Theory*, 74 U. Chi. L. Rev. 329, at 349. On the "*pari materia*" rule of interpretation, see Christopher J. Borgen, *Resolving Treaty Conflicts*, 37 Geo. Wash. Int'l L. Rev. 573, at 631, quoting William N. Eskridge *et. al.*, *Legislation and Statutory Interpretation* 381 (2000); ("similar statutes should be interpreted similarly, unless legislative purpose and history suggests material differences."); Jordan J. Paust, 'Race-Based Affirmative Action and International Law', 18 *Mich. J. Int'l L.* 659, at n. 35 ("Concerning the need to interpret treaties... also consider the maxim: laws pari materia (laws on the same subject must be construed with reference to each other"); Alex Glashausser, 'What We Must Never Forget When It is a Treaty We are Expounding', 73 *U. Cin. L. Rev.* 1243, at n. 516-18 ("when one statute is similar to another, the two are construed as a pair, unless legislative history shows that they should not be. Likewise, Courts sometimes interpret identical terms to mean the same thing not just within a single statute, but across different ones from the same jurisdiction."); W. Fletcher Fairey, 'The Helms-Burton Act: The Effect of International Law on Domestic Implementation', 46 *Am. U.L. Rev.* 1289, at n. 42; William N. Eskridge, Jr., 'Public Values in Statutory Interpretation,' 137 *U. Pa. L. Rev.* 1007, at 1039-42.

191. A related canon supports this interpretation: "*ex expressio unius est exclussio alterius*". In this regard, see Philip R. Principe, 'Secret Codes, Military Hospitals, and the Law of Armed Conflict: Could Military Medical Facilities' Use of Encrypted Communications Subject Them to Attack under International Law?,' 24 *U. Ark. Little Rock L. Rev.* 727, at 741 ("where a form of conduct, the manner of its performance and operation, and the persons and things to which it refers are designated, there is an inference that all omissions should be understood as exclusions. It, too, is applicable to treaty interpretation and is particularly illuminating in this context."), quoting Lord Arnold Duncan McNair, *Law of Treaties* 399-410 (1961) ("the maxim expressio unius exclusio alterius) would find a place in the logic of the nursery. If I agree that my brother may play with my railway engine and my motor car, it is obvious that I have not given him permission to play with my model aeroplane.... This maxim is also expressed as "inclusio unius est exclusio alterius," "expressum facit cessare tacitum," "affermatio est exclusio alterius," and "a contrario."... The maxim expressio unius est exclusio alterius is a rule of both law and logic and applicable to the construction of treaties.").

192. GATT Dispute Panel Report on *EEC: Regulation on Imports of Parts and Components*, 30 I.L.M. 1075, 1113 (May 16, 1990) (hereinafter EEC Regulation Panel).

193. Spring Assemblies Panel, at 124.

194. This is particularly important because the provisions of the GATT are to be read in light of their ordinary meaning. Augmenting or deleting the language of provisions clearly violates such a rule. See Vienna Convention on the Law of Treaties, opened for signature May 23, 1969, 8 I.L.M. 679, Article 31(1), "A treaty shall be interpreted in good faith in accordance with the ordinary meaning to be given to the terms of the treaty in their context...." at 691 and accompanying text (discussing ordinary meaning). See generally Appellate Body Report, *Canada: Certain Measures Affecting the Automotive Industry*, May 31, 2000, WTO Doc. DS142, 139, available at http:// www.wto.org/english/ tratop_e/dispu_e/distab_e.htm [hereinafter Automotive Industry Appellate Report] (examining the "ordinary meaning" of Article 3.1(b) to commence the analysis of its scope).

195. Bal, at 87-88.

196. See Garcia.

197. Bal, at 92.

198. See Reports of the International Law Commission on the Second Part of its Seventeenth Session and on its Eighteenth Session, U.N. Doc. A/6309/Rev.1 (1966), reprinted in [1966] 2 Y.B. Int'l Comm'n 247-48 (listing examples proposed by the International Law Commission including treaties contemplating an unlawful use of force contrary to the principles of the Charter, treaties contemplating the performance of any other criminal act under international law or treaties contemplating or conniving at the commission of acts, such as trade in slaves, piracy or genocide).

199. Barcelona Traction, Light and Power Company (Belg. v. Spain), 1970 I.C.J. 4, 32 [hereinafter Barcelona Traction]; see also Maurizio Ragazzi, the concept of International Obligations *erga omnes* (1997) (discussing the obligations *erga omnes*).

200. The International Court of Justice listed as examples of *erga omnes*: the outlawing of acts of aggression, of aggression and the protection of principles and rules concerning basic rights of the human person including the protection from slavery and racial discrimination. Barcelona Traction, at 32.

201. Barcelona Traction, at 32.

202. Shaw, at 247. See generally M.S. McDougal, H. Lasswell and L.C. Chen, *Human Rights And World Public Order* (1980); M. Moskowitz, *The Policies And Dynamics Of Human Rights* (1968).

203. Shaw, at 68-88 (2005). See generally, A. D'Amato, *The Concept Of Custom In International Law* (1971); M. Akehurst, *Custom as a Source of International Law*, 47 BYIL 1 (1974-75); B. Cheng, "Custom: The Future of General State Practice in a Divided World", in R. St. J. MacDonald and D. Johnston (eds.), *The Structure And Process Of International Law* (1983); G. Danilenko, The Theory of International Customary Law, 31 German YIL 9 (1988); K. Wolfke, *Custom in Present International Law* (1993); K. Wolfke, *Some Persistent Controversies Regarding Customary International Law*, Netherlands YIL (1993); M. Mendelson, *The Formation of Customary International Law*, 272 HR 259 (1999).

204. Shaw, at 77-80. See generally, A. D'Amato, *The Concept Of Custom In International Law* 2-3, 50-51, 88 (1971); M. Akehurst, *Custom as a Source of International Law*, 47 BYIL 1, at 2 *et. seq.* (1974-75); Brierly, *The Law of Nations* 63 (1960); I. Brownlie, *Principles Of Public International Law* 5 (1998).

205. Shaw, at 257. See also T. Meron, *Human Rights And Humanitarian Norms As Customary Law* (1989). See also Bruno Simma & Philip Alston, 'The Sources of Human Rights Law: Custom, Jus Cogens, and General Principles', 12 *Austrl. Y.B. Int'l L.* 82, 88-89, 107 (1989); Jordan J. Paust, 'Customary International Law: Its Nature, Sources and Status as Law of the United States', 12 *Mich. J. Int'l* L. 59, 61 (1990); Isabelle R. Gunning, 'Modernizing Customary International Law: The Challenge of Human Rights', 31 *Va. J. Int'l L.* 211, 221-22 (1991); Richard B. Lillich, 'The Growing Importance of Customary International Human Rights Law', 25 *Ga. J. Int'l & Comp. L.* 1; Jordan J. Paust, 'The Complex Nature, Sources and Evidences of Customary Human Rights', 25 *Ga. J. Int'l & Comp.* L. 147 (1995/1996).

206. Oscar Schachter, *International Law in Theory and Practice*, 343 (1991).

207. See *Infra* nn. 201-03. For the earliest *opinion juris*, see Egon Schwelb, 'The Influence of the Universal Declaration of Human Rights on International and National Law', 53 *Proc. Am. Soc'y Int'l L.* 217 (1959). See also Egon Schwelb, *Human Rights and the International Community* 34-74 (1964); Humphrey Waldock, "Human Rights in Contemporary International Law and the Significance of the European Convention", in *The European Convention on Human Rights* 15 *Int'l & Comp. L.Q.* Supp. No. 11, 1965.

208. ICJ, Barcelona traction ruling, 5/2/70, Rec., 1970, p. 32. See John P. Humphrey, 'The International Bill of Rights: Scope and

Implementation,' 17 *Wm. & Mary L. Rev.* 527 (1976); Louis B. Sohn, 'The Human Rights Law of the Charter', 12 *Tex. Int'l L.J.* 129, 133 (1977); M.S. McDougal, H. Lasswell and L.C. Chen, *Human Rights And World Public Order* 274, 320-22 (1980); Louis B. Sohn, *The New International Law: Protection of the Rights of Individuals Rather than States*, 32 Am. U.L. Rev. 1, 17 (1982); Philip Alston, *The Universal Declaration at 35: Western and Passe or Alive and Universal*, 31 Review 60, 69 (Int'l Comm'n Jurists ed., 1982); John P. Humphrey, *Human Rights and the United Nations: A Great Adventure* 75-76 (1984); John P. Humphrey, *No Distant Millennium: The International Law of Human Rights* 155 (1989); Richard B. Lillich, 'The Growing Importance of Customary International Human Rights Law', 25 *Ga. J. Int'l & Comp. L.* 1 (1995/1996); Hurst Hannum, *The Status of the Universal Declaration of Human Rights in National and International Law*, 25 GA. J. Int'l & Comp. L. 287, 324 (1995/96). See also Anne-Christine Habbard and Marie Guirard, International Federation for Human Rights (FIDH), *Report on the Primacy of Human Rights and for the Creation of an NGO Consultative Status*, Document No. 320/2, November 2001.

209. Anne-Christine Habbard and Marie Guirard, International Federation for Human Rights (FIDH), *Report on the Primacy of Human Rights and for the Creation of an NGO Consultative Status*, Document No. 320/2, November 2001; John Humphey, *No Distant Millennium: The International Law of Human Rights* (UNESCO, Paris, 1955).

210. Erika de Wet, 'The Prohibition of Torture as an International Norm of *Jus Cogens* and its Implications for National and Customary Law', *EJIL* (2004) Vol. 15, No. 1, 97. See also *Prosecutor* v. *Anto Furundzija*, Case No. IT–95–17/1-T10, International Criminal Tribunal Trial Chamber, 10 December 1998. See also I.D. Seiderman, *Hierarchy In International Law: The Human Rights Dimension* (2001) 58.

211. See Garcia.

212. Patricia Stirling, 'The Use of Trade Sanctions as an Enforcement Mechanism for Basic Human Rights: A Proposal for Addition to the World Trade Organization', 11 *Am. U. J. Int'l L. & Pol'y* 1, at 33 (1996); see Garcia, at n. 141; Blackett.

213. *Ibid. Addition to the World Trade Organization*, 11 Am. U. J. Int'l L. & Pol'y 1, at 39-40 (1996); see Garcia, at n. 144.

214. *Ibid.*

215. See Garcia.

216. See WTO Singapore Ministerial Declaration, WT/MIN(96)/ DEC/W (Dec. 13, 1996), available at http://www.wto.org/english/ thewto_e/minist_e/min96_ e/wtodec_e. htm
217. Nichols, at 709-12 (1996); see Garcia, at n. 147.
218. See Kevin C. Kennedy, 'Reforming U.S. Trade Policy to Protect the Global Environment: A Multilateral Approach', 18 *Harv. Envtl. L. Rev.* 185, 204 (1994) (arguing that amending GATT to draft new environmental exception is the best approach to the trade/environment linkage problems); see Garcia, at n. 148.
219. Nichols seems to blur this point, in that the operation of his exemption would still require an investigation by a dispute settlement panel into the measure's purpose. See Nichols, at 709-12 (1996) (positing implementation of Human Rights measures through modification or interpretation of the DSU); see Garcia, at n. 149.
220. This might resemble the practice under certain environmental treaties to provide for trade-restrictive measures to be taken with regard to delineated products which harm the environment. See Protocol on Substances that Deplete the Ozone Layer, Sept. 16, 1987, 26 I.L.M. 1550, Article 4 (entered into force Jan. 1, 1989); Convention on International Trade in Endangered Species of Wild Fauna and Flora, Mar. 3, 1973, Articles. III-V, VIII 12 I.L.M. 1085 (entered into force July 1, 1975) (both providing for the total ban of unlawful trade in covered substances, even with non-parties to the agreement). Of course, in the case of these treaties, the restrictions apply to products which themselves produce the harm.
221. The GATT already recognizes this principle in its exception for economic sanctions implemented in response to a U.N. Security Council Resolution. GATT, Article XXI(c). Particularly when one considers that such a measure would still be subject to multilateral review and constraint within its own system, such an exclusion may not be too broad for advocates of the trade system.
222. The "purity" of this proposed hierarchy of norms lies in the fact that it does not incorporate a trade-off mechanism requiring panel review.
223. On the distinction between legislative and adjudicatory approaches to the problem, see Nichols, at 691-99.
224. See Garcia, at nn. 118-24.
225. Moreover, the conflict at the norm-creation stage remains less constraining, in that States are free to reach negotiated compromises between different sets of values in the creation of a treaty, in a way that treaty-based dispute settlement mechanisms are not.

226. Such an exception could still be conditioned on the *chapeau* test for arbitrary discrimination or disguised restrictions on trade, and thus would not be a blanket invitation to protectionist legislation. Adding a *chapeau*-style test would change the nature of the exception from a limitation of jurisdiction to an amendment altering the nature of the trade-off device. It may also be possible to determine a rule or metric for distinguishing "authentic" from "protectionist" invocations of such a Human Rights exception, as Jeffrey Atik has proposed regarding linkage issues generally. See Jeffrey Atik, 'Identifying Antidemocratic Outcomes', 19 *U. Pa. J. Int'l Econ. L.* 229 (1998).

7

Human Rights of Children: A Study of Implementation of CRC in India

Nirmal Kanti Chakrabarti

Introductory Remarks

The slogan of the Convention on the Rights of the Child, 1989 (henceforth abbreviated as CRC) was "Human Rights begin with Children Rights". It is said that "There is no trust more sacred than the one the world holds with children. There is no duty more important than ensuring that their rights are respected, that their welfare is protected, that their lives are free from fear and want and that they grow up in peace".[1] It is a call to all people to respect Human Rights of children and to reaffirm their commitment to children. Sociologists argued that a child who is born innocent, if nourished with proper care and attention, he or she will blossom with faculties physical, mental, moral and spiritual, into a person of stature and excellence. So every effort should be made to provide children all possible opportunities for their development so that they become worthy citizens physically fit, mentally alert and morally healthy endowed with skills and motivations needed by society. With that end in view India ratified the CRC on 11th December, 1992. India is, therefore, accepted the need of basic Human Rights of children and started giving its children the hope to shape their own future protected by international as well as national legal regime. This paper is an attempt to present an overview of Human Rights of children recognized in

India through various legislative and administrative measures and critically review the problems and perspectives in the process of implementation of children rights as contemplated in the CRC.

Seeds of Human Rights of Children before CRC

The first international concern over the children came in 1923, when the Council of the then newly established non-governmental organization "Save the Children International Union" adopted a five point Declaration of the Rights of the Child. This Geneva Declaration was endorsed by the Fifth Assembly of the League of Nations in the following year. However, the International Labor Organization in 1919 initiated prohibition of industrial exploitation and prescribing minimum age of employment of children in any industrial undertakings to be fourteen years.[2] During 1920 to 1946 the ILO continued to express its concern on exploitation of child labor and prescribed minimum age for children to employment at sea,[3] agricultural activities,[4] non-industrial employment[5] night work of young persons,[6] medical examination of young persons.[7] The General Assembly in 1948 adopting the Universal Declaration of Human Rights[8] pledged themselves to achieve and promote "special protective care and assistance to children".[9] The Social Commission of the Economic and Social Council in 1950 adopted a draft of Declaration on the Rights of the Child on the lines of Geneva Declaration and forwarded the same to ECOSOC. In 1959 the General Assembly of the United Nations approved a slightly expanded version of the 1923 Declaration which contained 10 basic principles of child welfare and protection.[10] The 1959 Declaration was taken as the springboard for the preliminary initiative to draft the Convention on the Rights of the Child. The General Assembly called upon parents, local authorities, voluntary organizations and national governments to recognize the rights set out in the Declaration. The Government of Poland prepared a Draft Convention based on 1959 Declaration and submitted the same to the United Nations Commission on Human Rights in 1978. It reviews on the aforesaid draft throughout the 1980s. The Working Group ultimately came to consensus on the final version of the Convention on the Rights of Child for the United Nations General Assembly to adopt it on 20th November, 1989, the thirtieth anniversary of the 1959 Declaration.

The concern of the world community about Human Rights of the children had also been contained in Article 24(1) of the International Covenant on Civil and Political Rights 1966 which provided "that every child shall have, without any discrimination as to race, colour, sex, language, religion, national or social origin, property or birth, the right to such measures of protection as are required by his status as a minor, on the part of his family, society and the State."[11] These instruments aimed at creating an environment in which all children are able to live securely and realize their full potential in life.

Along with the development of international thinking and consciousness about the Human Rights for the children, the General Assembly constituted and established the United Nations International Children's Emergency Fund (UNICEF) in 1946.[12] The Assembly decided to continue this Organization indefinitely and recognized the need for continued action to relieve sufferings of children, particularly in the developing countries.[13] UNICEF assists programmes for children in more than 100 countries in Asia, Africa, America, and in Eastern Mediterraneans, with a combined population which includes approximately 960 million children.[14]

All the above development and international concerns have the character of setting up the standard of international morality to guide the national treatment to its children. Ultimately, these measures backed up by special programmes of UNICEF, WHO, ILO and other international bodies as well as sensitization over the issue world-wide in the International Year of the Child in 1979[15] set the stage right for legislating a Code of international legal standard towards the making of the CRC.

An Overview of the CRC

The Convention being international, it has to take account of different beliefs, values and traditions, as well as the wide range of socio-economic and political realities. Rather than a catalogue of rights, the Convention is a comprehensive listing of the obligations that States are prepared to recognize towards the child. These obligations may be direct-providing education facilities and ensuring proper administration of juvenile justice or indirect-enabling parents, the wider family or guardians to carry out their primary roles and responsibilities. In other words, this Convention is in no way a "children's liberation charter" and its content does not in any way reduce the importance of the family.

The CRC envisaged four types of rights of every child, *viz.*

(1) The Right to Survival;

(2) The Right to Protection;

(3) The Right to Development; and

(4) The Right to Participation.

The Right to Survival includes the right to life, the right to highest attainable standard of health, nutrition, right to a name and a nationality. The Right to Protection includes freedom from all forms of exploitation, abuses, inhuman and degrading treatment and neglect. The Right to Development includes the right to education, support for childhood development and care, social, social security and right to leisure, recreation and cultural activities. The Right to Participation includes respect for the views of the child, freedom of expression, access to appropriate information and freedom of thought, conscience and religion. Although Article 4 refers to these categories, the Articles themselves are not explicitly divided in this way. The whole thrust of the Convention is to emphasize that all rights mutually reinforce each other in ensuring what UNICEF calls the "survival and development" of children. Some have, nevertheless, found it useful to summarize the range of rights covered by the Convention as the **three "Ps": Provision, Protection and Participation**. Children have the right to be **provided** with certain things and services, ranging from a name and nationality to health care and education. They have a right to be **protected** from certain acts such as torture, exploitation, arbitrary detention and unwarranted removal from parental care. And children have the right to **participate** in decision affecting their lives as well as in community life.

The Convention sets out to do following three basic things:

(1) To reaffirm, for children, rights already given to human beings in general through other treaties, so as to underline the fact that children are human beings too, e.g. freedom of expression, freedom of religion etc.

(2) To strengthen certain basic Human Rights in order to take accounts of special needs and vulnerability of children, e.g. working conditions for children.

(3) To set standards in areas that are relevant particularly to children, e.g. adoption proceedings, access to primary education, protection from abuse and neglect within the family, etc.

The Convention also introduces two important concepts with important ramifications:

- The "best interests of the child"(Article 3) becomes a compulsory criterion "for all actions concerning children";
- The principle that parents (or others responsible for the child) should provide guidance to their child in exercising his/her rights (Article 5).[16]

The Committee on the Rights of Child has identified the following Articles as "general principles" that are basic to all rights contained in the Convention.

- Article 2 on non-discrimination.
- Article 3 on the best interests of the child.
- Article 6 on the right to life, survival and development.
- Article 12 on respect for the view of the child.

Impact and Implementation of CRC at International Level

Impact of CRC

The impact of CRC can be understood from the simple fact that just within five years of its adoption, the Convention had been ratified by almost 90 per cent of the member countries, a speed unprecedented in the history of international Human Rights law. This broad acceptance and equally unprecedented level of awareness of the provisions and obligations of the State in the Convention led to very high expectations as to its impact. But in practice this international Convention intended to have very little direct impact on children's lives and rather it provided guidance for Governments of Member States for legislative and administrative measures as well as programmes in matters of child welfare. Therefore, to assess the impact of the CRC we have to look into the extent to which its letter and spirit have been taken into account by national governments, institutions and related agencies. Thus, implementation of the Convention in any country can be measured by examining the law, infrastructure and mechanism existing and developing in the respective country.

Implementation at International Level

In pursuance of the Article 43 of the Convention a treaty body was contemplated to monitor States' compliance with their obligations under the treaty. This treaty body is known as the Committee on the Rights of the Child consisting of 10 independent experts elected by States Parties. This Committee meets for three month-long meeting each year in Geneva. The Committee reviews the obligatory Reports submitted by the States together with other information provided by other reliable sources.[17] This "monitoring" function is carried out by the Committee through a non-confrontational framework of dialogue and international solidarity. The NGOs are also involved in this monitoring process. There is a recognized international NGO Group which providing input into the Convention's implementation and is now privileged partner of the Committee along with UNICEF. This Committee has to face two limitations: first, that the monitoring by the

Committee has a limited direct effect because of the absence of sanctions, and second, that many countries have a limited capacity to comply fully with the Convention's provisions without technical and financial assistance from any UN agency. However, UNICEF has now developed as official agency of the UNO to the promotion and protection of children's rights. In 1996 the UNICEF has declared its Mission Statement which says that the Convention is the inspiration and foundation of its policies and work, and the framework within which it prepares its country programmes.[18] The first World Congress against Commercial Sexual Exploitation of Children was held in Stockholm (Sweden) in 1996 and the Age Agenda for Action of this World Congress set forth specific legal standards for the protection of children from sexual exploitation.[19] In 1999 the ILO adopted the Convention Concerning the Prohibition and Immediate Action for Elimination of the Worst Forms of Child Labor.[20] The Second World Congress against Commercial Sexual Exploitation of Children was held at Yokohama, Japan, from 17th to 20th December, 2001 where in total 700 representatives from the Governments of 132 countries participated in this World Congress in which efforts were concentrated more on the progress made on the global level so far and to assess the work that still remains.[21] Moreover, in May, 2000 the UN General Assembly adopted an optional Protocol to the Convention on the Rights of the Child on the sale of children, child prostitution and child pornography. This Optional Protocol has legal enforcement on 18th January, 2002 after getting the 16th ratification.[22]

Implementation of CRC in India

Government Policy

The Government of India adopted its National Policy for the Welfare of the Children in 1974. The said Policy starts with goal oriented perambulatory introduction: The nation's children are a supremely important asset. Their nurture and solicitude are our responsibility. Children's programmes should find a prominent part in our National Plans for the development of human resources, so that our children grow up to become robust citizens, physically fit, mentally alert and morally healthy, endowed with the skills and motivations needed by society. Equal opportunities for development to all children during the period of growth should be our aim, for this would serve our larger purpose of reducing inequality and ensuring social justice.[23] "The children as a class constitute the weakest, the most vulnerable and defenseless section of the human society. They are always at the mercy of their superiors in age even for sheer survival."[24] The founding fathers of our Constitution have formulated a State policy for protecting the children against exploitation.[25]

The Government of India ratified the Convention on Rights of the Child on November 12, 1992. By ratifying the CRC the Government obliges *first*, to review national and State legislations and bring it in the line with the provisions of the Convention and *secondly,* to develop appropriate administrative measures in implementing the Convention by all relevant government ministries and departments, international agencies, nongovernmental organizations and the legal profession. Also by endorsing the 27 survival and development goals for the year 2000 laid down by the World Summit for Children. Government of India has firmly reaffirmed its commitment to advance the cause of children in India. In fact, the CRC reiterates and elaborates what is already contained in the Constitution of India. According to Article 39 of the Directive Principles of State Policy:

The State shall, in particular, direct its policy towards securing:

(i) that the health and strength of workers, men and women, and the tender age of children are not abused and that citizens are not forced by economic necessity to enter avocations unsuited to their age and strength;

(ii) those children are given opportunities and facilities to develop in a healthy manner and in conditions of freedom and dignity and that childhood and youth are protected against exploitation and against moral and material abandonment.

The National Policy for Children in 1974 reaffirmed the Constitutional provisions and declared that "it shall be the policy of the State to provide adequate services to children, both before and after birth and through the period of growth, to ensure their full physical, mental and social development. The State shall progressively increase the scope of such services so that, within a reasonable time, all children in the country enjoy optimum conditions for their balanced growth".[26] The India Country Paper placed in the Sixth United Nations Congress on the Prevention of Crime the Treatment of Offenders states that the problem of children coming in conflict with law assumes a peculiar form in the Indian Society characterized by a wide range of culture variations, socio-economic developments and technological changes.[27]

However, the rising incidence of juvenile delinquency in developed as well as in developing countries drew attention of United Nations to work out some guiding principles for juvenile justice system. As a result of this, the seventh UN Congress on Prevention of Crime and Treatment of Offenders adopted the Standard Minimum Rules for Administration of Juvenile Justice[28] in September 1985. These Rules were subsequently adopted by the UN General Assembly in November 1985 which contained the following basic principles:

1. Juvenile in conflict with law should be leniently dealt with under the law.
2. They should not be lodged in prison where they are vulnerable to the evil influences of the adult prisoners.
3. Pre-trial detention of juvenile delinquents should be avoided as far as possible and they should not be incarcerated unless the imperatives of public safety so demanded.
4. Member nations should make efforts to provide adequate arrangements for the reformation and rehabilitation of juvenile offenders.

India being a member of the United Nations, responded favorably to this desired change and enacted the Juvenile Justice Act, 1986 which had now been replaced by the Juvenile Justice (Protection and Care of Children) Act, 2000 and it came into force on and from April 1, 2001.

Patterns of Implementation

To understand the patterns of implementation of the CRC in India we may analyze the administrative and/or legislative measures to be taken by the State in respect of each Article of the CRC (main provisions may be seen in the Annexure) below:

Article 1

For the purposes of the present Convention a child means every human being below the age of eighteen years unless, under the law applicable to the child, majority is attained earlier.

Administrative and legislative measures in India

In India eighteen years is the age when a child becomes an adult and attains majority for the purpose of entering into a contract or exercise the right to vote or can claim ancestral property. Under the Juvenile Justice (Care and Protection of Children) Act, 2000, (abbreviated JJ Act) "child" means a person who has not completed eighteen years of age. However there are a few labor legislations and in the Indian Penal Code where the age of a child is considered differently.[29]

Article 2

States Parties shall respect and ensure the rights set forth in the present Convention to each child within their jurisdiction without discrimination of any kind irrespective of the child's or his/her parent's or legal guardian's race, colour, sex, language, religion, political or other opinion, national, ethnic or social origin, property, disability, birth or other status.

Administrative and legislative measures in India

In the Constitution of India, Article 15 prohibits discrimination on grounds of religion, race, caste, sex or place of birth. Moreover Article 14 says: "State shall not deny to any person equality before law or equal protection before the laws within the territory of India." Article 15(3) in fact promised a discriminatory treatment for the children which is characterized as "protective right".[30]

Article 3

In all actions concerning children, whether undertaken by public or private social welfare institutions, courts of law, administrative authorities or legislative bodies, the best interests of the child shall be a primary consideration.

State Parties shall ensure that the institutions, services and facilities responsible for the care and protection of children shall conform to the standards established by competent authorities.

Administrative and legislative measures in India

In disposing a case by the Juvenile Welfare Committee under the JJ Act, the guiding principle is the best interest of the child. The State Government by rules made under the JJ Act recognizes and controls all Observation Homes, Special Homes, Children Homes or Shelter Homes, including standards and various types of services to be provided by them for rehabilitation and social reintegration of a child.[31]

Article 4

States Parties shall undertake all appropriate legislative, administrative, and other measures for the implementation of the rights recognizes in the present Convention.

Administrative and legislative measures in India

The Government of India has taken all possible administrative and legislative measures within its limited financial resources to implement rights under CRC.

Article 5

State Parties shall respect the responsibilities, rights and duties of parents or, where applicable, the members of the extended family or community as provided for by local custom, legal guardians or other persons legally responsible for the child, to provide, in a manner consistent with the evolving capacities of the child, appropriate direction and guidance in the exercise by the child of the rights recognized in the present Convention.

Administrative and legislative measures in India

In India, family continues to be the basic unit for the sustenance and development of the child. However, the socio-economic disabilities of parents on account of unemployment and poverty adversely affects the life chances of a child, especially of the girl child in a gender discriminatory culture.[32]

Article 6

1. States Parties recognize that every child has the inherent right to life.

2. States Parties shall ensure to the maximum extent possible the survival and development of the child.

Administrative and legislative measures in India

Under Article 21 of the Indian Constitution, the right to life is a fundamental right of all Indians. Survival of the girl child is a major question in India[33] as well as in the SAARC countries. The decade 1991-2000 was declared as the Decade of the Girl Child. To control selective abortion of female fetuses our Parliament enacted The Prenatal Diagnostic Techniques (Regulation and Prevention of Misuses) Act, 1994.

Article 7

The child shall be registered immediately after birth and shall have the right from birth to a name, the right to acquire a nationality and, as far as possible, the right to know and be cared for by his/her parents.

Administrative and legislative measures in India

In India an Act for Registration of Births and Deaths was passed which recognized the rights of a child as provided in Article 7 of CRC. However, due to illiteracy there is a strong son preference culture in India resulting neglect and abuse of girl child.[34]

Article 8

States Parties undertake to respect the right of the child to preserve his/her identity, including nationality, name and family relations as recognized by law without unlawful interference.

Administrative and legislative measures in India

By Birth and Death Registration Act the rights of a child to preserve his/her identity has been regularized in India.[35]

Article 9

States Parties shall ensure that a child shall not be separated from his/her parents against their will, except when competent authorities subject to judicial review determine in accordance with applicable law and procedures, that such separation is necessary for the best interests of the child.

Administrative and legislative measures in India

In India the principle that child is best developed under his/her parent has been followed and only in exceptional circumstances under due procedure of law children are separated from parents. The detailed provisions in this regard are provided in the Juvenile Justice (Care and Protection of Children), 2000 both for delinquent and neglected children.[36]

Article 10

In accordance with the obligation of States Parties under Article 9, paragraph 1, application by a child or his/her parents to enter or leave a State Party for the purpose of family reunification, shall be dealt with by States Parties in a positive, humane and expeditious manner.

Administrative and legislative measures in India

The Immigration Act, 1983 and Passports Act, 1967 in India give due priority in disposing of applications of children going abroad to meet their parents.

Article 11

State Parties shall take measures to combat the illicit transfer and non-return of children abroad.

To this end, States Parties shall promote the conclusion of multilateral agreements or accession to existing agreements.

Administrative and legislative measures in India

India abides by this Article regarding illicit transfer and non-return of children from abroad. With that end in view a Central Adoption Regulating Authority (CARA) has also been developed by the Government of India.

Article 12

States Parties shall assure to the child who is capable of forming his/her own views the right to express those views freely in all matters affecting the child, the views of the child, the views of the child being given due weight in accordance with the age and maturity of the child.

Administrative and legislative measures in India

According to Article 19 of the Constitution of India children have also right to freedom of expression. The Juvenile Justice Act, 2000 in Section 41(5)(c) also provides that "No child shall be offered for adoption-without his consent in the case of a child who can understand and express his consent".

Article 13

The child shall have the right to freedom of expression; this right shall include freedom to seek, receive and impart information and ideas of all kinds, regardless of frontiers, either orally, in writing or in print, in the form of art, or through any other media of the child's choice.

Administrative and legislative measures in India

Children in India are encouraged to read, write, paint, sing, perform by Government supported National Agencies like National Council of Educational Research and Training, National Book Trust, Children's Theatre, and other NGOs and provide opportunities to express their ideas through well organized essay, poem, drama, painting, writing competitions.

Article 14

1. States Parties shall respect the right of the child to freedom of thought, conscience and religion.

2. States Parties shall respect the rights and duties of the parents and, when applicable, legal guardians, to provide

direction to the child in the exercise of his/her right in a manner consistent with the evolving capacities of the child.

Administrative and legislative measures in India

The legal provisions and other institutional structure ensure the right of the child to freedom of thought, religion and conscience. The State protects the right of the minorities to develop their own educational institutions for their children. In some States in India including West Bengal there are legislations like Primary Education Act imposed duties upon the parents or legal guardians to send their children to school.[37]

Article 15

1. State Parties recognize the rights of the child to freedom of association and to freedom of peaceful assembly.

2. No restrictions may be placed on the exercise of these rights other than those imposed in conformity with the law and which are necessary in a democratic society in the interests of national security or public safety, public order, the protection of public health or morals or the protection of rights and freedoms of others.

Administrative and legislative measures in India

The Indian states fully support and protect these rights of the children who are often seen participating in organized peaceful protests meetings and procession and other social campaigns against social evils and hazards like HIV/AIDS, child labor, communalism, and the like.

Article 16

1. No child shall be subjected to arbitrary or unlawful interference with his/her privacy, family, home or correspondence, or to unlawful attacks on his/her honour and reputation.

2. The child has the right to the protection of the law against such interference or attacks.

Administrative and legislative measures in India

Section 23 of the Juvenile Justice (Care and Protection of Children) Act, 2000 provides punishment for causing a juvenile or a child unnecessary mental or physical suffering. However, data on crime against women in India reveals that girl child remains vulnerable in the family, in the street, in work place resulting into physical and mental trauma.

Article 17

States Parties recognize the important function performed by the mass media and shall ensure that the child has access to information and material from a diversity of national and international sources, especially those aimed at the promotion of his/her social, spiritual and moral well-being and physical and mental health. To this end, States Parties shall:

(a) encourage the mass media to disseminate information and material of social and cultural benefit to the child and in accordance with the spirit of Article 29;

(b) encourage international cooperation in the production, exchange and dissemination of such information and material from a diversity of cultural, national and international sources;

(c) encourage the production and dissemination of children's books;

(d) encourage the mass media to have particular regard to the linguistic needs of the child who belongs to a minority group or who is indigenous;

(e) encourage the development of appropriate guidelines for the protection of the child from information and material injurious to his/her well being, bearing in mind the provisions of Articles 13 and 18 of CRC.

Administrative and legislative measures in India

State media like Doordarshan (TV) and Akashwani (Radio) have played a very significant role in focusing on the issues and rights of children in India.

UNICEF and UNESCO have played a vital role assisting the national government in producing and disseminating relevant information with special focus on the girl child (UNICEF, 1995).

Children's books and literature are being developed by NCERT and NBT in addition to printing and supply of free of cost books in the primary schools by some State governments.

India being a multilingual country there is constitutional rights (Articles 348-350) of various linguistic groups to know as well as communicate to public authorities in their mother tongue.

In India besides general law of obscenity under Indian Penal Code there is a specific law in this regard, namely, Young Persons (Harmful Publications) Act, 1956 to control and prohibit "Pictorial and other publications containing stories of crime, violence, cruelty or incidents of repulsive or horrible nature that is likely to incite or encourage the young to commit such act".

Article 18

1. State Parties shall use their best efforts to ensure recognition of the principle that both parents have common responsibilities for the upbringing and development of the child. Parents or, as the case may be, legal guardians, have the primary responsibility for upbringing and development of the child. The best interests of the child will be their basic concern.

2. State Parties shall render appropriate assistance to parents and legal guardians in the performance of their childbearing responsibilities and shall ensure the development of institutions, facilities and services for the care of children.

3. States Parties shall take all appropriate measures to ensure that children of working parents have the right to benefit from child-care services and facilities for which they are eligible.

Administrative and legislative measures in India

In India the States have an extensive system of free and compulsory education for all children up to the age of 14 years in pursuance of Article 45 of the Constitution. Education is free for the girl child up to the secondary stage. Assistance is also given in the form of free noon meal scheme for primary school children. Under a Central Government scheme more than 100 million children are covered under the Integrated

Child Development Service Programme directed towards the children from 0-6 years through "Anganwadis" and pre-school education for children of urban poor.

In India a large network of institutional facilities and services exist for the care of children with a provision for crèche for working mothers. The coverage, however, is inadequate.[38]

Article 19

States Parties shall take all appropriate legislative, administrative, social and educational measures to protect the child from all forms of physical or mental violence, injury or abuse, neglect or negligent treatment, maltreatment or exploitation, including sexual abuse, while in the care of parent(s), legal guardian(s) or any other person who has the care of the child.

Administrative and legislative measures in India

The Indian family is severely patriarchal with the male head having overwhelming rights over women and children. No administrative or social measures are discernable to remove this absolute power of the male head of the family. However, Article 15 of the Constitution empowered the State to make protective rights for women and children. The JJ Act in Section 23 imposed punishment for cruelty to child in family or under custody such as assaults, abandons, exposes or willfully neglects the juvenile or causing the child unnecessary mental or physical sufferings.

Article 20

A child temporarily or permanently deprived of his/her family environment, or in whose own best interest cannot be allowed to remain in that environment, shall be entitled to special protection and assistance provided by the State.

Administrative and legislative measures in India

The JJ Act provides detailed programme of rehabilitation and reintegration of Child in need of care and protection who is found without any home or settled place or abode and without any ostensible means of subsistence or those whose parents or guardians are unfit to exercise control over the child.[39]

Article 21

States Parties recognize and/or permit the system of adoption shall ensure that the best interests of the child shall be the paramount consideration.

Administrative and legislative measures in India

Section 41 of the JJ Act provides principles to be followed in adoption for orphaned, abandoned, neglected or abused children through institutional and non-institutional methods in accordance with the guidelines issued by the State government from time to time in this regard.

Article 22

States Parties shall take appropriate measures to ensure that a child who is seeking refugee status or who is considered a refugee in accordance with applicable international or domestic law and procedures shall receive appropriate protection and humanitarian assistance.

Administrative and legislative measures in India

In India so far no specific legislation is being passed in this regard but there is a government department for refugee and some administrative measures had been taken for rehabilitation of the refugee children.

Article 23

States Parties recognize that a mentally or physically disabled child should enjoy a full and decent life, in conditions which ensure dignity, promote self-reliance and facilitate the child's dignity, promote self-reliance and facilitate the child's active participation in the community.

Subject to financial resources State Parties shall ensure that the disabled child has effective access to and receives education, training, health care services etc. in a manner conducive to the child's achieving the fullest possible social integration and individual development.

Administrative and legislative measures in India

In India under the Disability Act, 1995 all mentally or physically challenged persons are protected and conferred equal rights in all spheres of their life to promote self-reliance and equal participation in the community.[40]

Certain concession and retainers are made available for the disabled children such as travel concessions, wheel chairs, spare limbs, special shoes, hearing aids and specialized teaching and training aids on a minuscule scale.

Article 24

States Parties recognize the right of the child to the enjoyment of the highest attainable standard of health and to facilities for the treatment of illness and rehabilitation of health. States Parties shall strive to ensure that no child is deprived of his/her right to access to such health care services.

Administrative and legislative measures in India

In India the government hospitals are the main centres for health services and free treatment are provided to all poor people both adult and child alike though exclusive children's hospitals are very few compared to the needs.[41]

Article 25

States Parties recognize the right of a child who has been placed by the competent authorities for the purposes of care, protection or treatment of his/her physical or mental health, to a periodic review of the treatment provided to the child and all other circumstances relevant to his/her placement.

Administrative and legislative measures in India

The JJ Act authorized the Juvenile Welfare Committee to place any child in need of care and protection in any recognized Children Home or Shelter Home. The Social Welfare Departments of the State Governments are empowered to inspect those Homes periodically to review the situations in the Homes.

Article 26

States Parties shall recognize for every child the right to benefit from social security, including social insurance, and shall take the necessary measures to achieve the full realization of this right in accordance with their national law.

Administrative and legislative measures in India

In India measures are yet to be taken for realization of this right of social security including social insurance of children.

Article 27

States Parties recognize the right of every child to a standard of living adequate for the child's physical, mental, spiritual, moral, and social development.

States Parties...shall in case of need provide material assistance and support programmes, particularly with regard to nutrition, clothing and housing.

Administrative and legislative measures in India

In the case of neglected children, especially street children, there is a programme of the Social Welfare Department under the Vagrancy Law. In a very limited way under Integrated Child Development Schemes (ICDS) child health and nutrition care has been taken care of.

Article 28

States Parties recognize the right of the child to educate, and with a view to achieving this right progressively and on the basis of equal opportunity, they shall, in particular:

(a) make primary education compulsory and available free to all;

(b) encourage the development of different forms of secondary education, including general and vocational education;

(c) make higher education accessible to all on the basis of capacity by every appropriate means;

(d) make education and vocational information and guidance available and accessible to all children;

(e) take measures to encourage regular attendance at schools and the reduction of dropout rates.

Administrative and legislative measures in India

In pursuance of the Constitution of India (Article 45) the Government of India has launched nationwide primary education programmes with a strong girl child focus. Attempts are being made to draw more and more girls to general and vocational education facilities free ships, stipends, and financial assistance and residential facilities. Higher education is provided at nominal cost. Career guidance and counseling services are also started but not covered the required dimensions. Incentives like free noon meal, free books, free uniform and attendance scholarships for girls are provided. But the dropout from school, particularly girl child, is increasing alarmingly.

Article 29

States Parties agree that the education shall be directed to:

(a) the development of the child's personality, talent and mental and physical abilities to their fullest potential;

(b) the development of respect for Human Rights and fundamental freedoms, and for the principles enshrined in the Charter of the United Nations;

(c) the development of respect for the child's parents, his/her own cultural identity, language and values, for the national values of the country in which the child is living, the country from which he or she may originate, and for civilization different from his/her own;

(d) the preparation of the child for responsible life in a free society, in the spirit of understanding peace, tolerance, equality of sexes, and friendship among all peoples, ethnic, national and religious groups and persons of indigenous origin;

(e) the development of respect for the natural environment.

Administrative and legislative measures in India

In India a system of education has been developed based on a common educational structure, a national curricular framework and minimum levels of learning for each stage of education.

In pursuance of the constitutional values and framework for equality, freedom and justice, the National Framework for elementary and secondary education which among other aspects defined the following core components to include:

-The History of India's Freedom Movement

-Constitutional obligations

-Equality between sexes

-Small family norm

-Removal of social evils

-Environmental conservation

-National integration

-Scientific temper

-India's common Cultural Heritage

-Egalitarianism, Democracy and Secularism.

All the educational programmes are to strengthen India's philosophy of Peace and Understanding between Nations, the whole world as one family.

Article 30

In those States in which ethnic, religious or linguistic minorities or persons of indigenous origin exist, a child belonging to such a minority or who is indigenous shall not be denied the right, in community with other members of his/her group, to enjoy his/her own culture, to profess and practice his/her own religion, or to use his/her own language.

Administrative and legislative measures in India

The Constitution of India protects the rights of ethnic, religious and linguistic minorities to practice their own religion and language and makes it mandatory for the State (a) to provide instruction to linguistic minorities in their own language (within recognized official language) and (b) to give permission to minorities to run their own educational institutions with and without State aid. However, these institutions cannot force religious education on children of other groups attending these schools. But State run educational institutions do not impart religious instruction.

Article 31

States Parties recognize the right of the child to rest and leisure, to engage in play and recreational activities appropriate to the age of the child and to participate freely in cultural life and the arts.

Administrative and legislative measures in India

There are institutionalized recreational activities through more than a million formal and non-formal schools in India.

Article 32

1. States Parties recognize the right of the child to be protected from economic exploitation and from performing any work that is likely to be hazardous or to interfere with the child's education, or to be harmful to the child's health or physical, mental, spiritual, moral or social development.

2. States Parties shall take legislative, administrative, social and educational measures to ensure the implementation of the present Article. To this end, and having regard to the relevant provisions of other international instruments, States Parties shall in particular:

(a) provide a minimum age or minimum ages for admission to employment;

(b) provide for appropriate regulations of the hours and conditions of employment;

(c) provide for appropriate penalties or other sanctions to ensure the effective enforcement of the present Article.

Administrative and legislative measures in India

Article 24 of the Constitution of India prohibits employment of child labor in factories, mines and hazardous employment. Moreover, there are several legislations to safeguard children from economic exploitation and employment in hazardous occupations. Some important legislations are mentioned below:

(a) The Children (Pledging of Labour) Act, 1933 with the object of eradicating the evils arising from the pledging of labor of young children in lieu of loans and advances.

(b) The Child Labour (Prohibition and Regulation) Act, 1986 prohibits employment of children in any occupation mentioned in Schedule A and B.

(c) The Factories Act (1948) as amended in 1949, 1950 and 1954; Mines Act (1952); Plantation Labour Act (1951) and The Beedi and Cigar Workers (Conditions of Employment) Act, 1966, prohibit employment of children below the age of 14 years.[42]

But these provisions proved ineffective and child labor continues to flourish in the country.

Article 33

States Parties shall take all appropriate measures, including legislative, administrative, social and educational measures, to protect children from the illicit use of narcotic drugs and psychotropic substances as defined in international treaties, and to prevent the use of children in the illicit production and trafficking of such substances.

Administrative and legislative measures in India

In India there is a general law to control the abuse of drugs, namely Narcotic Drugs and Psychotropic Substances Act. For protection of children the JJ Act provides that State shall take care and protect child who is being or is likely to be induced into drug abuse.

Article 34

States Parties shall undertake to protect the child from all forms of sexual exploitation and sexual abuse. For these purposes, States Parties shall in particular take all appropriate national, bilateral and multilateral measures to prevent:

(a) the inducement or coercion of a child to engage in any unlawful sexual activity;

(b) the exploitative use of children in prostitution or other unlawful sexual practices;

(c) the exploitative use of children in pornographic performances and materials.

Administrative and legislative measures in India

In the Indian Penal Code there are penal provisions for acts of sexual abuse against children. Our Parliament had also passed the Immoral Traffic (Prevention) Act, 1956 to protect children being victims of trafficking.

Article 35

States Parties shall take all appropriate national, bilateral and multilateral measures to prevent the abduction of, the sale of or traffic in children for any purpose or in any form.

Administrative and legislative measures in India

To combat the problem of cross-border trafficking a multilateral SAARC Convention on Prevention and Combating Trafficking in Women and Children for Prostitution was adopted in January, 2002.[43]

Article 36

States Parties shall protect the child against all other forms of exploitation prejudicial to any aspects of the child's welfare.

Administrative and legislative measures in India

The JJ Act in Section 26 prohibits any kind of exploitation of juvenile or child employee. The street child or any other child who needs care and protections, such as, victim of any armed conflict, civil commotion or natural calamity, or who is being or is likely to be grossly abused, tortured or exploited for the purpose of sexual abuse or illegal acts.

Article 37

States Parties shall ensure that:

(a) no child shall be subjected to torture or other cruel, inhuman or degrading treatment or punishment. Neither capital punishment nor life imprisonment without possibility of releases shall be imposed for offences committed by persons below eighteen years of age; and

(b) no child shall be deprived of his/her liberty unlawfully or arbitrarily. The arrest, detention or imprisonment of a child shall be in conformity with the law and shall be used only a measure of last resort and for the shortest appropriate period of time;

(c) every child deprived of liberty shall be treated with humanity and respect for the inherent dignity of the human person, and in a manner which takes into account the needs of persons of his/her age. In particular, every child deprived of liberty shall be separated from adults unless it is considered in the child's best interest not to do so and shall have the right to maintain contact with his/her family through correspondence and visits, save in exceptional circumstances;

(d) every child deprived of his/her liberty shall have the right to prompt access to legal and other appropriate assistance, as well as the right to challenge the legality of the deprivation of his/her liberty before a court or other competent, independent and impartial authority, and to a prompt decision on any such action.

Administrative and legislative measures in India

Every citizen of India is entitled to fundamental rights to life and protection which include protection against cruel, inhuman torture, unlawful detention. The JJ Act in Section 16 provides that "Notwithstanding anything to the contrary contained in any other law for the time being in force, no juvenile in conflict with law (delinquent juvenile) shall be sentenced to death or life imprisonment, or commit to prison in default of payment of fine or in default of furnishing security. Moreover, the Supreme Court of India is now playing a pro-active role whenever any Public Interest Litigation comes before it to protect children from exploitation and abuse.

Under the Legal Services Authority Act 1987 every child in India is entitled to get services of a lawyer free of charge (Lawyer's Collective, 1992).

Article 38

1. States Parties undertake to respect and to ensure respect for rules of international humanitarian law applicable to them in armed conflicts which are relevant to the child.
2. States Parties shall refrain from recruiting any person who has not attained the age of fifteen years into their armed forces.

Administrative and legislative measures in India

The institutional structure in India to extend services to protect and care of children who are affected by an armed conflict is not adequate. However, Red Cross (India) takes active part in such situations. The law in India does not permit recruiting child soldier in any Defense Service.

Article 39

States Parties shall take all appropriate measures to promote physical and psychological recovery and social reintegration of a child victim of any form of neglect, exploitation, or abuse; torture or any other form of cruel, inhuman or degrading treatment or punishment; or armed conflicts. Such recovery and social reintegration shall take place in an environment which fosters the health, self-respect and dignity of the child.

Administrative and legislative measures in India

With a view to rehabilitate and reintegrate any child victim of any neglect, exploitation or abuse the JJ Act prescribed four processes, such as Adoption, Foster Care, Sponsorship and Aftercare (Ss. 40-44). The National Institute of Social Defense under Central Ministry of Social Justice is working to coordinate and to develop guidelines towards implementation of the JJ Act throughout the country.

Judicial Attitude to Human Rights of Children in India

The Indian Constitution in Article 253 provides that Parliament has the power to make any law for the whole or any part of the territory of India for implementing any treaty, agreement or convention with any other country or countries or any decision made at any international conference, association or other body. In view of this provisions Parliament passed many legislations to adapt in our legal system many international treaty obligations or Conventions ratified by it. The Supreme Court in *Visakha v. State of Rajasthan*[44] by wide interpretation of Article 253 says that in a matter on which there is no legislation of the Parliament the Court may invoke International Conventions or Instruments in support of its judgment. In fact by wide interpretation of Article 21 on *Right to Life* our Supreme Court has delivered a number of judgments recognizing various Human Rights of child as provided under CRC. Let us note some of these judgments. In *Unni Krishnan J.P. v. State of Andhra Pradesh*[45] the Supreme Court held that right to free education up to 14 years shall be regarded as Fundamental Right within the meaning of Article 21. In *People's Union for Democratic Rights v. Union of India*,[46] popularly known as Asiad Case, the Supreme Court had the occasion to dwell on the plight of child labor engaged in the construction work before the Asian Games and issued directions to the Central Government accordingly. In *M.C. Mehta v. State of Tamil Nadu*[47] the Supreme Court expressed great concern regarding the plight of child labor in firework and match manufacturing industries located in Sivakasi. The Court issued appropriate directions to uplift deplorable conditions of child labor in relation to wages, health, recreation and compulsory primary education.

The Supreme Court in a number of Public Interest Litigations also developed Human Rights jurisprudence for the children in India such as *Sheela Barsee v. State of Maharashtra*[48] on right of free legal aid of under trial children; *Salal Hydroelectric Project Case*[49] on payment of minimum wage for child labour; *Bandhua Mukti Morcha v. Union of India*[50] on freedom of children from bondage of bonded labour; *Vishal Jeet v. Union of India*[51] and *Gaurav Jain v. Union of India*[52] on protecting and rehabilitating children of prostitutes.

In issues relating to juvenile justice the Supreme Court also developed Human Rights jurisprudence in many cases. In *Bhola Bhagat v. State of Bihar*[53] the Supreme Court held that when a plea is raised on behalf of an accused that he was a child at the time of incidence of crime, in case of doubt, it is obligatory for the Court to make inquiry in the matter. In *Amireddi Rajagopala Rao v. Amireddi Sitharam Amma*[54] the Supreme Court held that illegitimate sons of *Sudra* from *Brahmin* concubine is entitled to maintenance from the *Brahmin.* In *Arnit Das v. State of Bihar*[55] the Supreme Court laid down that if the competent authority (i.e., JJ Board) is satisfied that at the beginning of enquiry the accused was a juvenile, his trial under the JJ Act would continue even if he crosses the prescribed maximum age during trial proceedings.

But on the question of the application of a death sentence or life imprisonment to a child the Supreme Court took a very conservative view. In *Amrutlal Someshwar Joshi v. State*[56] the convict was below 18 years of age and the Court held "there is no inflexible rule that a criminal aged about 17 or 18 years should never be sentenced to death irrespective of other circumstances, however, aggravating they may be." The convict in that case was a domestic servant and committed triple murder of the members of the family in cold blood, cruel and diabolical manner. The same line of judicial thinking was reiterated by the Supreme Court in *Ramdeo Chaudhuri v. State.*[57]

A Critical Appraisal of Implementation of CRC

The growing industrialization and urbanization has lead to increased marginalization of children, thus greater need for care and protection of children. The continued and even rise in the incidents of child labor in informal sector, the invariable rise of street children not only in large Metropolitan towns but even in smaller centers of trade and merchandise, the increase in number of school-dropouts is an indication of bulging numbers of the care and protection needing children. According to a study conducted by the International Food Policy Research Institute the number of malnourished children of aged five years and below in rural India alone can be placed at 250 million.[58] The pernicious evil of child labor in India is multiplying day in and day out. Legislative prescriptions and judicial responses have tried to make a dent in the situation.

But it is now realized that child labor in India is not a problem confined within the four walls of labor legislations rather it has its wide ramification in the overall development of a nation. Development of future progenies, and national commitment to social and juvenile justice, health and strength of civilized society are some of the pertinent issues which have been so intermixed with the issue of child labor that one cannot draw a framework in purely black letter law fashion.[59] From the study of the process of implementation of various child rights related legislations in India following barriers and flaws have been identified:

- Inexperience and untrained Adjudicatory Body
- Inactive Intake Agencies
- Inadequate infrastructure
- Lack of community participation
- Absence of coordination among various implementing agencies
- Traditional gender discrimination
- Inadequate fund allocation
- Absence of organized pressure group
- Absence of necessary database & feedback
- Lack of political will to focus on problems of children

To Conclude

Immediately after ratification of the CRC the Government of India formulated a National Plan of Action—A Commitment to the Child, 1992—which sets an illustrative list of *Goals for the Year 2000* on matters of Child Mortality, Health, Nutrition, Education, Children in specially difficult circumstances, the Girl Child, Children and Environment.

Some of these goals have been achieved to some extent while in the case of others, such as children in exploitative employment situations and the attitude of family to the girl child, much more needs to be done. Moreover, action needs to be taken along multiple fronts and by all agencies—government and nongovernmental, local, regional, national and international—to promote the Human Rights of children in India. This needs to be done immediately. The observation of the noted Nobel Laureate Gabrial Mistral is worth mentioning in this regard. He says "We are guilty of many errors and many faults, but our worst crime is abandoning the children, neglecting the foundation of life. Many of the things we need can wait, the child cannot, right now is the time whose bones are being formed, his blood is being made and his senses are being developed. To him, we cannot answer 'tomorrow'. His name is 'today'."[60]

To realize the rights of the child as declared in CRC the following initiatives are suggested: (i) promote pro-children development strategies; (ii) develop legislation that conforms to the Convention; (iii) encourage affirmative action to eliminate discrimination against girl child; (iv) support participatory and decentralized decision-making; (v) advocate child rights issues and (vi) monitor and report on the position of child rights by developing a set of indicators. In conclusion it may be said that the rights based development of children as propounded in CRC should be grounded on linkage between development and rights, accountability, empowerment, participation and non-discrimination.

Notes

1. Iyer, V.R. Krishna (2000), *Human Rights and Human Wrongs*, New Delhi, p. 10.
2. Article 2 of ILO Convention 5.
3. ILO Convention 7 of 1920.
4. Article 1 of ILO Convention 10 of 1921.
5. Convention No. 33 of 1932 which was revised in 1937 under Convention No. 60.
6. Convention No. 79 of 1946.
7. Convention No. 78 of 1946.
8. Vide Resolution No. 217A, 10th December, 1948.
9. Article 25(2) which states: Motherhood and childhood to special care and assistance. All children, whether born in or out of wedlock shall enjoy the same social protection.
10. Vide Resolution No. 1386(XIV) dated 20th November, 1959.
11. *See* Brownley, *op. cit.*

12. Vide Resolution No. 57(1) of 11th December, 1946.
13. United Nations Action in the Field of Human Rights, 1083, p. 207.
14. *Ibid.*
15. The General Assembly proclaimed the year 1979 as the International Year of the Child vide its Resolution No. 39/169 of 21st December, 1979.
16. *See* for more details Chowdhury, Dr. Baidyanath "Laws Concern on Children—On International and National Standard" in Dr. N.K. Chakrabarti et. el. Ed. *Law and Child* (2004), Kolkata, pp. 6-15.
17. ILO Report 1994.
18. Iyer, V.R. Krishna (1998), *Human Rights and Human Wrongs*, p. 58.
19. Profiting From Abuse, A Report submitted by the UNICEF to the United Nations, Geneva, 12th December 2001, p. 14.
20. Convention No. 182.
21. Kumar, Anuradha. "Protecting the Young", *The Telegraph*, December 26, 2001.
22. *UN Newsletter*, 2th Jan.-1st Feb, 2002, Vol. 57, No. 4, p. 12.
23. Mukherjee, Ashutosh (1989), *Juvenile Justice*, S.C. Sarkar, Kolkata, p. 30.
24. Rao, P. Koteswar, "Child, Constitution and Reality in India—A Socio-Legal Study", Paper presented in the All India Seminar on Child and the Law at Kurukshetra University during March 25-27, 1981.
25. Chowdhury, B.N., "Laws's Concern on Children: On International and National Standard" in N.K. Chakrabarti et.el. Ed. *Law and Child* (2004), *op. cit.* p. 16
26. Chakrabarti, N.K. (1997), "Administration of Criminal Justice: The Correctional Services", Vol. IV, *Juvenile Justice*, New Delhi, Deep and Deep Publications, p. 53.
27. *Government of India*, India Country Paper, presented in the Sixth U.N. Congress on the Prevention of Crime and Treatment of Offenders held at Caracas, Venezuela on 25th August to 5th September, 1980, pp. 15-16.
28. Also known as The Beijing Rules, 1985.
29. Factories Act, Plantation Act etc. and Ss. 82/83 of IPC.
30. Mitra, N.L., *Juvenile Delinquency and Indian Justice System* (1985), p. 114.
31. Chakrabarti, N.K., Ed. *Administration of Criminal Justice: The Correctional Services* (1997), Vol. IV.

32. Bhatia, J.C., "Ideal Number and Sex Preferences of Children", The Journal of Family Welfare, Vol. XXIV, No. 4, 1978.
33. Dutta Gupta, Bela, "The Girl Child" in Dr. N.K. Chakrabarti & Dr. Shachi Chakrabarty, Ed. *Gender Justice (*2006), Kolkata, p. 1.
34. Misra, Nidhi, "Legal Aspects of Foeticide and Infanticide: An Indian Perspective" in N.K. Chakrabarti, Ed. *Law and Child*, *op. cit.*, pp. 245-72.
35. *See* for details Shah, S.P., *Encyclopedia of Laws of the Child in India* (2000), Allahabad.
36. Sections 15(a) and 39 of the JJ Act.
37. *See* Chakrabarti, N.K., et.el. Ed. *Law and Child*, *op. cit.*, p. 86.
38. *Ibid.* p. 52.
39. Sec. 2(d) of JJ Act.
40. Karna, G.N. (1999), "United Nations Human Rights of the Disabled", New Delhi.
41. Nayer, Usha (1994), Seminar Paper, 4-8, July, 1994.
42. *See* MARG (1992), *Our Laws.*
43. Chakrabarty, N.K., Ed. *Law and Child*, *op. cit.*, p. 157.
44. 1997, 6 SCC 241.7.
45. AIR 1992 SC 2178.
46. AIR 1982 SC 1473.
47. AIR 1991 SC 417.
48. 1983, 2 SCC 96.
49. AIR 1984 SC 177.
50. AIR 1984 SC 802.
51. AIR 1990 SC 140.
52. AIR 1997 SC 3021.
53. AIR 1988 SC 236.
54. AIR 1965 SC 1970.
55. 2000, 5 SCC 488.
56. 1994, 6 SCC 200.
57. 2000, 7 SCC 455.
58. Pande, B.B., "Protection and Control of Children through Laws" in Chakrabarti, N.K., Ed. *Law and Child*, *op. cit.*, p. 36.
59. Akhtar, Saleem, "The Problem of Child Labour in India: Analysis and Solution" in Chakrabarti, N.K., Ed. *Law and Child*, *op. cit.*, pp. 343-64.
60. Iyer, V.R., Krishna, J., "Jurisprudence of Juvenile Justice: A Preambular Perspective", ILI, 1994.

8

The Administration of Juvenile Justice System in India: Many Miles to Go, Many Goals to Achieve and Many Children to Protect

Anuradha Saibaba Rajesh

Introduction

From times immemorial, in every civilization individuals, groups and communities rights have been denied due to prejudices based on religion, caste, economic status, gender etc. Children constitute one such social group. The varied manifestations of abuse experienced by children are unparalleled—child labor, female foeticide/infanticide, trafficking, child sexual abuse, juvenility, denial of education, child pornography and many more.

The vulnerability of children is not uniform and largely hinges on other aspects of their identity such as age, gender, ethnicity, religious background or economic status. The denial of one set of rights leads to the abuse of others. The pattern of abuse and exploitation of children also has not remained constant. It has undergone a sea change and today novel and more ominous areas have emerged.

Generally, girls have borne the brunt of all forms of abuse in myriad forms. However, the gender element of child rights violations is gradually blurring and increasingly boys are being recruited for work in hotels, factories, domestic households, construction sites and for the sex industry. All children are potential targets but undeniably children hailing from the minority religious and ethnic groups are more prone to abuse. Children from the lower castes and tribal belts remain more susceptible as low economic status and impoverished backgrounds leave children open for greater exploitation. Most children are also trafficked from rural to urban settings.

The protection and promotion of children's rights are vital to the very progress, development and stability of the country. Children are the torchbearers of a nation's future and thus their rights need to be secured and transgressions addressed effectively. The status of India's children is not shining. A lot needs to be accomplished before all our children dream of living a healthy, happy, safe and fulfilling childhood free from abuse and exploitation. Before delving into the specificities of the juvenile justice system in particular, it is imperative to comprehend why child rights today have assumed great significance.[1]

1. Children are Assets: Children are miniature adults and tomorrow's future belongs to them. Any nation's progress and development would be shaped by its citizens. Surely, the country's future would not be bright if a majority of its future citizens are malnourished, sickly, illiterate, semi-skilled, anti-social and dysfunctional. To invest in child rights today is to invest in the rights of the future generations.

2. Children Possess Distinct Rights and Personalities: They also possess a separate entity like men and women. Thus they are entitled to a whole spectrum of distinct rights. Also, due to their cognitive underdevelopment they deserve special protection and privileges as well.

3. Child Rights Subsumed under Women's Issues: Traditionally, women and children's rights have been construed together as one common social group. Consequently, children's issues have been ignored and unaddressed. The pertinent need thus is to affirm and recognize children distinct from other human beings.

4. Protection from Adults: Children are the most vulnerable of all the marginalized. Their issues remain at the periphery and often go unheeded and unheard. Their dependency on adults to highlight their concerns, needs and rights makes them soft targets—as often caregivers, parents turn abusers. Thus, it's imperative that children are recognized as distinct individuals with special and generic rights.

5. All Children Have Equal Rights: Any form of discrimination or distinction in both theory and practice would make child rights in essence and spirit futile. Children across classes, caste, sex, religion, economic strata have the same rights. Children who commit offences have rights as well.

6. Nascent Stage of Child Rights Movement in India: The emerging child rights movement necessitates sustained and concerted interventions on the part of all actors—bureaucracy, legislators, judicial fraternity, media, civil society groups, common man etc. We owe that much to our children.

The catalyst worldwide in accelerating the child rights movement is attributed to the landmark *Convention on the Rights of the Child, 1989*[2]—the most rapidly ratified and hugely subscribed Human Rights instrument. The CRC, 1989 is radical and path breaking in innumerable ways—apart from being the only child-centric and child specific instrument it guarantees a wide spectrum of diverse Human Rights to all children, some of which are unique and quite controversial.

Defining the Juvenile Justice System

Children constitute the weakest social group world over. Within this category itself there are some who are more marginalized and vulnerable—juveniles and abused children specially.[3]

The situation in India depicts the same reality. In most countries, the juvenile justice systems have an overarching and broad mandate. India is not different either. In several nations justice and welfare jurisdictions of children co-exist simultaneously in the juvenile justice system. The same is applicable in the Indian context.

The term 'Juvenile Justice' *per se* is capable of a myriad of connotations. At one level it represents a system that addresses issues pertaining to 'children in conflict with law' (hereinafter CICWL). It also refers to a system distinct from the adult criminal justice system and thus embodies rules and procedures governing the situation of alleged juveniles as well as convicted juveniles. It also symbolizes idealistic notions of rehabilitation, reintegration and a non-punitive approach to tackle deviant children. The presence of alternate sentencing dispositions as well as efforts towards decriminalization form the core thrusts of this system.

The juvenile justice system has traditionally always elucidated two vital beliefs about children who come in conflict with the law or are accused/convicted of committing offences. To begin with, children are cognitively and morally underdeveloped and thus should be precluded from being completely responsible for their deeds. Additionally, children and young offenders are more malleable and thus more inclined towards being successfully rehabilitated and reformed.[4] Most importantly the concept of juvenile justice system encompasses two ideal issues-fairness and justness to children and an alternate standard of justice.[5] The latter is a manifestation of the criminological elements as it's often visualized as an off-shoot of the adult criminal justice system. And that probably explains why traces of stigmatization, labeling and ostracization linger even today in the juvenile justice system.

In India like numerous other nations the Juvenile Justice System has an added flavor. It also focuses on children who have been abused, exploited, trafficked, abandoned, neglected etc., known as children in need of care and protection (hereinafter CINOCAP) The system herein again endeavors to provide for rehabilitation, treatment, development and restoration. The schemes envisaged here are to explore avenues for a stable and loving childhood and thus work towards foster care, community support, adoption and sponsorship.

Since an individual's childhood and growing years would determine his persona as a law abiding citizen or as an anti-social element, the doctrine of *parens patriae* has often been invoked to provide legitimacy to the State to take custody and control of children who either are bereft of parental care or who lack proper parental care. This paternalistic ideology of the State has resulted in a large group of abused, abandoned, trafficked, street, exploited children to receive protection and care through the State and its agencies.

Undeniably, the justice and welfare jurisdictions under the integrated juvenile justice system run parallel In India. The existing legislation—the *Juvenile Justice (Care and Protection of Children) Act 2000* that has been recently amended by the *Juvenile Justice (Care and Protection of Children) Amendment Act 2006* provides for separate statutory authorities, personnel, staff, homes, schemes, programmes, services etc. to assist and facilitate better and effective protection and development of both categories of children, yet there are several issues that remain common as well as distinct between both groups of children.

The Juvenile Justice System also traverses the path of discerning social, economic, familial, cultural factors that might have created 'conditions' for the child or youth in question either to turn deviant or pushed in labor, trafficking, commercial sexual exploitation etc. There is growing debate on the issue that at one level children who commit offences (CICWL) due to circumstances or dire straits can also fall under the category of being a child in need of care and protection actually.

The Genesis

The earliest legislation was the *Apprentice Act* in 1850 that catered to rehabilitation via thorough vocational training to children between 10 to 18 years who had been convicted by Courts. The *Reformatory Schools Act 1897* followed suit. A *Children's Act* in 1920 was passed in Madras and subsequently got replicated in other States like Bengal and Bombay in 1922 and 1924. The central enactment *The Children's Act* was legislated in 1960 for the Union Territories in India, which was subsequently amended into the *Children (Amendment) Act* of

1978. The Act covered neglected, delinquent and victimized children as well.

The *Juvenile Justice Act 1986* holds the distinction of being the first uniform and comprehensive legislation for the entire nation.[6] Though a central legislation, the erratic and piecemeal implementation by the state governments rendered the Act almost redundant. The inability of the Act to challenge the accepted and widely prevalent social practice of child labor in hazardous and non-hazardous sectors as well as lack of a right perspective towards all categories of children especially juveniles/children in conflict with law raised questions about the efficacy of the Act.[7] The term 'child' is conspicuously absent all through the legislation; instead the all pervasive word used has been 'juveniles'.

The ratification of the *Convention on the Rights of the Child, 1989 (hereinafter CRC, 1989)* by the Government of India accelerated the child rights movement in India. Growing international scrutiny on children's issues as well as increased awareness on child rights nationally, impacted the passage of the *Juvenile Justice (Care and Protection of Children) Act 2000.*[8] An attempt was made to internalize international standards and guidelines within the domestic framework.[9] The aim of this paper is to critically analyze the working of some of the core provisions of the Act.

The Catalyst

Most international Human Rights instruments have a sprinkling of provisions on child rights, child protection and child development.[10] The *Convention on the Rights of the Child, 1989* is credited for bring children's issues from a rights perspective to center stage. The CRC, 1989 holds the distinction of being the most rapidly ratified Human Rights Convention. CRC is also the first Human Rights treaty in contemporary times to exclusively concentrate on child rights only.[11] The treaty boasts of a wide and diverse spectrum of rights guaranteed to all children. Many of the rights are radical and controversial.

The core provisions that form the essence of the CRC, 1989 are:

(1) **The Right against Discrimination:** Article 2 of the CRC symbolizes this vital right to be made available to all children irrespective of any discrimination. The underlying theme being equal protection, equal opportunities and equal rights.

(2) **The Best Interest Principle:** Article 3 of the CRC embodies this crucial provision which mandates that in any decisions concerning or affecting a child, the child's best interest should be the driving and paramount concern. This adds a new dimension and vision to child rights issues.

(3) **The Right to Life, Survival and Development:** Article 6 of the CRC, 1989 reinforces the right to life as well as the right to the highest attainable standard of health, and adequate standards of living. Thus reiterating the fundamental right to survival, the term 'development' also encompasses guarantees cutting across not only physical health but also encompasses mention, emotional, cognitive development and growth.

(4) **The Right to Participate:** Article 12 of the CRC elucidates that a child possesses the right to articulate and express his views and opinion on all issues pertaining to him. This marked shift from treating children as 'objects' to 'subjects' of law makes this a key right in CRC. The right to participate includes not only right to express but also right to access appropriate information as well as right to freedom of thought, expression and religion.

The Juvenile Justice (Care and Protection of Children) Act 2000 and the Juvenile Justice (Care and Protection of Children) Amendment Act 2006: An Appraisal.

A progressive and successful juvenile justice system hinges on a myriad of factors and actors. The *Juvenile Justice (Care and Protection of Children) Act 2000* has been recently amended by the *Juvenile Justice (Care and Protection of Children) Amendment Act 2006*[12] in several arenas reflects a marked shift in mechanisms, systems and perceptions from its predecessor—*The Juvenile Justice Act of 1986.*

Under the existing law, two classifications of children come within the purview of the Act—*Children in Need of Care and Protection (CINOCAP)* and *Children in Conflict with Law (CICWL)*. Both the categories of children under the current Juvenile Justice System have separate statutory authorities—the Child Welfare Committees (CWCs) and the Juvenile Justice Boards (JJBs) respectively.

However, to laud the Act as a perfect piece of legislation in consonance with international standards and parameters embodied in *the Convention of the Rights of the Child, 1989* to which the Government of India is a party, would be a fallacy. Some areas of common concern are commented on below.

I. Children in Conflict with Law (CICWL)

(1) **Age Classification:** Under international Human Rights law, the definition of a child is generally directly or indirectly related to age. The same applies in the Indian context. However, the term 'juvenile' does not necessarily correspond to the concept of a child. The *JJ(C&PC)A 2000* defines a juvenile or a child (both boy and girl) to be someone who has not attained eighteen years of age.[13] This is marked shift from the erstwhile prevalent law on juvenile justice wherein protection was accorded to a boy juvenile till 16 years of age and a girl juvenile until18 years of age.[14] This discriminatory and artificial distinction has been done away with thereby bring the current law at par with the international standard proscribed in Article 1 of the CRC, 1989.

In reality, a lot of skepticism prevails regarding children in conflict with law—boy children *per se* in the bracket of 16-18 years. The argument being juveniles in this age group are aware of right and wrong and can make informed decisions and thus should be tried in the adult criminal justice system for their wrong doings. There is a concerted campaign to revert back to the age classification stipulated in the *JJA 1986*. Additionally, even after 7 years since the inception of the *JJ(C&PC)A 2000*, many stakeholders like police, lawyers are not aware of this law and still refer to the *JJA 1986*, doing grave injustice in the bargain.

(2) **Minimum Age of Criminal Responsibility:** The cognitive development of a CICWL determines whether the child should be brought within the juvenile justice framework or let away. This is reflected in the CRC, 1989, which categorically mandates the establishment by State parties of a minimum age of criminal responsibility.[15] The Indian Penal Code, 1860 has provided for such guarantees as well. Section 82 of the Indian Penal Code elucidates the concept of *doli incapax* and Section 83 lays down an act of child above 7 years and below 12 years with immature understanding to be exempted from the consequence of their actions—even if its criminal and anti-social in nature.[16]

In reality, these are flouted with impunity. Children as young as 4 and 6 years old have been accused of murder and treated as criminals. News items and real life depicting such incidents appear very frequently in print as well as electronic media.

(3) **Age Determination Procedure:** The determination of age is extremely crucial for a CICWL in addition to the issue of benefit of doubt being rendered to her if there is any ambiguity. As per the law, the determination of age needs to be verified in three ways—Birth Certificate, School Joining/Leaving Certificate, Medical Ossification Test. The presumption, if any, in case of ambiguity should go to the child alleged to have committed an offence.[17]

In real life, age of the CICWL is rarely verified. The magistrates do not send the children for age verification, more often than not the magistrate by a cursory visual examination by the eye decides whether the 'juvenile' is a child or otherwise. If a 'juvenile' looks well built and grown up, he is sent to the adult jail. If at all the parents can produce evidence of the age of their child, the child is released otherwise the child is treated as an adult offender and the case is instituted in the adult

Court. Often children lie about their age to the police, as they prefer to be kept in lock ups rather than being institutionalized in the observation homes.

(4) **The Competent Authority:** A major transition has meant not only re-christening the *JJA 1986* Juvenile Courts into Juvenile Justice Boards but inculcating changes in its composition as well. The current JJBs boast of a magistrate as well as two social workers forming a Bench. Herein the social workers have an equally important role to play and their presence provides ample scope of changing the nature and direction of inquiry in relation to a CICWL.[18] There is room to engage with not the intention of CICWL but the motive for him/her to commit the alleged offence thus analyzing the social background/family setting and compelling circumstances that pushed the child towards crime. The adjudicating authority thus transcends the punitive and criminalized approach towards CICWIL during inquiry proceedings to a more rehabilitative and reformative approach. The opinion of the majority in the Bench would prevail thus giving the social workers an equal platform while inquiring into cases. The Act also prescribes special qualification for the magistrates as well as social workers.[19]

In reality, the situation is mostly the opposite. Seldom do the Magistrates favor the participation of the social workers in decision-making. Additionally, the social workers also remain hesitant to undertake a more proactive role as lack of knowledge of procedural and substantive laws handicaps them. Most magistrates perceive postings to the JJBs as punishment posting. Rarely do magistrates possess the specialized skills, training or orientation that the situation demands. The social workers are also comparatively less sensitive towards a child who has committed an offence than a child in need of care and protection.

(5) **Due Process Rights not Protected:**[20] This is one area that is grossly violated. Apprehended children are not informed of the reasons for their arrest, they are handcuffed and jailed with adults, their families are not contacted. Their cases are not dealt with speedily and are more often than not denied bail

and even legal aid as well as contact with parents. The arrest, detention and imprisonment of children as stipulated in the CRC are to be used as a last resort but this is far from reality.[21]

Apprehended children are not produced within the mandated 24 hours period before a magistrate, they are kept overnight in lock up and often beaten and tortured. No record of their arrest is made and they are pressurized by the police to lie about the time of their arrest. Most children alleged to have committed offences, pending inquiry or later convicted for commission of an offence are hauled into Observation Homes for years wherein contact with family or outside world is minimal or even non-existent. Institutionalization remains the underlying mantra herein.

(6) **Orders Passed:** The *JJ(&PC)A 2000* clearly articulates that no imprisonment let alone life imprisonment or the death penalty can be inflicted on a CICWL.[22] The focus of the juvenile justice system being reformative and rehabilitative, no penal or punitive sanctions are to be imposed on a CICWL. In fact, the *JJ(C&PC)A 2000* provides for alternate methods of addressing wrongdoing or instilling notions of self-realization of wrongdoing in the CICWL. Community-based sentencing are provided for in the Act.

In practice however, punitive and penal orders are regularly passed against a CICWL. Imprisonment and life imprisonment for minors is a common sentencing adopted by several Courts in India. In the infamous case of murder of Australian Missionary Graham Staines and his two sons, the Orissa High Court in 2000 awarded a minor 14 years of imprisonment.[23] The judicial fraternity are often not aware of the kinds of orders that can be passed or that are prohibited under the *JJ(C&PC)A 2000*. The community-based reformative sentencing option is rarely exercised. Only recently in Delhi, the JJB sentenced a CICWL to assist a traffic cop in navigating heavy traffic as a measure of community service for the offence of rash driving.[24] Such sentences are far and few.

(7) **Ambience of JJB:** The whole idea of establishing a Juvenile Justice System is to facilitate services distinct from the adult criminal justice to children who come in conflict with

law.[25] The setting is crucial to reassure the child that he is in safe hands and the functionaries present are there to assist him. A non-threatening and friendly atmosphere is the need of the hour.

However, most JJBs resemble miniature adult Court rooms/halls. The atmosphere remains gloomy, intimating and hostile. Though the JJBs are special Courts the personnel in these Courts are not aware of the specialized approach. To a large extent the JJBs have functioned like second-class criminal Courts with the adult criminal justice system, terminology and perceptions prevailing in full force.[26] The entire system is intimidating and traumatic for the child.

(8) **Role of Police:** The *JJ(C&PC)A 2000*, clearly provides for the presence of a specially trained police officer to exclusively handle cases of CICWL. The investigating officer under the system is the regular police. The role of the police is crucial as it is the police that provides the first contact point in the juvenile justice system to the child. The juvenile justice system prescribes a critical and specific role for the police not only in terms of their dress code while dealing with children but also in their mannerisms, interactions, etc. with the child. The system also envisages special juvenile police units in every police station wherein specially trained police officers exclusively handle cases of children.

In actuality, the police often are responsible for meting out harsh treatment to apprehended juvenile-ranging from housing them in lock ups to beatings to torturing them. The police are often very insensitive in handling cases of CICWL. This often jeopardizes successful rehabilitation of these children.[27] Moreover, for most police officials investigating/inquiring into children's issue is neither a mainstream duty nor a task of priority. Many remain unaware of the special provisions of the Act. This is further compounded by the conspicuous absence of training in child rights issues in most police training curriculum and programmes.

II. Children in Need of Care and Protection (CINOCAP)

(1) **Powers of the Statutory Body CWCs:** The Powers of CWCs are ambiguous. Though technically per the Act they possess powers of JFMCs or MMs, in practices they rarely exercise it.[28] The CWCs are a Bench of Magistrates per the Act but they are generally not regarded so, especially those accused of committing an offence against a child.

Two schools of thought exists on this—one that the juvenile justice system is an alternate justice system so they cannot execute powers and functions as per the Code of Criminal Procedure like regular judges in adult Courts do. For example, issuing summons to employer of child laborers, if done does it mean the juvenile justice system is not distinct from the adult criminal system as same procedures/processes/formats are used. This added with the fact that most CWC members are not qualified/trained in law so procedural irregularities could damage the case. The second school of thought reflects on the fact that the law clearly stipulates their powers and thus they possess the requisite magisterial powers and can be oriented on basis procedures of law to prevent any irregularities that may arise.

(2) **Balancing Parental and Child's Interest:** The prevailing *JJ(C&P)C A 2000* and *JJ(C&P)C AA 2006* are novel in several aspects. One redeeming feature is the issue of termination of parental rights in case it is found that the parents are unable or incapacitated to provide for adequate and appropriate parents care and support.[29] This has rarely been used in the Indian context and often the child's interest takes backseat when parents claim custody of their child. This is especially true in cases of rescued child laborers who are often sent by their parents for work and thereafter face abuse and exploitation and when rescued the parents demand custody of their child. The child is often not given an opportunity to express his views and it is deemed that parents and adults know what is best for the child. This balancing act between parents' right to custody and a child's best interest is a grey area for the CWC members.

(3) **Issue of Rehabilitation and after Care:** The rehabilitation component remains the weakest link of the entire system. Similarly, there is no adequate mechanism in place for after the child turns 18 and moves beyond the confines of the State institutions under the juvenile justice system. The rehabilitation programmes otherwise are also lackluster, they are often archaic and outdated and not relevant in contemporary situations. The existing rehabilitation and care plans are applied alike to all children, they don't take into account special and specific needs, desires and interests of the child in question. The rehabilitation plans are seldom tailor-made or innovative and most importantly often lack the very pertinent livelihood and social skills that are so crucial for these children.

Also many a time society and families refuse to accept a child back within their folds for a variety of reasons and this stigmatization and labeling prevents successful and effecting reintegration of a child to where he/she actually belongs.

(4) **Limited or Negligible Convergence with other Laws:** The moot problem in India context remains the definition of a 'Child'. The legal age of a 'child' has varied according to the purpose it seeks to achieve. A whole plethora of laws on CINOCAP are present in India. For example, there are separate laws addressing issues of child labor, child marriage, child trafficking/prostitution, adoption, guardianship, juvenile justice etc. Different laws stipulate different age cut offs for a person to qualify as a child/minor.[30]

There is an absolute *lacunae* in terms of convergence of these laws to strengthen the child rights and child protection issue. Often the CWC members are not aware of the existence of other laws relating to children. And this renders the juvenile justice system ineffective.

(5) **Lack of a Licensing Regime:** The proliferation of NGOs, charity homes and faith based organizations has gone unchecked. No stringent laws regulate the mushrooming of these institutions resulting in violation of minimal standards of institutional care as a pre-requisite to house CINOCAP. The existing law on this issue is the *Orphanages and Charitable*

Homes Act (Supervision and Control Act, 1960). However, the implementation of the concerned Act remains defunct, as many State governments have not formulated rules under the Act. Even in the few State that have framed these rules, the implementation and supervision of the Act remains lax giving rise to many discrepancies in procedures, standards of institutions etc.

Often these institutions have become emerging hubs for trafficking and abuse of hapless and vulnerable children. Many a time, poor parents are compelled to admit their children in these institutions professing support and help but parental contact with child remains almost zilch. Many institutions also offer admissions based on conditions like payment of some money, a promise never to meet the child or claim custody of the child and often impoverished parents succumb to these demands. It's rather ironical that penury and impoverishment results in children with parents, siblings and extended families growing up as orphans in these homes. The licensing regime needs to be implemented vigorously to avoid further abuse and victimization of marginalized children.

(6) **Outreach of CWCs Minuscule:** The *JJ(C&PC)A 2000* and *JJ(C&PC)AA 2006* provide for establishment of a CWC in every district or group of districts.[31] In many States, no CWCs have been constituted to date. And in still many more just a few have been instituted without taking into consideration issues like appropriate geographical location, adequate and equal representation etc. And in many, though CWCs have been established, members have not been recruited or the committees are defunct.

This literally implies that the number of children who are deprived and marginalized are innumerable but the outreach of CWC remains limited. Moreover, often the mapping of CWC is haphazard resulting in lop sided protection being provided to the CINOCAP. Moreover, the CWCs in urban settings in comparison to those in districts are in a position to offer more sustained and varied services for children. This lack of accessibility translates into the CWCs failing to emerge and consolidate themselves as a principal point of contact for marginalized and vulnerable children.

Common Concerns Affecting Both CICWL and CINOCAP

(1) **Institutionalization:** The omnipresent institutional and custodial approach permeating the juvenile justice system remains a sore area of concern. This coupled with lack of Protocols and guidelines on minimum standards of institutional care and lack of any supervisory mechanism on the ever-mushrooming institutions basically leave the children more vulnerable. Incidents of sodomy, neglect, beatings, rape, corruption etc. are often commonplace behind closed doors of these institutions. The CRC 1989 categorically entails institutionalization and detention as a last resort and that too for the shortest possible period of time. Institutionalization can have grave repercussions on a child's psyche and hamper his familial and social bonding, yet this trend continues unabated.

The pressing need of the hour is restorative strategies for the child—CINOCAP or CICWL—through home and community based approaches. Non-institutional and family-based services should be the standard approach and be made mandatory. In addition, institutional care incurs huge infrastructure costs and the funds herein could be diverted for a more cost effective and child friendly non-institutional care. Non-institutional care like foster care, sponsorship, day/night care shelter adoption etc. have tremendous scope in facilitating better services and protection for children.

(2) **Strengthening Family Settings:** Family preservation as a key concept is categorically articulated in the CRC, 1989.[32] The State mechanism and community initiatives should be geared towards strengthening family bonding and the family as a unit of child care and child protection. Lack of schemes and programmes to assist BPL (below poverty line) families should be activated with full vigor. State's coercive interventions in family settings should be received with caution and only when absolutely essential. Parental control and choice for their child's care plans and future should be respected.

Parental contact with institutionalized children should be fostered and promoted. In a nut shell, all decisions to be based on 'best interest' of the child. Non-institutional approach endorses the child's right to a family and strengthens the family as a unit and prevents its disintegration.[33] Even marginalized children have a right to a decent, stable and loving home environment and this should be zealously protected and promoted. The underpinnings of schemes and programmes for 'families at risks' should be proactively implemented to prevent juvenile and familial problems.

(3) Boosting Staff Support: It is of utmost importance that staff support is increased in numbers. Often the inadequate number of staff hinders the smooth functioning of the system. Also, constant orientation and skill enhancement of all staff involved in the juvenile justice system is vital. Specialized skill training should be imparted to staff handling cases of children with special needs or interacting with children with extreme trauma. Personnel working and associated with the system are prime stakeholders. Identification of skilled staff, constant training and upgrading of skills, is a necessary component for an effective juvenile justice system.

The staff should be adequately trained to recognize and develop the common and distinct social, educational and treatment requirements of children and their family is crisis. The staff works under tremendous pressure and duress and thus the need to take care of the care givers as well so that the children are not deprived of professional and experienced hands. Thus incentives and rewards for exemplary services and punishment for dereliction of duties by staff/personnel should be formulated.

(4) Integrated Approach: Often the juvenile justice system appears fragmented and in a disarray. An integrated justice system wherein all stakeholders work towards the common vision of effective and sustained protection of children and justice to children is required. Convergence, collaboration, joint management and partnership should be the driving force behind all the stakeholders' initiatives and programmes. Child welfare and protection intervention, facilities and services have to be conceptualized in the socio-economic, religious, cultural and political realities. Constant information sharing between all actors in the juvenile justice system and coordinated and collaborative initiatives would add succor and strength to the juvenile justice system.

The Road Ahead[34]

A progressive juvenile justice system would inculcate practices and procedures that optimally benefit the children in question. It would be based on the 3 Rs—reform, rehabilitation and reintegration. 'Child rights' as jargon or rhetoric needs to be replaced with an actual practice and culture of child rights. In the rapidly transforming socio-economic and cultural milieu of India, child rights have remained on the threshold. The need is to transcend that and work collectively and concertedly towards establishing, promoting and making child rights in every domain a reality. Recognition of children as a distinct social group with identifiable rights is one such small step.

Some proposed landmark initiatives which hold a promise of transforming the face of child rights in India are mentioned below.

(1) The National Commission on Children

A National Commission on Children has been established in February 2007 in India. The advent of the Children's Commission and hopeful replication of it in different states hopes to reinvigorate the entire child rights scenario in India. The effective functioning of the Commission will go a long way in giving children especially those who are marginalized and vulnerable a greater visibility in all quarters-law, policies, schemes, programmes. As an ombudsman for child rights, child protection and child development the onus remains on the Commission to propel the child rights movement ahead. It is hopeful that the Commission's mandate and functioning is in tandem with child rights and interests.

(2) The Offences against Children's Bill 2006

This marks the beginning of the first comprehensive legislation on child rights issues. Within its ambit, the OAC Bill

2006 purports to address the multitude of offences perpetuated against children in diverse fields. The proposed enactment on children includes provisions covering sale/transfer, sexual assault, sexual/physical/emotional abuse, commercial sexual exploitation, child pornography, grooming for sexual purpose, incest, corporal punishment, bullying and economic exploitation. These provisions would co-exist with other laws on children's issues thus further strengthening the legal mechanism for child protection.

(3) The proposed Integrated Child Protection Scheme

On the lines of the Integrated Child Development Scheme (ICDS) the government is contemplating introducing an Integrated Child Protection Scheme (ICPS) to address issues of child protection and child safety in a more concerted and sustainable manner. The ICPS advocates strong partnership and linkages between civil society groups and the State to facilitate better delivery of services. The ICPS aims to mitigate the lip service paid to child protection issues which for long has been a neglected area and attempts to boost this by financial support as well as revamping programmes/schemes for vulnerable and marginalized children. The ICPS is poised to take child protection and child development to new heights with its holistic and exclusive concentration on protection issues.

(4) Rights of the disabled persons

The *UN International Convention on the Protection and Promotion of the Rights and Dignity of Persons with Disabilities* was opened for ratification to the States in 2007. The Indian Government signed the Convention in March 2007. By doing so India is endorsing its commitment to promoting, protecting and ensuring full and equal enjoyment of all Human Rights by people with disabilities, including children with any form of disability. However, India needs to do more than simply sign the convention.

(5) The Optional Protocols to Convention on the Rights of the Child

India has ratified the *Optional Protocol to the Convention on the Rights of the Child on the Involvement of Children in*

Armed Conflict in the year 2005 as well as the *Optional Protocol to the Convention on the Rights of the Child on the sale of children, child prostitution and child pornography*. By doing so the message sent to the international community reflects India's commitment to effectively address and curb trafficking and use of children in armed conflicts, commercial sex industry, pornography, sex tourisms etc. Despite this, trafficking of children for sexual exploitation continues unabated. With the exception of the State of Goa, no other Indian State has laws to address child trafficking and child commercial sexual exploitation. In fact, there is no central legislation on this crucial area at all.

(6) Children and Immoral Trafficking

The existing *Immoral Trafficking (Prevention) Act 1986* is fraught with shortcomings. Children are identified differently in terms of their age under this legislation—if below 16 years then deemed to be a 'child' and if between 16 to 18 years then deemed to be a 'minor'. The forthcoming *Immoral Trafficking Prevention (Amendment) Bill 2006* yet again is deficient in many quarters still it is an attempt to tighten the noose further on the issue of trafficking and prostitution of children.

(7) The Child Marriage Prohibition Act, 2006

This unlike its predecessor is vested with more teeth. However more than the law, social awareness and stringent action against erring officials/perpetrators on the issue is crucial.

The Convention on the Rights of the Child, 1989 affirms the rights of children to an adequate living standard and adequate health care, social security and education. Delivering on this commitment is an enormous challenge for any government, requiring a combination of legal, economic and social measures. A critical and complementary synthesis of all existing child labour laws needs to be undertaken. The need of the hour demands a collaborative, constructive yet critical relationship between the community and the State to ensure justice in its truest form to children. The challenge is therefore to shift collectively from the predominant custodial, institutional and State centric approach towards a more sensitive, inclusive and child friendly and child-centric justice system.

Conclusion

The plain reading of the article reflects the perception that the implementation and administration of the juvenile justice system has taken the shape of a marginalized justice system still deeply entrenched in the adult criminal justice system. This current status of the varying juvenile justice mechanisms is far from what it was initially perceived to be. This scenario is definitely disturbing. In the twenty-first century, the juvenile justice system has to be modeled on responding to the social, psychological and developmental needs of subaltern children—children in conflict with law as well as children in need of care and protection.

One way of addressing the issues raised would be to revisit the domestic legislation and embark on a sincere and rigorous road of implanting basic international norms prescribed under the *Convention on the Rights of the Child 1989, Beijing Rules of 1985, Riyadh Guidelines of 1990,* other UN Resolutions, comparative practices etc. to ensure law reforms are incorporated in the real and true sense. Finally '*the best interest of the child*' should be the omnipresent and overriding principle followed by all stakeholders pursuing child rights, child protection and child development concerns under the juvenile justice set up.

It would not be farfetched to reiterate that the Human Rights culture of a nation is determined largely by the protection and rights that it guarantees to the most vulnerable of all its citizens-children *per se*.

Children may be small but their problems are definitely not small issues!!!

Notes

1. "A Handbook on Implementing the Juvenile Justice (Care and Protection of Children) Act 2000 and the Juvenile Justice (Care and Protection of Children) Amendment Act 2006", Using the 'Best Interest Principle', *A Child Welfare Committee Handbook* (under print) by Ms. Nina. P. Nayak and Anuradha Saibaba, published by ChildFund India, 2007.

2. Hereinafter termed as CRC, 1989.
3. In common parlance children who commit offences are referred to as 'juveniles', 'delinquents and children who are abused/exploited known as 'neglected' juveniles. Similar terminology was also used in the erstwhile *Juvenile Justice Act, 1986*—the first uniform and comprehensive juvenile justice legislation for the whole of the country.
4. "The Courts Effectiveness in Protecting Rights Juveniles in Delinquency Cases", Janet. E. Ainsworth, *The Future of Children*, Volume 6, No. 3, The Juvenile Court (Winter 1996), pp. 64-74.
5. "The India Juvenile Justice Jurisprudence & the Convention on the Rights of the Child", Prof. B.B. Pande, NHRC Consultant. Unpublished source.
6. The backdrop of *JJA* 1986 can be traced to the UN General Assembly adoption of the Standard Minimum Rules Regulating Administration of Juvenile Justice called the 'The Beijing Rules, 1985', UN Document Resolution 4, sixth UN Congress on Prevention of Crime and Treatment of Offenders.
7. The *JJA 1986* categorized a 'juvenile' as a boy child under 16 years of age and a girl child as someone who had not attained 18 years of age. Juveniles were further categorized as 'Neglected & Delinquent Juveniles.'
8. Unlike erstwhile legislation an international treaty resulted in enactment of the *JJ(C&PC)A 2000.*
9. Eg. Under Section 2(k) of the *JJ(C&PC)A 2000*, a child or juvenile means a person who has not completed 18 years of age. The CRC, 1989 also defines a child on the same lines.
10. Articles 5(b), 16(1)(d) of CEDAW, Articles 10, 10(3), 12, 13(1) in ICCPR, Articles 1(1), 14(3)(f) in ICESCR.
11. The "Declaration of the Rights of the Child", *1924* adopted by the League of Nations is deemed to be the first international treaty focusing on child rights. Records of the Fifth Assembly, 1924, Supplement No. 23, Legue of Nations Official Journal.
12. Hereinafter *JJ(C&PC)A 2000 and JJ(C&PC)A 2006.*
13. As per Section 2(k), in this Act, unless the context otherwise requires 'juvenile or child' means a person who has not completed eighteenth year of age.
14. As per the Juvenile Justice Act of 1986.
15. Section 40(2b)(vii)(a), the establishment of a minimum age below which children shall be presumed not to have the capacity to infringe the penal law.
16. *The Indian Penal Code, 1860* via Section 82 stipulates 'Act of a child under seven years of age. Nothing is an offence which is done

by a child under seven years of age. Section 83 provides that 'Act of child above seven and under twelve of immature understanding.—Nothing is an offence which is done by a child above seven years of age and under twelve, who has not attained sufficient maturity of understanding to judge of the nature and consequences of his conduct on that occasion.

17. Section 49 of the *JJ(C&PC) A 2000*, the JJB is mandate to conduct an inquiry into the age of a child alleged to have committed an offence.
18. As per *JJA 1986*, the Juvenile Courts would consist of Magistrates who would be assisted by a panel of two social workers. In contrast Section 4(2) of *JJ(C&PC) A 2000*, the Magistrate and two social workers will form a Bench and sit as a quorum.
19. Section 4(3) furthers states that the Magistrate should have training or knowledge of child psychology and social workers, a history of involvement in children's welfare issues.
20. Article 37(b), 40(3)(b), 40(2)(b)(1) of CRC.
21. Section 160 of the Code of Criminal Procedure, 1973 prohibits detention of males under 15 or females under any age for purpose of investigation or questioning by police.
22. Section 16 of JJ(C&PC)A 2000. Also Article 37(a) of the CRC 1989 holds that neither capital punishment nor life imprisonment shall be imposed for offences committed by persons below 18 years of age.
23. "14 yrs jail for juvenile in Staines murder case", *The Times of India*, News Service, Bhubaneswar, October 2000, Website:http:// www.barodabibleclub.org/news/TI_14_yrs_jail_Staines_murder_oc t_ 03.html
24. Article 40(4) of CRC, 1989 provides for a variety of disposition orders to be made available to ensure that children are dealt with in a manner appropriate to their well being and proportionate to both their circumstances and the offence.
25. Article 40(3) of CRC, 1989 lays down that State parties shall seek to promote the establishment of laws, procedures, authorities and institutions specifically applicable to children allege or accused of or recognized as having infringed penal law.
26. Child Rights in India: Law, Policy and Practice, Asha Bajpai, oxford University Press, 2003, p. 289.
27. "Police Flouts Law, Parades Juveniles before Media; Minors Charged with Theft, Pick-pocketing", Jupinderjit Singh, *Tribune News Service*, February 2005, Website: http://www.tribune india.com/2005/ 20050206/ldh1.htm

28. As per Section 29(5) of the *JJ(C&PC) A 2000*, the committee shall function as a bench of Magistrates and shall have the powers conferred by the Code of Criminal Procedure, 1973 on a Metropolitan Magistrate or as the case may be of a Judicial Magistrate of first class.
29. Section 2(d)(iv) a Cinocap is one 'who has a parent or guardian and such parent or guardian is unfit or incapacitated to exercise control over the child'.
30. *The Prohibition of Child Marriage Act 2006*, herein under Section 2(a) 'Child' means a person if a male below 21 years and if female below 18 years. *The Immoral Trafficking (Prevention) Act 1986*, herein child means a person below 16 years of age and minor means a person below 18 years. *Indian Contract Act 1870,* A person below the age of 18 years has no capacity to contract. As per *Child Labour (Prohibition and Regulation) Act 1986*, child means a person below 14 years of age. Under *The Factories Act 1948,* Child means a person who has not completed 14 years, Adolescent means a person who has completed 15 years of age but not 18 years.
31. Section 29(1) of the JJ(C&PC)A 2000 stipulates that the State Government may by notification constitute for every district or groups of districts one or more Child Welfare Committees for exercising the powers and discharge the duties conferred on such Committees in relation to child in need of care and protection under the Act.
32. As per Articles 23 & 27 of the CRC 1989.
33. As per Article 9 of the CRC, 1989.
34. "A Handbook on Implementing the Juvenile Justice (Care and Protection of Children) Act 2000 and the Juvenile Justice (Care and Protection of Children) Amendment Act 2006", Using the 'Best Interest Principle', *A Child Welfare Committee Handbook* (Draft version) by Ms. Nina. P. Nayak & Anuradha Saibaba, 2007.

9

Role of United Nations in Protection and Promotion of Human Rights

Sadiq A.J. Syed

> *"It is for you to realize these rights, now and for all time. Human Rights are your rights. Seize them. Defend them. Promote them. Understand them and insist on them. Nourish and enrich them."*
>
> Former United Nations Secretary-General Kofi Annan

I. Introduction

Human Rights issues and abuses are a subject throughout human history. Be it the *Bible*, the *Quran*, the Vedic scriptures, the Babylonian Code of Hammurabi or the Analects of Confucius, which are considered as the most authentic and oldest documents advocated for people's rights, duties and responsibilities and the principles of equality and justice. The history of modern Human Rights is very much connected to World War II and the foundation of the United Nations. The term Human Rights denote those basic standards without which one cannot live as a human being. Human Rights are 'inalienable' and 'indivisible', which means that no one can lose or be deprived of these rights. At the same time it has undergone some radical, even evolutionary changes.

The United Nations Organization (UNO) joined by the international community has adopted various Conventions, Declarations and other documents aimed to protect and promote Human Rights. Over the years the definition of

Human Rights has undergone some radical, even evolutionary changes and has been broadened and incorporated a list of rights to be termed as 'basic rights'. The Universal Declaration of Human Rights (UDHR),[1] which contains a list of basic principles, has been unequivocally endorsed and most of the principles were integrated into national Constitutions by various Governments around the world. Some of the rights provided under the UDHR include, the 'Right to: life, liberty and security of person; freedom from slavery and servitude; freedom from torture or cruel, inhuman or degrading treatment or punishment; equality before the law and equal protection of laws; not being subjected to arbitrary arrest, detention or exile; freedom of movement and residence; nationality; marriage and to found a family; freedom of thought, conscience and religion; peaceful assembly and association; work; health and education. For example, the UDHR[2] states: "Everyone has the right to life, liberty and security of person" and "Everyone is entitled to a social and international order in which the rights and freedoms set forth in this declaration can be fully realized."

Since its adoption the UDHR has been considered by the national governments, judiciary and civil society as a benchmark to judge what Human Rights are and thereby analyze what constitute the abuses, and issues surrounding Human Rights. Mary Robinson, the former United Nations High Commissioner for Human Rights,[3] emphasized the need to broaden the definition of Human Rights to include not only the "civil and political rights" that industrialized democracies emphasize but also "economic, social and cultural rights" such as the right to food, clothing, housing, medical care and education that are lacking in many countries.

II. Strategies for Protection of Human Rights

The United Nations, which was created on October 24, 1945, has continued to grow and has progressively diversified its activities. It is not merely confined to 'save the succeeding generations from scourge of war' but to safeguard their rights and to bring new hope to the States and to men and women around the world under a social contract.[4] The UN has played a significant role towards the development of international legal principles and standards towards the protection of Human Rights. The UN since its inception has adopted more than 500 treaties and other documents which include over 100 treaties having direct bearing on Human Rights. The Secretary-General is the depository for the multilateral treaties. The Office of Legal Affairs of the United Nations is responsible for the registration and publication of treaties submitted to the Secretariat pursuant to Article 102[5] of the Charter of the United Nations.

Some of the landmark treaties adopted by the United Nations include: Universal Declaration of Human Rights (UDHR); International Covenant on Economic, Social and Cultural Rights (ICESCR);[6] International Covenant on Civil and Political Rights (ICCPR);[7] Convention on the Elimination of all Forms of Racial Discrimination (CERD);[8] Convention on the Elimination of all Forms of Discrimination Against Women (CEDAW);[9] Optional Protocol to the Convention on the Elimination of all Forms of Discrimination Against Women (CEDAWOP); Convention Against Torture and Other Cruel, Inhuman or Degrading Treatment or Punishment (CAT);[10] Convention on the Rights of the Child (CRC);[11] Optional Protocol to the Convention on the Rights of the Child (CRCOPSC); Convention on the Protection of the Rights of All Migrant Workers and Members of Their Family;[12] Beijing Declaration and Platform of Action, 1995[13] etc.

Protection of Human Rights through UN peacekeeping

The history of warfare, especially during the 20th Century, reveals that the growing number of those killed were civilians. The rise in the proportion of death of civilians, especially women and children has been a matter of concern to the international community in general and the United Nations in particular. While the conflict impacts on the society as a whole, women are susceptible to poverty and suffering in situations of armed conflict as they lose their breadwinners, father, husband, sons, property and in addition, they have to earn a living for the remaining children and relatives. Women are at great risk during and after the war and need special protection from sexual abuse and exploitation. Peacekeeping is an instrument that was developed by the United Nations to promote and achieve its objective of "maintaining international peace and security". Besides, the Preamble, Chapter VI and Chapter VII of the UN Charter specifically provide for pacific settlement of disputes and military enforcement.[14] Former UN Secretary-General Boutros Ghali defined peacekeeping as, "The deployment of a United Nations presence in the field, hitherto with the consent of all the parties concerned, normally involving United Nations military and/or police personnel and frequently civilians as well."[15]

As of August 2007, there are more than 100,000 personnel serving on 18 Department of Peacekeeping Operations (DPKO)-led peace operations on four continents in twelve time zones,[16] directly impacting the lives of hundreds of millions of people. The UN does not have its own military forces; it depends on contributions from Member States. 115 countries contribute military and police personnel to UN peacekeeping. Almost 73,000 of those currently serving are troops and military observers and about 9,500 are police personnel. In addition, there are almost 5,700 international civilian personnel, more than 12,400 local civilian staff and some 2,000 UN Volunteers. Nearly 2,000 uniformed personnel and more than 5,000 civilian staff serving on UN peacekeeping operations are women.[17]

The UN Security Council Resolution 1325, calls for the prosecution of crimes against women, increased protection of women and children during war, appointment of more women to peacekeeping operations, and ensuring that more women participate in peace-building decision-making processes. The Resolution also advocates developing a consolidated database on the impact of conflict on women and girls.

III. Accountability Mechanisms

International law has graduated in the last half century from an orientation on the relationships between States to one that focuses on the protection of rights of individuals regardless of their nationality. The advancement of the definition of basic Human Rights is reflected in the UN

Conventions and other documents such as the International Covenant on Civil and Political Rights and the Optional Protocols to the Convention on the Rights of the Child and the CEDAW. The concept of accountability for serious Human Rights violations has been a core of the issues and has attained much significance in the wake of large scale attacks, killings and displacements. The Charters of the two *ad hoc* Tribunals, for former Yugoslavia and Rwanda, as well as the Rome Statute establishing the International Criminal Court, are examples of the proliferation of accountability enshrined in Human Rights documents.

Human Rights Council

The General Assembly through its Resolution[18] established the Human Rights Council as a subsidiary organ of the General Assembly.[19] The Human Rights Council, which replaced the Commission on Human Rights on 18 June 2007, one year after its first meeting, agreed on a package of elements that establish the procedures, mechanisms and structures that will form the basis of its future work. Among others, the Council is mandated to promote universal respect for the protection of all Human Rights and fundamental freedoms for all, without distinction of any kind and in a fair and equal manner; address situations of violations of Human Rights, including gross and systematic violations, and make recommendations thereon. It should also promote the effective coordination and the mainstreaming of Human Rights within the United Nations system; promote Human Rights education and learning as well as advisory services, technical assistance and capacity-building, in consultation with and with the consent of Member States concerned.[20]

Charter and treaty based mechanisms for the realization of global peace and Human Rights

One of the outstanding developments at the international level towards the monitoring and implementation of commitments under the UN Charter and Treaties is the setting-up of mechanisms to monitor the implementation. In this context the UN has setup Charter Based bodies such as: (i) The General Assembly; (ii) The Security Council;

(iii) The Economic and Social Council (ECOSOC); (iv) The Commission on Human Rights (CHR);[21] (v) The Sub-Commission on the Promotion and Protection of Human Rights; (vi) The Commission on the Status of Women;[22] (vii) The Commission on Crime Prevention and Criminal Justice. Quite apart from these, there came to exist in recent times Conventional mechanisms popularly known as "Human Rights Treaty-Monitoring Bodies" to review and monitor Human Rights violations such as:

(a) **Human Rights Committee:** monitors the implementation of the *International Covenant on Civil and Political Rights*;

(b) **Committee on Economic, Social and Cultural Rights:** monitors the implementation of the *International Covenant on Economic, Social and Cultural Rights*;

(c) **Committee on the Elimination of Discrimination against Women:** monitors the implementation of the *Convention on the Elimination of all Forms of Discrimination against Women*;

(d) **Committee on the Rights of the Child:** monitors the implementation of the *Convention on the Rights of the Child*;

(e) **Committee Against Torture:** monitors the implementation of the *Convention Against Torture and Other Cruel, Inhuman or Degrading Treatment or Punishment*;

(f) **Committee on the Elimination of Racial Discrimination:** monitors the implementation of the *International Convention for the Elimination of all Forms of Racial Discrimination*;

(g) **Committee on Migrant Workers** (CMW): examines the implementation of the *International Convention on the Protection of the Rights of All Migrant Workers and Members of Their Families*.

Apart from the above Charter based and Treaty-Monitoring bodies there exist "Extra-Conventional Mechanisms" in the form of Special Rapporteurs, Special

Representatives, Special envoys and Independent Experts, Working Groups—thematic or country (Urgent Actions) for the promotion and effective monitoring of the implementation of Human Rights standards.

The Council's "special procedures" system includes 41 independent Human Rights experts or working groups focusing either on particular themes, like violence against women and arbitrary detention, or on Human Rights situations in specific countries, including Myanmar and Sudan.

Individual complaints procedure

The Optional Protocol to the International Covenant on Civil and Political Rights, the Optional Protocol to the Convention on the Elimination of all Forms of Discrimination against Women, Article 22 of the Convention Against Torture, and Article 14 of the International Convention on the Elimination of Racial Discrimination provide for an individual complaints procedure.

The communication procedure set out in the Optional Protocol to the ICCPR—Article 22 (Convention Against Torture) and Article 14 (Convention on the Elimination of Racial Discrimination) is conditional on the following:[23]

- That the individual must first exhaust local remedies. In other words, the individual must have explored available legal remedies in the State concerned including appeal to the highest Court, unless: there is no legal process in that country to protect the rights alleged to have been violated; access to remedies through the local Courts has been denied or prevented; there has been an unreasonable delay locally in hearing the complaint; a consistent pattern of gross violations of Human Rights makes any prospect of remedies meaningless; the remedies are unlikely to bring effective relief to the victim.
- The communication must not be anonymous or abusive.
- The communication must allege violations of rights as stipulated in the treaty which the committee oversees.

- The communication must come from an individual who lives under the jurisdiction of a State, which is party to the particular treaty.
- The communication must not be under current or past investigation in another international procedure.
- The allegations set out in the communication must be substantiated.

Communications, submissions or correspondence for these treaty bodies may be directed to: (The relevant committee), Support Services Branch, c/o Office of the High Commissioner for Human Rights, United Nations Office at Geneva.[24]

The 1503 procedure[25]

Every year the United Nations receives thousands of communications alleging the existence of gross and systematic violations of Human Rights and fundamental freedoms. The Economic and Social Council consequently adopted a procedure for dealing with such communications. This is known as the *1503 Procedure* pursuant to the adoption of the Resolution 1503 of 27 May 1970. It does not deal with individual cases but with situations affecting a large number of people over a protracted period of time.

Application of International treaties by the states parties

The United Nations Conventions, Declarations and other documents have a greater impact on the States Parties towards promotion and protection of Human Rights. Following ratification many States have incorporated these provisions into the national Constitutions and also enacted legislations at par with these provisions.[26] Quite apart from these, the judiciary in most of the jurisdictions played a significant role in respect to and implementation of law in respective jurisdictions. For example, the Indian Supreme Court while highlighting the need for implementing the International Conventions held: 'India is a State Party to many International Treaties, Declarations, Conventions and Resolutions which prohibit gender discrimination and the Courts have given effect to the same in a series of cases'.[27] In its path-breaking judgment in *Vishaka case*[28] while formulating the guidelines for prevention of sexual harassment of women at workplace the Supreme Court of India observed that"[t]here is no reason why these international conventional and norms cannot, therefore, be used for construing the Fundamental Rights expressly guaranteed in the Constitution of India, which embody the basic concept of gender equality in all spheres of human activity."[29] The Court further held:

> It is now an accepted rule of judicial construction that regard must be had to the International Conventions and norms for construing domestic law when there is no inconsistency between them and there is a void in the domestic law. In the absence of domestic law occupying the field, to formulate effective measures to check the evil of sexual harassment of working women at all work places, the contents of International Conventions and norms are significant for the purpose of interpretation of the guarantee of gender equality, right to work with human dignity in Articles 14, 15, 19(1)(g) and 21 of the Constitution and the safeguards against sexual harassment implicit therein. Any International Convention not inconsistent with the Fundamental Rights and in harmony with its spirit must be read into these provisions to enlarge the meaning and content thereof, to promote the object of the Constitutional guarantees.

IV. Promotion of Human Rights: Role of United Nations

Promotion of Human Rights has been one of the major priorities of the United Nations Organization since its inception. Provisions on Human Rights education have been incorporated in many international instruments, including the Universal Declaration of Human Rights (Article 26), the International Covenant on Economic, Social and Cultural Rights (Article 13), the Convention on the Rights of the Child (Article 29), the Convention on the Elimination of all Forms of Discrimination Against Women (Article 10), the International Convention on the Elimination of all Forms of Racial Discrimination (Article 7), the Vienna Declaration and Programme of Action[30] and the Declaration and Programme of

Action of the World Conference against Racism, Racial Discrimination, Xenophobia and Related Intolerance, held in Durban, South Africa, in 2001.[31] For example, the Universal Declaration of Human Rights specifically provides that: "Education programmes should be designed to promote the full development of the human personality and strengthen respect for Human Rights and fundamental freedoms".[32] Further the General Assembly also called upon all Member countries to publicize the text of the Declaration and "to cause it to be disseminated, displayed, read and expounded principally in schools and other educational institutions, without distinction based on the political status of countries or territories."[33]

With an aim to encouraging Human Rights education initiatives, Member States have adopted various specific international frameworks for action, such as the World Public Information Campaign on Human Rights, focusing on the development and dissemination of Human Rights information materials, the United Nations Decade for Human Rights Education, 1995-2004 and its Plan of Action, encouraging the elaboration and implementation of comprehensive, effective and sustainable strategies for Human Rights education at the national level, and the International Decade for a Culture of Peace and Non-Violence for the Children of the World (2001-2010). Besides, the Economic and Social Council, welcoming Commission on Human Rights Resolution 2004/71, requested the General Assembly to proclaim, at its fifty-ninth session, a world programme for Human Rights education, to begin on 1 January 2005 and to be structured in consecutive phases, in order to further focus national Human Rights education efforts on specific sectors/issues periodically identified by what was then the Commission on Human Rights.

Quite apart from this, the Dakar Framework for Action spelt out the strategy that:

> Schools should be respected and protected as sanctuaries and zones of peace. Education programmes should be designed to promote the full development of the human personality and strengthen respect for Human Rights

and fundamental freedoms as proclaimed in the Universal Declaration of Human Rights (Article 26). Such programmes should promote understanding, tolerance and friendship among all nations, and all ethnic and religious groups; should be sensitive to cultural and linguistic identities and respectful of diversity; and reinforce a culture of peace. Education should promote not only skills such as the prevention and peaceful resolution of conflict but also social and ethical values.

The Dakar Framework refers particularly to primary and secondary education, but what it proposes is equally valid for tertiary and other professional or technical education, such as that of police and judicial officers. The Dakar framework calls for all education to intrinsically and continuously facilitate processes for learning *about* and *for* Human Rights.

The various initiatives by the United Nations more specifically, the United Nations Decade for Human Rights Education, 1995-2004 and its Plan of Action, joined by the added commitment and contributions by the States Parties, UN agencies, NGOs, had tremendous impact on the international community and contributed significantly in developing and implementing Human Rights Education (HRE) programmes for various groups including school children, police, judiciary, NGOs and other functionaries and civil society. In the wake of globalization and the increased conflicts including grave violation of Human Rights, the UN has a greater role to play. It is hoped that the ongoing reforms, concerted efforts by States Parties and enforced action will contribute significantly in accomplishing its goal of 'saving the succeeding generations from the scourge of war' and in making the slogan "Human Rights for All" a reality.

Notes

1. Adopted by the General Assembly on 10 December 1948. UDHR is the primary UN document establishing Human Rights standards and norms.
2. Articles 3 and 28, Universal Declaration of Human Rights.
3. Wesson Lecture at Kresge Auditorium on November 2, 1999.

4. Sadiq A.J. Syed, *Women in India: Legal and Human Rights,* Women's Studies and Development Centre, University of Delhi (2001).
5. Article 102 provides that every treaty and every international agreement entered into by a Member of the United Nations, after entry into force of the Charter, shall be registered with and published by the Secretariat.
6. As of 14 February 2009, ICESCR has 160 States Parties to it.
7. As of 14 February 2009, ICCPR has 164 States Parties. The UDHR together with ICESCR and ICCPR are termed as the "International Bill of Rights".
8. As of 14 February 2009 CERD has 173 States Parties to it.
9. As of 14 February 2009, CEDAW has 185 States Parties, CEDAW-OP has 96 States Parties.
10. As of 14 February 2009, CAT has 146 States Parties and CAT-OP has 44 States Parties to it.
11. As of 14 February 2009, CRC has 193 States Parties and CRC-OP-AC has 127 and CRC-OP-SC has 130 States Parties.
12. As of 14 February 2009, CMW has 40 States Parties.
13. The Fourth World Conference on Women, held in Beijing in 1995 significantly contributing towards attaining women's equality. The Declaration and Platform for Action adopted by the Fourth World Conference on Women, identifies "12 critical areas of action" needed to empower women and ensure their Human Rights. These include, women and poverty; education and training of women; violence against women; women and health; women and the economy; women and armed conflict; women in power and decision-making; institutional mechanisms for the advancement of women; Human Rights of women; women and the media; women and the environment; and the girl-child.
14. There are more than 100,000 personnel serving on 18 DPKO-led peace operations on four continents in twelve time zones, directly impacting the lives of hundreds of millions of people.
15. United Nations, *Agenda for Peace,* (1992).
16. These statistics don't include the highly complex African Union-United Nations Hybrid Operations in Darfur.
17. United Nations, *Peacekeeping Fact-sheet,* (DPKO, 2007). Since 1945, UN peacekeepers have undertaken over 60 field missions and negotiated 172 peaceful settlements that have ended regional conflicts, and enabled people in more than 45 countries to participate in free and fair elections.
18. GA Resolution No. 60/251 dated 6 April 2006.

19. For the moment it is a subsidiary organ of the Assembly. But within five years the Assembly will review its status. I venture to hope—and I suggest it should be your ambition—that within five years your work will have so clearly established the Human Rights Council's authority that there will be a general will to amend the Charter, and to elevate it to the status of a Principal Organ of the United Nations. (UN Secretary-General address to the Human Rights Council, 19 June 2006).
20. *Ibid.*
21. The Commission on Human Rights met for the first time with an objective to oversee the drafting of the Universal Declaration of Human Rights. The task was accomplished. Currently the Commission on Human Rights serves as the main subsidiary organ of the United Nations dealing with Human Rights matters. Under this the Sub-Commission on the Promotion and Protection of Human Rights (formerly Sub-Commission on Prevention of Discrimination and Protection of Minorities) also functions. The Sub-Commission is assisted by working groups and special rapporteurs. The Commission on Human Rights was replaced by the Human Rights Council in accordance with the General Assembly Resolution 60/251.
22. The Commission on the Status of Women is the principal technical body of the United Nations towards the development of substantive policy guidance with regard to the advancement of women. The Commission presently consists of 45 government experts elected by the Economic and Social Council for a period of four years.
23. *Human Rights: A Basic Handbook for UN Staff,* Office of the High Commissioner for Human Rights, United Nations.
24. The Committee for the Elimination of All Forms of Discrimination against Women is serviced by the Division for the Advancement of Women. Submissions or correspondence may be directed to: c/o Division for the Advancement of Women Attention Women's Rights United Nations, United Nations Headquarters, DC2, 1 UN Plaza, NY 10017.
25. *Ibid.*
26. For example, Article 51 of the Constitution of India mandates the State, among others, to endeavor to "foster respect for international law and treaty obligations in the dealings of organized peoples with one another". Further it also empowers the Parliament to enact a law for implementing any treaty, agreement or Convention (Article 253).
27. See. *Valasamma Paul v. Cochin University* (1996) 3 SCC 545.

28. *Vishaka and others v. State of Rajasthan and others* (1997) 6 SCC 242.
29. *Ibid.*
30. Part I, paras. 33-34 and Part II, paras. 78-82.
31. Declaration, paras. 95-97 and Programme of Action, paras. 129-39.
32. Article 26(2) Universal Declaration of Human Rights.
33. *Adopted and Proclaimed by General Assembly Resolution 217 A (III) of 10 December 1948.* The Office of the High Commissioner for Human Rights has been awarded the Guinness World Record for having collected, translated and disseminated the Universal Declaration of Human.

10

Role of Non-Governmental Organizations in the Promotion of Human Rights

*V. Seshaiah Shasthri** and *A.S. Dalal*

1. Introduction

Nature and quality of information being provided coupled with the opportunity to utilize the same in distinct fact situations demonstrates the level of progress of a civil society and its responses to the promotion and safeguarding of the Human Rights. For this precise reason, various stakeholders of the civil society demonstrate their concern for the well being of all concerned and to contribute in their own chosen way. The continuing calls for the upholding the basic dignity of human beings regardless of the territorial and manmade boundaries, have for times immemorial sounded like funeral chimes. Onus of transforming the same into wedding bells has remained as a daunting challenge before the international community. During the twentieth century it came to be realized that an important stakeholder in the creation of (i) the pool of information; (ii) dissemination of knowledge; (iii) evolving of strategies and interventions for their permeation into the grassroot levels of

* The Author profoundly thanks Ms. Saakshi Khatri, 3rd year B.P.Sc. LLB (Hons), National Law University, Jodhpur for being the key researcher and providing all academic assistance in the development of this chapter.

the society is the Non-Governmental Organizations (NGOs) which have emerged as entities, serving best, the interests of inducing activism in civil society.

At the international and national Levels, NGOs occupy a prominent role in making (a) public authorities accountable; (b) system of governance transparent; and in turn, (c) rights of the beneficiaries to be rightly addressed. From the stereotyped roles and restricted contours, the modern NGOs have come a long way in redefining their roles to induce humanitarian perspective, spur a cosmopolitan outlook and promote community participation to strive for the promotion of the Human Rights. By undertaking mass awakening strides and importantly aligning themselves with the UN Millennium Development Goals, the NGOs have marched way ahead in contributing to the various national programs which include for example, (i) training youth for nation building, (ii) religious revivalism, (iii) promoting community and religious tolerance etc., and thereby promoting the social, political and cultural Human Rights.

Hence, this study (i) investigates into the manner in which, in building positive public opinion and pressure on bodies of policy making, the NGOs furthered their agenda to realize their common goals; (ii) looks into and focuses up on the role of the NGOs in the creation of awareness and ensuring the internalization of the same through various educational means; (iii) outlines the salient features of these internationalized institutions and their common agendas so as to integrate the mutual concerns into concrete courses of actions; (iv) identifies the typologies of these institutions and their functional commonalities; (v) brings to the forefront the success stories; and importantly, (vi) puts forth, formidably and concretely a futuristic agenda for the ultimate realization of their unending commitment to the human community.

2. Importance of Human Rights Education

Human Rights education is a key and important component of the protection of Human Rights. Human Rights education can be seen in both narrow and broad perspectives. While in its literal and narrow sense Human Rights education concerns with the teaching of Human Rights norms to the public at large and encompasses issues such as curriculum development, civics education, tertiary education and research, in its broader context, it involves shaping of a nation's political culture such that respect for Human Rights is seen as an integral part of the public life of that nation. For example, a culture of respect for Human Rights will ensure that (i) minority voices are heard; (ii) women are fairly represented; and, importantly, (iii) mechanisms of oversight of government function honestly. It further allows the opposition and the media to perform its tasks and encourages the activism of civil society and thus paves way for the full utilization of a nation's social capital. In this manner, the electoral democracies transform themselves into participatory, deliberative, liberal democracies.

3. Role of Human Rights NGOs in the Promotion of Human Rights Education

From the viewpoint of the work of the NGOs associated with the promotion of Human Rights standards it is important to remember that the preparation of reports under various Human Rights treaties (for example, International Covenant on Civil and Political Rights, 1966 and International Covenant on Social, Economic and Cultural Rights, 1966) is not to be seen as a mechanical chore of reporting to an international body. Rather, it needs to be appreciated as important document reporting to one's own people about the state of Human Rights in a given country. The periodic reports required under the six major Human Rights treaties create a process whereby a nation can 'take its own temperature' in relation to the promotion and protection of Human Rights.

This demonstrates the need to prepare the report in a context of consultation with affected groups, writing the report in the local vernacular as well as in one of the UN languages, using a non-legalistic style that is accessible to a broad segment of the population and publishing the reports in such a way that many people can have access to them. Posting them on the internet is important and is undertaken by the Office of the High Commission for Human Rights with the website address being made known locally. Thus, the NGOs can play an important role in facilitating the accomplishment of the important goals and objectives of the Human Rights education.

It is important to understand how Human Rights education may be promoted so as to contribute to a culture of peace and in that process what role NGOs have to play. This is essential because respecting Human Rights is the surest basis on which to build a culture of peace and on that note, Human Rights education is an indispensable means of ensuring respect for Human Rights. The importance of Human Rights education has long been recognized. The prominence accorded to it at the Vienna World Conference and that the United Nations decided to establish the International Decade for Human Rights Education are evidence of this. If one were to ask why Human Rights education holds so much of importance, it is because, in the first place, the right to education is being elevated from the status of ordinary legal right to a fundamental right and Human Rights provide the essence of a quality education.

4. Design and Conduct of Training Programs and Role of Human Rights NGOs

While designing the Human Rights communication processes, it becomes incumbent on the part of the Human Rights NGOs to ensure the most effective means of promoting Human Rights is to undertake educational and training programs. In this regard, one must pay due attention to the nature and kind of education and training being provided to the region's future lawyers and policymakers of the region as well as the education and training programs being offered to current and future leaders, in both the public and private sectors. For example, providing workshops for those who are teachers and trainers can bring in a multiplier effect. This will ensure that the benefit of the workshops extends beyond the actual participants in the long run. Therefore, the efforts of the NGOs shall be oriented towards enabling the educators and trainers in the region, in the law schools as well as in other contexts, to acquire the skills and knowledge needed to design and teach Human Rights programs. Such continuing endeavors will result in a vast variety of valuable outcomes like,

(i) Identification of Human Rights priorities for their respective countries or professional environments;

(ii) Enhancement in the understanding level of the participants to either implement their courses of action or recommend the same for due and effective implementation;

(iii) Enhanced understanding of the key principles for developing training courses and education programmes; and

(iv) importantly transformation of the course participants to pass on the skills and knowledge gained from the workshop to others.

These outcomes will in turn empower the participants to train others, and thus achieves the aim of the course to produce a multiplier effect; and, enhance long-term impact of these courses. Such workshops will also provide a good model for further 'train-the-trainers' approaches to the teaching of Human Rights in the given specific region. Very importantly, questions from and within each of the delegations centering on nation's Human Rights promotion 'framework' will develop an interesting framework for the participants to understand as to how best they can further to promote the study of Human Rights; encourage centers of excellence in Human Rights research and advocacy, and develop a relationship between government and Human Rights advocates. Thus, the basic skills developed can be applied not only to Human Rights programmes, but to any form of teaching or training.

5. Role of Human Rights NGOs in Strengthening the Civil Society

In the promotion of democracy through governance training, the issue of Human Rights is of critical importance. To examine the clearly evolving link between Human Rights and democracy as envisaged in the 1993 Vienna Declaration and Plan of Action:

> Democracy, development and respect for Human Rights and fundamental freedoms are interdependent and mutually reinforcing. Democracy is based on the freely expressed will of the people to determine their own political, economic, social and cultural systems and their full participation in all aspects of their lives. In the context of the above, the promotion and protection of Human Rights and fundamental freedoms at the national and international levels should be universal and conducted without conditions attached. The international community should support the strengthening and promoting of democracy, development and respect for Human Rights and fundamental freedoms in the entire world.[1]

Thus, participation is a key to develop the quality of democracy. To unlock the productivity of a country's social capital it is critical to find ways of working with and strengthening civil society. If the Human Rights NGOs continue to advance their endeavors and organize more and more Human Rights training and promotion programs with a focus on Leadership and Advocacy of the representatives of the given civil society members, such a training can result in:

(i) increased understanding of the democratic process in the given States and the role of the members of the Civil Society in that process;

(ii) broader understanding of global forces shaping the given society;

(iii) an understanding of the nation's parliamentary processes;

(iv) increased knowledge of and ability to use the media;

(v) experience of how both government and civil society can develop policies and enter into constructive policy dialogue;

(vi) greater appreciation of the applicability of international Human Rights obligations; and,

(vii) a reinforcement of the interdependence of nations and the importance of friendship and mutual support. At a practical level, these efforts will facilitate the development of the organizational capacity of the NGOs.

6. Subject Matter of the Focus of the Work of the Human Rights NGOs

At the most basic level, knowledge of one's rights is a prerequisite to establishing and defending those rights. But Human Rights education goes beyond these frontiers. In the words of the General Assembly Resolution (49/184) establishing the Decade, Human Rights education is intended to be "a life-long process by which people at all levels of development and in all strata of society learn respect for the dignity of others and the means of ensuring that respect in all societies".[2] The key word is "lifelong": the educational process is not confined to one phase of the human life but continues throughout the existence. It is important that the need to respect the dignity and rights of every individual be understood as early as possible. Children should be the focus of particular attention. Children demonstrate an open mind about the world, for example, they will play and live with children of a different race or color without attaching importance to difference. Prejudice and intolerance are not natural to children. So, it is vital to convey the importance of Human Rights to children in the classroom, in the home, in all of their activities. Learning by example is as important as the civics class: children derive many of their attitudes from parents and friends. Young people have great reserves of energy, creativity and enthusiasm which should be drawn on. Similarly, in the adult life need for Human Rights education is important and pertinent. This takes on a special urgency in societies in conflict and in societies where gross violations have been committed. Whether it is the Democratic Republic of Congo, East Timor or Colombia, the urge to know more about Human Rights and how they can be meaningful in people's lives is very strong since the people, especially those caught up in conflict situations see Human Rights as a basis on which to build a better life.

However, the startling reality is that despite the importance and significance of the Human Rights education, often one gets to realize that the governments have not been putting as much emphasis on the Human Rights education and creation of Human Rights awareness nor have they been directing adequate resources to this area. It may be that governments harbor residual fears that Human Rights are threatening. That would be a very short sighted approach. All the evidence shows that Human Rights, by empowering people, strengthen democracy and social cohesion and greatly benefit societies. Governments have nothing to fear from Human Rights education, quite the reverse. One who is familiar with Human Rights knows that it is a complex subject and growing even more complex by the day. The array of Covenants, conventions, Protocols and other treaties is formidable, the literature on the subject vast. This is another reason why Human Rights education which should translate those documents into people's daily lives plays such an important role.

7. The Level of Operation of the Human Rights Education

Human Rights education operates at different levels. At the local level the objective is to provide individuals with practical knowledge about Human Rights and mechanisms for their protection. At the national and international levels, Human Rights education promotes values, beliefs and attitudes that inspire action in upholding Human Rights. Human Rights education thus encourages all from the individual to the international community to take action to defend Human Rights and prevent abuses.

An area of particular importance is the training of those engaged in careers where Human Rights play a central or especially sensitive role. Judges, lawyers and other members of the legal community constitute this category and the need for Human Rights training geared to their particular duties is clear. This is true also of law enforcement agents, immigration officials, professionals involved in health and social services; local administrators who deal with members of minority communities. Therefore, according to the authors, the role of

NGOs in promoting Human Rights education is vital and crucial in the promotion of human standards and protections and what is required is the will and the focus to do it.

Thus, the findings that flow from the foregoing are:

(i) Human Rights education should form an integral part of democracy promotion activities;

(ii) democracy promotion should be seen as part of the promotion of Human Rights;

(iii) the national projects in this field in each one of the States shall work to strengthen the capacity of institutions and individuals in regional countries to deliver Human Rights training;

(iv) the reports to Human Rights treaty committees should be drafted in part for the purpose of educating domestic readers about the Human Rights situation in their countries; and finally,

(v) projects working on Human Rights education in the region should strive to include civil society representatives in their programs of work.

8. Characteristic Features of Third World/Asian Human Right NGOs[3]

In Asia to a greater extent, several alarming and intolerable trends have started emerging over a period of time namely:

(i) the growing impoverishment, exploitation, and powerlessness of a majority of the poor rural and urban population;

(ii) the growing incidence of malnutrition, hunger, and starvation;

(iii) the growing levels of degradation of the physical environment for the production of food and the meeting of survival needs;

(iv) the worsening of already intolerable conditions of those subject to multiple oppression and exploitation of vulnerable sections such as women, children, and religious or ethnic minorities;

(v) the routine debasement of human beings leading to the very devaluation of human life itself;

(vi) the increasing adoption, by the elites in such countries, of a life-style whose affluence can only be sustained by the pauperization and exploitation of others;

(vii) the growth of fundamentalist trends in religious revivalism, making religion a divisive, rather than a cohesive force;

(viii) the increasing incidence of ethnic violence and cultural genocide;

(ix) the growth of material and moral corruption among the bureaucracy and their virtually total lack of accountability;

(x) the increasingly authoritarian nature of political institutions despite their democratic facade and the growing trend towards governmental (especially executive) lawlessness and abuse of power, authority, and position;

(xi) the growing militarization of developing countries achieved through governmental expenditure on arms at the expense of programs to alleviate poverty; and lastly,

(xii) the imposition of hazards and harms upon powerless workers and communities through indiscriminate industrialization employing hazardous technologies.

In the light of the above referred, it becomes pertinent to closely examine the social, economic, and political climate prevailing in the third world countries in which the Human Rights NGOs, and in particular, Asian NGOs, operate, for a variety of reasons. Some of these organizations to be named are Tibetan Centre for Human Rights and Democracy (TCHRD);[4] The South Asia Human Rights Documentation Centre (SAHRDC);[5] People's Union for Civil Liberties, (PUCL);[6] Manabadhikar Suraksha Mancha, (MASUM);[7] The Ad Hoc Human Rights Tribunal in Indonesia and the Special Panels for Serious Crimes in Timor Leste, JSMP;[8] The Human

Rights Congress for Bangladesh Minorities, (HRCBM);[9] End Child Prostitution, Child Pornography and Trafficking of Children for Sexual Purposes, (ECPAT);[10] Democracy Watch;[11] Chin Human Rights Organization (CHRO);[12] Centre for Human Rights and Democratic Studies, (CEHURDES);[13] Bhutan Women and Children Organization, (BWCO);[14] and importantly, The Asian Legal Resource Centre, (ALRC).[15] Primarily, these Human Rights NGOs have evolved on account of the:

(i) Human Rights scholarship and action which is different and distinct from that of the First World;

(ii) Mixed participation from both the public sector and private sector;

(iii) Outcomes of social action, history and culture;

(iv) Growing perception among international organizations and among northern governments that they have the potential of being more effective agents of development than government agencies, especially when working with or attempting to reach the poor;

(v) Increase in the supply of funding support to the work of Asian NGOs;

(vi) Explosive emergence of NGOs as a major collective actor in development activities. With the capability to assert itself with increasing forcefulness;

(vii) Qualitative and steadily progressive emergence of NGOs and their assertion to play an important role in the policy formulation and international development assistance processes;

(viii) Steady increase in the emergence of the Peoples Organizations, which have become internally more sophisticated, better organized, more aware of their power, and thus have increased their mobilization capabilities; and finally,

(ix) Emergence than to an explicit Human Rights agenda, rather to activities involving the promotion, assertion, and protection of Human Rights.

Thus and while the Human Rights movement in Asia has emerged in response to the above referred intolerable trends and conditions it has also lead to the emergence of three distinct strands within the Asian Human Rights movement namely:

(a) *Grassroot Human Rights NGOs*: which are operating at grassroot level in order to mobilize local communities for protracted political efforts as a part of struggle against the prevailing, authoritarian political regime;

(b) *Campaign-centric Human Rights NGOs*: which are involving in the delivery of educational activities in response to the ineffective government programs regarding the delivery of basic services so as to develop the communities' capacities to meet their own needs in the future by asserting the entitlement of local impoverished communities to resources from the State to meet such needs; and,

(c) *The human right NGOs*: which are disillusioned with the results and the direction of the development model adopted by the country and are deeply concerned about the national development projects and developmental decisions of the government authorities and are seeking their accountability by asserting the rights of indigenous people and other poor communities displaced by development projects of the State.

Interestingly, all these Human Rights NGOs look towards 'Human Rights' as a means to:

(i) *Empowerment:* It is increasingly felt that Human Rights can play a significant role in the empowerment of the impoverished. The oppressed can become more self-reliant through an understanding of their rights. Indeed, the right to organize and rights of association are vital to impoverished groups seeking to mobilize and organize themselves and thus develop countervailing power.

(ii) *Security Accountability:* Human Rights can play a significant role in securing the accountability of those who wield power and control resources essential to the satisfaction of basic human needs. Rights to secure *mandamus* or *prohibition* are important checks on abuse of power. Rights of access to information, rights to a public hearing and freedom of speech and of the press, are crucial in checking governmental lawlessness and abuse of discretion or powers by bureaucratic and government officials.

(iii) *Participation:* Human Rights have an important role to play in combating exclusion as well as in asserting the right to participate in key decisions affecting resource allocation or relating to technology choice.

(iv) *Assert Values:* Human Rights are also being increasingly viewed as a means to express and reinforce social values and ethical principles which should underlie the much needed restructuring of social orders.

9. Forces behind the Asian Human Rights Organizations

In order to understand Human Rights activism as it has evolved in Asia and to underpin the interface between this growth and the contribution of the NGOs, one needs to take a closer look at the people involved in these organizations. Three main categories have been involved: intellectuals, professionals, and activists. Prominent among the professionals have been members of the legal elite—leaders of the legal profession, former members of the judiciary and prominent legal academics. Involvement of these people has been of a more conventional kind, which included on their part, efforts in providing legal services and legal representation to indigents, or to those whose civil and political rights have been violated, or in "test cases" and "public interest litigation". Their approach has been mainly to work within the existing law, using existing legal processes to enforce Human Rights or to help bring about incremental development of the content of specific Human Rights. Their approach has been the conventional liberal approach to Human Rights which presumes that compliance with rights is the societal norm and rights enforcement is only necessary in a few deviant cases.

However, in most of the Third World societies, this presumption has not held to be true, and an alternative breed of Human Rights activist started emerging so as to arouse the public awareness of gross and widespread violations of Human Rights (especially, but not exclusively, economic, social and cultural rights) and seeking assertion of those rights through both legal and extra-legal methods, including protest and direct action. This category of NGOs would not be contented with the working within the existing legal order. Rather, they aim at helping reforms as a part of a process of securing social change and structural transformations. The influence of these Human Rights organizations and activists upon the professionals and intellectuals in the society has led to their gradual reorientation and professional resocialization. Consequently, the professionals and intellectuals in Asia have attempted to reach out to Human Rights activists through a variety of intellectual and professional movements of which two specific movements will deserve a specific mention and enunciation.

9.1. The Alternative Movement

This has challenged the "development models" adopted by the Third World countries in general and Asian countries in particular, by emphasizing on the modernization, industrialization, economic growth, and integration into the global capitalist system. This movement had, over a period of time, stimulated Human Rights activism in support of the victims (e.g., indigenous people, displaced people) of development policies and projects. It has also stimulated activism centered round formulation and implementation of policies and programs of "alternative development", that are built upon concepts of community mobilization and organization, participation, self-reliance, and the adoption of alternatives to western consumer-oriented life-styles. This movement has brought out a variety of interdisciplinary perspectives and skills into Human Rights thought and activism in Asia and a fresh "alternative" set of values. It has helped to foster the perception that law is too serious matter to be left entirely to lawyers; for, the issue of Human Rights is not merely a legal one but a potent political and social issue. Further, it has also helped the stimulation of the process of deprofessionalization of law through "bare-foot lawyers" and "community dispute-settlement mechanisms". By far the greatest impact of an intellectual movement on Human Rights in Asia has been the movement towards participatory action research. The concept of participatory action research (PAR) originated in Latin America but soon gained acceptance in Asia. PAR emphasizes the importance of participatory development of knowledge, action strategies and Human Rights through close interaction with grassroots communities. PAR has fundamentally changed Human Rights thinking and activism in Asia by broadening the base of Human Rights actors to include those who are victims of Human Rights violations.[16]

9.2. The Alternative Law Movement

This movement has called attention to deep-rooted pathologies that exist in law and the legal profession in most Asian countries. The movement has been iconoclastic by debunking legal sacred cows and myths and by calling attention to the wide gap that exists between the law on the books and the law in action, i.e. between law and justice. Thus, the movement has worked towards securing fundamental changes in the legal system to make it more accessible, more indigenous, more just (by fostering notions of redistributive justice) and more supportive of social change.[17]

Human Rights activists in Asia have also increasingly reached out to intellectuals and professionals as a result of a number of action strategies they have adopted. Originally, most social activists adopted an attitude of "legal nihilism": the less contact with law and lawyers, the better. But they found themselves being dragged into contact with the legal system particularly the criminal justice system as their work gathered momentum. They soon began to shed such an attitude. Contacts between activists, intellectuals and professionals constantly increased within the context of specific action strategies which necessitated new forms of association and organization namely (i) *Campaigns* such as the Infant Formula Campaign; (ii) *Coalitions* such as the International Coalition for Justice in Bhopal; (iii) *Solidarity and Protest Organizations* such as Greenpeace; (iv) *Lobby Groups* such as the Asian Pacific Forum for Women, Law, and Development; (v) *Regional Networks* such as the Asian Regional Council on Human Rights; (vi) *Social Movements* such as the consumer movement, the women's movement, and the environmental movement etc.

To sum up, intellectual movements, social movements, pragmatic-action strategies and campaigns have brought the main Human Rights actors in Asia namely victims, activists, intellectuals, and professions together in a variety of situations of interaction. As a result, Human Rights organizations in Asia have become more interdisciplinary in nature and more broad-based in composition. They have also become harder to identify and define. A few Asian NGOs wear the label of Human Rights.

But the vast majority of Asian NGOs, concerned primarily with education, or development, or delivery of support and services, have adopted Human Rights into their agendas and programs of action. A broad definition of Human Rights organizations in Asia would have to include all these "non-specialist" NGOs which are undertaking significant Human Rights activities.

10. Typologies of Asian Human Rights NGOs

It would not be possible, desirable, or sensible to attempt to construct a single, comprehensive, all-encompassing typology of Asian Human Rights organizations. Rather, one might suggest the many ways that loose typologies might be drawn.

10.1. Governmental/non-governmental/intergovernmental

While the majority of Human Rights organizations in Asia are non-governmental, there has been the recent trend (especially in countries like the Philippines, which are undergoing a process of re-democratization) to establish governmental Human Rights commissions.

10.2. International/regional/national/local

In Asia, where the governments have firmly rejected any regional intergovernmental Human Rights organizations, a number of regional non-governmental organizations have sprung up.

10.3. Membership

In Asia, a distinction is usually drawn between people-based organizations (PBOs) and participatory organizations of the rural poor (PORPs) on the one hand, which are primary-level organizations (e.g. of small farmers, fisherfolk), and support groups which render services to PBOs and which are referred to as secondary-level organizations.

Human Rights organizations may also be classified on the basis of membership drawn on professional lines.

10.4. Victim-group served

While certain Human Rights organizations serve only single target groups, e.g., women, children, indigenous people certain others serve a variety of victim groups.

10.5. Functions

Distinctions are being made between Human Rights organizations performing mobilizational roles, advocacy roles, or service-providing roles. Thus, terms such as social action group; support or service organization; solidarity group; legal resource group; representational or advocacy group; documentation centre; communications or clearing-house centre; training centre; networking or coordination centre; forum; coalition; or campaign, are used to describe a range of Human Rights organizations in Asia. Most of them tend to be multifunctional or, at least, bi-functional.

10.6. Category of Human Rights specialization

This, essentially Western categorization of groups focusing on civil and political rights, and those focusing on economic, social, and cultural rights, is not much used in Asia, where organizations tend to focus on both categories of rights. However, because of the gravity of the problem in some countries, Human Rights organizations have emerged focusing on particular sets of rights such as those relating to ethnicity.

11. Roles and Functions of Asian Human Rights Organizations[18]

Many Asian Human Rights organizations did not start as explicit Human Rights organizations at all. Rather by their nature of development they were essentially associated with activities like emergency aid; philanthropic; developmental; or environmental concerns. This fact is often reflected in the roles and functions they would play upon in their address of a specifically Human Rights-oriented agenda. While the Asian Human Rights organizations are not a mirror image of their First World counterparts, it is possible to study them in the following terms of the conventional roles of Human Rights activism.

11.1. Promotion

Many Asian Human Rights organizations embarked on conventional typical Human Rights promotion activities employing locally appropriate devices such as comic books, folk theatre, or folk music, poster competitions, etc. However and more often, the promotional work on their part would form an inherent component of a rights awareness program, i.e. fostering rights assertiveness as a means towards mobilization, and organization for direct action.

11.2. Standard setting

Asian Human Rights organizations have increasingly recognized the importance of participating in standard-setting work, both at the international level (e.g., in relation to the right to development, or the Convention on the Rights of the Child) as well as at the national level (e.g., in the Philippines, to develop comprehensive national codes on agrarian reform and on fisheries' resources).

11.3. Monitoring

Asian Human Rights groups have been actively monitoring implementation of national legislation (e.g., dealing with women's rights and child labor in India) and are beginning to be concerned with international Human Rights law (e.g., by bringing complaints before the Sub-Commission on Rights of Minorities and Indigenous People).

11.4. Enforcement

Asian Human Rights Groups have made impressive strides in assisting enforcement of rights through the courts (e.g., in India through social action litigation) or through direct action (e.g., by adoption of meta-legal tactics in the Philippines).

11.5. Lobbying for !aw reform

On account of the continued efforts of the Human Rights activist groups, especially in countries like the Philippines and Nepal, parliamentary, legislative processes have been restored after a long lapse of time.

In addition to these conventional roles, Human Rights organizations in the Third World have also played unique roles which result from their Human Rights activism originating in community and victim-group mobilization and organization.

11.6. Creation of grassroots organizations and their organizational development

They have helped organize people to make better use of their own local productive resources, to create new resources and services, to promote equity and alleviate poverty, to influence government actions towards the same objectives and to establish new institutional frameworks that will durably sustain humane people-powered development.

11.7 Developing the capacity for strengthen community-based resource management

With an emphasis on participation, equality and equity the Human Rights organizations working in neglected rural areas have helped in setting up of local production-related organizations such as water-user societies, pastoral-grazing associations, credit, production or consumer cooperatives, food-processing cooperatives, farm equipment purchase or lease associations, tree grower associations, fisherman cooperatives, etc. At first glance, these activities seem far away from the focus of Human Rights concerns. However, it is these kinds of organizations which have proved to be the critical instruments, not only for participatory local development but also for grassroots realization of Human Rights. At times, these organizations have averted serious denials of Human Rights which would have resulted had their efforts not prevented ecological degradation imperiling the very survival of the most depressed sections of the local community.

11.8. Residuary

In addition to the above referred two important aspects, the Human Rights organizations also contributed in:

(i) Liaising as intermediaries between local government and community organizations;

(ii) Raising of funding and directing the same towards the local community organizations in necessary circumstances;

(iii) Creating the means for

(a) community organizing,

(b) community self-defense,

(c) assertion of community rights,

(d) rising of community awareness and expectations, and

(e) protecting the activists against reprisals from highhanded administrators. Thus, Human Rights organizations in Asia have had to constantly undergo a process of self-development.

12. Specific Asian Experiences in the Protection and Promotion of Human Rights[19]

Besides the abstract or conceptual generalizations in the context of promotion of Human Rights awareness, it is important to look into and examine the vast variety and wide range of activities with which the Asian Human Rights NGOs are deeply associated with. This demonstrates how in their own unique and imaginative ways the Asian NGOs have been posed with grave, often virtually insurmountable problems in the field of creation of awareness and promotion of Human Rights. Hence, the authors, at this stage, present the following specific kinds of activities around which the roles of these NGOs were centered around.

12.1. Monitoring and documenting Human Rights violations

Asian NGOs such as Lawasia, and the Asian Human Rights Commission, conducted the conventional "fact-finding missions" either entirely on their own or in partnership with other international Human Rights organizations such as the International Commission of Jurists, e.g. on the Philippines, Sri Lanka, Singapore, Malaysia, Burma, China, etc. In May 2005, an informal South Asian peoples-to-peoples initiative was launched in the form of a SAARC Jurists Mission on Bhutan wherein the idea was to involve the retired Supreme Court Justices from the SAARC countries to convene *ad hoc* missions as appropriate, for purposes of fact-finding as well as to study and appraise the laws, constitutions, and jurisprudence in the countries of the SAARC region in terms of their conformity with international Human Rights principles and standards. Similarly, a unique and pioneering fact-finding mission was undertaken several years ago in the Philippines focusing on "internally displaced persons", especially in the Cordilleras and in the South.

Several years ago, Human Rights NGOs in Switzerland and the Philippines worked together and convinced MIGROS, the giant European Super-Market chain (which was a significant importer of pineapples grown on large agribusiness plantations in the Philippines) to send a Human Rights fact-finding mission to investigate Human Rights abuses on the plantations which were supplying them the fruit. Respected international Human Rights scholar and activist, Virginia Leary (who has also undertaken reports in the Philippines and Sri Lanka for the International Commission of Jurists), was a special advisor to the mission on workers rights. The mission, after discussions and negotiations, was also to furnish a "no nonsense" report and several protective measures were introduced on the plantations as a result. Documentation of Human Rights violations is taking place all over Asia—using both the HURIDOCS standard format as well as other formal methods. Groups (like INFORM in Sri Lanka) have sprung up specializing in Human Rights documentation. A variety of national level magazines, bulletins, reports, and information sheets are also being produced locally within Asia. For example, the bi-monthly INSEC Bulletin published from Nepal (and now into its second year) focuses on Human Rights under especially difficult circumstances, e.g., Burma. Such "tough case" country situations as Burma, Sri Lanka, and Nepal (especially earlier) have also become the focus of Thai Human Rights groups working together to develop better and more up-to-date information on these countries as well. Over the last year an Asian Human Rights Documentation Centre has been created in Taipei, and next year one will be established in Osaka. Fax machines and mobile telephones have been used most effectively to disseminate Human Rights information, e.g., in Nepal and in Thailand during democracy struggles.

12.2. Asian urgent actions: Disseminating and acting on Human Rights information

Hot Line and various National Commissions on Justice and Peace put forward, regularly, a steady stream of "urgent action appeals". National Human Rights organizations (like the Bangladesh Human Rights Commission and Lawyers for Human Rights and Development in Sri Lanka) release reports on national situations of Human Rights violations which can form the basis of regional Asian and international campaigns. FLAG's reports on attacks on Human Rights lawyers in the Philippines proved tellingly effective. Thai Human Rights NGOs have repeatedly come together to form Friends of Burma, Friends of Sri Lanka, and Thai solidarity action campaigns. The international NGO FIAN (Food Information Action Network) now has a significant presence in certain Asian countries and has been releasing "urgent action appeals" regarding Human Rights situations in Asian countries which displace people, threaten their food security, and generally violate economic, social, and cultural rights. The Pastoral Letters in the Philippines have proved a unique and effective way of disseminating information and issuing calls to action. At the Asia-Pacific NGO Dialogue held in Fiji earlier this year, an interesting follow-up action was adopted. A State of Human Rights Report will be prepared on each of three countries: Japan, the United States, and Australia. These reports will be prepared jointly by NGOs in those countries and by NGOs in Asia-Pacific countries focusing on Human Rights abuses within those three countries as well as Human Rights abuses which emanate from those countries and result in violations in the countries of the Asia-Pacific Region. These reports would then form the basis of regional action campaigns.

12.3. Learning about Human Rights by listening

Increasingly, NGOs in Asia are giving importance to listening to the voices of victims of Human Rights abuses. Fisherfolk from eleven Asian Countries, for example, came together at Songkla, Thailand, earlier this year and presented their situations, demands and priorities expressed in Human Rights terms. Later, in several Asian countries, a series of Forums of the Forgotten People (i.e., people forgotten by the Human Rights movements in their own countries) were convened in India (of child workers), Nepal (of women), Thailand (of community forest dwellers), and in the Philippines (of subsistence fisher folk). A project to compile a publication entitled Documenting Peoples Struggles for Justice in Development in Asia was undertaken. This publication, compiled various Declarations of peoples' organizations, specific groups in struggles, and victims' voices in respect of Human Rights, abuses that resulted from development projects and activities in Asia. ARENA (a Hong Kong based NGO) published a series of country studies entitled "State of the Asian Peoples Report". Emphasis was placed on South—South sharing among peoples organizations (e.g., fisher folk, peasants, workers) and among Asian Human Rights NGOs (e.g., working on women's rights issues organized by the Asia Pacific Forum on Women, Law and Development). In Bogota, Colombia, the first ever South—South Sharing Workshop was held, bringing together representatives from six Asian Human Rights and alternative law NGOs, with four of their African counterparts and some 20 representatives from Latin America, Central America, and the Caribbean. As a result, some of the materials being produced by Asian NGOs are now being published in Spanish in Latin America, and new, Third World solidarity links forged.

12.4. Participating in standard-setting

Asian NGOs have tried, albeit within severe limitations of resources and time, to participate in UN level standard-setting efforts on the rights of the child, rights of indigenous peoples, and presently on rights of minorities. An Asian NGO consultation submitted, through the International Commission of Jurists, its own Declaration on the Right to Development to the UN Working Group that was preparing the draft of the UN General Assembly resolution at the time. Two other ongoing Asian initiatives bear mention. ACFOD (the Asian Cultural Forum on Development) undertook an effort to produce an Asian Peoples Code of Conduct on Multinationals, which will focus, not on the conduct of the multinationals, but on the conduct of Asian governments who, in dealing with multinationals, must not default in their obligation to preserve and protect the Human Rights of their own peoples, especially workers. Secondly, an Asian initiative launched at the last two sessions of TOES (The Other Economic Summit) involves the formulation of "peoples conditions in development lending". These conditions, drawn from existing international law, will restate the protective measures which experience has shown must be taken in respect of typical development projects (e.g., large-scale infrastructure building, tourism promotion) to protect the Human Rights of what the World Bank has euphemistically come to describe as PAPs (project-affected peoples) in "risk-prone projects". In the Philippines, India, and elsewhere, a special focus has been on standard-settle efforts at the national level through articulation and lobbying for people-initiated law reform (e.g., of squatter rights, the fishery code, and the comprehensive agrarian reform program in the Philippines). In India, law students have been drawn upon to work with local groups and communities in the generation of such people-initiated law reform measures.

12.5. Action campaigns

These have focused on a single (often corporate) target group, e.g., Nestles, Union Carbide, Reebok, or on specific issues, e.g., tropical timber, carpets using harmful child labor, etc. One Bangladesh NGO (CARITAS) has declared its entire office grounds to be a "tobacco free-zone!" These action campaigns involve a number of methods of direct action such as rallies, marches, boycotts, etc.

12.6. Solidarity campaigns

These have tended to focus on the grave situation in a single country, e.g., the Philippines (Hindi ka nagiisa), Nepal, Burma, East Timor, and Bhutan, and mobilize collective solidarity actions by Human Rights groups in several Asian countries.

12.7. Regional Asian Human Rights campaigns[20]

These kinds of campaigns have been of more recent origin and seek: (a) to articulate an Asian voice and position on Human Rights issues, e.g., women's rights are Human Rights and the signature campaign on violence against women (of APFWLD), and the signature campaign launched recently by Chandra Muzzafar at a meeting of Asian Human Rights NGOs in Tokyo on the inter-relatedness of economic, social, and cultural rights and civil and political rights; (b) to *participate* in an organized Asian manner in the UN World Conference on Human Rights and in other similar UN World Conferences. At a regional South Asian level, there is an attempt, also, to develop a People's SAARC as a parallel to the inter-governmental SAARC.

12.8. Campaigns against multinational corporations

Asian NGOs are joining with their counterparts in the West (e.g., Korean women workers abandoned by the PICCO corporation) to demand the accountability of the multinational corporation through litigation (against PICCO; and thus far, unsuccessfully, against Union Carbide); or through submissions and interventions at the annual stockholders meetings of such corporations. The Inter-Faith Center on Corporate Responsibility and other like-minded NGOs in the US are working towards developing a Directory for Sound Investments in Corporations as a mechanism for improving the social responsibility of large corporations.

12.9. *People's tribunals*

Given the inadequacy of international (and often national) judicial fora, Asian NGOs are increasingly turning to "people's tribunals" invoking international bodies like the Permanent People's Tribunal (on Bhopal and other hazardous industrialization) and the International River Waters Tribunal (e.g., on Narmada and the Bangladesh Flood Control Plan). An *ad hoc* people's tribunal was convened in Bangkok (during the meeting there last year of the IMF and World Bank Governors) at which Thai victims of Thai development activity wished to tell their story. This has had to a wider call for the creation of an Asia-Pacific People's Tribunal on Justice in Development. The need for such a forum through which public awareness can be raised by listening to the voices of victims, is one being increasingly reiterated in Asia and the Pacific.

13. Regional Task Forces

Especially in South Asia, there has been recent but growing recognition of the need for regional NGO task forces to work on Human Rights problems which are typical of the region such as the South Asian Judiciary Task Force (to help safeguard judicial independence, autonomy, accountability, and Human Rights activism) and the South-Asian Election Monitoring Group (that has been forged by the International Centre for Ethnic Studies, Sri Lanka). A second type of South Asian NGO Task Force focuses on Human Rights problems which do not respect country boundaries, e.g., trafficking in women and migrant workers.

13.1. *Asian Human Rights NGO task force on migrant workers*

Several Asian countries have large-scale "out migration" of workers (often women) to other Asian countries, the Middle East, and Europe. Although the country benefits from (and therefore encourages) the income repatriated by its workers, they rarely intervene when workers face appalling conditions of near slavery, general exploitation, or harassment. There is a need for improved controls on recruitment, better worker education programs, and programs for immediate relief of distressed workers. At the receiving country level there is a need to press for enforcement of national laws and international Human Rights standards. ACFOD would assemble a task force comprising NGO representatives from both countries which are sending, and countries which are receiving, migrant workers. Such a commission would formulate specific policies and actions to deal with the needs outlined above. Where appropriate, it would also undertake fact-finding missions regarding specific situations of alleged violations and malpractices.

13.2. Asian Human Rights NGO task force on the trafficking of women and children

A flourishing trade in babies exists in and between several Asian countries. The situation is similar regarding the trafficking in women. ACFOD would convene an Asian Task Force of NGOs (similar in concept to the one on migrant workers) which would undertake several tasks namely (i) Fact finding and dissemination of reports; (ii) Formulation and lobbying for policy and legal measures to combat trafficking; (iii) Creation of more sustained links between NGOs in the various Asian countries through which the trafficking or transit occurs; (iv) Promoting greater public awareness and media exposure of the issues; and, (v) Establishing Human Rights commissions. Several Asian countries are experimenting with the media of national, governmental Human Rights commissions. In the Philippines, such a commission has already existed for a long enough period of time to enable a careful evaluation to be undertaken thereof. In India (largely in response to critical reports on the Human Rights situation in India released by international Human Rights NGOs) and in Nepal, there are plans for establishment of such commissions, and Human Rights NGOs' attitudes in such countries range from ambivalence to hostility towards such plans. For example, Pakistan has successfully experimented with a non-governmental Human Rights commission, and that seems to be the case with Bangladesh as well. Several years ago, a regional, non-governmental Asian Human Rights Commission was established with mixed, but hopefully optimistic prospects of success. Over the last year, there have been calls in several "people's forums" and Asia-Pacific NGO meetings for the establishment of an Asia-Pacific People's Commission on Justice in Development.

14. Human Rights Education[21]

There has been growing recognition among Asian NGOs of the importance of grassroots Human Rights education for empowerment and thereby the protection and promotion of Human Rights. Two regional initiatives are especially significant: the movement for a Nuclear Free and Independent Pacific, and the recently established Asia-Pacific Regional Resource Centre on Human Rights Education. First of all, at the national level, there has been produced a very rich assortment of materials for Human Rights education which includes posters (e.g., on gender justice); games (e.g., on children's rights); comics; T-shirts (e.g., proclaiming "Arrest without warrant is illegal"); bumper stickers (e.g., proclaiming "Exxon spills, Carbide kills"); calendars (to ensure that Human Rights are remembered all year round and not just on December 10); buttons, etc. There have been poster and essay competitions for children; music; art and film festivals; street theater; traditional dance and drama festivals; and now a rapidly growing collection of video materials.

The power of popular, non-formal Human Rights education has increasingly been recognized in Asia, and so, too, has the importance of Human Rights education. In South Asia, the special role that journalists (especially those publishing in the local vernacular languages) can play has led to serious efforts at forming a South Asian Forum of Journalists on Human Rights. Similarly, in South Asia, the special role that law students can play prompted the recent convening in Sri Lanka of the first-ever South Asian Law Student Debating Competition on "Justice, Equity and Democracy". In Nepal, in particular, after the success of the mass-based people's movement for democracy, highly successful "constitutional literacy", "election literacy", and "rural Human Rights awareness" programs have been conducted. The training of Human Rights educators for grassroots popular education has also received much attention in Asia.

The Asian NGO Task Force has completed two highly successful Asia level training programs for "the middle-level leadership" of Asian NGOs. Recently, in Dhaka, the first-ever South Asian Training of Trainers in Human Rights education was successfully conducted by the South Asian Forum for Human Rights (SAFHR). Similarly, at national levels, there have been a number of deep Human Rights training programs conducted for women (in India and Bangladesh, for example), and for workers (in the Philippines), etc. The Alternative Law School of the Philippines regularly conducts "courses" or specialized subjects and issues for NGO and PO representatives. Thus, a great deal is going on in Asia in the field of Human Rights education for empowerment.

15. Resurgence of Constitutionalism

Especially in South Asia, but also in Kampuchea, Thailand, and, to a certain extent, the Philippines, Human Rights NGOs have expressed a new interest in reconstructing or renovating "constitutional and legal orders" as an essential first task for the rebuilding of civil society; the protection and realization of Human Rights; and the establishment of genuine representative and participatory democracy. Especially in South Asia, NGOs are striving to establish particularly processes to achieve the task so that "constitutions" are not just bestowed by legal experts but emerge from truly participatory consensus. So that "constitutions" are not just dry words and dry ink on paper but are truly a "social compact" that lives in the hearts and minds of its people.

16. Asian Peoples Forums, Congresses and Happenings

For solidarity as well as other purposes, Asian POs and NGOs are increasingly finding the need to come together in large numbers, not only nationally (as in the andolans and padayatras in India), but at a regional Asia-Pacific level. The month-long events that took place in Japan (culminating in Minamata in 1990) under the People's Plan for the 21st Century; the highly effective People's Forum that was held in

Bangkok in 1991 during the IMF/World Bank Governors' Meeting; the Second Session of the People's Plan for the 21st Century; and the International Congress on Democratic Alternative held in Kathmandu in April 1993—all represent mass gatherings of the peoples of Asia, coming from all walks of life, to find new strength from one another in their quest for a just, participator, and sustainable future. The above highly selective review of the activities of Human Rights NGOs in Asia is bound to be woefully inadequate. So rich, diverse, innovative, and ever-changing are the roles and activities of Asian NGOs in the protection and promotion of Human Rights. Of course, there is no room for complacency and little room for romanticized, Pollyanna optimism. Vast remains yet to be achieved for the realization of all Human Rights of all peoples of Asia. But if it remains unachieved it will not be for want of trying on the part of Asian NGOs and POs.

17. Challenges before the Asian NGOs[22]

(i) In certain instances, Human Rights activism has proved to be counterproductive. For example, in India the legal rights movements in support of child labor, female labor, and bonded labor resulted in the enactment of beneficial legislations. However, the rights created by such legislations could be enjoyed by only a few. Female laborers ended up getting pushed into the unorganized, informal sector. While the Child labor has considerably decreased in industries unregulated by child welfare law, such as match factories and fireworks' factories, they became exposed to new hazards and bonded labor became free only in name.

(ii) In other instances, Human Rights activism has proved ineffective. Much of the social-action litigation undertaken in India (e.g., that relating to bonded labor and to the rights of those pending trial) has resulted in victory. But this victory has proved pyrrhic. Remedies and reliefs ordered by the Court have proved to be illusory since those ordered by the Court to provide such relief have ignored the decree of the Court. The Supreme Court, lacking an effective enforcement mechanism, has stood by powerless, watching its decrees being flouted with impunity. Human Rights organizations, thus, have a vital role to play in ensuring that hard-won victories in Court result in more than cosmetic changes and illusory remedies. Balancing the rights of collective entities and groups over those of individuals has also created cruel dilemmas for Human Rights activists.

(iii) The relationship between ethnicity and survival struggles can also pose cruel dilemmas for Human Rights activists. Curtailment of the rights of a tribal minority for the greater good of all (e.g., by displacing a tribal community to build a multipurpose dam) has led to virtual cultural genocide. In times of economic hardship for all, defense of the rights of a minority becomes a most unpopular task. Yet, lasting relationship of trust between ethnic groups can perhaps only be forged through the active defense of the rights of the minority in times of such crisis. In some instances, a significant increase in the level of Human Rights activism has resulted, in the short term, in a closure of the political in times of such crisis.

(iv) Asian NGOs also continue to face extremely perplexing challenges in their relationship with State. On the one hand, there is a real need to devolve power from the State to people because without such devolution, accountability becomes minimal and participation virtually nonexistent. However, on the other hand, there is a need for a strong state to protect its people from multinational corporations and other increasingly monolithic forces of global trans-national power. Yet a strong nation state calls for forced integration of ethnic and other minority groups, and all too often the insecurity of a government causes it to project a threat to the security of State and results in the invocation of

> emergency powers and suspension of the rights of its peoples. Asian NGOs are increasingly aware of the dilemmas and challenges they face and they are seeking new ways of coming together to surmount the obstacles they face. They are moving from networking to strategic linkages and solidarity actions. Indeed, the`challenge for Asian Human Rights NGOs and the newly emergent grassroots movements of Human Rights activism in Asia lies precisely in the satisfactory resolution of dilemmas such as those posed above. It is a challenge that they can well rise up to.

At the end, Asian Human Rights organizations have brought fresh approaches, both theoretical and strategic, to Human Rights activism. On the theoretical plane they have focused attention not only on Human Rights but also on inhuman wrongs; not only on Human Rights but also on the right to be human. They have sought to address Human Rights violations resulting both from government lawlessness and Human Rights violations in the domain of civil society. They have often had to wage their struggles in situations where vindication of rights is essential for continued survival. Yet they have struggled to establish not only the right to survive but also the right to survive with dignity and equality. They have grappled with the violence, both of Human Rights violators and as the violence out of which Human Rights was born. They have worked to generate not only a jurisprudence of rights but also to generate truth, indignation, and shame regarding Human Rights violations. They are constantly struggling to keep Human Rights truly human for all. Despite all the difficulties they can expect to encounter in the changed global realities of a "New World Order" one thing is certain: Asian Human Rights NGOs and POs will not go gently into the night but will continue to rage, and rage "against the dying of the light".

Notes

1. The 1993 Vienna Declaration and Plan of Action, para 8, http://www.unhchr.ch/huridocda/huridoca.nsf/(Symbol)/A.CONF.157.23.En, (last visited on 2nd July 2007).
2. http://www.un-documents.net/a49r184.htm, (last visited on 5th July 2007).
3. http://www.hrdc.net/sahrdc/hrfchr58/Issue5.htm, (last visited on 10th July 2007).
4. TCHRD is the first Tibetan non-governmental Human Rights organization that had been established in exile in India. Having been founded in 1996, TCHRD is registered as an NGO under Section 2 of the Indian Societies Registration Act, 1860 and is based in Dharamsala, North India. Its mission includes (i) Promotion and protection of Human Rights of the Tibetan people in Tibet; and, (ii) Educating the exile Tibetan community on Human Rights principles and democratic concepts. To this end, TCHRD (a) conducts regular, systematic investigations of Human Rights situation in Tibet; (b) monitors Human Rights policies of the People's Republic of China (PRC); (c) On issues of Human Rights concerns that confront Tibetans inside Tibet, every year brings out an annual report, thematic reports, profiles of former political prisoners, monthly newsletters, and press releases and news briefs; (d) organizes workshops, talk series, public discussions and campaigns to engender a culture of Human Rights and democracy within the exile Tibetan community; (e) TCHRD staff visits schools, institutions and settlements to give talks on Human Rights and democracy; (f) launches various public campaign activities and also organizes in-depth awareness programs to broaden their awareness and support; (g) regularly attends the UN Commission on Human Rights as well as other regional, national and international conferences in order to highlight Human Rights situation in Tibet and to lobby and to network on the promotion and protection of Human Rights in Tibet; and (h) conducts campaigns of international scope such as letter writing and signature appeals, and submits memoranda to visiting delegations and media on actual Human Rights condition in Tibet.
5. The South Asia Human Rights Documentation Centre (SAHRDC) is a network of individuals across the region which seeks to investigate, document and disseminate information about Human Rights treaties and conventions, Human Rights education, refugees, media freedom, prison reforms, political imprisonment, torture, summary executions, disappearances and other cruel, inhuman or degrading treatment. SAHRDC has Special

Consultative Status with the Economic and Social Council of the United Nations. Its office is based in New Delhi. The core volunteers help on request on a specific issue (i.e. lawyers, medical practitioners, journalists, computer programmers and other resource persons). SAHRDC collects information on Human Rights, specifically on violation of civil and political rights in relation to Human Rights education; arrest, detention and disappearances; refugees and asylum; torture, capital punishment and other cruel, inhuman or degrading treatment; freedom of the media; custodial deaths; extrajudicial killings. The type or form of information collated includes international instruments, national legislation, court documents, affidavits, data questionnaires, reports, leaflets, letters, and clippings from media reports and books. While the information sources are individuals, Human Rights activists and groups, lawyers, journalists, media and national and international organizations, as the information reaches the office, it is classified into thematic and geographic areas which are given internally developed call numbers, and filed accordingly. Before the information goes into the manual files, it is recorded on the computer worksheets (CDS/ISIS) according to the standard formats, which eventually enables us to retrieve it whenever we want with the help of key words. Whenever it is necessary as a solidarity measure, SAHRDC sends Action Alerts requesting the national and international Human Rights community to appeal to governments in South Asia to stop violation of Human Rights in their countries. SAHRDC's Executive Director is on the board of the Geneva based International Service for Human Rights (ISHR). SAHRDC is a part of the Geneva based SOS Torture Network. It is also the South Asian Representative on the Bangkok based Asia-Pacific Human Rights NGOs Facilitating Team. SAHRDC is also represented on the International Editorial Board of the Ottawa based Human Rights Tribune, on the Robert F Kennedy Memorial Human Rights Award and the International Board of the International Service for Human Rights, Geneva. SAHRDC is also consulted on occasion by the diplomatic missions of the Australia, Austria, Belgium, Canada, Croatia, Czech Republic, Denmark, Finland, Germany, Italy, Ireland, Netherlands, New Zealand, Norway, Slovak Republic, Sweden, Switzerland, United States of America, United Kingdom, and the Mission of the European Union in India. It has been received by senior officials of the South Asia Department in the Dutch Foreign Ministry in the Hague, the South Asia and Human Rights Division of the Danish Foreign Ministry in Copenhagen, the Ministry of Foreign Affairs and the Ministry of Home Affairs of his Majesty's Government of Nepal, the Human Rights Department in the Swiss Foreign Ministry in Berne, the Human Rights and South Asia Department at the US State Department in Washington, the South Asia Departments of the Foreign and Commonwealth Office in London and the Law Minister in Bangladesh. The SAHRDC is also consulted by the New Delhi office of the International Committee of the Red Cross (ICRC) and has been received by the Delegate General for Asia of the ICRC in Geneva. SAHRDC interacts with the United Nations Human Rights machinery on a regular basis.

6. Veteran leader Jaya Prakash Narayan (JP) founded the People's Union for Civil Liberties and Democratic Rights (PUCLDR), in 1976 with a view to make it as an organization free from political ideologies, so that people belonging to various political parties may come together on one platform for the defense of Civil Liberties and Human Rights. The Janata Party, formed with blessings of JP, came to power. A very large number of people who had worked with him assumed power at the centre and an impression started floating that now the liberties of the people were secure. The dynamic element in the PUCLDR subsided. Jaya Prakash Narayan died on October 8, 1979, after a prolonged kidney problem. The year 1980 saw the return of Indira Gandhi to power. A consensus emerged among civil liberties activists and various political parties that such an organization should remain non-partisan. The organization was re-christened as the People's Union for Civil Liberties (PUCL). The founding conference, held in November 1980, drafted and adopted the Constitution of the PUCL and made it a membership based organization, aiming to have branches all over the country. The Constitution laid down that the members of a political party will not have the right to hold any office if they joined the organization; the number of members, belonging to political parties, in the national or state executive committees shall not be more than 50% of the members of the National Council and the National Executive Committee respectively (and also the corresponding bodies at the state and local level). Not more than 10% shall be members of any single political party. This founding conference elected V M Tarkunde as its President and Arun Shourie as the General Secretary. Later, Y P Chhibbar was appointed as Executive Secretary. Those elected as President and General secretary(ies) in the following year(s) were: President: V M Tarkunde (1982 to 1984); Rajni Kothari (1984 to 1986); Rajindar Sachar (1986 to 1995); K G Kannabiran (1995, continuing). General Secretary: Arun Shourie (1982 to 1986); Rajni Kothari (1982 to 1984); Y P Chhibbar (1984, continuing); Dalip Swami (1986 to 1990). V M Tarkunde was named Advisor in 1986. The PUCL (i) publishes a monthly journal, *The PUCL*

Bulletin, in English; (ii) organizes a JP Memorial Lecture on March 23rd every year and in the same function presents its 'Journalism for Human Rights' Award which carries a citation and an award of Rs. 20,000/—to enthuse interest in civil liberties and Human Rights amongst journalists and also to bring to light the dedication and the work of those working in this field; (iii) takes up instances of violations of democratic rights, covering most parts of the country and involving the rights of many sections of society; (iv) conducts investigations, issues statements, distributes leaflets, organizes public meetings, demonstrations and dharnas, and fights legal cases to highlight the violation of people's rights, and to help towards their redress; (v) takes up issues of general importance that affect the rights of people through general campaigns, publications and legal interventions. These include: gender equality; rights of forest-dwellers and forest policy; working class rights; agrarian conflict; caste oppression; deaths, rapes and torture in police custody; and undemocratic legislation, in particular the various incarnations of the 'terrorist act' (TADA and POTA) etc.; (vi) engages actively in legal defense of civil liberties and democratic rights. It has taken up hundreds of cases in the last two decades, including many of constitutional importance, such as the Asiad labor petition which opened the doors to public interest litigation in India. Importantly, being an entirely voluntary organization its members are not paid for their time, and funds are generated entirely from sale of its literature and from small donations. PUDR does not accept foreign funds, or funds from any institutional funding agencies, foreign or national.

7. Manabadhikar Suraksha Mancha (MASUM) took shape in 1998, to form a platform for the Human Rights activists based in Calcutta. The activists who were working for Human Rights (HR) movement with different organizations for more than a decade came together to create a new forum to strengthen the movement from different perspectives. MASUM aims at bringing back the spirit of exploring different dimensions of Human Rights, and to provide a forum for dialogues on different aspects of HR movement. MASUM is therefore an organization of any activists of the HR movement who shares these thoughts and works for that. MASUM has no new manifesto, no ideological hang-ups. It sees itself as an agent to spread HR movement on its own strength supplementing the initiatives of existing HR groups. It wants to continue uncompromising fight against all forms of Human Rights violation. Based on a loose organizational structure, devoid of any structural hierarchy MASUM has no formal membership. It depends solely on a meager fund constituted out of donations and contributions from its activists. MASUM's aims include:

Developing a broad based HR movement. Investigation in the cases of abuses of Human Rights legal intervention in specific cases searching new avenues in awareness campaign Documentation & Publication.

8. Having been established in April 2001 to monitor the processes of the Ad Hoc Human Rights Tribunal in Indonesia and the Special Panels for Serious Crimes in Timor Leste, JSMP very quickly extended court monitoring and judicial system analysis to include the operations of Timor Leste's District Courts. It undertakes (i) legislative analysis; (ii) extensive outreach work in Dili and throughout Timor Leste in order to inform East Timorese people of the decisions of the Ad Hoc Tribunal and Special Panels for Serious Crimes wherein its outreach work has expanded to include Human Rights training, training of judicial officials and district workshops explaining judicial processes and civil and political rights. In 2004 JSMP created the Women's Justice Unit to focus on cases involving women victims of domestic violence as a result of researching the situation of women in the formal justice sector. In 2005 JSMP has established a Victim's Support Service, a legal referral and legal aid service for women. The vision of JSMP is to be the foremost independent organization in Timor Leste that contributes to the development and improvement of the justice and legislative system through objective monitoring, analysis, advocacy and training in order to: (i) support and advance the rule of law and Human Rights; (ii) advance the independence of the judiciary and the legal profession and the administration of justice in full compliance with standards of international law; (iii) promote the adoption and implementation of international Human Rights standards and other legal rules and principles that advance Human Rights and the rule of law; (iv) promote the establishment and enforcement of a legal system which protects individuals and groups against violations of their Human Rights; (v) promote understanding of and compliance with the rule of law and Human Rights and provide assistance to those to whom the rule of law and Human Rights are denied; (vi) promote equality and the right of everyone to receive equal and fair access to justice and treatment under the law.
9. HRCBM is a worldwide campaigning movement dedicated to protecting the Human Rights of people in Bangladesh. It (i) works for minorities in Bangladesh; (ii) stands with victims and activists to prevent discrimination, to uphold political freedom, to protect people from inhumane conduct, and to bring offenders to justice; (iii) investigates and exposes Human Rights violations and hold abusers accountable; (iv) demands governments and those who hold power to end abusive practices and respect international

Human Rights law; (v) follows the guideline enshrined in UDHR, International Bill of Rights and other standards; (vi) work to end xenophobia, Human Rights abuse, racial discrimination, civil resentment, brutality and oppression against minorities in Bangladesh. As a Human Rights organization it does not evince any political interest of any sort, but continues to oppose any government law that discriminates minorities; calls for the racial discrimination and xenophobia in Bangladesh to be ended and seeks the prosecution of all offenders and pursues its activities through worldwide campaign and followed by appeal to government of Bangladesh and world leaders to end Human Rights abuses in Bangladesh. The Human Rights Congress for Bangladesh Minorities being a world-wide organization aims to (a) promote Human Rights, help stop Human Rights abuses against minorities in Bangladesh and bring offenders to justice for their criminal conducts of present and past; (b) encourage and promote worldwide campaign on "The Plights of Bangladesh Minorities"; (c) provide all required humanitarian assistance to refugees and destitute minorities of Bangladesh; (d) provide the required assistance to the organizations/individual serving "Destitute Bangladesh Minorities"; (e) encourages communication and collaboration among the organizations serving "Bangladesh Minorities"; (f) works with UN to help the oppressed Bangladesh Minorities and provide assistance to improve their living condition and safeguard them to live enjoying full rights as enshrined in UDHR; (g) ensure and monitor that Bangladesh Government implements UDHR in its entirety and record any violation of such guidelines; (h) works with international community to ensure that Bangladesh Government enforces laws of international norm and safeguard Bangladesh minorities irrespective of any political situation and provides dignity and recognition to minorities in Bangladesh which includes but not limited to immediate abolishment of any discriminatory act written and unwritten; (i) encourages individuals/organizations to continue uninterrupted social service specific to the well being of "Bangladesh Minorities"; (j) provides all required services to families belonging to "Bangladesh Minorities" at home and abroad.

10. ECPAT is a network of organizations and individuals working together to eliminate the commercial sexual exploitation of children. It seeks to encourage the world community to ensure that children everywhere enjoy their Fundamental Rights free from all forms of commercial sexual exploitation. ECPAT has Special Consultative Status with the Economic and Social Council of the United Nations (ECOSOC). The main thrust of ECPAT's work is to make a reality of the *Agenda for Action adopted by 122*

countries at the First World Congress against the Commercial Sexual Exploitation of Children in Stockholm, Sweden in 1996. This work takes different forms. ECPAT follows on (i) what governments are doing, and have done, to combat commercial sexual exploitation of children, and publishes the results; (ii) explore good models for prevention work, and share those models and experiences; (iii) finds and develops training modules to help caregivers to do their work better; (iv) develops learning tools for police training curricula; (v) provides advice and information to groups who are trying to make a national plan for their country, or to implement an existing plan; (vi) carries out research and develop research methodologies; and (vii) promotes the participation of young people in seeking solutions to the problems and in providing support to victims.

11. Democracy watch is a development and educational institution working to promote and strengthen democracy and good governance by creating awareness about rights and values through research, training for leadership, advocacy and mobilization of media to fight against injustice and Human Rights violation. It provides different kinds of training especially to the youth to build up their career and leadership quality. As an NGO working in promotion of democracy and good governance in Bangladesh since 1995 it conducts training and runs projects with a vision to build awareness on democracy and good governance; carries out research and opinion poll on different social and political dimensions; emphasizes most on education and awareness building of the young adults and women in the society. Towards this end, it runs courses on Lifestyle, Democracy Training Program, Internship Project with the Parliamentarians, IELTS, Basic Computing and English for General Purpose. Side by side, quiz, debate, dialogue session, and workshop on various issues of democracy are regularly carried out in an attempt to raise the confidence level of the youths. Skill development training and awareness building is necessary in terms of creating employment opportunities. In this context, Bangladeshi workforces are not quite adaptable in line with the international standards. This is why skill building training should spread all over the country. Apart from the Dhaka office, it has a branch at Mymensingh. Regular activities are also carried out in Chittagong, Comilla, Sylhet and in some other districts in Bangladesh. It also targets women as the core field of development in near future because we believe no development can be possible as long as the young and women are not conscious. As a non-government organization working to promote and strengthen democracy and good governance it aims at creating awareness about rights and values

through research, training for leadership, advocacy and mobilization of media to fight against injustice and Human Rights violation.

12. CHRO is working to protect and promote the rights of the Chin people in the areas relating to violation of the rights of women and children, forced labor, political suppression, racial discrimination religious persecutions committed by the Burmese military regime etc. The aims and objectives of CHRO are to (i) Promote Human Rights and democratic principles among Chin people; (ii) Empower the people, especially the victims of Human Rights violations, who have been suffering so long under the Burmese military regime; (iii) Provide accurate and reliable information about Human Rights situation in Chin state and western part of Burma to the international community. Being established in 1995, and registered as not for profit organization in Canada in its efforts to restore democracy and Human Rights to Burma, CHRO has been independently documenting Human Rights violations perpetrated by Burma's military regime against the Chin of Burma. Abuses such as racial discrimination, forced labor, rape, and religious persecution are commonplace for the Chin as well as many other peoples in Burma. CHRO produces a news bulletin six times a year, which is disseminated to Human Rights institutions and individual supporters around the world. Accordingly, CHRO has become a key advocate internationally for the support of the Chins and people from Western Burma, those living in Burma as well as those living as refugees in other countries. Over the years the CHRO has grown from a small and inexperienced organization run on a shoe-string budget to a well-respected and professionally managed Human Rights organization. CHRO fact-finders actively document Human Rights violations in most parts of Chinland, as well as other Chin inhabited areas of Burma and among the Chin people in other countries. CHRO is also promoting Human Rights and democratic principle among Chin people inside and outside of the country. CHRO produces Rhododendron Human Rights news bulletin six times a year and has already published a Book; *Religious Persecution: A Campaign of Ethnocide against Chin Christian in Burma* (February 2004); "Assessment Report on Burmese Refugees in Mizoram and Delhi" with the other Media of New Delhi, India and with MAP, Thailand (June 2004); "Nowhere to Go: Chin Refugees in Malaysia" (July 2005); "A Struggle for Survival: The Chin People of Burma" Winter 2006.

13. The main aims and objectives of CEHURDES are to (i) work for the protection and promotion of Human Rights under the policies and guidelines adopted by the United Nations; (ii) carry out

Human Rights awareness activities to raise the level of consciousness of people to materialize the theme "all Human Rights for all"; (iii) conduct Human Rights education programs at the grassroots level both in formal and informal education sector; (iv) work to ensure press freedom and freedom of expression, including the rights of media workers and journalists as guaranteed by the country's Constitution and international Human Rights instruments; (v) conduct research, study, interaction programs etc. in the areas of Human Rights, press freedom and freedom of expression, democracy and peace in Nepal in the context of regional experience; (vi) advocate for safeguarding the rights of women, children, disabled people, disadvantaged communities, refugees and victims of torture; (vii) coordinate and monitor the implementation of the international Human Rights instruments adopted by the United Nations and ratified by Nepal.

14. Established as an independent non-profit and non-governmental Human Rights organization on November 23, 1991 in exile by Bhutanese women for the establishment of democracy; protection, promotion and defense of democratic values, Human Rights, women's and child rights in Bhutan through peaceful and non-violent means, BWCO is dedicated for the establishment of Human Rights and democracy in Bhutan and promoting the principles of democracy, Human Rights, democratic values, women's rights, gender justice, social justice, child rights, rule of law among Bhutanese people and creating a culture of peace through education, training, publication and dissemination. By implementing principles of democracy, nondiscrimination, Human Rights, women's rights, child rights, civil, political, social, economic, cultural rights and fostering international public law instruments through peaceful and non-violent means, BWCO aims to reformulate the existing discriminatory system in public policies and social system and cultivate social justice in the development of a sustainable peaceful and democratic Bhutanese society. Its goals are to (i) work for the establishment of Human Rights in Bhutan through peaceful and non-violent means; (ii) promote and propagate the principles, ideals and values of democracy; rule of law, principles, and provisions of non-discrimination, equality, women's Human Rights, and social justice enshrined in the international Human Rights instruments including CEDAW, and CRC among Bhutanese people; (iii) work for the empowerment and advancement of Bhutanese women through better opportunities of education, gainful and equal employment, economic, political and legal empowerment, gender equality and an equitable share in decision-making and for their full

participation in all spheres of society; (iv) combat against all forms of discrimination, injustices, exploitation, and oppression against women and work for their elimination; (v) work for the protection and promotion of the rights of Bhutanese children and work for elimination of all forms of exploitation and discrimination against children; (vi) work for the early repatriation of Bhutanese refugees with dignity and honor.

15. ALRC is an NGO having General Consultative status with the Economic and Social Council of the United Nations. The ALRC was founded in 1986 by a prominent group of jurists and Human Rights activists in Asia. It is a body committed to the development of legal self-reliance and empowerment of people. It will place particular emphasis in its work on the areas of cultural, social and economic rights and the right of development. ALRC will work closely with and support regional, national, and local groups involved in this field, taking care, at the same time, to protect the autonomy and independence of such groups. The Centre will promote the development of, and support specific legal service and resource programs promoting self-help at the local level. It will also seek to strengthen and encourage positive action on legal and Human Rights issues by the bar and other legal bodies and personnel, at local and national levels. The Centre will press, where appropriate, for the introduction and improvement of effective government legal services. During the last three years (1996-98), ALRC has done extensive work in several countries in Asia. More notable ones are: the judges' and lawyers' programs conducted in Cambodia and Sri Lanka. At such meetings judges and lawyers from a particular country are brought together with other experts from the region and discussions are conducted for arriving at conclusions on what changes are to be recommended to the governments concerned. These programs have been well documented. The Centre focuses on (i) Coordinating and sharing amongst local, national and sub-regional groups and individuals information on legal service programs and legal initiatives being taken in Asian countries, through such means as e-mail, newsletters, publications, exchange of materials and workshops; (ii) facilitating exchanges of people working in the field of Human Rights and legal resources, and to encourage sharing of information and skills. Development of such programs in places where they do not currently exist through visits, internships, and the like; (iii) develop training schemes to assist the creation and operation of legal resource and paralegal programs, and promoting the running of such programs on a sub-regional basis; and, (iv) researching and analyzing current legal issues, Human Rights violations and oppression of people within Asia and to

encourage development of a macro-perspective on these problems and provide such information for the Asian Human Rights Commission. The broad Principles that guide AHRC and LARC Programs are (i) Victims-directed approach must be combined with structural reforms needed to prevent Human Rights abuse and to promote rights; (ii) Protest work will be combined with a community-based approach. In this, building of a support base in church and religious groups will be given priority; (iii) UN-directed approach must be combined with regional and country based Human Rights promotional activities; (iv) Human Rights promotion must be combined with promotion of democracy and rule of law; and importantly, (v) the issues of poverty eradication, gender equality, caste, indigenous peoples' and minorities' rights must be brought into all programs.

16. http://www2.fhs.usyd.edu.au/arow/arer/004.htm, (last visited on 15th July 2007).
17. http://www.altlawforum.org/law%20and%20social, (last visited on 22nd July 2007).
18. http://www.arrc-hre.com/publications/hrepack1/page56.html, (last visited on 24th July 2007).
19. *Ibid.*
20. http://www.forum-asia.org/index.php?option=com_content&task=view&id=310&Itemid=114, (last visited on 27th July 2007).
21. http://www.ohchr.org/english/about/publications/docs/50kit4.htm, (last visited on 28th July 2007).
22. http://www.forum-asia.org/index.php?option=com_content&task=view&id=174&Itemid=34, (last visited on 29th July 2007).

11

Promoting and Protecting Human Rights Education*

Subhram Rajkhowa and *Stuti Deka*

Introduction

According to Article 1 of the Universal Declaration of Human Rights, all human beings are born free and equal in dignity and rights. Hence, it may be stated that the system of Human Rights is founded on the recognition of the inherent dignity of every human being,[1] which include the right to life, liberty, equality and dignity of an individual. The Declaration has attained the status of *jus cogens* in international law, for which countries are expected to incorporate the same in their domestic legal system and facilitate the exercise thereof. These inherent rights cannot be taken away or declared as void by any authority through State made laws or legislation. It involves the relationship among individuals and the State[2] and is primarily a responsibility of the State. Therefore, regardless of their political, economic and cultural system, it is the duty of the State to promote and protect all Human Rights and fundamental freedoms.[3] Further, the effective exercise of Human Rights is also contingent upon the degree of responsibility by individuals towards the community.

---

* This is a modified version of the original article titled "Imperative of Human Rights Education Towards Promoting Human Rights Awareness". Published in *Human Rights Some Reflections*, 2006.

It has been universally recognized that the concept of Human Rights is closely related to human dignity. It constitutes a strong device to ensure the protection of dignity of each and every individual in society. Dignity in turn provides a sense of value. Therefore, the observance of Human Rights may be considered an indicator of awareness of and individual of the dignity of others.

Though the existence of Human Rights is as old as the 'natural law theory', reference has been made to the Universal Declaration only, since from the practical point of view the term has been in use in modern times and understood as such after the world wars. The experience of the two world wars and immense sufferings of mankind, lead to the realization among the international community that a device had to be evolved to minimize or control the sufferings of mankind on the basis of international law.

Literacy and Awareness

In a society for the effective exercise of Human Rights there has to be mutual respect for the principles of Human Rights enshrined in various international instruments as well as the provisions enshrined in the respective domestic legal systems. Realization of Human Rights demands a legal regime for its protection as well as for economic and cultural developments; literacy and consciousness of the people of their rights have also to be facilitated through an effective machinery of supervision.[4]

An ideal society wherein Human Rights are observed in letter and spirit is perhaps a rare phenomenon, but in reality it has been observed that there has been a wide disparity between the proclaimed ideals, declared intentions and actual situation. The prevailing situation has been occasioned by an ignorance of the rights. This may be attributed to illiteracy as one of the causes for the low level of observance of Human Rights. This is further compounded by a lack of commitment on the part of official agencies which only help impinge upon the elementary norms of Human Rights.[5]

Over 510 million young women and 540 million young men live in the world today according to United Nations (UN) estimates. In this population, approximately one person in five is between the ages of 15 and 24 years, or youth comprise almost 18 per cent of the world's population. About 27 per cent of the world population comprise youths out of a population of about 6.6 billion as of September, 2007. Although the proportion of youth in the world is dwindling, and by 2025 it is forecast to fall to 16 per cent, in numerical terms the absolute number has increased and is expected to continue to do so well into the twenty-first century. It has been ascertained that the majority of young people, 85 per cent, live in developing countries, with approximately 60 per cent in Asia alone. Vast numbers of people still today happen to be unaware of their rights as human beings. Even today 103 million children and 771 million adults of the world population are stated to be illiterate. UNESCO estimates that approximately 96 million young women and 57 million young men are illiterate, most of them in developing countries. This is so, because despite progress towards universal primary education in many regions, access is still limited in some countries and more so for some groups. It also reflects the poor quality and relevance of basic education in many countries. Illiteracy rates are highest in northern Africa and significantly high in sub-Saharan Africa and south-central Asia, with a significant gender differential: women are much more likely to be illiterate than men. The greatest differential is said to prevail in northern Africa, where twice as many women as men are illiterate (40 per cent for women, 20 per cent for men). Again youth illiteracy is much higher in rural than in urban areas since in the rural areas educational institutions are not found to be established in adequate numbers. Illiteracy rates are negligible in developed regions where primary education is universal and compulsory. But in the developing world, though elementary education is gradually being considered to be compulsory, it has remained so more on paper rather than being translated into action. Reducing illiteracy and improving the coverage and quality of basic education are potentially powerful instruments for reducing inequality in the size and distribution of income and for raising the productivity and earnings of the poor. They also offer an access route to training and through this to better jobs and higher incomes.[6]

It is precisely for this reason that the Millennium Development Goals (MDGs) aims at ensuring that all boys and girls complete a full course of primary schooling. Universal schooling has already been achieved in some less developed countries; particularly in Latin America. A concerted international effort can extend this experience to other parts of the world. As of now, only 37 of 155 developing countries have achieved universal primary school completion.[7]

About 85% of illiterate people are concentrated in 34 countries, particularly in rural areas. UNESCO's new Literacy Initiative for Empowerment (LIFE) strategy aims at helping accelerate the literacy drive in countries where the rate of illiteracy is higher than 50% and/or the number of illiterate people is more than 10 million. LIFE is designed to further the goals of the United Nations Literacy Decade (2003-2012). Irrespective of the background of the child, the right to education is absolutely central. Migrant children too should be ensured access to compulsory education—irrespective of their or their parents' legal status. Such pupils should receive qualitative education and the component of Human Rights education is all the more necessary as it is also relevant. Their fate is ours and they have much to contribute—if given a chance. The first step is to recognize that they have Human Rights and it has to be provided to young children if the world community expects an orderly and response society, based on Human Rights values. In order to facilitate such an exercise, the various international and regional instruments pertaining to the rights of the child in particular and other Human Rights instruments have to be introduced in a meaningful manner. The Database on Human Rights education and training provided in connection with the UN decade for Human Rights education can be very much profitably adopted by nations to provide for effective Human Rights education not only among young children and youth but also among common people in general who have so long been left out of the process of having exposure to Human Rights education.[8]

It bears mention that among the illiterate, gender disparity is very much in evidence. Presently, over 55% of children out of school are girls, and fully two-thirds of adults without access to literacy are women. According to a recent recalculation, there are about 77 million children not enrolled in school and an estimated 781 million adults have not yet had the opportunity to learn, read and write—two-thirds of them are women. Hence there is a need for adoption of a positive and realistic approach towards educating the illiterate masses. In doing so, the four basic aims of education have to be kept in mind. These being:

- The full development of the individual's personality, talents and abilities;
- The strengthening of respect for Human Rights and fundamental freedoms;
- The enabling of all persons to participate effectively and responsibly in a free society;
- The promotion of understanding, tolerance and friendship among all nations;
- Racial, ethnic or religious groups and the furtherance of activities of the UN for maintenance of peace.

Education brings about all-round and harmonious development of the personality of individuals, such as physical, intellectual, aesthetic, social, economic, religious, cultural, and spiritual, along with realization of social needs. Human Rights education as the very name indicates is to do with learning and practice of Human Rights. It can help people to develop to the point where they can gain a proper understanding of Human Rights, which enables them to develop a feeling of being important and being able to defend themselves as well as others. Human Rights education should not only aim at contributing trained professional workers, but also at contributing to the development of those who possess the skills to interact in a society. This education provides the student the ability to accommodate and produce societal change. It is seen as a way to empower people to improve their quality of life, increase their capacity to participate in the decision making process.[9] Such education can lead to development of a sense of respect, need to protect and promote Human Rights in a dispassionate manner. It can promote communication skills and critical thinking in societies as diverse as multicultural ones. It is a fact that people who know their rights stand the best chance of realizing them. What is of utmost importance is that it enables them to develop respect for the rights of others and points the way to a more tolerant and peaceful society.[10] According to Emilio Gercia Mendez "in the current stage of technological development, in which access to knowledge constitutes the decisive and fundamental factor allowing for an existence worthy of human dignity, which is the ultimate purpose of human rights, the right to education cannot be submitted to any form of negotiation and must be considered to be as much an absolute priority as abolition of slavery or of torture."[11]

The denial of human right and fundamental freedom is not only an individual and personal tragedy, but also creates conditions of social and political unrest, sowing the seeds of violence and conflict within and between societies and nations.[12] The most dangerous aspect of it is that it creates conditions of social and political unrest, violence and conflicts among the members of the society.

Mechanisms Facilitating Human Rights Education

The existing laws and instruments could in many cases defend against and counter abuses, but people must first know where they may turn to for help.[13] Various international instruments or national laws pertaining to Human Rights can be meaningful to the people only when they are made aware of their existence, purpose and utility. Only then can they effectively exercise various provisions in the society or vouch for their implementation through the judicial system. There is, therefore, a need to inform and to educate about Human Rights in order to foster the development of values and attitudes which uphold Human Rights.

This will make participants aware of which laws in the legal system can protect them and encourage action aimed at defending Human Rights from violation. Human Rights culture will survive only when one knows of both his rights and obligations through a process of reasoning, for a Human Rights culture attempts to define the principles for a positive conduct of all human behavior.[14]

Respect for Human Rights can be achieved by making the people aware of the rights and duties of individuals, social groups and nations towards each other. Making people aware of their rights can lead to their participation in problem solving of their community, country and ultimately the world at large.[15] It was in this context that the Universal Declaration of Human Rights stressed upon the "understanding and respect for all peoples, their cultures, civilization, values and ways of life, including domestic, ethnic, cultural and the cultures of all nations". With this in view, Article 26(2) of the Universal Declaration stressed the necessity of educating the people by providing that "education shall be directed to the full development of the human personality and to the strengthening of respect for human rights and fundamental freedoms". In fact, while adopting the Universal Declaration, the General Assembly recommended to the governments that the text be distributed in schools and other educational institutions.[16] But even after almost six decades, many a country is yet to comply with this elementary formality. This prompted the Vienna meet to reiterate the emphasis on Human Rights education. The Vienna Declaration provided that "States should strive to eradicate illiteracy and should direct its education towards the full development of the human personality and to the strengthening of respect for human rights and fundamental freedoms in formal and non formal settings".[17] There are now over 300 translated versions of the Declaration.

The emphasis on Human Rights education to young people should be the primary concern of every society in order to prepare them for a plural society. Education should include the development of the spirit of tolerance and fostering the human capacity for sympathy. It should include means of non-violent resolution of conflict besides developing respect for other people. Hence, Article 26(2) goes on to state that "it shall promote understanding, tolerance and friendship among all nations, racial or religious groups, and shall further the activities of the United Nations for the maintenance of peace". Education helps for the development of inherent powers of men. Education has always been a lifelong and comprehensive affair. The purpose of education is to give people enhanced awareness, greater openness, the courage to question and perseverance in searching for solution. The objective of initial education is to equip one with basic minimum levels of knowledge, attitude, values and scale to begin one's life journey. Education is an instrument of development and factor of social change.[18]

To inform and to educate is to create awareness and knowledge of Human Rights. The protection of Human Rights depends on the people knowing about their rights to which they are entitled and the mechanisms that are available to enforce these rights. The topics should include equal rights and opportunities across the spectrum of civil, cultural, economic, political and social rights, including dignity, identity, liberty, the Human Rights of women, elimination of racial, ethnic and religious discrimination, life in a free and democratic society, the rights of the child, sense of moral and social responsibility, the rights of disabled, self-determination, decolonization, Human Rights in development process, peace and so on.

Human Rights education should encompass both theoretical dimension and practical application. That includes Human Rights education provided at school level, that is in primary education, in secondary education and in institutions of higher learning as well. Adult education and formal and non-formal education are likewise to be employed. At different levels Human Rights are to be incorporated in a variety of subject matters, such as history, the social sciences and medicine, and also taught in courses specially designed for this purpose. Human Rights education can lead to strengthening respect for Human Rights and freedoms, development of human personality and sense of dignity, development of proper attitude and behavior towards promotion of proper respect for others, besides helping in the promotion of understanding and tolerance. It can empower people enabling them to actively participate in social and community life. The UNESCO congress on Education of Human Rights and Democracy held about a decade and half back in the year 1993 observed that Human Rights education is a Human Right, a precondition for sustainable development. It further held that "human rights education provides protection from discrimination, unfair treatment, undemocratic attitude, deterioration of cultural values, exploitation, bondage, human right illiteracy, abuse of human rights at any level."

Referring to Human Rights education as a 'universal priority', the then UN Commission on Human Rights recommended that 'knowledge of Human Rights, both in its theoretical dimension and in its practical application, should be established as a priority in educational policies' and that international agencies for financial and technical cooperation should include support for such programmes. (Paragraphs 6 and 8 of Res. 1993/56).

The instruments attach special importance to the teaching about different civilizations, cultures and languages for the purpose of improving ethnic and religious relations. The right to Human Rights education is thus a major component in the realization of the rights of minorities and indigenous peoples.

According to the United Nations publications on National Human Rights Institutions,[19] knowledge of Human Rights requires constant internal and external vigilance. Internal vigilance is instilled by sensitizing an individual to his or her own potential for violative behavior. External vigilance is aimed at encouraging groups or individuals to act in defense of Human Rights. Such defensive action presupposes the existence of adequate protective mechanisms and programmes that seek to promote knowledge and, the exercise of these mechanisms. Dissemination of knowledge of Human Rights in the community is certainly the first and surest defense against the danger that these rights will not be trampled upon.

The International Congress on Education for Human Rights and Democracy[20] held in the year 1993 to stress upon the need "to educate individuals and groups about human rights conduct leading to a denial of rights will be changed, all rights will be respected and civil society will be transformed into a peaceful and participatory model." Such "education should be participatory and operational, creative and innovative and empowering at all levels of civil society. Education should aim to nurture democratic values, sustain impulses for democratization and promote social transformation based upon human rights and democracy."[21]

The World Plan of Action[22] conceives of education in its broadest sense, among all age, gender, class, ethnic, national, religious and linguistic groups and in all sections of society. It takes a global view of education through strategies of learning in formal and non-formal setting including popular and adult education, education in the family, out of school, education of youth, education of specialized groups, and education in difficult situations. In fact, the plan of action calls for "a framework of action to be implemented in accordance with their priorities, upon all actors including grassroots education workers in the villages, refugee camps, inner cities and war zones throughout the world".[23] The United Nations General Assembly while proclaiming the Decade for Human Rights Education from January 1, 1995 to 31st December, 2004 called upon the United Nations High Commissioner for Human Rights to facilitate implementation of the plan. The mid-term and end-term review of the Plan of Action left much to be desired resulting in the adoption of the two year emphasis on primary education from the year 2005 till 2007.

As stated earlier, the Vienna Declaration too stressed upon Human Rights education, training and public information as essential components for the promotion and achievements of stability and harmonious relationship among communities and for fostering mutual understanding and peace.[24] It observed "education should promote understanding, tolerance, peace and friendly relations between the nations and all racial or religious groups and encourage the development of UN activities in pursuance of these objectives". Therefore, education on Human Rights and the dissemination of proper information, both theoretical and practical, play an important role in the promotion and respect of Human Rights with regard to all individuals without distinction of any kind...and this should be integrated in the educational policies at the national as well as international level.[25] In order to promote Human Rights it called for "broad based education and public information" as components of the Human Rights programme,[26] calling upon the States to "develop scientific programmes and strategies for ensuring the widest Human Rights education and the dissemination of public information, taking particular account of the Human Rights needs of women"[27] in order to "promote and increase awareness of Human Rights and mutual tolerance".[28] While reaffirming the commitment towards Human Rights it stated that States are duty bound, as stipulated in the Universal Declaration of Human Rights and the International Covenant of Economic, Social and Cultural Rights as well as other instruments, to ensure that education is aimed at strengthening the respect of Human Rights and fundamental freedoms.

Earlier the first world conference held in Tehran resolved to call upon all States to ensure "all means of education" be used to provide youth with an opportunity to grow up in a spirit of respect for human dignity and equal rights. In the year 1978 the United Nations Educational Scientific and Cultural Organization organized an international congress in Vienna on teaching Human Rights—a landmark event that gathered together wide range of governmental and non-governmental education specialists. This was followed by a similar conference in Malta in 1987. That very year a training course on teaching of Human Rights for Asia and Pacific Region was organized by the Economic and Social Commission for Asia and Pacific (ESCAP) at Bangkok. Another important seminar was held at Geneva the following year on the teaching of Human Rights wherein representatives from 40 countries inter-governmental and non-governmental organizations took part.[29] However, these efforts have not been matched by practical measures. Hence the role of formal and non-formal education in the promotion and protection of Human Rights is considered to be very vital.

Methodology

With respect to formal education, educational and academic institutions are considered to be the most important means for fashioning a Human Rights culture.[30] Educational institutions have a tremendous responsibility to embark upon a broad based comprehensive program of championing the cause of Human Rights through its wide network, undertaking various Human Rights implementation programs. Therefore, the role of educational institutions should not be confined to delivering sermons but ensure to have an effective impact, enabling effective implementation in the social fabric. Practical courses and tasks in the Human Rights discipline may be designed for the students, since students learn best by doing interesting and varied things.[31]

Students should be made aware that Human Rights are not something relevant only for other people somewhere else. They concern us all as we are in the same world, no matter who 'we' are. Students should be encouraged to consider how they might best use what they have learned to promote and protect Human Rights in their respective societies.[32] They should be able to illustrate what is right and what is wrong.

It has to be realized that children of different strata require different training of Human Rights for the reason that due to circumstances their needs are different and accordingly their actions will differ. Human Rights are closely related to morality, and therefore, they may be prescribed in schools as a moral science. Taking school children for outing and showing reality also works well, as for example showing poor homes, old age homes, orphanages, prisons will definitely help out to imprint on their mind the need of respecting Human Rights.[33] The sharing of experience by children from different background enables a better appreciation of problems and be sympathetic to each other's problems.[34] Knowledge of Human Rights should be accorded to school children according to their age and circumstances. Topics should include Human Rights, duties, obligations and responsibilities, various forms of injustice, inequality and discrimination so that the study of Human Rights in schools should lead to an understanding of, and sympathy for the concept of justice, equality, freedom, peace, dignity, rights and democracy. Schools should thus provide opportunities for pupils to experience effective involvement in Human Rights and to express their feeling through drama, art, music, creative writings and audio visual media. An appropriate climate is therefore an essential component to effective learning of Human Rights.[35]

Ideally, a culture of Human Rights should be built into the whole curriculum, yet in practice, particularly at the secondary level it is treated piecemeal as part of the established disciplines within the social and economic sciences and humanities, involving philosophical, political and legal concepts.[36] At the post-secondary stage, Human Rights can be a field of study within almost every discipline including law, media studies, medicine, political and social sciences.[37] It is essential to build an integral and broad based curriculum that is both persuasive across subject disciplines and taught as a separate subject so that Human Rights are dealt with repeatedly throughout a person's basic education. The curriculum should be so structured as to provide an understanding of the fundamental Human Rights principles and values underlying awareness of the Human Rights principles. They should be encouraged to develop a spirit of tolerance and of democratic participation which can foster a national culture of justice, tolerance and fairness, through case studies, role plays, mock trials, stimulations, small group discussions and debates. Basic skills including the ability to reason, communicate and think critically are the other characteristics.[38]

There should be systematic revision of textbooks aimed at cost effective and sustainable programs.[39] Access to up-to-date information and documentation and the availability of practical and inexpensive teaching materials are much essential to develop intellectual and social skills for a proper understanding of Human Rights issues.

The teacher carries a great responsibility in the communication of the Human Rights message. The moral influence that teachers have on their pupils should be properly utilized in the dissemination of Human Rights education. Teachers have to teach in such a way as to respect Human Rights in the class room and the school environment itself. The teachers should be able to stimulate discussion and ideas and thus hopefully help children to develop an objective, basic understanding of the rights and obligations so as to apply Human Rights principles to the fullest extent of our human existence.[40]

The teacher should spend, where appropriate, a few minutes of the day with his or her own class discussing news items from the press, radio, television or local talk. This will provide more opportunities to look at Human Rights issues in a less fraught or formal way.[41] It is imperative that a teacher remains open to discuss adversity or even conflict situation. However, the emphasis on teaching and learning should be positive instances of progress and success.[42] They should use methods which appeal to the creative imagination of children.

While formal Human Rights education concerns the primary, secondary, post-secondary and university education, alternative Human Rights education poses the greater challenge of teaching Human Rights to the underprivileged sections of society who will never have the opportunity to access formal education for various reasons. Any such programs should be arranged in collaboration with professional groups, trade unions, community based organizations and non-governmental organizations as the case may be so as to develop non-formal education for particular constituencies. This would make available information about Human Rights norms and instruments as well as enable recognition of procedures and mechanisms against violations with the purpose of creating a culture of Human Rights, facilitating solutions of disagreements and conflicts by use of non-violent means. Such an approach "calls for identification of the most appropriate target groups so as to ensure rapid and effective implementation".[43] In other words, there has to be a focus on educational support where it is most needed and most empowering and ensuring that projects are suitable for potential users. Target groups should be imparted practical training, imbibing equality in response to the real needs of the people. It should include approaches which assist people to understand and analyze their relation with power as well as leadership styles and abuses.

The aim of such exercise should be to involve groups of adults and young people, including those not attending school, in out of school education, work places, institutes, groupings etc. Programs should aim at increasing the awareness of individuals in both formal and informal groups to their rights and responsibilities and to their full participation towards society. Common tools employed in such processes include audio visuals, transparencies, music, toy and other forms appropriate for reaching neo-literate people and children. In other words, Human Rights should be translated into social norms and behavior.

Education should develop a sense of social responsibility and solidarity with the less privileged groups and should lead to the observance of the principles of equality in everyday conduct, besides enabling the ability to critically understand problems and express opinions leading to value based judgments.[44]

Educators should use methods that appeal to the creative imagination of children and adolescents and to their social activities so as to prepare them to exercise their rights while recognizing and respecting the rights of others.[45] Such measures will empower communities to partake in matters of their rights and also to enhance personality development. Juvenile inmates and prison inmates may be taught Human Rights by way of painting Human Rights murals at the prison, which has been so effectively employed in South Africa under the Street Law program.[46] In this process the juveniles could express what they have learnt as well as vent of their willingness to learn.

Human Rights education is essential as it forms part of a person's beliefs and attitudes; therefore, the process of educating the people about Human Rights should be a continuing one. It is crucial that people know their rights, demand them and defend them. Such education should aim at the ethical, civil and cultural aspects which can only be provided by people with motivation, commitment to ethics and Human Rights, who have in them an ingrained aim of changing society, so that Human Rights is applied in practice.[47] It has to be appreciated that the inner strength of respecting Human Rights does not come just in one day. It comes through intensive training during young age.

Human Rights attitudes have to be inculcated so that humanism and respect for Human Rights is reflected in one's actions in later years.

National Human Rights institutions have a major role to play in promoting Human Rights awareness. Stressing the significance of national Human Rights institutions the former High Commissioner for Human Rights, Mr. Jose Ayala Lasso observed that "the role of national institutions is clearly complementary, and their strengthening can clearly enhance the effectiveness of both national and international systems for the promotion and protection of human rights".[48] The most effective education and information campaigns for example are likely to be those which are designed and carried out at the national and local level for it can take the local, cultural and traditional context into account. Its functions normally include the task of educating the people about Human Rights, fostering the development of values and attitudes in order to uphold Human Rights from violation.

Considering the important role of national institutions, the first International Workshop on National Institutions for the Promotion and Protection of Human Rights held in Paris, among others, proposed national institutions "to assist in formulating and executing Human Rights teaching and research programmes and to increase public awareness of Human Rights through information and education".[49]

The Second International Workshop for the Asia and Pacific Region held in Jakarta considered the establishment of national institutions in the region. Further, the Second

International Workshop on National Institutions held in 1993 in Tunis too considered the role of national institutions.

The same year the Vienna Declaration and Programme of Action adopted by the World Conference on Human Rights reaffirmed:

> ...the important and constructive role played by national institutions for the promotion and protection of human rights, in particular in their advisory capacity to the competent authorities, their role in remedying human rights violations, in the dissemination of human rights information, and education in human rights....[50]

National institutions, along with inter-governmental and non-governmental organizations can play an important role in promoting Human Rights at the domestic level. Non-governmental and community-based organizations are in a unique position to identify those individuals and groups within a society who are most vulnerable to Human Rights violations, and therefore, in a position to obtain greatest benefit from the services of a national Human Rights institution.

It is also necessary that Human Rights institutions should have high visibility so that the potential complainants are made aware of their rights to complain as well as of the necessary procedures for filing a complaint.[51]

National institutions should educate various groups about international and domestic Human Rights standards; develop training courses which transform knowledge about Human Rights into operational skills. The target audience for training should properly be selected so that they can act as a vehicle in the process of learning and unlearning. Such training should also be imparted to persons associated with the administration of justice, government officials, social workers, armed forces, media, nongovernmental organizations, teachers, community leaders and the like.

Training and educational efforts must be directly targeted and appropriately addressed and structured to a particular audience who are in a position to benefit from a Human Rights training course. Training should also focus on Human Rights issues or problems which a target group is most likely to encounter. Instructions should be imparted by persons familiar with the background and working environment with the audience. Trainers should be well versed in effective techniques for training of audience through a process of creative interactive teaching methods for securing the attention of active engaged participation of the audience. The participants should also be equipped and motivated to continue the training process after completion of the course, such as to equip those persons already involved in educating others with the knowledge and skills necessary to incorporate effectively into their own teaching programs.[52]

Self produced materials can be targeted precisely to those sectors of society most in need of information and education. By providing its own materials, the national institutions can incorporate local laws and the realities in a way which makes those materials more accessible than those produced elsewhere. Information collection and production are of little value without a strategy for ensuring the effective dissemination of materials. A dissemination strategy must begin with identification of appropriate target audiences in order to synthesize the data into easily readable and readily accessible style. Ensuring the accessibility of documentation materials for students and for scholars may only be a matter of developing an appropriate classification system providing facilities for reading, writing and copying.[53]

Further, national institutions should provide expert assistance in the adoption or modification of curricula, provide instruction and assistance to teachers and teacher trainers, and work together with educators in producing educational resource tools. Simultaneously, general information materials intended for widespread distribution may be effectively disseminated via schools, libraries, government offices and community organizations.

Conclusion

The full realization of Human Rights cannot be achieved solely through adequate legislation and appropriate administrative arrangements. In recognition of this fact, commissions are often entrusted with the responsibility of improving community awareness of Human Rights. Promoting and educating about Human Rights may also improve informing the commission's own function and purposes, provoking discussions about various important questions in the field of Human Rights, organizing seminars and training courses, which have already been discussed, besides providing counseling services and meetings and producing and disseminating Human Rights publications.

Further, the national institutions and commissions can very effectively utilize the media in promoting awareness of Human Rights. The people may be made aware of the rights that they are entitled to, the duties which they owe to others as well as the structure that has been developed to implement those rights and duties.

It hardly needs stressing that Human Rights education is a powerful means of influencing and bringing attitudinal change in the citizens in general and professional groups in particular. Without education, one cannot see beyond the narrow surroundings, hence they are unable to appreciate the reality of global interdependence. Only through Human Rights education it is possible to provide for knowledge, values, beliefs and attitudes, thereby enabling one not only to defend him- or her-self but also to prevent Human Rights abuse on others. Steps taken at the domestic level by respective countries to meet the international efforts are what matters most in translating ideas into action. In doing so, the domestic cultures and values should definitely find a place of priority in the domestic policy framework in order to achieve success.[54] Hence, the ingrained local values and cultures have to be recognized in promoting Human Rights education through school curriculum, adult education programmes—formal and informal as well as higher education. Human Rights education should be all comprehensive from the primary to tertiary level.

Knowledge must lead to action, it should be empowering and learning, should lead to a participatory process wherein the learner is considered a teacher and *vice versa*, only then can Human Rights education be considered to reach the widest number of people. It has to be realized that people who are aware of their rights stand the best chance of realizing them.

Notes

1. Asbjourn Eide, "History of Human Rights: Summary of Lectures, Collection of Lectures, International Institute of Human Rights", Strasbourg, 1996, p. 47.
2. Jose Ayala Lasso, *National Human Rights Institutions*—A Handbook on the Establishment and Strengthening of National Institutions for the Promotion and Protection of Human Rights, Center for Human Rights, p. V.
3. Mona Rishmawi, "Human Rights Development within the League of Arab States and in Asia", in *Collection of Lectures, International Institute of Human Rights*, Strasbourg, France, 1996, p. 364.
4. "UNESCO World Plan of Action on Education for Human Rights and Democracy", Montreal, Canada 8-11v March, 1993, p. 3.
5. Md M Shah Alam, "Role of Law Faculties and the Law Schools in the Protection of Human Rights in Developing Countries", Paper presented at the CLEA Conference on Economic Policies, Human Rights and the Legal Order, June 4-5, 1993, p. 149.
6. Young people in today's world, ILO 2001.
7. goals.ca/goals.html—29k.
8. http://www.ohchr.org/english/library/index.htm
9. C. Naseema, *Human Rights Education, Concept and Pedagogical Aspects*, Kanishka Publishers and Distributors, 2002 pp. 170-71.
10. Human Rights Educators Network, Amnesty International, USA, January, 1991.
11. Quoted in Brazilian Common Law and How It Restricts The Efficacy of Human Right to Education, Sargio Branco SUR International Journal on Human Rights, No 6, 2007.
12. "United Nations ABC Teaching Human Rights—Practical Activities for Primary and Secondary Schools", New York, 1989, p. 5.
13. "United Nations, World Public Information Campaign for Human Rights", Fact Sheet No B, p. 3.
14. *Supra* n. 11, pp. 9, 31.
15. "UNESCO Recommendation Concerning Education for International Understanding, Co-operation and Peace and Education Relating to Human Rights and Fundamental Freedoms", no. 1974, p. 2.
16. *Supra* n. 7, p. 11.

17. "United Nations Vienna Declaration and Programme of Action", A/conf. 157, p. 23 dated 12 July 1993, Para 79.
18. Chiranjivi J. Nirmal, (ed) *Human Rights in India*, Oxford University Press, 1999, pp. 72-77.
19. United Nations, *Supra,* n. 2, p. 18.
20. *Supra* n. 4, p. 2.
21. *Ibid* p. 3.
22. *Ibid* p. 1.
23. *Ibid.*
24. *Supra* n. 16, para 28.
25. *Ibid* para 23.
26. *Ibid* para 68.
27. *Ibid* para 81.
28. *Ibid* para 82.
29. *Supra* n. 11, p. 3.
30. *Supra* n. 12, p. 12.
31. *Supra* n. 11, p. 7.
32. *Ibid* p. 52.
33. Sandhya De, "Human Rights Teaching to the Children in Schools and to The Public", Paper presented at the CLEA conference at Durban, South Africa, 15-17 December, 1995.
34. David Mc Quoid Mason, "Street Law and Human Rights Education as Means of Achieving Social Integration in Culturally Divided Societies", CLEA Conference at Durban, South Africa, 1995, p. 3.
35. Council of Europe, Recommendation No. (85) 7 of the Committee of Ministers to Member States On Teaching and Learning About Human Rights in Schools, 14.5.1985, p. 3.
36. *Supra* n. 11, p. 10.
37. *Supra* n. 2, p. 22.
38. *Supra* n. 11, p. 3.
39. *Supra* n. 4, p. 6.
40. *Supra* n. 14, p. 3.
41. *Ibid* p. 18.
42. *Supra* n. 34, p. 3.
43. *Supra* n. 4, p. 6.
44. *Supra* n. 14, p. 2.
45. *Ibid* p. 3.
46. Street Law currents, Newsletter of the National Street Law, vol. 2 No 4, December 1995.

47. *Supra* n. 14, p. 5.
48. *Supra* n. 2.
49. E/CN/4/1992/43add I.
50. *Ibid* para 36.
51. *Supra* n. 2, p. 8.
52. *Ibid* p. 21.
53. *Ibid* p. 19.
54. Amiya Kumar Bhuyan, Unpublished Ph.D thesis, "A Critical Legal Study of Human Rights Education in India", Gauhati University, 2005.

12

Humanizing the Criminal Justice System: The Victim Perspective

Dipa Dube

> *Rape is a crime against basic Human Rights. It is violative of the victim's most cherished of the Fundamental Rights, namely, the Right to Life.*

Introduction

The purpose of criminal justice is to protect the rights of individuals and the State against intentional invasion of the criminals who violate the basic norms of society. In the modern welfare state, this protection is sought to be achieved by punishing the accused in accordance with the provisions of law. However, criminal law, which reflects the social ambitions and norms of society and punishes perpetrators thereof, hardly takes any notice of the 'by products' of crime, its victims.[1] As lamented by Krishna Iyer J., "It is a weakness of our jurisprudence that victims of crime and the distress of the dependants of the victim do not attract the attention of law. In fact, the victim reparation is still the vanishing point of our criminal law. This is the deficiency in the system, which must be rectified by the legislature."[2]

This article reviews the present role and place of victims *vis-à-vis* the offender and the criminal justice machinery in force and offers suggestions for an improved system based on victims' needs. It focuses specially on victims of rape offences. The reasons underlying the same are:

(a) Rape is one of the most heinous offences perpetrated on womanhood. It is an act of violence which subjects the victim to physical and emotional humiliation besides pain, fear and serious injury.

(b) Despite efforts to curb its occurrence, the offence has never ceased to exist. The Medical Girl rape case of Delhi, the Rajasthan University rape case or the German Lady rape case—the list continues unabated, drawing serious concerns from every corner.[3]

(c) Myths traditionally associated with women have tended to overshadow their plight. The picture of the woman as a seducer, as a vengeful virgin in love and many others have made the machinery to falsify and negate claims of rape and instead, accuse the woman for what has befallen her.

(d) It is popularly said that a woman is raped twice—once, if the tragedy occurs and next, when she approaches the police and the Court to seek justice. Reliving every moment of that dreaded nightmare reduces her to a mental wreck and at the end, while the offender and the State emerges as triumphant parties, the victim stands as a living corpse, with no means to stand again in the battle of life.

Administration of Criminal Justice: Offender-Victim Perspectives

The criminal justice system in India, based on the adversarial model, focuses heavily on the offender and his rights. The plea of innocence, of rights against arbitrary arrest, of fair trial and adequate legal aid services are, amongst others, various measures designed to ensure the Human Rights of the accused. The development of this edifice has been most significant step in the Indian criminal law framework. However, a consequential grey area has been the neglect and apathy of the system towards the victims.

For every crime committed, there are at least two victims: society, which suffers a violation of its laws, and the actual victim who suffers an injury to body or property. The former regards a criminal act as essentially disturbing the equilibrium of social order and harmony and therefore takes on its part the responsibility of restoring peace by punishing the criminal and/ or reforming him. It therefore occupies the center stage in the criminal justice system. The second victim, the 'principal affected' in terms of loss of life or limb or property is relegated to a secondary status with little or no role to play in the complex process of dispensation of justice. He is merely transformed to a witness to watch the entire play being enacted by the accused and the State as the protagonists.

Simply speaking, the victim is a forgotten party to the criminal justice system. While the entire focus of the law is on the offender, to protect his rights, to punish him and thereby bring about his reformation and rehabilitation with all the resources and goodwill available through Courts and other agencies, the victim, more often, is left to fend for himself with little or no assistance coming his way. The violation of his rights, the invasion of his dignity, the actual losses incurred by him do not constitute matters of concern for anyone but himself. Strange but true, justice fails to redress the wrong perpetrated by the offender on the victim; on the contrary, it aggravates the injustice by focusing solely on the offender, sidelining the victims minimum needs and requirements.

The situation is more averse when it comes to victims of rape. In the backdrop of a conservative society, one can well imagine the shame and ignominy attached to the lives of such women. More often than not, women prefer to remain silent and hush up the matter.[4] For those who dare face the society, hurdles await at every step. Lodging a First Information Report (FIR) becomes the first and most difficult aspect with the police either refusing to record the statement or passing remarks about the veracity of the complaint. The next tedious process comes in the form of medical examination. In most cases, delays are a common matter with crucial evidences being lost; in those where examinations are conducted, an unsympathetic and unconcerned medical officer comes heavy. Many times, the doctors are more keen to probe whether the victim is habituated to sexual intercourse than examining whether she might have been subjected to such an act.[5] The trial is the next impending danger awaiting the victims turn. With little or no information coming as to the developments made during investigation, the victim is made to stand in the box to face a forceful cross examination and her tormentor. Silence on the part on the victim as well as her refusal to answer indecent and suggestive questions, are interpreted to mean 'consent', the litmus test of the offence of rape, and very soon the victim finds herself more dejected and humiliated than ever before.[6] The final blow comes with the acquittal of the accused. In cases where the trial results in conviction of the accused, sentencing follows subject to the stipulations laid down in the Indian Penal Code.[7] That spells the end of the case and justice is said to be done.

While analyzing the entire sequence of events, it becomes clear that the criminal justice system fails to ameliorate the condition of the victim as well as re-socialize and re-assimilate them in society. From lodging the FIR to the final disposition of the case by the Court, nothing comes in the way of the victim. She is left to fight the battle of justice with her own might, ignore taunts and sneers, brave the deadly Court environs and come out empty handed with no succor for herself. Compensation, counseling, medical care, none are available leaving the rape victims in a wretched and pitiful condition.

Indian Legal Framework

What is the present role the victim is assigned under the existing criminal law? When a person who has been the victim of a cognizable offence gives information to the police regarding the same, the police are required to reduce the information into writing and read it over to the informant. The informant is required to sign it and get a copy of the FIR.[8] If the police refuse to record the information, the victim—informant is allowed to send it in writing and by post to the Superintendent of Police concerned.[9] If the police refuse to investigate the case for whatever reason, the police officer is required to notify the informant of that fact.[10] Alternatively, victims are enabled by Section 190 of the Code of Criminal

Procedure (Cr.P.C.) 1973 to avoid going to the Police Station for redress and directly approach the Magistrate with his complaint.

The investigation process is exclusively a police function and the victim has a role only if the police consider it necessary. There are administrative instructions given by police departments of certain States to give information on progress of investigation to the victim when asked for. Otherwise, till police report (charge sheet) is filed under Section 173 Cr.P.C. 1973, the victim is neglected.

The victim has a say in the grant of bail to an accused S. 439(2) Cr.P.C., as interpreted by the Courts, recognizes the right of the complainant or any "aggrieved party" to move the High Court or the Court of Sessions for cancellation of a bail granted to the accused. A closure of report by the prosecution cannot be accepted by the Court without hearing the informant. Also, compounding of an offence cannot possibly happen without the participation of the complainant.[11] The victim of a crime may move the government to appoint a special prosecutor for a given case[12] though S. 301(2) mandates that such lawyer of the private party "shall act under the directions of the public prosecutor...and may, with the permission of the Court, submit written arguments after the evidence is closed in the case". Further, though there is no legal provision in the code for providing legal aid to victims of crime, S. 12(1) of the Legal Services Authorities Act, 1987 entitles every person "who has to file or defend a case:" to legal services subject to the fulfillment of the means test and the "prima facie" criteria.[13]

The victims' right of participation in the post trial stage of the proceedings are recognized. An appeal against an order of acquittal can be preferred, with the prior leave of the High Court by both the government[14] and the complainant.[15]

Some other provisions worth mentioning, so far as rape victims are concerned, are S. 228A Indian Penal Code, 1860 which prohibits the disclosure of the identity of the victim in any publication concerning the offence, S. 327(2) Cr.P.C. 1973 which provides for in camera proceedings in trials and repeal of S. 155(4) Indian Evidence Act, 1872 which permitted the impeachment of the credibility of an accuser by referring to her "immoral character".

Section 357, Cr.P.C., empowers a Court imposing a sentence of fine or a sentence (including a sentence of death) of which fine forms a part, in its discretion, *inter alia*, to order payment of compensation, out of the fine recovered, to a person for any loss or injury caused to him by the offence.[16]

However, Section 357(1) is subject to some limitations as may be stated below:

1. Compensation to victims can be awarded only when substantive sentence is imposed and not in cases of acquittal.
2. Quantum of compensation is limited to the fine levied and not in addition to it or exceed the fine imposed.
3. Compensation can be ordered only out of fine realized and if no fine is realized, compensation to victim cannot be directed to be realized.
4. In very rare cases under IPC, the maximum amount of fine is imposed. Moreover, the maximum fine as prescribed in IPC amount 150 years back is now inadequate in terms of real losses to victims.
5. Compensation to victim under this Section can be allowed by the Court if it is of the opinion that the compensation is recoverable by such person in a Civil Court.[17]

The right to compensation has also been recognized as an integral part of right to life and liberty under Article 21 of the Indian Constitution. As early as in 1983, the Supreme Court recognized the petitioner's right to claim compensation for illegal detention and awarded a total sum of Rs. 35,000 by way of compensation. In delivering the judgment, Chief Justice Chandrachud observed: "Art 21 which guarantees the right to life and liberty will be denuded of its significance content if the power of this Court were limited to passing orders of relief from illegal detention. One of the telling ways in which the violation of that right can reasonably be prevented and due compliance with the mandate of Art 21 secured is to mullet its violators in the payment of monetary compensation".[18] In several cases thereafter, the apex Court has repeated its order, making compensation an integral aspect of right to life.[19]

While these above provisions have encompassed the entire gamut of victims' rights, the judiciary has had a remarkable impact on victim justice movement.

In 1995,[20] a public interest litigation was filed to espouse the pathetic plight of four domestic servants who were raped in a moving train by some military personnel. The apex Court highlighted the ordeals of the victims of rape and the defects in the criminal law system in vogue.

It is rather unfortunate that in recent times, there has been an increase in violence against women causing serious concern. Rape does indeed pose a series of problems for the criminal justice system. There are cries for the harshest penalties, but often times such cries eclipse the real plight of the victim. Rape is an experience, which shakes the foundations of the lives of the victims. For many, its effect is a long-term one, impairing their capacity for personal relationships, altering their behavior and values and generating endless fear. In addition to the trauma of the rape itself, victims have had to suffer further agony during legal proceedings.

> We will only point out the defects of the existing system. Firstly, complaints are handled roughly and are not given such attention as is warranted. The victims, more often than not, are humiliated by the police. The victims have invariably found rape trials a traumatic experience. The experience of giving evidence in court has been negative and destructive. The victims often say, they considered the ordeal to be even worse than the rape itself. Undoubtedly, the court proceedings added to and prolonged the psychological stress they had had to suffer as a result of the rape itself.

In this background, the Court indicated the broad parameters in assisting the victims:

(1) The complainants of sexual assault cases should be provided with legal representation. It is important to have someone who is well-acquainted with the criminal justice system. The role of the victim's advocate would not only be to explain to the victim the nature of the proceedings, to prepare her for the case and to assist her in the police station and in Court but to provide her with guidance as to how she might obtain help of a different nature from other agencies, for example, mind counseling or medical assistance. It is important to secure continuity of assistance by ensuring that the same person who looked after the complainant's interests in the police station represents her till the end of the case.

(2) Legal assistance should be provided at the police station since the victim of sexual assault might very well be in a distressed state upon arrival at the police station, the guidance and support of a lawyer at this stage and whilst she was being questioned would be of great assistance to her.

(3) The police should be under a duty to inform the victim of her right to representation before any questions were asked of her and that the police report should state that the victim was so informed.

(4) A list of advocates willing to act in these cases should be kept at the police station for victims who did not have a particular lawyer in mind or whose own lawyer was unavailable.

(5) In all rape trials anonymity of the victim must be maintained, as far as necessary.

(6) It is necessary, having regard to the Directive Principles contained under Article 38(1) of the Constitution of India to set up Criminal Injuries Compensation Board. Rape victims frequently incur substantial financial loss. Some, for example, are too traumatized to continue in employment.

(7) Compensation for victims should be awarded by the Court on conviction of the offender and by the Criminal Injuries Compensation Board whether or not a conviction has taken place. The Board should take into account pain, suffering and shock as well as loss of earnings due to pregnancy and the expenses of child birth if this occurred as a result of the rape.

An increased sensitivity towards the plight of the victims was also noticeable in the landmark case of *State of Punjab* v. *Gurmit Singh*[21] where the Court made some revolutionary and ground breaking observations:

- Trial of sexual offences should be in-camera and invariably by lady judges, wherever available.
- The Court must share responsibility and restrain from making loose observations about the character of the accuser.
- The Court is under an obligation to ensure that the accuser is not unnecessarily harassed and humiliated in cross-examination in case of rape trial.

In 2004, the apex Court expressed concern over the plight of child victims of sexual assault, who often, have to describe their experiences of the assault in Court. It has a tremendous effect on the psyche of the child, and her physical and mental well-being. The Court accordingly prescribed the following guidelines:[22]

(i) A screen or some such arrangements may be made where the victim or witnesses (who may be equally vulnerable like the victim) do not see the body or face of the accused.

(ii) The questions put in cross-examination on behalf of the accused, in so far as they relate directly to the incident should be given in writing to the Presiding Officer of the Court who may put them to the victim or witnesses in a language which is clear and is not embarrassing.

(iii) The victim of child abuse or rape, while giving testimony in Court, should be allowed sufficient breaks as and when required.

The judiciary has also delivered several judgments reinforcing its views with regard to compensation.

In the case of *Gudalure M.J. Cherian* v. *Union of India*,[23] a compensation of two lakhs fifty thousand rupees was awarded to the victims of rape. In this case, some miscreants had entered a convent and committed rape on nuns. The case was investigated in a perfunctory manner and vital clues and evidence was lost. The Supreme Court, while ordering the Government to suspend the police officers and initiate disciplinary action against them, also directed it to pay compensation to the victims.

In *Bodhisattwa Gautam* v. *Subhra Chakraborty*,[24] the accused established sexual relations with a woman on the pretext of marriage and even falsely married her before the family deity. The woman underwent abortions as a result of such relations but in spite of repeated requests, the accused refused to make their relation known to his family members and finally, abandoned her. A complaint was registered against him when he abandoned his wife, under Sections 312, 420, 496 and 498A IPC. These were mainly offences relating to marriage. But, in its judgment, the Supreme Court equated the plight of the woman to that of a victim of rape and gave an eloquent exposition of the heinousness of the offence and the need to assist the victim to overcome the physical, psychological and financial loss suffered by her. In its opinion, rape is a crime against the entire society. It shatters the equilibrium of the social order. At the same time, it is a devastating experience for a woman and pushes her into deep emotional crisis. It is of paramount importance to rehabilitate the woman who has suffered such a trauma in rape. Referring to the decision in Delhi Domestic Working Women's case, the apex Court pointed out that

> This decision recognizes the right of the victim for compensation by providing that it shall be awarded by the Court on conviction of the offender subject to the

> finalization of Scheme by the Central Government. If the Court trying an offence of rape has jurisdiction to award the compensation at the final stage, there is no reason to deny to the Court the right to award interim compensation which should also be pervaded in the Scheme. The jurisdiction to pay interim compensation shall be treated as part of the overall jurisdiction of the Court trying the offences of rape which...is an offence against the basic Human Rights as also the fundamental right of personal liberty and life.[25]

Accordingly, the accused was ordered to pay an interim compensation of Rs. 1,000 per month during the pendency of the case.

Similarly, in *Jarnail Singh* v. *State of Punjab*[26] where the appellant was convicted under Section 376 IPC, for raping a girl below 16 years, the apex Court directed him to pay an amount of twelve thousand rupees as compensation to the victim.

In yet another landmark decision, *Chairman Railway Board* v. *Chandrima Das*[27] a Bangladeshi woman was raped by some railway officials in the railway yatri niwas. The apex Court asked the railways to pay Rs. 10,00,000 as compensation for the infringement of her right to life under Article 21 of the Constitution. In the opinion of the Court,

> Smt. Hanuffa Khatoon, who was not the citizen of this country but came here as a citizen of Bangladesh was, nevertheless, entitled to all the constitutional rights available to a citizen so far as "Right to Life" was concerned. She was entitled to be treated with dignity and was also entitled to the protection of her person as guaranteed under Article 21 of the Constitution. As a national of another country, she could not be subjected to a treatment which was below dignity nor could she be subjected to physical violence at the hands of Govt. employees who outraged her modesty. The right available to her under Article 21 was thus violated. Consequently, the State was under the constitutional liability to pay compensation to her.

In *Brijesh* v. *State of Haryana*[28] where an 18 year old girl was gang raped by three young men, the High Court ordered compensation to the tune of Rs. 50,000. In the words of the Court, since, the Fundamental Right of the prosecutrix—Nisha under Article 21 of the Constitution of India i.e. right to life which included right to live with human dignity has been violated, so it will be in the fitness of the circumstances, if a sum of Rs. 50,000 is awarded as compensation to Nisha which shall be shared jointly and severally by all the three appellants.

In *Chandradevi, Kamalanantha & others* v. *State of Tamil Nadu*[29] a sensational news item appeared in the *Indian Express* which captured the attention of its readers. It spoke of the rape of 13 minor girls by the Swami of an ashram. Subsequently on investigation, the case came up before the Court and it was revealed that Swami Premananda committed rape on 13 girls in his ashram. He used to commit rape immediately some time after the girls attained puberty while they were put on guard duty during nights and at other odd hours and places. The Court ordered life imprisonment in addition to payment of fine. It opined,

> While imposing the fine amount on A-1, the learned Sessions Judge has taken into consideration the age of the victim girls, the trauma which they have undergone and the damage which they have suffered and hence ordered a fine of Rs. 5,00,000 on A-1 to be paid as compensation to each of the victim girl. We find that the fine imposed is commensurate with the crime and the capacity of A-1 to compensate. It is not in dispute that A-1 is holding a Joint Account...to a tune of Rs. 89,00,000 and the operation of this account had been frozen under the orders of the Court. Though an attempt had been made by a third party to represent that this amount represents the amount of a Trust and that it cannot be utilized by A-1 for paying the fine ordered to be paid by him, we have no hesitation in rejecting such a representation made without any pleading and records. It only fortifies our apprehension that the appellants are trying to see that the fine amount is not recovered

> and thereby deprive the victim girls of their due compensation. As the amount in the bank is in the joint account of A-1, the said amount is liable to be utilized for payment of the compensation. Therefore, we direct the concerned, including the bank and the revenue authorities, to permit and release the fine amount of Rs. 61,30,000 (Rs. 61,20,000 + Rs. 10,000) and the compensation as ordered by the Court, viz., Rs. 5,00,000 be paid to each of the victim girls.

Another path breaking judgment by the Rajasthan High Court deserves specific mention.[30] It was a case of rape of a German Lady Tourist in the city of Jodhpur by two auto-rickshaw drivers. Under instructions of the Hon'ble High Court of Rajasthan, the fast track Court decided the case within a period of two weeks of its occurrence. The investigation, including medical tests and DNA, was completed and charge sheet laid within a record time of 36 hours. The accused persons were represented by competent lawyers and the judge gave full opportunity for defense to cross-examine the victim, thereby ensuring a fair and speedy trial. The accused were thereafter convicted and sentenced to imprisonment for life. From the victim's perspective what was remarkable was that she was provided boarding and lodging by the State Government and all expenses during the days of trial was borne by the former. Additionally, an amount of Rs. 3 lacs was awarded as compensation by the High Court of Rajasthan. While disposing of the civil writ petition, the High Court passed the following directions:

- The Registrar General should ensure that the trial in cases of Sexual Violence is completed within a period of four months from the date of filing the charge sheet.
- The State Government must prepare a scheme to ensure that victims of violence are immediately provided necessary financial, medical, psychological and social assistance and where the victims are foreigners, their statements be recorded immediately.

- Courts trying sexual offences must ensure that victims are not harassed, victims are not made to wait for long hours to tender evidence, evidence is recorded in an atmosphere conducive to the woman. Any disrespectful language to victim used by a court officer including the lawyer shall be construed as a misconduct to be appropriately dealt with by the respective authorities.

International Concerns

The plight of victims of crime and rape, in particular, has been a cause of concern at the global level. International Conventions, Declarations and victim specific legislations have been passed to ameliorate their condition and ensure a life of dignity and well being.[31] The Declaration of Basic Principles of Justice for Victims of Crime and Abuse of Power[32] is a positive acknowledgement of the basic need "of adopting national and international measures in order to secure the universal and effective recognition, of and respect for, the rights of victims of crime and of abuse of power". It enjoins the Member States to establish judicial and administrative mechanisms to enable victims to obtain redress through formal or informal procedures that are expeditious, fair, inexpensive and accessible. Victims should be informed of their rights in seeking redress through such mechanisms. Some of the crucial steps underlined towards a victim oriented approach are:

- Informing victims of their role and the scope, timing and progress of the proceedings and of the disposition of their cases;
- Allowing the views and concerns of victims to be presented and considered at appropriate stages of the proceedings where their personal interests are affected, without prejudice to the accused and consistent with the relevant national criminal justice system;
- Providing proper assistance to victims throughout the legal process;

- Taking measures to minimize inconvenience to victims, protect their privacy, when necessary, and ensure their safety, as well as that of their families and witnesses on their behalf, from intimidation and retaliation;
- Avoiding unnecessary delay in the disposition of cases and the execution of orders or decrees granting awards to victims;
- Making fair restitution to victims, their families of dependants;
- Providing adequate compensation to the victims and families, by offender or State.

Ensuring the availability of necessary material, medical, psychological and social assistance through governmental, voluntary, community-based and indigenous means.

The European Convention on the Compensation of Victims of Violent Crimes[33] also calls upon its Member States "for reasons of equality and social solidarity" to "introduce or develop schemes for the compensation of...victims by the State in whose territory such crimes were committed, in particular when the offender has not been identified or is without resources". Countries of the World, from United Kingdom to Australia, New Zealand, Canada, USA and several others have taken prominent steps to appreciate victim perspectives, *viz.*,

- Passing of special legislations regarding crime victims so that pro-victim practices are made obligatory on the part of police, prosecution and Courts.
- Enforcement of UN Declaration of Basic Principles for protecting the interests of victims.
- Facilitation of victim participation in the criminal justice process by allowing him to be heard at various stages of the case, to have information about the progress made, to present Victim Impact Statements enabling the judge to decide the quantum of punishment.
- Compensation as a right of the victim.

- Entitlement to receive assistance, guidance and many types of welfare benefits from governmental and voluntary agencies.

Ensuring Human Rights of Victims

A holistic approach is required to ensure the Human Rights of victims in the dire need of the times. They may be categorized as under:

Right to Compensation: In the first place, compensation to victims must be drawn up as a matter of right. So far as rape victims are concerned, the offence involves infliction of wounds on the body as well as the soul of the woman. Hence, it requires years to recover from the traumatic experience. In fact victims have opined that in most cases it is difficult to forget the nightmarish experience of rape. It overshadows the happiness of their entire lives. Whether married or unmarried, a woman is never again able to enjoy the thrills of sexual life; she suffers from anxiety, shock, intense fear, depression, suicidal ideation, and post-traumatic stress disorder. Long-term effects also include disordered eating, sleep problems, sexual dysfunction and increased negative feelings about themselves. Apart from the psychological part, in forced or violent rapes, the victim may have severe injuries over her body. Recovery from the deep-seated problem involves long-term treatment involving lakhs of rupees. The State must provide for payment of adequate compensation to the victim. Furthermore, payment of compensation should not be dependent on the conviction and/or acquittal of the offender. In all cases where an allegation of the commission of such offence is made by the victim and it *prima facie* appears from medical reports and/or otherwise to the concerned authorities that such an act has taken place, payment of compensation may be ordered. Immediacy in payment of compensation is a dire requirement as, much of its efficacies/needs may be lost with the passage of time. Thus, payment of money after two or five years of the incident would be of no utility; rather its immediate access would benefit the victim to tide over the physical as well as mental distress through proper medical/psychological care and treatment.

Determination of the quantum of compensation must be a matter of discretion for the Court/Board. However, in no case should it fall below the bare minimum fixed by the State or be a mere token amount for the satisfaction of the Court and the accused. Having regard to the heinousness of the crime, the Court should be stern in ordering a hefty amount as compensation. The nature of injuries caused, the gravity of the injuries, the impact of the incident on the victim, the present situation of the victim should be factors for the Court to consider in the matter of fixation of compensation.

Institutionalized Care and Treatment: The next important aspect is the setting up of Rape Crises Centers in all over the country. These centers would operate as after care institutions for the victims as well as place of temporary stay and comfort. To be run primarily by NGOs with the financial assistance of the State Governments, these centers would employ trained women as doctors, nurses, counseling experts, psychologists to enable the victims to tide over their physical problems and mental stress. Rehabilitation of the victim would be the final goal of such institutions. While it may not be compulsory for all victims to take recourse to these centers, and the facilities offered by them, those who desire and/or approach must necessarily be extended the services. The Court may also, having regard to the condition of the victim, in specific cases, direct that she be treated or kept at the centers for a substantial period of time.

Economic Assistance and Establishment: India being a tradition-bound conservative society, victims are treated with much intemperance and brutality. Once a woman is raped, she is discarded by her relatives and left to fend for herself. It is also true that in India, most women are still brought up as homemakers with little or no education to rescue them in times of distress. In such scenario, the writer, may well imagine the plight of the victim. With minimum education and no skills whatsoever, she is left with no alternative but to beg and/or die. To avert such misfortune, the State may provide for vocational training programs, financial assistance for small-scale business opportunities etc. A slight liberal and sympathetic approach from the part of the authorities would help in devising better means *vis-à-vis* the victim.

Humane Treatment: Victims should not be made to relive their experiences in Court. In other words, the Court should not be a forum for re-enactment of the drama of rape. As psychologists have revealed, victims prefer to remain silent in fear of the shameful and indecent treatment they would have to face during trials. This has to be done away with. The hostile treatment meted out to the victims by the defense counsel, in particular, and the Judge, at times, should be greatly discouraged. A predetermined prejudicial mental set up has to be completely wiped out. Thus the basic notion that the victim is also responsible for the occurrence must not haunt the Honorable justice. He must consider the facts and the evidence adduced before him impartially, not with an eye of suspicion. In line with this thought, he must regulate the questions put forward by the defense counsel. Any attempt to hurt the dignity of the woman standing as a victim must not be tolerated; rather all questions directed at her must be carefully scrutinized so as not to offend her sensibilities.

A hostile climate inside the Court must necessarily be avoided. The victim must be made to feel at ease; she must be kept out of the public gaze. Hence, trials must compulsorily be held in camera; identities of victims must necessarily be withheld. The victim may also be given the opportunity to decide on whether to face her attacker as it may have, in cases, severe effects on her psyche. In other words, while she must be present in the Court for examination and cross-examination, arrangements may be made whereby she does not come face to face with her attacker. A screen separating the accused and the victim while enabling the Judge to see either of them may be made use of.

Participation in Trials: The victim must not be a left out party in the entire trial procedure. As her interests are of prime concern, she must be given the opportunity to intimately associate herself if she so desires. She must be allowed to provide a counsel of her choice, in addition to the State counsel, as in criminal proceedings, the aggrieved party is the State. This, in many cases, may improve the effectiveness of the entire process and in turn secure conviction. She must also be intimated of the day-today progress in the trial. She must be consulted and taken into confidence in every matter and/or argument that the State proposes to bring up before the Court. Such an approach would reassure the faith of victim in the system and help to create a full proof trial procedure.

As suggested by the Committee on Reforms of Criminal Justice System constituted under the Chairmanship of Dr. V.S. Malimath,[34] The victim may be made a party to assist the Court in discovering truth. He may be permitted to put questions or suggest questions to be put by the Court to the witnesses produced by the parties. He can also point out the availability of other evidence that would assist the Court in discovering truth. On the victim furnishing such information the Court may cause production of such evidence as it considers necessary to discover truth. It has further reiterated[35] that active participation of the victim during investigation would be helpful in discovering truth. He can assist investigation in finding out the real offender and in collecting evidence to prove the commission of the offence by the assailant. He can also offer suggestions for proper investigation of the case. When the investigation proceeds on wrong lines, the victim can move the Court for appropriate directions to ensure proper investigation of the case.

Speedy Justice: Finally, and most importantly, 'speedy justice' should be the motto of the criminal justice system. Speedy disposal of cases would help the victims, since they would not be made to relive their experiences for years in Court rooms. That would also help build the confidence of the victims in the system. As suggested by the Malimath Committee:

> The Committee...recommends that so far as offences of rape and other sexual offences against women are concerned, a suitable provision should be made

requiring the investigation agency to complete the investigation within the prescribed time and for the Court to dispose of such cases on priority basis within a period of four months.[36]

Concluding Note

Today in the 21st century, Human Rights not only enjoy positive recognition at the national level but international recognition as well. In fact, Human Rights have become the yardstick in determining the status of a country's civilization. In determining a nation's rank in the political civilization, no test can be so decisive than the degree in which Human Rights as defined by law is actually realized. It is not uncommon that every problem of today has been infested with some Human Rights dimensions in one way or other, criminal justice system too is not an exception to this general rule. The Constitution of India envisages a welfare State that secures social justice to all the people of India. Administration of criminal justice by the welfare State is one such means through which the State can provide social justice.[37]

The Indian criminal justice system needs an overhaul. Among the other significant reforms, a major area remains that of victim orientation. Greater respect and consideration towards victims and their rights in the investigative and prosecution processes, provision for greater choices to victims in trial and disposition of the accused, and a scheme of compensation, aftercare and rehabilitation in society[38] is particularly called for if the country has to respond to the international call for a Human Rights protected regime. The winds of change are gradually paving the path,[39] but a more pragmatic and prompt initiative on the part of the legislature will be appreciated.

Notes

1. K.D. Gaur, "Justice to Victims of Crime: A Human Rights Approach" in K.I. Vibhute (ed.), *Criminal Justice* (Lucknow: Eastern Book Company, 1st Edn. 2004) p. 350.
2. *Rattan Singh* v. *State of Punjab* (1979) 4 SCC 719.
3. In 1971, the reported cases of rape in India were 2487, in 1981 it was 5409, in 1991, it was 10,410 and in 2002 it is 16373. The

increase in the cases as represented by the figures is staggering. However, these figures are indicative of the reported cases and not the actual figures, since many hundreds and thousands of such cases go unreported due to fear of social stigma, ostracization, family honor etc.

According to the Crime in India, 2002, rape cases have reported a mixed trend over last five years with a decrease of 2.5% in the year 2001 and an increase of 1.8% in the 2002. Madhya Pradesh reported the highest number of cases (2891), contributing 17.6% to total cases reported in the country, followed by Uttar Pradesh (1415), Maharashtra (1352), Rajasthan (1051) and Bihar (1040).

4. "In the Indian setting,...[R]arely will a girl or a woman make false allegation of sexual assault.... Because: (1) A girl or a woman in the tradition-bound society of India would be extremely reluctant even to admit that any incident which is likely to reflect on her chastity has ever occurred. (2) She would be conscious of the damage of being ostracized by the society or being looked down by the society including her own family members, relatives, friends and neighbors. (3) She would have to brave the whole world. (4) She would face the right of losing the love and respect of her own husband and near relatives, and of her matrimonial home, and happiness being shattered. (5) If she is unmarried she would apprehend that it would be difficult to secure an alliance with a suitable match from a respectable or an acceptable family. (6) It would almost inevitably and invariably result in mental torture and suffering to herself. (7) The fear of being taunted by others will always haunt her. (8) She would feel extremely embarrassed in relating the incident to others being overpowered by a feeling of shame on account of the upbringing in a tradition-bound society where by and large sex is taboo. (9) The natural inclination would be to avoid giving publicity to the incident lest the family name and family honor should be brought into controversy. (10) The parents of an unmarried girl as also the husband and members of her husband's family of a married woman would also more often than not, want to avoid publicity on account of the fear of social stigma on the family name and family honor. (11) The fear of the victim herself being considered to be promiscuous, or, in some way responsible for the incident regardless of her innocence. (12) The reluctance to face interrogation by the investigating agency, to face the Court, to face the cross-examination by counsel for the culprit and the risk of being disbelieved, act as a deterrent..." *B.B. Hirjibhai* v. *State of Gujrat* AIR 1983 SC 753.
5. The concept of being 'habituated' to sexual intercourse was initially thought to indicate 'consensual sex', though the Supreme Court in *Sanju Gope v. State* 1998 Cri. L.J. 1984 held, "A woman

may be of immoral character and yet if sexual intercourse is committed with her against her will or without her consent, the person committing it must be held guilty of rape." *Milind Ambadas Mhaske v. State of Maharashtra* 1998 Cri. L.J. 1357. See, *Tukaram* v. *State of Maharashtra* AIR 1979 SC 185.

6. Swayam, "Gender Equality and the Judicial System in West Bengal" in N.K. Chakrabarti and Shachi Chakrabarty (ed.), *Gender Justice* (Kolkata: R. Cambray & Co. 2006) pp. 386-87. "The responses of the litigants who had taken cases of violence against them to Court paint a gloomy picture of what they experience in the hands of the judicial system...They are mistreated, misinformed, and ignored or even sexually harassed by their own lawyers. The judges often do not consider them reliable or truthful witnessed(sic). The judges, lawyers, Court officials, members of the public behave rudely with them or are at best dismissive of them."
7. Section 376, Indian Penal Code 1860.
8. Section 154(1) and (2) Code of Criminal Procedure 1973.
9. Section 154(3) Code of Criminal Procedure 1973.
10. Section 157(2) Code of Criminal Procedure 1973.
11. Section 320 Code of Criminal Procedure 1973.
12. Section 24(8) Code of Criminal Procedure 1973.
13. Section 12(1)(h) and S. 13(1) of the Legal Aid Services Act 1987.
14. Section 378(1) read with S. 378(3) Code of Criminal Procedure 1973.
15. Section 378(4) Code of Criminal Procedure 1973.
16. Sub-section (1) of Section 357 reads as: When a Court imposes a sentence or fine or a sentence (including a sentence of death) of which fine forms a part, the Court may, when passing judgment, order the whole or any part of the fine recovered to be applied: (a) in defraying the expenses properly incurred in the prosecution; (b) in the payment to any person of compensation for any loss or injury caused by the offence, when compensation is, in the opinion of the Court, recoverable by such person in a Civil Court; (c) when any person is convicted of any offence for having caused death of another person or of having abetted the commission of such an offence, in paying compensation to the persons who are, under the Fatal Accidents Act, 1855 entitled to recover damages from the person sentenced for the loss resulting to them from such death; (d) when any person is convicted of any offence which includes theft, criminal misappropriation, criminal breach of trust, or cheating or of having dishonestly assisted in disposing of, stolen property knowing or having reason to believe the same to be

stolen, in compensation any *bona fide* purchaser of such property for the loss of the same if such property is restored to the possession of the person entitled thereto.

17. N.K. Chakraborty, "Victim Assistance and Compensation to Crime Victims under Indian Criminal Justice System" in National Seminar on Victimology, May 12-14, 1998, Organized by Punjab Police Academy, pp. 9-10.
18. *Rudul Sah* v. *State of Bihar* AIR 1983 SC 1086.
19. See also, *Bhim Singh v. State of Jammu & Kashmir* (1985) 4 SCC 577; *People's Union for Democratic Rights v. State of Bihar,* 1987 1 SCR 631; *People's Union for Democratic Rights Thru. Its Secy. v. Police Commissioner, Delhi Police Headquarters,* (1989) 4 SCC 730; *Arvinder Singh Bagga v. State of U.P. (1994) 6 SCC 565; Dr. Jacob George v. State of Kerala* (1994) 3 SCC 430; *Paschim Bangal Khet Mazdoor Samity v. State of West Bengal & Ors.* (1996) 4 SCC 37 *and Mrs. Manju Bhatia v. N.D.M.C.* (1997) 6 SCC 370; *Nilabeti Behera v.State of Orissa* (1993) 2 SCC 746.
20. *Delhi Domestic Working Women's Forum* v. *Union of India* (1995) 1 SCC 14.
21. AIR 1996 SC 1393.
22. *Saakshi* v. *Union of India* AIR 2004 SC 3566.
23. 1995 SCC (Cr) 925.
24. AIR 1996 SC 922.
25. *Ibid.,* at p. 928.
26. (1998) 8 SCC 629.
27. MANU/SC/0046/2000.
28. MANU/PH/0482/2003.
29. MANU/TN/2335/2002.
30. *Suo Moto v. State of Rajasthan* RLW 2005 (2) Raj. 1385.
31. Refer to the Universal Declaration of Human Rights, 1948; Article 3 of U.N. Declaration on the Elimination of Violence against Women which says that: Women are entitled to the equal enjoyment and protection of all Human Rights and fundamental freedoms in the political, economic, social, cultural, civil or any other field. These rights include, *inter alia*: (a) The right to life;... (b) The right not to be subjected to torture, or other cruel, inhuman or degrading treatment or punishment.
32. UN Resolution No. 40/34 of 29th November, 1985.
33. Strasbourg, 24.XI.1983.
34. Government of India, *Committee on Reforms of Criminal Justice System* (Ministry of Home Affairs, New Delhi, March 2003) para. 2.20.2.

35. *Ibid.*, at para. 2.20.3.
36. *Supra* n. 34, para. 16.6.2
37. David Ambrose, "Law of Confessions and Right against Torture: Balancing Societal Interest and Individual's Right—Need for Legislative Action" in K.I. Vibhute (ed.), *Criminal Justice* (Lucknow: Eastern Book Company, 1st Edn. 2004) p. 243.
38. N.R. Madhava Menon, "Victim Compensation Law and Criminal Justice—A Plea for a Victim Orientation in Criminal Justice" in K.I. Vibhute (ed.), *Criminal Justice* (Lucknow: Eastern Book Company, 1st Edn. 2004) p. 362. See also, S. Muralidharan, "Rights of Victims in the Indian Criminal Justice System" (http://www.ielrc.org/content/ a0402.pdf).
39. For proposals for reform, see Law Commission of India, *Forty Second Report: Indian Penal Code* (Government of India, New Delhi, 1971); Law Commission of India, *One Hundred and Fifty Sixth Report on the Indian Penal Code* (Government of India, New Delhi, 1997); Law Commission of India, *One Hundred and Fifty Fourth Report on the Code of Criminal Procedure, 1973* (Government of India, New Delhi, 1996); Draft Bill 'The Victim' (Criminal Injuries) Right to Assistance Bill, 1996; The Victims (Crimnal Violence) Compensation Bill, 1996.

13

Revisiting Award of Compensation for Violation of Fundamental Rights: An Analysis of Indian Supreme Court Decisions

J.L. Kaul and *Anju Vali Tikoo**

I. Introduction

The language of Human Rights has over the years gathered great momentum in all legal systems of the world. The idea of Human Rights itself has become universalized, even though no convergence between socio-legal systems about the exact content and systems of protection of Human Rights is easily forthcoming. Indeed, despite this, Human Rights have been described as "common language of humanity".[1] The Human Rights discourses have sought meaningfully to interpose Human Rights in every conceivable area of human activity. The national and international Human Rights law, which has grown over the years has been so interpreted that it provides broad content to the rights regime of individuals, groups, sub-groups and minorities. Various theoretical justifications have been offered to the growing affirmation of 'the universal rights of man'.[2]

---

* We are grateful to Susheel Bala for providing immense research support. We also thank Niraj. Shortcomings, if any, however, are ours only.

The methodology for implementation of Human Rights at both national and international levels has not been free from difficulties. Even though the national constitutions and the legal regimes guarantee the Human Rights, yet the enforcement of these rights has been far from satisfactory. It is eventually the superior Courts, which have an onerous task towards enforcement of Human Rights. Broadly speaking, the Courts and National Human Rights Commissions[3] and other designated authorities, have been empowered to uphold and enforce Human Rights and pass appropriate orders in this regard. Also the emergence of the victim protection jurisprudence[4] has enlarged the scope of protection of Human Rights. However, this jurisprudence includes the protection programs for victims of crime, as well as victims of abuse of power.[5] While as the former is the subject matter of criminal justice system, the latter is the subject matter of public law, and hence falls within the rubric of protection and enforcement of Human Rights regime. In our submission, compensatory jurisprudence falls within the realm of public law remedy, against abuse of power, resulting in abridgement of right to life and liberty. However, not all abuse of power, resulting in victimization can be brought under public law enforcement category particularly under compensatory jurisprudence.

In India too, the Human Rights are catalogued in the Constitution. The Constitution of India guarantees civil and political rights in Part III and social, cultural and economic rights in Part IV.[6] It also confers power on the Supreme Court[7] and the High Courts[8] to protect and enforce fundamental Human Rights in Part III. The Supreme Court acts as 'sentinel on the qui vive' in relation to fundamental Human Rights. Over the years, and particularly in post-emergency era, the Indian Supreme Court has interpreted the rights regime broadly and enthusiastically. It has also resorted to judicial activism[9] in key constitutional and legal interpretations, which has supported the cause of protection of Human Rights. In the process it has devised newer strategies to enforce the fundamental Human Rights. The Supreme Court and the High Courts have even awarded compensation to the victims of violation of Human Rights in the exercise of their inherent constitutional powers. This remedy of claim of compensation is apart from the remedies available to such victims under ordinary law of tort. The compensatory remedy may be seen as important fallout of constitutional tort litigation, which has increased in India in recent years. This is indeed a progressive way of looking at promotion and enforcement of Human Rights and has found general support in the Indian legal scenario. Even though the Courts have not been consistent in awarding such damages/compensation in violation of right to life, it exhibits a rich interplay between compensation as an individual remedy and the development of important constitutional norms. Indeed of late, Indian Supreme Court has been actively contributing to such constitutionalism.[10] Looking at how the Supreme Court has embarked upon the compensation as a remedy for violation of Fundamental Rights, it has given rise to arguments that every violation of such right under Article 21[11] of Indian Constitution should be accompanied by appropriate compensation, and should always be legally enforceable. This is so, because Supreme Court has taken into account the doctrine of strict liability in constitutional tort litigation.[12] Secondly, should this right be forthcoming even in cases involving violation of other Fundamental Rights apart from Article 21?

This paper analyzes the doctrine of award of compensation in case of violation of Fundamental Human Rights, as enunciated by the Indian Supreme Court. It tries to look at the justifications given by the Court for such awards. Part II of the paper highlights the position of Human Rights in Indian Constitution. It argues that these rights are justifiably included in our Constitution. Part III of the paper examines the way in which Supreme Court has positioned itself in protection and enforcement of Fundamental Human Rights. Part IV and Part V analyze the concept of compensatory jurisprudence as enunciated and developed by the Indian Supreme Court. It also explains the theoretical basis as expounded by the Court. Various judgments of the Indian Supreme Court in this connection are also discussed. Lastly, Part VI as usual deals with the conclusions.

II. Legitimacy of Human Rights

Human Rights as a concept have evolved gradually over several centuries.[13] They have been given a plurality of names, like rights of man, natural rights, Human Rights or Fundamental Rights, each one of them referring to different sets of non-derogable rights which individuals must possess.[14] Such a nomenclature has been the product of juristic thought emanating at particular periods of progressive evolution and realization of these rights. Even though the theoretical explanations of the legitimacy of Human Rights differ, they have made us believe that they are indispensable for the holistic development of individual's personality. These rights are of such a nature that the State is under a duty not to violate these rights and the individuals have a right to enforcement of these rights.[15]

Every legal system, India being no exception, recognizes the legitimacy of Human Rights in their social and legal conscience. These rights are overwhelmingly necessary for overall human welfare. The United Nations has been a pioneer in building a universal consensus for the protection and promotion of Human Rights. Indeed the Universal Declaration of Human Rights, 1948 was a milestone in the progressive realization of Human Rights throughout the world. It has provided a framework for all shades of Human Rights development. In fact, the 1948 Declaration emphasizes that recognition of the inherent dignity and of equal and inalienable rights of all members of the human family, is the foundation of freedom, justice and peace in the world.[16] Dereze and Sen rightly observe that integrity of democracy can deeply be threatened by widespread Human Rights violations.[17] After the 1948 Declaration, the United Nations has worked well in the drafting of various Conventions, Treaties and Protocols concerning universal realization of Human Rights.[18] Human Rights activists, trade union groups and others have even relied upon the 1948 Declaration, and subsequent international Covenants, in their struggles for liberation and empowerment.

Consequently, the provisions of the UN Declaration find significant place in national constitutions throughout the world. It may be argued that the inscription of these rights in the constitutions of the world bear testimony to the legitimacy and importance of Human Rights. This gives us an impression of a trend of convergence of legal cultures towards universal protection of Human Rights.[19] However, a visionary commitment to building institutions, laws and enabling conditions to secure fundamental freedom for all Human Rights, for all people in all countries has to be emphasized.[20]

The making of India's Constitution also demonstrates the greatest concern for fundamental Human Rights and freedoms for people of India. Far before the UN Charter concern for the protection of Human Rights, the concern for Human Rights of people of India was a recurrent theme in the freedom struggle. The persistent demands for their protection reverberated throughout the freedom struggle. It was made as far back as in 1895 in the Constitution of India Bill, popularly called the Swaraj Bill, which was inspired by Lokmanya Tilak. The demand was repeated in Mrs. Annie Besant's Commonwealth of India Bill finalized by the National Convention of Political Parties in 1925, by the Motilal Nehru Committee in 1928 at the Karachi Session of the Indian National Congress in 1932, and by the Tej Bahadur Sapru Committee in 1944-1945.[21]

The drafters of Indian Constitution had before them important documents like the Magna Carta, Declaration of Rights of Man, US Constitution, as well as the UN Charter and other social welfare laws of several countries. As rightly pointed out by Seervai, the emphasis on Human Rights, in the UN Charter, to which India was a party, was not without its impact on our Constitution.[22] In our submission many provisions in our Constitution bear the imprint of UN provisions. The Constituent Assembly discussed the subject of fundamental Human Rights extensively and painstakingly. Thereafter, the Assembly embodied in Preamble to the Constitution, the resolution to secure to all its citizens, justice social, economic and political; liberty of thought, expression, belief, faith and worship; equality of status and of opportunity;

and to promote fraternity assuring the dignity of the individual and unity of the nation. The Preamble is the mirror of our Constitution.[23] The Preamble avows to secure the basic Human Rights to the people. The dignity of the individual secured by the Preamble and some of the Fundamental Rights are one of the basic features of the Constitution.[24]

Along with other common law countries India has also incorporated within its constitution a justiciable bill of rights.[25] It may be noted that entire Human Rights jurisprudence of India centers on Part III and Part IV of the Constitution. Part III of the Constitution, under the caption of Fundamental Rights, guarantees a fairly comprehensive array of basic Human Rights to citizens and casts a duty on the State not to violate these rights.[26] While as Part III rights are enforceable rights, Part IV, the Directive Principles of State Policy incorporating socio-economic rights, are not enforceable, nevertheless they are fundamental in the governance of the country.[27] Part III supplemented by Part IV and the Preamble represent the compendium of Human Rights and fundamental freedoms as enshrined in the Constitution of India.[28] These rights cover a wide spectrum such as equality,[29] freedom of expression, assembly and association, freedom of movement, freedom to carry on profession or business,[30] freedom of conscience and freedom of religion.[31] There are guarantees against retrospective criminal laws, double jeopardy and self-incrimination[32] and against deprivation of life and personal liberty.[33] Fundamental Rights as enacted in our Constitution not only recognize the dignity of individual, but also recognize the necessity for the full development of the individual and for preserving the unity of India. Minorities are guaranteed linguistic and cultural rights, and the right to establish and administer educational institutions of their choice.[34] Seervai observes, "[t]hese religious and cultural freedoms remove the most potential sources of discord in a multi-racial society".[35] At the same time, the Constitution provides an elaborate mechanism for the enforcement of such Human Rights. Part III of the Constitution itself guarantees the enforcement of these Fundamental Rights.[36]

Commenting upon the legitimacy of these Human Rights, it has been observed that they inhere in the dignity of human beings and are therefore inalienable rights.[37] Human Rights are not gifts conferred by the State. Constitution and law do not create Human Rights. They are enacted to protect Human Rights, which inhere in individual's antecedent to constitutions and the laws. Fundamental Human Rights are essential for development of the human personality and for full realization of the human potential. Chief Justice Subba Rao observed, "[f]undamental Rights are the modern name for what have been traditionally known as natural rights. They are moral rights, which every human being everywhere at all times ought to have simply because of the fact that in contradistinction with other beings he is rational or moral."[38] Similarly, Mathew, J. in *Kesavananda Bharti* v. *Union of India* observed, "they are rights, which are inherent in human beings, because they are human beings, whether you call them by human rights or any other appellation. It was to secure the basic human rights like liberty and equality that people gave unto themselves the constitution. These basic rights are essential features of our constitution."[39] Similar sentiments have been echoed by Bhagwati J, when he observed,

> these fundamental rights represent the basic values cherished by the people of India, since the Vedic times and they are calculated to protect the dignity of individuals and create conditions in which every human being can develop his personality to the fullest extent. They weave a "pattern of guarantee" on the basic structure of human rights and impose negative obligations on the state not to encroach on individual liberty in its various dimensions.[40]

Actual working of the Constitution shows that the inclusion of Fundamental Rights has been more than justified. They have also acted as restraint on executive and legislative power. That is precisely the reason that under Article, 13(2), any law made by the State inconsistent with or violating Fundamental Rights will be *protanto void*. Commenting upon the necessity and relevance of the fundamental Human Rights, the Supreme Court has observed:

> ...The Fundamental Rights are intended not only to protect individual's rights but they are based on high public policy. Liberty of the individual and the protection of his Fundamental Rights are the very essence of the democratic way of life adopted by the Constitution.... This Court would refuse to circumscribe them or to curtail them except as provided by the Constitution.[41]

Secondly, the Court has broadened the scope of these rights by interpretative techniques. The Court has rightly observed:

> it must be remembered that Fundamental Rights are constitutional guarantees given to the people of India and are not merely paper hopes or fleeting promises and so long as they find a place in the Constitution, they should not be allowed to be emasculated in their application by narrow and constricted judicial interpretation.[42]

Thirdly, the legitimacy of the Fundamental Rights springs from the fact that, constitutionally if the effect of any legislation is that it violates rights in Part III, the legislation would be unconstitutional; the motive of the legislature is of no consequence.[43] Furthermore, even a constitutional amendment that takes away or abridges basic/essential features of Part III (Fundamental Rights) will be void and unconstitutional.[44] The Court has even legitimized the Directive Principles as providing support and content to the Fundamental Rights. Although, initially it ruled that Directive Principles were subservient to Fundamental Rights. However, over the years, it has followed a "collaborative and synergetic approach", and has even ruled that harmony between Fundamental Rights and Directive Principles is one of the basic features of the Constitution.[45] If need be, Part III rights may be given restricted interpretation in order to uphold Part IV rights. Indeed, if the social-welfare functions of the State is any indicator; one does not see any difficulty in accepting this thesis of reading Directive Principles of State Policy into the Fundamental Rights part. Of course, the State's willingness and capacities to act as a social welfare agent and thus efficiently protect Human Rights and entitlements in the face of liberalization of economy and globalization remains doubtful.

III. Supreme Court and Fundamental Human Rights

The Indian judiciary has played an effective role in promoting and enforcing the culture of Human Rights. The Supreme Court being the ultimate interpreter of the Constitution has displayed its concern for Fundamental Rights from time to time. The Court acts as the protector and guardian of these rights. Secondly, the Court as an interpreter of the Fundamental Rights has interpreted these rights in most liberal manner.[46] It has shown highest judicial creativity in catalyzing Human Rights and fundamental freedoms in Indian Constitutionalism. The Courts have exercised judicial review most profitably in the area of Fundamental Rights.[47]

Article 32 and Article 226 of the Constitution are the pivotal provisions empowering Supreme Court and High Courts to enforce the Fundamental Rights. Article 32 guarantees the right to move the Supreme Court by appropriate proceedings for the enforcement of the Fundamental Rights. The Supreme Court is also empowered to issue appropriate writs for the enforcement of the Fundamental Rights. The significance of Article 32 is further highlighted by the fact that this provision not only empowers the court to issue directions or orders or certain writs for the enforcement of Fundamental Rights, but it also provides a guaranteed remedy, as this enforcement right is itself made a fundamental right. This provision cannot even be suspended in respect of Articles 20 and 21.[48]

Commenting upon the importance of Article 32 the chairman of the Drafting Committee B.R. Ambedkar has remarked:

> If I was asked to name any particular Article in this constitution as the most important, an Article without which this constitution will be nullity, I could not refer

to any other Article except this one. It is the very soul of the constitution, and the very heart of it and I am glad that the House has realized its importance.[49]

Apart from the powers being exercised by the Supreme Court under this Article, the Court also exercises appellate jurisdiction,[50] and even has original jurisdiction[51] in several matters. Article 226 of the Constitution empowers the High Courts to issue orders, directions or writs not only for the enforcement of Fundamental Rights but also for any other purposes.

These two Articles combined form the citadel of judicial review under Indian Constitution. These powers of the superior Courts enable them to judicially review legislative actions, judicial, quasi-judicial decisions and administrative actions to examine whether they conform to the Constitutional provisions, including the Fundamental Rights in Part III. The scope and extent of power of judicial review has been the subject matter of several decisions. Despite several doubts over the way the superior Courts particularly the Supreme Court has exercised the judicial review, it is now a settled legal proposition that the Constitution confers powers on the superior Courts to review not only legislations, but also the constitutional amendments in order that they do not violate Fundamental Rights. It is also a settled legal proposition that judicial review is the basic feature of the Constitution, which cannot be taken away even by a constitutional amendment.[52]

Judicial review has been resorted to most profitably in the areas of protection of individual freedoms and Human Rights. The last two decades of working of the judicial review has demonstrated that Supreme Court and High Courts have enthusiastically entertained petitions relating to violation of Human Rights.[53] The cases involving violation of Human Rights have come to the Supreme Court and High Courts not only as private litigations, but also under the banner of Public Interest Litigation (PIL). The Supreme Court has liberalized *locus standi* in PIL, and thus any public-spirited citizen having no private interest can approach the Supreme Court and High Courts for prosecuting violation of Fundamental Rights.[54] The

Court exercising its powers under the banner of public interest litigation has made an immense contribution to Human Rights jurisprudence in India by creating a new regime of Human Rights by expanding the meaning of fundamental right to equality, life and personal liberty; by fashioning new kinds of reliefs under the Court's writ jurisdiction; and by judicial monitoring of State institutions, such as jails, women's protective homes, mental asylums and the like.[55] Issues relating to Human Rights concern relating to criminal justice administration alongside right to life and liberty under Court has even enunciated the doctrine of implied Article 21 have been profusely dealt with the Fundamental Rights. The Court has asserted that in order to treat a right as a fundamental right, it is not necessary that it should be expressly stated in the Constitution as a fundamental right. Political, social and economic changes occurring in the country may entail the recognition of new rights and the law in its eternal youth grows to meet social demands.[56] Most significantly, custodial deaths,[57] illegal detentions,[58] prison administration,[59] right to shelter,[60] rehabilitation of mentally retarded and physically handicapped persons,[61] rights of women and children,[62] protection against exploitation,[63] telephone tapping and other privacy rights,[64] have been ably and legitimately dealt with by the Indian Supreme Court and High Courts. Simultaneously, the socio-economic rights have also been agitated before the Courts and Courts have not shied away from giving relief in these areas. Issues relating to bonded labor, better environmental standards,[65] consumer rights,[66] rights against exposure to hazardous substances,[67] inter-country adoptions[68] fall in this area. The Courts have even taken up the subject matter of good governance of the country under the public interest litigation. Therefore, issues relating to public life, corruption, the criminal-politician nexus, allotment of plots, disinvestments of public sector undertakings, violation of building laws and byelaws have raked judicial attention.[69]

The procedure followed by Supreme Court under Article 32 has given new dimension to the enforcement of Human Rights in India. Not only has it liberalized the *locus standi* rule, to the extent of permitting any member of the public acting in a *bona fide* manner to espouse the cause of Human Rights violations by the State. It has developed epistolary jurisdiction, whereunder any member can invoke Court's jurisdiction by writing a simple letter or sending a telegram. The Court has also permitted new forms of fact finding authorities such as socio-legal commissions of enquiry and even handed over the investigation to National Human Rights Commission or even Central Bureau of Investigation. It has also taken the help of lawyers, journalists, retired judges, District Judges, and others for ascertaining the facts of violations of Human Rights. It has also stated that the Supreme Court rules pertaining to private litigations may not be appropriate in such public interest litigations involving Human Rights violations of class or classes of people.[70] It has been rightly argued that there are no limitations on the powers of Supreme Court and High Courts to award *appropriate* relief and remedy, except the ones that may be imposed by the Courts themselves.[71] Consequently, in dealing with the cases of violations of Human Rights, the Courts have fashioned newer kinds of relief. These reliefs stand in contrast to the reliefs available under private law and private litigations. [72] These reliefs are preventive, curative, restitutive, rehabilitative and compensatory.[73] The compensatory relief is essentially a relief based on the doctrine of constitutional tort applied in constitutional litigations in Human Rights litigations. This type of remedy is available in other legal jurisdictions also. The Supreme Court has heavily relied on this doctrine in legitimizing payment of compensation to the victims of Human Rights violations. This relief does not prevent the victim of Human Rights violation from claiming damages from a civil Court.

IV. Constitutional Tort and Compensatory Relief

The liability of the State for tortious acts of its servants has for some time posed immense difficulties. Even though the concept is recognized in all jurisdictions, yet the doctrine of sovereign immunity was interposed to deny the liability of the State. However, in the event of state donning various activities for the welfare of its citizens, the immunity rule has been diluted by the judicial reasoning in upholding the liability of State for tortious acts of its employees.

A tort is generally viewed as the breach of a duty owed to the public in general (as distinguished from a duty owed to an individual). In India, we do not have a legislation which deals with the liability of State for tortious liability of its servants. The vicarious liability of Union of India and the State Govt. for the tortious acts of its employees is regulated by Article 300 of the Constitution of India.[74] However, the Supreme Court has also enunciated the concept of 'constitutional tort'. A constitutional tort occurs, when an act or omission violates a constitutional right, particularly, a Fundamental Right. In cases of relief on account of Fundamental Right violations, the Courts applying 'constitutional tort' doctrine have done away with some of the doctrines generally applicable in law of torts that make liability dependent on fault. Some of these doctrines have created controversies", e.g. State liability for acts committed in the course of 'sovereign' functions.[75] The Supreme Court of India has also accorded recognition to what may be called the 'tort of misfeasance' in public office, where Union Ministers were ordered to pay damages to the State for *mala fide* official action amounting to abuse of power.[76]

R.M. Sahai, J., has finally laid down the entire concept of tortious liability of State at rest in *N. Nagender Rao and Company* v. *State of Andhra Pradesh*.[77] The Court held:

> ...No civilised system can permit an executive to play with the people of its country and claim that it is entitled to act in any manner as it is sovereign. The concept of public interest has changed with structural changes in the society. No legal or political system today can place the state above the law.... From sincerity, efficiency and dignity of state as a juristic person, propounded in nineteenth century as sound sociological basis for state immunity the circle has gone round and the emphasis is now more on liberty, equality and the rule of law. The modern social thinking of progressive societies and the judicial approach is to do away with archaic state protection and place the state or the government on the

path with any other juristic legal entity. Any watertight compartmentalisation of the functions of the state as "sovereign and non-sovereign" or "governmental of nongovernmental" is not sound. It is contrary to modern jurisprudential thinking. The need of the state to have extraordinary powers can't be doubted but with the conceptual change in the statutory powers being statuary duty for the sake of the society and the people the claim of the common man or ordinary citizen can't be thrown out merely because it was done by an officer of the state even though it was against law and negligent. Needs of the state, duty of its officials and right of the citizens are required to be reconciled so that the rule of law in a welfare state is not shaken.... In welfare State, functions of the State are not only defense of the country or administration of justice or maintaining law and order but extends to regulating and controlling the activities of people in almost every sphere, educational, commercial, social, economic, political and even marital. The demarcating line between sovereign and non-sovereign powers for which no rational basis survives has largely disappeared. Therefore, barring functions such as administration of justice, maintenance of law and order and repression of crime etc. which are among the primary and inalienable functions of a government, the State can't claim any immunity.

V. Supreme Court and Award of Compensation

The Supreme Court by interpreting Article 32 of the Constitution has innovated new methods, techniques and strategies for purposes of securing the enforcement of Fundamental Rights of the individuals. The purpose of such an activist interpretation is to entrench rule of law and to secure the sacrosanct nature and inalienability of the Fundamental Human Rights. However, as we shall see later, the Supreme Court and even the High Courts have put "right to life and liberty" on a higher pedestal than other Fundamental Rights.

The powers under Article 32 are not subject to any limitations, except the ones self-imposed by the Court.[78]

Judicial review has also been held to be part of the basic structure of the Constitution.[79] The powers under the said Article have been used by the Court for preventing as well as remedying the infringement of Fundamental Human Rights. The Court has evolved the award of monetary compensation as one of the means of remedying encroachment of Fundamental Rights as well as providing relief to the victims of said violation. This remedy, it may be mentioned is provided in the International Covenant on Civil and Political Rights[80] that has been relied upon by the Court in some of its decisions, as we shall see later.

Before 1983 the Court refused to award such compensation under Article 32 for violation of Fundamental Rights. In such a scenario, the victim had to file a civil suit under the ordinary law of torts for claiming compensation, which by all means was dilatory and time consuming and subject to other statutory limitations. The Court for the first time in *Khatri* v. *State Bihar*[81] (infamously known as Bhagalpur Blinding Case) considered the issue of award of monetary compensation to the victim of violation of right to life and liberty by the State. Speaking for the Court, Bhagwati, J. stated:

> Why should the Court not be prepared to forge new tools and devise new remedies for the purpose of vindicating the most precious of the precious Fundamental Right to life and personal liberty?[82]

An important question considered by the Court in *Khatri* was, would the State be liable to pay compensation for the acts of its servants outside the scope of their power and authority affecting the life or personal liberty of a person and infringing Article 21 of the Constitution? The Court answered the question in affirmative, saying that otherwise Article 21 would be reduced to a nullity, a mere rope of sand. This way if the officer of the State is acting according to law, there will be no violation of Article 21, and if he were acting without the authority of law, the State would be able to contend that it is not responsible for his actions and therefore there is no violation of Article 21. This case also interposed new dimensions of the constituency of the right to life and personal liberty, which has over the years been continued by the Court.[83]

Even though in *Khatri* the Court did not award compensation to the victims of violation, the Court upheld the doctrine that the Supreme Court under Article 32 and the High Courts under Article 226 can award compensation in the event of infringement of Fundamental Right to life and liberty. It is because of the reasons that the Supreme Court and High Courts under their writ jurisdiction have the powers to issue appropriate orders for remedying the situation.

Rudul Sah v. *State of Bihar*[84] is a landmark decision in compensatory jurisprudence evolved by the Court. The State and its machinery illegally incarcerated the petitioner in jail for 14 years, even after his acquittal by a Criminal Court, demonstrating absolute administrative laxity and scant respect for life and liberty. The Court in a *habeas corpus* petition awarded damages against the State for breach of petitioners' right of personal liberty. The Court observed that the instant case revealed "a sordid and disturbing state of affairs" for which the State was accountable. Taking an activist rather than a traditional approach, in which the Court would have released the petitioner with liberty to file a suit for compensation against the State, the Court awarded compensation in favor of the petitioner. The Court stated, "Not doing so would be doing a mere lip service to the Fundamental Right to liberty which the State Government has so grossly violated". The Court further observed:

> One of the telling ways in which the violation of the right can reasonably be prevented and due compliance with the mandate of Article 21 secured, is to mulct the violators in the payment of monetary compensation.... The right to compensation is some palliative to the unlawful acts of the instrumentalities of the State which act in the name of public interest and which present for their protection the powers of the State as a shield....[85]

It is submitted that had the Court allowed legal technicalities to prevail; it would have amounted to surrendering its powers to State's lawlessness, conveying indifference to the personal liberty of the peoples and their sufferings. It would also have conveyed a message that the gross violations of life and liberties go unpunished. Judicial response to Human Rights cannot be blunted by legal jugglery, as rightly stated by the Supreme Court.[86]

Again in *Sebastian M. Hongray* v. *Union of India*,[87] a *habeas corpus* petition was filed to produce the two missing persons before the Supreme Court. The persons having been taken away by army officers went missing mysteriously. The Government failed to produce them and asserted that they left the military camp alive. The Court found this assertion untenable and incorrect. It came to a conclusion that they were not alive and had met an unnatural death. The Supreme Court keeping in view the torture, agony and mental oppression, through which the wives of these persons had to pass, directed the government to pay Rupees one lakh as a measure of exemplary cost to each of the two women. It also directed that a complaint should be filed under Cr. P.C. to take actions against persons responsible for what *prima facie* appeared to be a case of murder. The Court used the term *exemplary costs* and not the term *exemplary damages*. The award of exemplary costs is permissible in such cases. The Court also did not cite any precedents nor did it support its findings on any jurisprudential doctrines. The object of awarding such costs, in our opinion is reflecting both a deterrent policy and a relief to the victims of such gross violations of life and liberty of persons.

Bhim Singh v. *State of J&K*[88] involved illegal detention of the petitioner, who was a member of legislative assembly of Jammu and Kashmir. The police officers obtained remand orders from the executive magistrate and the sub-judge without production of the petitioner before them. The law required such production before the magistrate. He was detained with malicious intent, and thus deprived of his right to attend the session of the assembly. The Court found that there was gross violation of the petitioner's constitutional rights under Articles 21 & 22 of the Constitution. The Court opined that the deprivation of constitutional rights might not be washed away by mere release of the petitioner. It further observed that in appropriate cases the Court has the power to compensate the victim by awarding suitable monetary compensation. It directed the State of J&K to pay the petitioner a sum of Rupees 50,000. It may be noted here that unlike *Rudul Shah* where the compensation was an interim measure and in the form of exemplary costs, in *Bhim Singh* the award was to compensate the victim, even though in the form of exemplary costs. It is to be noted that the Court relied on *Rudul Shah* and *Sebastian* to substantiate its order of award of compensation.

Nilabati Behera v. *State of Orissa*[89] seems to have firmly settled the issue of award of compensation as a measure of enforcement of Fundamental Rights. This case involved the death in public custody. It is the first time that the Court acknowledged the award of compensation as a remedy under public law in contradistinction to private law claim. It also held that the concept of sovereign immunity is not applicable in cases of violation of the right to life and liberty guaranteed by Article 21 of the Constitution. The Court observed:

> The public law proceedings serve a different purpose than the private law proceedings. The relief of monetary compensation as exemplary damages, in proceedings under Article 32 by this Court or under Article 226 by the High Courts, for established infringement of indefeasible right guaranteed under Article 21 of the Constitution, is a remedy available under public law and is based upon strict liability for contravention of the guaranteed basic and indefeasible rights of the citizens. The purpose of public law is not only to civilize public power but also to assure the citizens that they live under a legal system, which aims to protect their interest and preserve their rights. Therefore, when the Court moulds the relief by granting "compensation" in proceedings under Articles 32 or 226 of the Constitution seeking enforcement or protection of Fundamental Rights, it does so under the public law by way of penalizing the wrongdoer and fixing the liability for the *public wrong* on the State which has failed in its public duty to protect

> the Fundamental Rights of the citizens. The payment of compensation is to be understood in the broader sense of providing relief by an order of making "amends" under the public law for the wrong done due to breach of public duty, of not protecting the Fundamental Rights of the citizen. The compensation is in the nature of "exemplary damages" awarded against the wrongdoer for the breach of its public law duty, and is independent of the rights available to the aggrieved party to claim compensation under the private law in an action based on tort, through a suit instituted in a Court of competent jurisdiction or/and prosecute the offender under the penal law.[90]

It is for the first time that a clear principle and philosophy underlying the doctrine of award of compensation for violation of fundamental right to life can be discerned. The distinction between the remedy of damages under the private law, where sovereign immunity is available, and the public law of compensation, where it is not available, indicates the basis of award of compensation as a remedy. The Court introduced strict liability in public law claims pertaining to Fundamental Rights and particularly the right to life and liberty.[91]

The doctrine of sovereign immunity was again relied on by the State in denying its liability of payment of compensation to the victim of violation of fundamental right of life and liberty. In *State of Andhra Pradesh* v. *Challa Ramakrishna Reddy*[92] where the respondents were in judicial custody, some persons entered the jail premises and hurled bombs, thus killing one of them. The suit for damages of the respondents was decreed by the High Court. The State argued in the appeal before the Supreme Court that the suit for compensation was not maintainable, as the establishment and maintenance of prisons was a sovereign function. The Court speaking through S. Sagir Ahmad, J. observed: "that right to life is one of the basic human rights of a prisoner, be he a convict or an under trial or a detenu does not cease to be a human being. Claiming sovereign immunity cannot defeat a prisoner's Fundamental Right." The Court dismissed the appeal and upheld the decree of the High Court awarding compensation to the dependants of the deceased. It is significant to note here that the Court in exercise of its appellate jurisdiction discussed, considered and relied upon the cases of award of compensation under public law remedy under Article 32 of the Constitution.

In *D.K. Basu* v. *State of West Bengal*,[93] compensatory jurisprudence was firmly approved as a measure relevant to the protection of Human Rights in India. It also invoked reimbursement of the compensation money from the erring State officials who were found guilty of the violation of Human Rights. The Court discussed extensively the law pertaining to claim of compensation against the State for the wrong of police officers depriving citizen's rights under Article 21 of the Constitution. The Court examined in detail the issues relating to torture, custodial violence and deaths in lock ups, along with the liability of State to compensate the victims of such wrongs. It also discussed the accountability of police officers to reimburse the State. A.S. Anand, C.J. speaking for the Court issued mandatory guidelines for the police officers and other investigating officials in all cases of arrest and detention till legal provisions are made in that behalf by the competent legislature. With reference to the vicarious liability of the State he discussed the punitive provisions of Indian Penal Code, 1860 and lamented the inadequacy of these provisions to repair the wrong done to the victim. He further observed:

> ...That a mere prosecution of the police officers or declaration of his action being invalid does not by itself provide any meaningful remedy to a person whose fundamental rights to life have been infringed. According to him, the civil action for damages is a long drawn and cumbersome judicial process. Hence, where the infringement of fundamental rights is established the Court must proceed further and give compensatory relief to the victim. The compensation shall not be by way of damages as in a civil action but by way of compensation under the public law jurisdiction, wherein the State is made liable to pay compensation as it has committed a breach of public duty of protecting the fundamental

> right to life of citizen.... The claim of the citizens for compensation is based on the principle of strict liability, to which the defense of sovereign immunity is not available...the citizens must receive the compensation from the State, which in turn shall be indemnified by the wrongdoer.[94]

The Court reiterated that the award of compensation for established invasion of Fundamental Rights of citizens under public law jurisdiction, in addition to traditional remedy under the law of tort. Secondly, The Court did not accept the reservation, which the Govt. of India had attached to Article 9(5) of International Covenant on Civil and Political Covenant (1966).[95]

Once the Court firmly established the award of compensation as a measure of enforcement of fundamental right to life and liberty, it did apply this measure to violations of other Fundamental Rights also. Thus in *Common Cause* v. *Union of India*,[96] the Court while referring to the law in England, stated:

> There is therefore, not much of a difference between the powers of the Court exercised here in this country under Article 32 or Article 226 and those exercised in England for judicial review. Public law remedies are available in both the countries and the Courts can award damages against public authorities to compensate for the loss or injury caused to the plaintiff/petitioner, provided the case involves, in this country, the violation of fundamental rights by the government or other public authorities or their action was wholly arbitrary or oppressive in violation of Article 14 or in breach of statutory duty and is not purely a private matter directed against a private individual.

Reiterating the same theme in *Chairman, Railaway Board and Ors*, v. *Chandrima Das*[97] and others, the Supreme Court held that the public law remedies have also been extended to the realm of tort. It was a case of gang rape of a Bangladeshi national by the employees of the Indian Railways in a room at Yatri Niwas at Howrah Station. These employees managed the

Yatri Niwas. The Government contended that it could not be held liable under the law of torts, as the offence was not committed during the course of official duty. However, the Court did not accept this argument and stated as under:

> The employees of the Union of India, who are deputed to run the railways and to manage the establishment, including the railway stations and the yatri niwas, are essential components of the government machinery which carries on the commercial activity. If any of such employees commits an act of tort, the Union government, of which they are the employees, can, subject to other legal requirements being satisfied, be held vicariously liable in damages to the person wronged by those employees.

This case is noteworthy for two important reasons; firstly, the Court stated the need of reading the principles of international Covenants into the domestic jurisprudence for purposes of effective implementation of Human Rights. Secondly, the Court held that even a non-citizen could claim compensation for violation of Article 21 of the Constitution. The Court ruled:

> Just as the State is under an obligation to protect the life of every citizen in this country, so also the State is under an obligation to protect the life of the persons who are not citizens.... As a national of another country, she could not be subjected to a treatment which was below dignity nor could she be subjected to physical violence at the hands of government employees who outraged her modesty. The right available to her under Article 21 was thus violated. Consequently, the State was under a constitutional liability to pay compensation to her.

It would appear that the Court has extended the compensatory principles to violations of any fundamental right and entitling the victim to compensation. However, this has not been accepted in later formulations of the Court. Thus in *Hindustan Paper Corporation Ltd.* v. *Ananta Bhattacharjee*[98] the Court stated:

> Public law remedy for the purpose of grant of compensation can be resorted to only when the Fundamental Right of a citizen under Article 21 of the Constitution is violated and not otherwise. It is not every violation of the provisions of the Constitution or a statute, which would enable the Court to direct grant of compensation. The power of Court of judicial review to grant compensation in public law remedy is limited.

A perusal of the Apex Court decisions discussed above reflects that the relief of compensation is a judicial innovation in the inherent powers of the Court. Since the award of compensation by the Court is not consistent, it follows that the remedy is discretionary in nature, as we noted earlier. Considering this, it cannot be stated with firmness that the right to claim compensation in India has settled as a fundamental remedial right. However, it has a cascading effect in greater evolution of Human Rights protections at the level of judiciary. Moreover, as seen above the Court has awarded compensation, when the violation occurred under Article 21 concerning rights to life and liberty. The Court has thus impressed upon the State to take these rights seriously and seizing any opportunity to pronounce itself upon such violations of rights to life and liberty. As a matter of fact, post emergency, the Court has truthfully and courageously embarked upon a journey towards sensitizing Indian legal order towards greater Human Rights protection programs. However, in our submission, the Indian legal order has still to go a long way in assuring each individual about the sanctity of his individual Human Rights, despite bolder attempts by the Indian Supreme Court.

VI. Appraisal

Over the years, it has become clear that Courts are heavily relying on the Constitution, Bill of Rights, and even international norms to protect and enforce rule of law. They are equally using their powers and new strategies and tools to restrict parliamentary and executive autonomy, so that it conforms to constitutional norms, particularly relating to fundamental Human Rights. The interdependence between judicial conscience and reasoning has equally led to greater concerns being shown about rights by the Courts. The Supreme Court of India is not an exception to this legal compass.

The Supreme Court has enlarged the scope and protection of the fundamental Human Rights guaranteed under the Constitution, as analyzed above. It has devised new tools to promote a right-based administration. The Public Interest Litigation has been an important strategy towards increasing access of people to the Court. It has also helped the Court to address violations of fundamental Human Rights in India and give appropriate relief. The Court has visualized the award of compensation as an important methodology not only to redress the violation but also as a deterrent. Consequently, it has awarded compensation to the victims of violation of Fundamental Right to life and liberty. This is so even though the Constitution of India does not expressly provide for a *right to compensation* unlike other legal systems. Nor is there any legislation, which deals with such compensatory relief in case of infringement of Fundamental Rights, unlike other common law and continental jurisdictions. Despite this the Court has awarded compensation, exercising its inherent power to do complete justice and awarding appropriate relief under Article 32. In the initial phase of evolution of compensatory relief, the Court did not offer any firm jurisprudential basis for such a remedy. It used different terminology like exemplary costs, and exemplary damages. However, the Court later relied on constitutional tort theory to justify the award of compensation. The Supreme Court has taken a view that a claim in public law for compensation is distinct from, and in addition to, the remedy in private law for damages for the tort resulting from the contravention of Fundamental Rights. The Court has also relied on Article 9(5) of International Covenant on Civil and Political Rights, 1966, while justifying the award of compensation under Article 32 of the Constitution. This is despite India having put a reservation to Article 9 of the Covenant, stating that the reservation has lost its importance.

In a welfare State the State must strive to establish just relations between the rights of the individual and the responsibilities of the State. The award of compensation as a remedial measure has been established by interpretative techniques of the Supreme Court, even though the Court has not been consistent in awarding the same. The award of compensation by the Court has evolved as a discretionary relief, even though it has emphasized justifications for such a relief. In our submission, the compensatory relief serves both deterrent as well as restitutive purposes. It is pertinent to note that despite many objections to the Courts awarding compensation as a remedy for violation of fundamental Human Rights, the Courts have leaned in favor of compensating the individuals for injuries suffered at the hands of State and its employees. It is submitted that preventing and remedying injury to an individual is the bedrock of many constitutional protections. Also the Court's attention is focused towards establishing constitutional rights so that individuals are protected from State lawlessness. Such an approach is warranted for establishment of astute constitutionalism and rights conscious and accountable executive. Indeed, such individual protection would have been considerably enhanced, had this right to compensation been made an enforceable right in India also.

Notes

1. *See* Boutros Ghali, "The Common Language of Humanity", Inaugural Address at the United Nations World Conference on Human Rights, Vienna Declaration and Program of Action. 1993.
2. *See* Shad Saleem Faruqi, "Human Rights: Asian and Western Perspectives" in *Criminal Justice* (2004) K.I. Vibhute (ed.) 62-81. For an analysis of various paradigms in this regard, See Archana Parashar, "Human Rights: Imperatives of Theoretical Change", 40 *JILI* (1998), No. 1-4, 6-38.
3. In India, the National Human Rights Commission has been established under *Protection of Human Rights Act*, 1993.
4. *See* Justice A.S. Anand, "Rights of Victims of Crime" XXVI *Delhi Law Review* (2004) 1-11.
5. *UN Declaration of Basic Principles of Justice for Victims of Crime and Abuse of Power, 1985*. The Declaration defined victim as including not only the victims of Crime, but also victim of abuse of power. However, for our purposes the abuse of power resulting

into abridgement of Human Rights particularly, relating to life and liberty is important and relevant.

6. Articles 12-35 are included in Part III under the nomenclature of Fundamental Rights, and Articles 36-51 are included in Part IV under the nomenclature of Directive Principles of State Policy. The main difference between the two is that while as the former is justiciable, the latter is not. However, this distinction has of late become more illusory rather than substantial one, as some of rights in Part IV have been interposed in Part III by judicial reasoning. There have been strong arguments in favor of inclusion of some Part IV rights in Part III, and we also endorse this view. See e.g. *National Commission to Review the Working of the Constitution* (2001), *See* also, M.P. Singh, "The Statics and the Dynamics of the Fundamental Rights and the Directive Principles—A Human Rights Perspective" (2003) *5 SCC (J)* 1.
7. Article 32. Arms the Supreme Court with a power to issue appropriate writs, orders or directions to prevent the violation of a Fundamental Right.
8. Article 226. Similarly empowers the High Courts to issue appropriate writs, orders or directions to prevent the violation of a Fundamental Right.
9. The legitimacy of judicial activism on the part of Indian Supreme Court has been questioned. See S.P. Sathe, *Judicial Activism in India* (2002). For legitimacy of judicial activism, See Anirudh Rastogi, "A Jurisprudential Affirmation of Judicial Activism", II *Delhi Law Review* (Student Edition) 2005-06, 140-44.... Its activism is to be advocated on grounds of functionalism in today's era, wherein the context for a popular revolution against the all pervasive State is missing. It is in this context that inevitable and legitimate activism attains its own significance", *Id* at 144.
10. One of the important exercises in Indian constitutionalism has been the liberalization of *locus standi* in Public Interest Litigation (PIL). See P.M. Bakshi, *Public Interest Litigation* (2002).
11. Article 21 States: No person shall be deprived of his life or personal liberty except according to procedure established by law. The procedure established by law has to be just, fair and reasonable, as held by Indian Supreme Court. See e.g. *Maneka Gandhi* v. *Union of India*, AIR 1978 S.C.596.
12. *See Nilabati Behera* v. *State of Orissa*, (1993) 2SCC 746, *See infra.*
13. See generally, Jawahar L. Kaul, *Human Rights: Issues and Perspectives* (1996).
14. However, over the' years, not only rights, but also even entitlements have been brought under the rubric of Human Rights. Dereze and Sen, the noble laureate, rightly States, it may not be

appropriate to define Human Rights simply as rights that ideally should be legally recognized. A human right can be invoked in many contexts, even when its legal enforcement as opposed to giving it general support, would be inappropriate and unhelpful. Jean Dereze and Amartya Sen, *India: Development and Participation* (2002) at 372. It is precisely because of this reason that even entitlements have been clubbed together in right to life. "Right to life includes the right to live with human dignity and all that goes along with it namely, the bare necessaries of life such as adequate nutrition, clothing and shelter over the head and facilities for reading, writing and expressing oneself in diverse forms freely moving about and mixing and comingling with fellow human beings"..... See *Francis Coralie* v., *Union Territory of Delhi*, AIR 1981 SC 746.

15. Article 13(1) and 13(2) of Constitution of India obligates the State not to make any law, which takes away or abridges the rights conferred by Part III. Any such law, if made shall be void to the extent of contravention/abridgement. Under Article 32, the right to move the Supreme Court and High Courts under Article 226, for the enforcement of Fundamental Rights is itself a Fundamental Right under Part III of the Constitution.
16. Preamble of UDHR, para 2nd. Even though UN Declaration did not provide for easily discernible enforcement mechanism, yet over the years, UN has served the cause of Human Rights objectives in many ways. See V.S. Mani, "Human Rights and the United Nations: A Survey", 40 *JILI* (1998) no. 1-4, 38-66 at 45.
17. *See Supra* note 14.
18. *See* generally, Steiner and Alston, *International Human Rights in Context* (1996).
19. However, despite this, much difference exists between legal orders about the scope and content of Human Rights protection. See Faruqi, *Supra* note 2 at 65.
20. Human Development Report 2000 has dovetailed the necessity of such a commitment. See UNDP, *Human Development Report* (2000).
21. *Supra* note 6, para 6.
22. H.M. Seervai, *Constitutional Law of India*, Vol. 1 (1991), 154-55.
23. Even though Preamble does not grant any power but it gives a direction and purpose to the Constitution. It contains the fundamentals of the Constitution, and therefore the Supreme Court has many a times referred to it while interpreting the Constitutional provisions. See e.g. *Kesavananda Bharati* v. *State of Kerala*, AIR 1973 S.C.1461, *In Re Kerala Education Bill, 1957*, AIR 1958 S.C.956.

24. According to *Kesvananda* formulation, the Parliament has the power to amend any part of the Constitution, but it has no power to amend the "basic features/structure" of the Constitution. See *Id.*
25. Justice Sujata Manohar, "Human Rights Protection: Current Challenges", XXII *Delhi Law Review* (2000) 15-20 at 16. However, other countries like Bangladesh and Pakistan have also incorporated such justiciable Bill of rights in their constitutions. See www.elaw.org/resources/text.asp?id and www.sdpi.org/know your rigths/The constitution of pakistan (last visited October 4, 2007).
26. *See Supra* note 15. Human Rights and Fundamental Rights are used interchangeably. The State for purposes of Part III includes Parliament, State Legislature, Governments and all local and other authorities. In order that these rights are protected in a meaningful way, the Supreme Court has given a wide interpretation to the term "other authorities" in Article 12 of the Constitution. See particularly, *Ajay Hasia* v. *Khalid Mujib Sehravardi,* (1981) 1SCC 722.
27. Article 37, Constitution of India. The Supreme Court has of late given a strong meaning and orientation to these Directive Principles. See M.P. Singh, *Supra* note 6.
28. The Supreme Court has innovatively recognized the 'trinity' of Fundamental Rights, directive principles and preamble, an important backbone of Human Rights jurisprudence in India. See *Delhi Road Transport Corporation* v. *DTC Mazdoor Congress*, AIR 1991 SC 101 at 193.
29. Article 14.
30. Article 19.
31. Article 25.
32. Article 20.
33. Articles 21 and 22.
34. Articles 29 and 30.
35. *Supra* note 22.
36. Guaranteeing enforcement of Fundamental Rights is vital to the protection and enforcement of fundamental freedoms and Human Rights in any legal order. Under Article 32, the right to move the Supreme Court by *appropriate* proceedings for enforcement of Part III right is guaranteed (*emphasis* added). The Court has the power to issue appropriate orders, directions or writs, like *habeas corpus*, *mandamus*, prohibition, *quo warranto* and *certiorari*. However, looking at the ambit of this Article, despite being

guaranteed right, the discretionary element in these writs cannot be overlooked, in our submission.

37. *State of West Bengal* v. *Subodh Gopal Bose*, AIR 1954 SC 95.
38. *I.C. Golaknath* v. *State of Punjab* AIR 1967 SC 1656. Golaknath also ruled that Parliament has no power to take away the Fundamental Rights, even by an amendment, which was later overruled by Kesavananda. See *infra* note, 44.
39. *Supra* note 23.
40. *Maneka Gandhi* v. *Union of India* AIR 1978 2 S.C.R. 621.
41. *Daryao* v. *State of Uttar Pradesh*, AIR 1961 SC 211.
42. *Ajay Hasia* v. *Khalid Mujib* AIR 1981 SC 487 at 493.
43. *Bennett Coleman* v. *Union of India* (1980) A.SC. 898.
44. *I.R.Coelho* v. *State of Tamil Nadu*, 2007(1) SCALE 197. *Keshavananda*, *Supra* note, 23 had ruled that Parliament has the powers to amend any part of the Constitution including Part III, but it has no powers to amend the basic/essential features of the Constitution. *Coelho* is important, as Article 31(B) and IX schedule of Constitution of India, protected all laws put in IX schedule from judicial attack, which now stands reversed by this judgement.

    In our submission, Coelho is a partial return to Golaknath, Supra note 38 which had ruled that any amendment of the Constitution abridging the Fundamental Rights is impermissible and unconstitutional.
45. *Minerva Mills Ltd* v. *Union of India,* (1981) S.C.R. 206.
46. See M.P. Jain, *Indian Constitutional Law* (2003) 827-854.
47. *Id* at 832, See also P.N. Singh *Infra* note 53.
48. Article 359(1).
49. *Constituent Assembly Debates*. Vol. VII, 953.
50. Articles 132-36.
51. Article 131.
52. *Minerva Mills*, *Supra* note 40.
53. See P.N. Singh, "Promises and Perils of Public Interest Litigation in Protecting the Rights of the Poor and the Oppressed", XXVII DLR (2005) 8-25.
54. *S.P. Gupta* v. *Union of India,* 1981 (Supp) SCC 87, See also *Bandhua Mukti Morcha* v. *Union of India,* (1984) 4 SCC 161.
55. By invoking epistolary jurisdiction, the Court entertains a petition even in the form of a letter or a telegram addressed to the Court. The Court also does not apply the usual technical procedures in such petitions. See Parmanand Singh, "Human Rights Protection

Through Public Interest Litigation in India," XLV *IJPA* (1999) 731-49 at 734 See Bakshi, *Supra* note, 10. For a valuable critique of PIL, See Upendra Baxi, "The Avatars of Indian Judicial Activism: Explorations in the Geographies of (In) Justice" in *Fifty Years of The Supreme Court of India* (2003) Verma and Kusum (Eds), 156-209.

56. *Unnikrishnan, J.P.* v. *State of Andhra Pradesh* AIR 1993 SC 2178.
57. *In Re Death of Sawinder Singh Grover*, 1995 (Supp) 4 SCC 450.
58. *D.K. Basu* v. *State of West Bengal*, AIR 1997 S.C. 610, See also *Joginder Kumar* v. *State of U.P.* AIR 1994 SC 1349, *Nilabati Behera* v. *State of Orissa*, AIR 1993 SC 1960.
59. *Supreme Court Legal Aid Committee* v. *Union of India* (1994) 6 SCC 731.
60. *Desh Raj Khurana* v. *Delhi Administration*, 1987 (1) SCALE 1313.
61. *Sheela Barse* v. *Union of India*, (1995) 5 SCALE 159.
62. *Sheela Barse* v. *Union of India*, (1986) 3 SCR 443.
63. *Bandhua Mukhti Morcha, Supra* note 49, See also, *P.U.D.R. v. Union of India* (1982) 3SCC 235.
64. *P.U.C.L.* v. *Union of India*, (1997) 1SCC 301.
65. *M.C. Mehta* v. *Union of India*, 1996(5) SCALE (Sp) 3.
66. *Common Cause, a Registered Society* v. *Union of India* (1997) 10 SCC 729.
67. *Research Foundation for Science, Technology Policy v. Union of India,* SCALE(PIL) 1981-97, 1670.
68. *Lakshmi Kant Pandey* v. *Union of India*, 1989 (2) SCALE 691.
69. *M.C. Mehta* v. *Union of India*, (1997) 8SCC770; *Delhi Development Authority v. Skipper Construction Co. (p) Ltd.* (1996) 4SCC 622; *Vineet Narain v. Union of India*, (1996) 2SCC199.
70. *See* P.N. Singh, *Supra* note, 48, and also Bakshi, *Supra* note, 10.
71. Seervai, *Supra* note 15.
72. *See also*, Justice Madan B. Lokur, "Some Recent Developments in Indian Public Law-Forging New Tools", VII *Nyaya Deep* (2006) Issue 2, 40-56.
73. P.N. Singh, *Supra* note, 48 at 10.
74. According to Supreme Court Article 300 confers juristic personality on the State, and therefore State can be held liable for acts of its employees. See e.g. *State of Rajasthan* v. *Vidyawati*, AIR 1962 SC 933. See *Infra* note 75 and the accompanying text.

75. *Nilabati Behera* v. *State of* Orrisa (1993) 2SCC 746. *Kasturilal Raliaram Jain* v. *State of U.P.* AIR 1965 SC 1039 made a distinction between "sovereign and non-sovereign functions" of the State being exercised by the officers of the State. The liability of the State was only confined in non-sovereign functions only, thus effectively undoing *State of Rajasthan* v. *Vidyawati* AIR 1962 SC 933 which did not accept any justification for not holding the State liable for the tortious acts of its servants. For a comparative analysis of the doctrine of sovereign immunity, See A. Raghunadha Reddy, "Reparation of the Wrong: Problems and Perspectives", 46 *Indian Journal of International Law* (2006), No 4, 572-85.
76. *Common Cause v. Union of India* (1996) 8 SCALE 127, 130.
77. AIR 1994 SC 2663.
78. Seervai, *Supra* note 15.
79. *L. Chandra Kumar v. Union of India,* AIR 1997 SC 1125. See also, *Subhash v. Union of India* AIR 1991 SC 63: *Shri Kumar v. Union of India,* 1992 (2) SCC 428.
80. Article 9(5) *International Covenant on Civil and Political Rights* 1966. The Court has also relied on international treaties and Covenants for protection of Fundamental Rights. See e.g. *Vishaka* v. *State of Rajasthan* AIR 1997 SC 3 011, *Delhi Domestic Working Womens Forum* v. *Union of India* (1995) 1 SCC 14.
81. AIR 1981 SC 928 at 1068.
82. *Ibid* at 930.
83. *Ibid.* Lokur, *Supra* note, 66, See also *Sunil Batra* v. *Delhi Administration* AIR 1978 SC 1675, *Indian Council for Enviro-legal Action* v. *Union of India* AIR 1996 SC 1446, *M.C. Mehta* v. *Union of India* AIR 2004 SC 4016, *Vishakha* v. *State of Rajasthan* AIR 1997 SC 3011, *P.U.D.R.* v. *State of Bihar* AIR 1987 SC 355.
84. AIR 1983 SC 1086.
85. *Ibid* at 1089.
86. *Bhupinder Sharma* v. *State of Himachal Pradesh* 2003 (8) SCC 551.
87. AIR 1984 SC 1026, See also *Nilabati Behara* v. *State of Orissa, Infra* note 89.
88. AIR 1986 SC 494, at 499.
89. (1993) 2 SCC 746.
90. *Ibid*, paras 10 and 17.
91. Lokur *Supra* note 66 at 43.
92. AIR 2000 SC 2083.
93. (1997) 1 SCC 416, also See *In Re Death of Sawinder Singh Grover* 1995 Supp. (4) SCC 450 wherein the deceased died in the custody

of Directorate of Enforcement and the Union of India was made to pay ex-gratia payment of Rupees 200,000 to the widow of the deceased as an interim measure.

94. *Ibid,* para 44 & 54.
95. *Ibid,* para 46.
96. (1999) 6 SCC 667.
97. AIR 2000 SC 988.
98. (2004) 6SCC 213.

14

The Presumption of Innocence and Fair Trial

Nimushakavi Vasanthi

Introduction

The presumption of innocence is one of the cardinal principles of the adversarial system of criminal trials in all common law countries. This presumption arose out of the public outrage against inquisitorial investigations where the presumption was of guilt and the accused had to prove their innocence. In the earlier trial by ordeal methods of investigations in the Star Chambers of these countries, confessions were forced out of the accused under duress. The presumption of innocence and the adversarial system of criminal trial seeks to provide for a more humane and fair system of trial where the accused is given the benefit of doubt and the State had to prove guilt beyond reasonable doubt. Thus the presumption of innocence becomes an indispensable aspect of fair trial.

The presumption of innocence is also an integral part of the due process model of criminal justice, a model that is based on securing justice in a manner that is respectful of the rights of the suspect. Its hallmark is its attempt to ensure that no injustice is done. Both the utilitarian approach to criminal justice, which states that the effect that a wrongful conviction of an innocent person has on society is far outweighed by the merits of securing the lives of the citizens against crime[1] and the moral theorists who argue that though the utilitarian justification is unacceptable, innocence and its protection must be of prime importance to the State, as not convicting the guilty is an error of omission whereas convicting an innocent person is an unwarranted intrusion into the rights of the individual and an error of commission.[2] Thus the presumption of innocence is of value even in conflicting theories of justice such as the utilitarian and the moral theorists.

The presumption of innocence can be argued as an integral part of the right to life enshrined in various international instruments.[3] The right to life includes the right against the deprivation of freedom by arbitrary methods. The American due process clause states that, no person may be deprived of his life or liberty except by procedure established by law. The procedure established by law believes in the presumption of innocence and any procedure violating that presumption is violative of the right to life. Thus the process of fair trial is an integral part of Fundamental Human Rights. The ICCPR also recognizes that this presumption as a basic right.[4]

Recent trends indicate a steady reversal of this presumption. Since the horrors of the old criminal law receded, the justifications for these elements of fair trial have also dimmed. In the context of the new wave of anti-terrorism laws across the world the relevance of this presumption and the protections it offers in the context of international Human Rights are worth examining. In India the Parliament bombing case, the conviction and subsequent acquittal of key accused and the imposition of death sentence of one of the accused while acquitting others also raises questions about the protections to citizens during these trials and the relevancy of this presumption.

This paper is divided into the following sections:

1. The origin of the doctrine and its development (using case law from India and England, as common law countries and the doctrine being a principle of common law).
2. The exceptions to the doctrine.

3. The new terror legislations in India and the USA.
4. The Innocence Protection Act 2004 in the United States of America.
5. The Committee on Criminal Justice Reforms in India 2003.
6. Conclusion.

PART 1: ORIGIN OF THE DOCTRINE

Odiosa et inhonesta non sunt in lege proesumenda

(Odious and dishonest things are not to be presumed in law)

The origin of the doctrine can be traced back in English law to the case of *Woolmington* v. *Director of Public Prosecutions*[5] in the year 1935 and to an even earlier case in India in *Weston* v. *Peary Mohun* dassi[6] wherein the Court was pleased to say that there is a general presumption against misconduct of all kinds, no presumption being more highly favored in the law than that of innocence. And the more heinous and improbable a crime is, the greater is the force of the evidence required to overcome this presumption. The usual way of directing the jury in cases of jury trial is to tell them to start presuming that the accused is innocent and the burden of proof is on the prosecution to prove the guilt of the accused. The rationale for this presumption is also explained in terms of the right to reputation of every person and the right to life.

The doctrine has found favor with jurists across countries and is often placed higher than other presumptions in law. Since this presumption is an integral aspect of fair trial it is not on par with other presumptions that the legislation may expressly provide for. For instance in the Indian Law of Evidence there is no express mention of this presumption even though several presumptions of law are provided for in the code. In India then the presumption operates as an unwritten norm.

In the absence of a clear enunciation of the presumption it is often argued that the presumption of innocence is nothing but the rule of proof beyond reasonable doubt.

The presumption of innocence in criminal cases signifies nothing more than that if the commission of a crime is directly in issue, it must be proved beyond reasonable doubt.[7]

But in civil cases as in criminal cases, especially in matters of misconduct there is a presumption that the accused has not acted in a manner that is fraudulent but in an innocent manner and not illegally or wickedly. Fraud has to be proved by the prosecution, there is no presumption of fraud. In civil cases the presumption is that a person who is shown to have done any act is presumed to have done it innocently and honestly and not fraudulently, illegally or wickedly.

Thus the presumption of innocence is of wide ranging application being used in criminal and civil cases such as:

Fraud

The presumption is of constant application and there is a presumption against fraud in the sense that without evidence fraud will not be presumed and all transactions being presumed to be in fairness and honesty.

Marriage and children

There is a presumption in favor of marriage, such that cohabitation and reputation are held to be presumptive evidence of marriage. In the same way the law presumes the legitimacy of children who are born in wedlock.[8]

Misconduct

There is a legal presumption that a deed or a will is validly made and every effort is made by the Courts to read it to have a lawful meaning. Where a deed or a will is capable of two meanings the law will construe it in a manner to have a lawful intent. Wrongful or tortuous conduct will not be presumed. All persons will be presumed to have duly discharged any obligation imposed on them by law. Thus, the judgments of Courts of competent jurisdiction, are presumed to be well founded, and their record to be correctly made; judges and juror's are presumed to do nothing causelessly or maliciously; public officers are presumed to do their duty, and the like.[9] Further perjury is not to be presumed.[10]

There is presumption of good faith in every statute. Officers who have acted under the authority of that legislation are presumed to have acted in good faith.

Negligence

There is no more reason to presume fraud than to presume negligence.[11] Negligence too is not to be presumed unless the facts are so obvious as to attract the responsibility to prove that proper care was taken. The State for example will be presumed to have taken proper care and it is for the person alleging negligence to prove it.

Apart from the initial stage of the trial this doctrine of presumption of innocence is also used during the trial. It is generally said that there is no such presumption but merely a rule of the shifting of the burden. It is argued that the rule in burden of proof in all cases is that the party alleging a particular fact has to prove it. In a civil case the party maintaining a case has to prove it and similarly the State while maintaining a case against the accused has to prove it and there is no presumption beyond this.

However, it has been held that a *prima facie* case does not take away from a defendant the presumption of innocence, though it may in the opinion of the jury, be such as to rebut and control it; but that presumption remains, in aid of any other proof offered by the defendant, to rebut the prosecutor's *prima facie* case.[12]

Some commentators have distinguished between the two kinds of burden in law. The two burdens are the legal burden and the evidentiary burden. The legal burden is a burden of proof, which is a burden if not proved, will go against him. The evidentiary burden is not a burden of proof as much a duty to adduce evidence to a particular point. This evidentiary burden will vary depending on who is discharging it. For example, the prosecution carries a heavier burden in that it has to prove an issue beyond reasonable doubt whereas the burden on the defense is merely to prove a balance of probabilities.

This distinction is brought out quite well in the case, which is the leading case on the presumption of innocence,

Woolmington v. *Director of Public Prosecutions.*[13] In the case Woolmington was charged with the murder of his wife. He had visited her with a sawn-off shotgun concealed under his coat, and when they met she was killed by a shot from such a gun. Woolmington said that it went off accidentally. The judge directed the jury that, once it was proved that Woolmington shot his wife, he bore the burden of proving that it was unintentional. The House of Lords holding that as incorrect laid down what is still today said to be the statement of the presumption of innocence:

> But while the prosecution must prove the guilt of the prisoner, there is no such burden laid on the prisoner to prove his innocence and it is sufficient for him to raise a doubt as to his guilt; he is not bound to satisfy the jury of his innocence....
>
> Throughout the web of the English Criminal law one golden thread is always to be seen, that it is the duty of the prosecution to prove the prisoner's guilt....
>
> It is not the law of England to say as was said in the present case; 'if the Crown satisfy you that this woman died at the prisoner's hands then he has to show that there are circumstances to be found...which alleviate the crime'....

Position in international criminal law

The presumption of innocence and the rule of the prosecution proving the case beyond reasonable doubt are to be found in international criminal law as well.

> An accused is to be acquitted if the prosecution cannot prove that the accused is guilty beyond any reasonable doubt of the crime he is charged with. However, if after the prosecution's presentation of its case-in-chief the Court considers that there is lack of sufficient evidence to substantiate the charge against the accused, then there is no case for the Defense to answer, and the accused must be released. Thus, in Jelisic, after the prosecution had come to the end of its presentation of evidence against the accused and trial Chamber I of the ICTY had

> considered that the evidence was not sufficient to substantiate the charge of genocide against the accused, the Trial Chamber ruled that the accused could not be found guilty of genocide. This was despite the fact that the defense still had not commenced its case.[14]

Article 21 of the ICTY Statute in the rights for the accused provides for the presumption.[15] Article 66 of the ICC Statute provides explicitly for the presumption.[16] The International Covenant on Civil and Political Rights provides that every one charged with a criminal offence shall have the right to be presumed innocent until he is proved guilty according to law.[17]

PART 2: The Exceptions

There have always been exceptions to this doctrine. The Supreme Court of India has observed that there is a need to moderate this presumption with a view to make criminal justice potent and realistic.[18] Similarly, when the accused raises the private defense of provocation or the defense of insanity he will bear the burden of proving it.[19] Similarly, statute may cast on the accused the burden of proving a particular issue or issues. The legal burden in relation to all other issues in such cases will remain on the prosecution. For instance, the Indian Evidence Act, 1872 clearly provides for the burden to prove innocence on the accused by Section 113A which reads:

> When the question is whether the commission of suicide by a woman had been abetted by her husband or any relative of her husband and it is shown that she had committed suicide within a period of seven years from the date of her marriage and that her husband or such relative of her husband had subjected her to cruelty, the court may presume, having regard to all the other circumstances of the case, that such suicide had been abetted by her husband or by such relative of her husband.

Similarly, Section 113B of the same Act reads:

> When the question is whether a person has committed the dowry death of a woman and it is shown that soon before her death such woman had been subjected by

such person to cruelty or harassment for, or in connection with, any demand for dowry, the Court shall presume that such person had caused the dowry death.

Similarly, the Court may in the facts of the case also presume that a person in possession of stolen goods soon after the theft, is either the thief or a receiver of stolen goods. When the incident cannot be determined with certainty the accused is entitled to the benefit of doubt, but when the act constitutes an offence even though there is no intention to commit it, the commission of the offence even with the best of intentions, amounts to an offence and the accused cannot be entitled to the benefit of doubt. Section114-A[20] of the Indian Evidence Act, 1872 also shifts the burden onto the accused.

These exceptions, however, are meant to balance the inequitable position of parties before the law. In a case of rape, the victim is already under severe emotional and mental stress and her position is vulnerable. In these circumstances, to cast the burden of proof on the accused only serves to enable justice. In all the cases that the burden is shifted on to the accused, either they are situations where the accused is the best person to lead evidence in that regard i.e. the general defense of provocation, of saving oneself etc., or the victim of the crime is socially recognized as being in a vulnerable position.

Thus, even when the presumption is set aside it is done to ensure that justice is done and not merely to expedite trial or repress crime, especially when witnesses may be unwilling to testify against the accused, which are the defenses offered in the case of preventive detention and the new anti-terrorism legislations.

PART 3: Innocence and the New Terror Laws

In the post 9/11 era there has been a rise in the number of legislations in all parts of the world to deal more firmly with terror. The United States came out with the Patriot Act and another legislation dubbed as the Patriot II which raises some serious concerns about the future of traditional criminal law and theory.

The new terror legislations

In a wave of new legislations traditional norms of criminal justice have been deliberately ignored. The PATRIOT Act, (the Uniting and Strengthening America by Providing Appropriate Tools Required to Intercept and Obstruct Terrorism (USA PATRIOT) Act of 2001 in the United States, the Prevention of Terrorism Act in the United Kingdom and the Prevention of Terrorism Act (POTA), 2001 in India reflect a common premise that terrorism cannot be dealt with under the existing criminal law systems. One feature common to these legislations is the presumption of guilt, of the suspects rather than the presumption of innocence. The procedural safeguard of presumption of innocence is seen as a delaying procedure and an impediment to the law enforcement agencies especially claiming difficulty in getting evidence. The cases of *Rasul* v. *Bush* and the *Jose Padilla* cases in the United States post 9/11 have brought to light the denial of basic protections under criminal law, like the filing of charges under which the accused are held. In *Rasul* v. *Bush* the U.S. Government argued that individuals detained in Afghanistan had no right to challenge their detention in the Courts of the country, which detained them. In the other case, *José Padilla* who is a citizen of the United States was detained on the suspicion that he belonged to the terrorist outfit Al Qaeda and had entered the United States with the intention of exploding a 'dirty bomb' (a bomb with conventional explosives and radioactive material). The Court hearing the case proceeded on the ground that the State had 'some evidence' to hold that Padilla was an unlawful enemy combatant. While under traditional criminal law, no suspect may be punishable for a crime unless they are found guilty "beyond a reasonable doubt", under the "unlawful enemy combatant" standard, the executive branch may indefinitely detain a suspected terrorist without bringing formal charges against them so long as they have "some evidence" to do so.[21]

It has been observed in the United States as well as India that anti-terrorist legislations have been widely abused. These legislations are not used against terrorists and crimes related to terrorism but against persons who would ordinarily come under existing laws. They are used merely as methods of subverting the protections available under traditional criminal law to the accused. For example, in India Human Rights Watch has documented the Act's use against political opponents, religious minorities, Dalits (untouchables), tribals, and children.[22] The POTA has been used to characterize struggle for worker's rights as membership in the banned, extreme leftist Maoist-Leninist groups known collectively as Naxalites.

Such legislation is however not new in India. India inherited these laws from its colonial masters and has found it useful to retain them. Preventive Detention laws have been many since India's independence. The latest law is the Prevention of Terrorism Act, 2001 which has been repealed in 2004 only with the promise that a new law will be drafted.

Such Preventive Detention laws are the exception to the constitutional guarantees of being deprived of life and liberty only after suitable cause has been shown. Article 22 of the Constitution of India provides for protections against arbitrary arrests and detention, but preventive detention is the exception to this.[23]

The Armed Forces Special Powers Act, 1958 is one of the legislations, which are not preventive detention legislation but still retain several powers, which are similar to the preventive detention laws like the Terrorist and Disruptive Activities (Prevention) Act (TADA), 1987 and the Prevention of Terrorism Act, POTA 2001.

Anti-terror legislations and the presumption of guilt

One of the features of these legislations is the presumption of guilt that is found in several of its provisions. Under the TADA the burden of proof against suspected terrorists is not upon the State. In contrast to the traditional criminal procedure which presumed the innocence of a detainee prior to their being found guilty by a Court of law, TADA presumed a suspect guilty if they were found to be in possession of arms, weapons, or explosives specified by prior legislation, or if the fingerprints of the accused were found at the scene of the terrorist act. The presumption of guilt also applies to cases where the detainee has been accused of involvement in the act by the confession of a co-accused party, or if the accused has made a confession to anyone other than a police officer.[24]

Eventually, when the legislation was repealed for reasons of rampant abuse and total failure in containing terror the National Human Rights Commission of India (NHRC) applauded the decision and noted that TADA was "incompatible with [India's] cultural traditions, legal history and treaty obligations".[25]

However soon after the Parliament bombing on December 13th, the Indian Government introduced another legislation and also justified POTA by pointing to the United Kingdom's adoption of the Prevention of Terrorism Act (POTA) and the United States' PATRIOT Act as evidence that other countries had acknowledged the need to move beyond traditional domestic criminal procedure in order to properly battle terrorism. The dominant theme running through the government position in this debate was that the current laws left law enforcement ill-equipped to handle the new threats brought on by terrorism and, as such, new legislation was necessary.

POTA also significantly departs from traditional Indian Criminal Procedure by allowing the pretrial detention of a suspected terrorist for up to 180 days.[26]

This prolonged detention before being brought in front of a Court leaves the door open for police brutality and arbitrary detention of political opponents.

Since its enactment over one year ago, POTA has provided ample evidence that its opponents' worries about abuse were well founded. In the year since POTA has been in force, Human Rights Watch has documented the Act's use against political opponents, religious minorities, Dalits (untouchables), tribals, and children.[27]

Discussions are underway regarding new anti-terrorist legislation that will "definitely be milder than the old law", and tries to ensure that "innocents don't suffer".[28] But given the basic premise of all preventive detention law and anti-terrorism legislations unless the basic protections available in the adversarial system of litigation and the components of fair trial are observed, it is highly unlikely that any "new mild law" will fare better than the older laws have. In an era of new threats to society the older protections will have to be revived in order to protect the most basic of all rights—the right to life.

In these legislations the questions of innocents being convicted for lack of adequate protections in the legislations is a major concern. The questions of innocents being convicted and sentenced to capital punishments have been raised in a big way in the United States. The Innocence Projects as they are called brought to light several cases of such convictions. Since then it has been a major concern for the criminal justice system in general and capital punishment in particular.

PART 4: The Innocence Protection Act 2004

The Innocence Protection Act 2004 enacted in the United States is the result of a long sustained campaign against wrongful convictions. Through innocence projects in various parts of the country several convicted death row inmates were acquitted. Pioneering work done by Innocence Project founders Barry Scheck and Peter Neufeld resulted in the exoneration of some long time prisoners using DNA evidence, which was not available at the time of the sentencing of these convicts.

This called for a closer look at the death penalty in order to protect the innocent. In this context the Innocence Protection Bill came to be proposed. The original Bill contained proposals by which State appoints defense lawyers for indigent capital punishment convicts, improving instructions to the jury, and that juveniles and the mentally retarded should not be executed. The bill also contained entitlement to scientific testing to all convicts. These proposals were however dropped in the final Act and the Act became a law as Title IV of H.R.5107, the Justice for All Act. The Act contains two parts, one that a convict can obtain post-conviction DNA testing by showing that the testing would raise a reasonable probability that the inmate did not commit the offence and the other authorizes grants to improve the quality of legal representation in capital punishment cases. The Act specifically provides that the convict must maintain that he was innocent. The applicant could have pleaded guilty also and in many cases where the applicant has pleaded guilty it could be due to fear or any other reason and hence such persons are not excluded. The inadequacy of competent legal representation is a major flaw in the criminal justice system and this has been specifically taken note of especially for indigent persons. It has been observed that the Act establishes a framework for improving the administration of capital punishment and is a turning point in the debate over the death penalty and the criminal justice system as a whole.[29]

PART 5: Criminal Justice Reform in India

The Committee on Criminal Justice Reforms headed by Justice Malimath gave in its report in 2003.[30] The report discussed a wide range of issues regarding criminal justice reforms and in the course of its discussions also gave attention to the presumption of innocence. The Committee accepts that the presumption of innocence and the concept of proof is one of the most important contributions of Roman law to the criminal law jurisprudence; however, it has expressed its reservations on the burden of proof that it places on the prosecution. The committee asserts that the principle is based on fairness, good sense and practical utility and accepted in the English Common law but has always been subject to exceptions.

> It is therefore clear that "proof beyond reasonable doubt" is not an absolute principle of universal application and deviations can be made by the legislature. Deviations can take different forms such as shifting the burden of proof to the prosecution or prescribing a standard of proof lower than "proof beyond reasonable doubt". As long as the accused has the opportunity to adduce evidence to nullify the adverse effect such deviation will not offend Article 14 or 21 of the Constitution. Even in England the principle in

> Woolmington case would apply only in the absence of a statutory provision to the contrary.[31]

The committee ignores the fact that the presumption of innocence is tied to the fundamental right to life contained in Article 21 of the Constitution of India. Similarly, the right against any arbitrary action clearly falls within the right to equality under Article 14. When an innocent person is wrongfully deprived of his life by procedures, which are arbitrary, it must be violative of both Fundamental Rights. Further Article 22 of the Constitution also prescribes procedures for a lawful exercise of power. The only exception to procedures under Article 22 of the Constitution of India is the Preventive Detention Laws, and these are being constantly challenged and repealed.

After stating that the presumption of innocence is a principle based on fairness, good sense and practical utility the Committee suggests that there is a need for reform of this principle as it is a principle that is not within the comprehension of the layman. It has been suggested that the principle is responsible for fewer convictions and the acquittal of the guilty. Since the acquittal of the guilty leads to a demoralization of the law enforcement authorities the committee calls for reforms, which do not impose a higher standard of proof in criminal cases from civil cases.

> The protagonists of reforms contend that there is no justification for applying a higher standard of proof than the one prescribed by the law made by Parliament, in criminal cases. They argue that "proof beyond reasonable doubt" is a vague, unreasonable, unfair, unjust and impractical standard, which has done more harm than good to the society. They want that the lower standard of "preponderance of probabilities" should govern criminal cases. We should examine the arguments against the higher standard of "proof beyond reasonable doubt" in the context of the new ethos of quest for truth.[32]

The Committee contends that the Courts have already watered down the presumption from its original position and the level of proof that is required is now a more relaxed standard, which is that of reasonable certainty rather than reasonable doubt.[33] The Committee argues that to set the guilty free is not doing justice and hence the standard of proof of being beyond reasonable doubt needs to be modified, as it is not capable of a clear definition. There is no distinction made between the presumption and the burden of proof between the presumption of innocence and the burden or the standards of proof that are required.

In England where the doctrine has its origin the standard of beyond reasonable doubt prescribes a standard for the jury. The Committee opines that the jury being composed of non-law persons cannot be expected to make any fine distinctions between reasonable doubt and the preponderance of probabilities.

> 5.26 Though the trial judge in the jury system asks the jury to take a decision bearing in mind that the burden is on the prosecution of proving the case beyond reasonable doubt, it is doubtful whether in practice the members of the jury would make a conscious effort to apply this principle in deciding the case. As the jury consists of laymen who are not used to the judicial ways of assessing evidence, they would decide the matter in the same manner they take decisions in their day-to-day affairs and not following the uncommon way of looking for reasonable doubt. That standard which a prudent man would apply is of "preponderance of probabilities.[34]

The Committee is of the opinion that since the jury in England is composed on persons who may not be well versed in law or in the hairsplitting differences as to when an offence is proved and when it is proved beyond reasonable doubt there is a need to shift the burden of proving the case onto the suspect. This argument may not be relevant in India as we do not follow the jury system and the judges are normally presumed capable of establishing guilt on the basis of reasonable evidence of guilt. The committee strangely does not refer to the Preventive Detentions Acts or the Armed Forces Special Powers Act, which have done away with this presumption. The rationale for diluting the presumption is given in the following manner:

> Requirement of "proof beyond reasonable doubt" was laid down long back with regard to the prevailing circumstances of the time. At that time offences were few, ways and habits of the people were simple, people were more honest, by and large witnesses readily came forward to give truthful evidence before the Court. The modes adopted for committing the offences were simple. Now there is a sea change in all these aspects. People now-a-days are better informed. The Press, the radio, the T.V., films and various types of literature have enormous influence in educating and enlightening people of different ways of committing crimes. They use sophisticated weapons and employ techniques so as not to leave any trace of evidence that may implicate them. The accused are becoming more daring and reckless. The level of morality has gone down and regard for truth is waning. Witnesses do not come forward to give evidence on account of threats or inducements and those who come, quite often turn hostile. It looks as though the criminals are emerging stronger than the law enforcing agency. The existing laws and procedures are proving inadequate to meet the new challenges. The changing scenario has to be taken into account to evaluate the efficacy of the present standard and to find suitable solutions to meet the new challenges.[35]

The Committee is of the opinion that in the changed social circumstances the traditional protections offered to the accused can be replaced with only those protections that are offered in civil law. To quote from the report.

> 5.29 While proof on "preponderance of probabilities" followed in civil cases provides a lower standard of proof, "proof beyond reasonable doubt" followed in criminal cases provides a higher standard of proof bordering on certainty. The cherished object of the criminal justice system is to ensure that every guilty person is punished and every innocent person is

> protected. Our experience shows that operation of the standard "proof beyond reasonable doubt" has contributed to large number of guilty persons escaping punishment. This standard followed all these years has failed to achieve the main object of ensuring that the guilty are punished. What then is the answer and what are the options available to remedy the mischief? Should we opt for the standard of "proof on preponderance of probabilities" that is applied in civil cases? On a careful examination the Committee is of the view that this standard is not adequate to lend assurance that the innocent will be protected. Therefore, we have to find standard of proof which, while protecting the innocent, is adequate to prevent the guilty escaping punishment. A standard in between these two standards seems to be the answer.[36]
>
> The middle course, in our opinion, makes a proper balance between the rights of the accused on one hand and public interest and rights of the victim on the other. This standard is just, fair and reasonable.[37]

The Committee states that the standard of preponderance of probabilities rather than proof beyond reasonable doubt can be substituted in criminal cases. The question of it being violative of fundamental criminal principles is dismissed on the ground that the doctrine at common law already envisaged exceptions. Further it meets with the constitutional protections under Article 21. But the presumption of innocence is not merely about any particular stage of the trial but is intended to permeate the trial process and constantly remind the officers of the system that they cannot presume guilt and accordingly treat the suspect in that manner. The presumption of innocence is linked to the entire method of investigation, trial and the right of the suspects during trial. It is linked to a humane treatment of all persons in custody under the premise that they are innocent until proved guilty and cannot be subjected to unnecessary restrictions. It is also linked to the right to bail which is recognized as a part of the right to life. Unless a strong case is made out regarding interference bail must be granted as a matter of right. To limit the discussion of the presumption to the question of burden of proof alone is to reduce this fundamental premise of the criminal justice system to a legal rule, which can be changed.

While prescribing these standards the committee does not distinguish between cases of preventive detention or terrorism and other criminal cases. Nor is it indicative if there is to be change in these cases.

In addition to the proof beyond reasonable doubt, there is another maxim that is the standard of a reasonable person. Often called the Wednesbury rule, this standard is often invoked to determine whether the action taken is reasonable and is based on the standard of a reasonable person who can be any person on the street. The Committee does not explain how the "reasonable person" standard, which is well settled in law to mean the reasoning of a common person, is different from the standard of "beyond reasonable doubt". If the law presumes that a reasonable person in a given situation would come to a certain conclusion there is nothing to preclude him from using that standard to that of reasonable doubt. The term reasonable doubt as against any standard of conclusive proof or beyond all doubt itself should be sufficient to suggest that what is expected is that any doubt which is reasonable as to the guilt of the suspect needs to be eliminated before a conviction and that if the suspect is not guilty beyond doubt he must be given the benefit of it.

There is no discussion on the fact that the investigation agencies need to be strengthened, the types of evidence needs to be updated and sophisticated fact-finding methods need to be used instead of the time tested mechanisms of coercion of the suspect. However, the rationale used by the Committee is not in these terms, but in entirely different terms.

Conclusion

Two theories, the due process model and the crime control model have influenced the criminal justice system. Both these theories emphasize on different methods of dealing with crime. The crime control model focuses on an aggressive method of crime control one could say a no holds barred method while the other is said to reflect a "solicitude" for the right of the individual.[38] This labeling was done by Herbert Packer which has been disputed and differed from but which gives us a starting point of discussion for the attitude of the criminal justice system towards crime and suspected criminals.

> According to this classification the crime control model is based on the proposition that the repression of criminal conduct is by far the most important function to be performed by the criminal process.[39]

And the key to achieving that end is

> The efficiency with which the criminal process operates to screen suspects, determine guilt, and secure appropriate dispositions of persons convicted of crime.[40]

This model relies on high apprehension and conviction and speed and finality are the key words. The emphasis on speed leads to an emphasis on informality and processes such as interrogation at the police station and cases treated in an administrative and routine manner. The theory is that this leads to a prompt and successful conviction and cases are speedily eliminated when the available evidence does not point to guilt and those cases where there is available evidence will be pursued in a quick expeditious manner with little occasion for challenge and "post-audit". The model is dependent on availability of informal fact-finding and the only restrictions are those, which enhance reliability of such fact-finding rather than restrict them. Inevitably with such a system is the fact that the presumption is one of guilt rather than innocence. The element of mistakes are not discounted but even if there are mistakes if the overall goal of crime repression is attained the model is deemed successful.

The due process model tries to minimize the possibility of error and is a system with protections, which emphasize on the rights of the individual and offer him protections against wrongful convictions. The adversarial system allows for evidence to be disputed and is conceived as a restriction on power and permits the guilty to escape when evidence is procured in an unreliable manner. The presumption is of innocence and the oft-quoted phrase is that a hundred guilty may escape provided no innocent is punished by the system. Evidence collected in a wrongful manner is excluded and convictions may be reversed even when the evidence points to guilt if due process is not followed. Packer notes two forces behind this model:

> a concern for equality of justice and a skepticism about the morality and utility of the criminal sanction itself.[41]

The ideological underpinnings of the due-process model are thus broader than those of the crime-control model, and the confluence of these various themes results in a model that emphasizes formal processes, individualized consideration, and the opportunity for careful review.[42]

The due process model has been preferred by utilitarianism. The utilitarian argument for a presumption in favor of the accused is in the words of Bentham:

> Generally speaking, a too easy acquittal excites regret and uneasiness only among men of reflection; while the condemnation of an accused, who turns out to have been innocent, spreads general dismay; all security appears to be destroyed; no defense can any longer be found, when even innocence is insufficient.[43]

The utilitarian arguments believe that taking a lenient rule in favor of the accused does a better job at protecting citizens from crime as the cost of deterrence may outweigh the benefits the strict principle affords.

The moral theorists while rejecting utilitarian arguments have defended the presumption of innocence on the grounds that to do otherwise and risk a wrongful conviction is an unwarranted intrusion into individual rights and must not be done even at the cost of not repressing crime as insufficient crime control is an omission on the part of the State whereas to hold an innocent man guilty would constitute an active wrong on the part of the State.[44]

Thus, the presumption of innocence is an integral model of what has been termed as a due process model and of extreme importance and cannot be treated merely as a rule of evidence and be dispensed with. To dispense with it would mean to contradict the Constitution of India as Articles 21 and 14 clearly provide for the protection of life and liberty. The presumption permeates the criminal justice process and is of wide ranging application is civil and criminal cases. The exceptions to the doctrine also point to the doing of justice in the end and the presumption is withdrawn depending on the nature of the crime and in order to address the inequities between the persons before the Court. To treat the parties as equals as in civil case defeats the purposes of justice. In not addressing this issue the Malimath Committee fails to uphold the Human Rights of the citizens of India. The legislations against terrorism have invoked the spectre of terrorism to do away with this presumption. Such legislations have failed to prove the worth of doing away with basic protections of the law. There is no purpose served then by ignoring this essential principle of law in any situation.

While arguing for greater crime control and more convictions we really need to address the issue as to whether confessions of the suspects are the only evidence we need to come to a conclusion of guilt. When there are confessions and no corroborating evidence does the confession overwhelm other evidence? An attempt must be made to study how likely are false confessions to lead to wrongful arrests, prosecutions, convictions and imprisonment or death of the innocent. This has a profound impact on the study of miscarriage of justice and the proper administration of justice.[45]

The fact that the guilty are acquitted does not necessarily mean that everything has been done to eliminate the risks that an innocent person is convicted.[46] "Perversely, the fact that the guilty are regularly acquitted obscures the difficulties that the adjudicatory system poses for the innocent."[47]

Notes

1. Bentham, J., 1825. *A Treatise on Judicial Evidence.* London: Paget, p. 197.
2. Dworkin, R., 1986. "Principle, Policy, Procedure," in R. Dworkin: *A Matter of Principle.* Oxford: Oxford University Press, pp. 81-84.

3. Such as the ICCPR, UNDHR etc.
4. Article 14(2).
5. AIR 1935 AC 462.
6. AIR 1914 Cal 396.
7. *Amrita Lal Hazra v. Emperor*, AIR 1916 Cal 188.
8. Section 112 of the Indian Evidence Act, 1872 reads: the fact that any person was born during the continuance of a valid marriage between his mother and any man, or within two hundred and eighty days after its dissolution the mother remaining unmarried, shall be conclusively proof that he is the legitimate son of that man, unless it can be shown that parties to the marriage had no access to each other at any time when he could have been begotten.
9. Section 114 of the Indian Evidence Act, 1872. Section 114: The Court may presume the existence of any fact which it thinks likely to have happened, regard being had to the common course of natural events, human conduct and public and private business in their relation to the facts of the particular case. Illustrations (e) that judicial and official acts have been regularly performed; (f) that the common course of business has been followed in particular cases.
10. Best, Ev., Sections 35 and 352 from law of Evidence Section 114-N5, p. 2886 to 2892.
11. Lawson, Pres. Ev., 93; *Savalappa v. Devchand*, (1901) 26 B 132.
12. *Law of Evidence* p. 2891, *Commonwealth v. Kaimball*, 24 pick (Mass) 373 (Amer).
13. AIR 1935 AC 462.
14. *International Criminal Law*, p. 294, *Prosecutor v. Goran Jelisic*, Case No. IT-95-10, ICTY T.Ch.1, Oral Judgment of 19t Oct. 1999.
15. Rights of the accused: The accused shall be presumed innocent until proved guilty according to the provisions of the present statute.
16. Presumption of innocence: Everyone shall be presumed innocent until proved guilty before the Court in accordance with the applicable law. The onus is on the Prosecutor to prove the guilt of the accused. In order to convict the accused, the Court must be convinced of the guilt of the accused beyond reasonable doubt.
17. Article 14(2) of the International Covenant on Civil and Political Rights, 1966.
18. *Shivaji Sahebrao Badade v. State of Maharashtra*, (1973) 2 SCC 793.

19. Section 105 Indian Evidence Act, 1872: When a person is accused of any offence the burden of proving the existence of circumstances bringing the case within any of the General Exceptions in the Indian Penal Code (45 of 1860), or within any special exception of proviso contained in any other part of the same Code, or in any law defining the offence, is upon him, and the Court shall presume the absence of such circumstances.
20. Where sexual intercourse by the accused is proved and the victim states in her evidence that she did not consent, the Court shall presume that she did not consent and the burden shifts to the accused to prove that she had given her consent.
21. Manas Mohapatra, "Learning Lessons from India: The Recent History of Antiterrorist Legislation on the Subcontinent" 95, *Journal of Criminal Law and Criminology*, 315, Fall 2004.
22. "Human Rights Watch, In the Name of Counter-Terrorism: Human Rights Abuses Worldwide" (2003), at 15, available at http://www.hrw.org/un/chr59/counter-terrorism-bck4.htm#P252_51825 [hereinafter HRW India Report].
23. No person who is arrested shall be detained in custody without being informed, as soon as may be, of the grounds for such arrest nor shall he be denied the right to consult, and to be defended by, a legal practitioner of his choice.

    Every person who is arrested and detained in custody shall be produced before the nearest magistrate within a period of twenty-four hours of such arrest excluding the time necessary for the journey from the place of arrest to the Court of the magistrate and no such person shall be detained in custody beyond the said period without the authority of a magistrate.
24. Sections 3(1)(a), 21(1)(b), (1)(c), and (1)(d).
25. South Asia Human Rights Documentation Centre, Human Rights Documentation Center, Prevention of Terrorism Ordinance 2001: Government Decides To Play Judge And Jury 24, (2001).
26. Section 49(2)(b).
27. "Human Rights Watch, In the Name of Counter-Terrorism: Human Rights Abuses Worldwide" (2003), at 15, available at http://www.hrw.org/un/chr59/counter-terrorism-bck4.htm#P252_51825.
28. Manas Mohapatra, "Learning Lessons from India: The Recent History of Antiterrorist Legislation on the Subcontinent" 95, *Journal of Criminal Law and Criminology*, 315, Fall 2004.
29. Ronald Weich, senior counsel and counsel for the justice project which advocated the passage of the act, "Innocence Protection Act

of 2004: A Small Step Forward and a Framework for Larger Reforms" 29-MAR Champion 28, Champion, March, 2005.

30. *Committee on Reforms of Criminal Justice System*, Government of India, Ministry of Home Affairs, India, March 2003.
31. *Committee on Reforms of Criminal Justice System*, Government of India, Ministry of Home Affairs, Volume I, p. 67 Para 5.8, India, March 2003.
32. *Ibid.*, at 5.13, p. 68.
33. *Ibid.*, at 5.17, p. 70.
34. *Ibid.*, p. 72.
35. *Ibid.*, p. 73.
36. *Ibid.*, at 5.28, 5.29, p. 73.
37. *Ibid.*, at 5.31, p. 73.
38. Daniel H. Foote, "The Benevolent Paternalism of Japanese Criminal Justice", 80, *California Law Review*, March, 1992 quoting Herbert L. Parker "The Limits of the Criminal Sanction: Conceptualizing Two Models of the Criminal Process" 149-73, *California Law Review* (1968).
39. *Ibid.*
40. *Ibid.*
41. *Ibid.*
42. *Ibid.*
43. Alon Harel, Zvi Safra and Uri Seqal, "Ex-post Egalitarianism and Legal Justice" using Bentham (1825:197), 21 J.L. Econ. & Org. 57, *Journal of Law, Economics and Organization*, OUP April, 2005.
44. *Ibid*, (Dworkin, 1986: 72, 81-84).
45. Steven A. Drizin and Richard A. Leo "The Problem of False Confessions in the Post-DNA World" *82 North Carolina Law Review 891*, March 2004.
46. Daniel Givelber, "Meaningless acquittals, meaningful convictions: do we reliably acquit the innocent?" 49 *Rutgers Law Review*, 1317, Summer 1997.
47. *Ibid.*

15

Terrorism and Human Rights: A Saga of Opposites?

Shameek Sen

Terrorism— A Brief Introduction

The world has, in its different stages of development and structural adaptations, confronted problems of varied natures and magnitudes. However, even without the ever-presence of a global consensus in many of them, a reasonable working formula has been developed to resolve most of them. The underlying reason for such resolutions can be attributed to, among other reasons, the countries' constant thrust for amicability and interdependence, a precursor for growth and development. However powerful a country might be, at some plane, it has to depend on others for, if not anything else, trade proliferation. The countries therefore tend to exercise a degree of mutual concern and co-operation in solving issues that are universal in nature and operation.

However, the biggest stumbling block to maintenance of world peace and order, a global need also highlighted by the UN Charter, has been, in the recent years, the huge surge in the magnitude and intensity of terrorist and disruptive activities. The 9/11 and the 7/7, are now household tales of universal dread and there is a constant threat perception involving the question— where next? Seldom does one realize the reason behind such actions—many say the reason is theological, but strictly speaking, there can be no religion that turns its backs towards people's welfare, and development. Hence, blaming religion for everything would be improper and unjustified. What is to be blamed is the unscrupulous nature of these people who perpetrate such dastardly acts on the existence of peace and security, and the global community must strongly address such issues.

Though so far, an exact definition of the term 'Terrorism' has not been achieved to be culled out due to national differences on the extent of the concept, it can be safely said that *Terrorism refers to a strategy of using violence, or threat of violence targeted against non-combatants to generate fear, cause disruption, and ultimately, to bring about compliance with specific political, religious, ideological, and personal demands.*[1] The targets of terrorist attacks typically are not the individuals who are killed, injured, or taken hostage, but rather the societies to which these individuals belong. It is a type of unconventional warfare designed to weaken or supplant existing political landscapes through capitulation or acquiescence, as opposed to subversion or direct military action.

However, as poetic justice would have it, it has also been noticed that the fear psychosis that terrorism seems to have developed among the nations of the world has given rise to a phenomenon that is as despicable as terrorism itself. That is the gross violation of established standards of Human Rights while carrying out counter-terrorism measures. It is not denied that terrorists carry out acts that cannot be justified under any stretch of imagination, yet the global community cannot take the primitive 'eye-for-an-eye' approach to counter these. What needs to be addressed is the inherent dan'er in the acts, and fair, yet stringent means to prevent them. This might, owing to the peculiar and serious nature of the situations, require some amount of deviation from the established practices, but the question is—how much? This paper attempts to analyze this question, based on latest global developments in the realm of international Human Rights jurisprudence.

Hypothesis

Considering the Utilitarian Principle of the Greatest Good for the Greatest Number and the Balance of Interests between a Private Right and a Public Right, the stringency of the laws prohibiting and punishing terrorism must have a degree of stringency associated with them. However, given the universal need for ensuring Human Rights protection to everyone, as also ordained by the International and regional organizations including the UN, the anti-terrorism laws and measures must necessarily conform to the Human Rights standards. Nevertheless, considering the needs for achieving the ends, it should also be said that a minimum deviation from the set norms can be justified in certain occasions, but the deviation must not cross the limits of necessity and proportionality.

Terrorism— Key Features

Before going into a discussion on the issue of terrorism and Human Rights, one must clearly outline the key components of what can be called a terrorist act:[2]

Violence: The only general characteristic of terrorism generally agreed upon is that terrorism involves violence and the threat of violence.

Psychological impact and fear: Any act of terrorism is a "performance", a product of internal logic, devised to have an impact on many large audiences. Terrorists also attack national symbols to show their power and to shake the foundation of the country or society they are opposed to. This may negatively affect a government's legitimacy, while trying to increase the legitimacy of the given terrorist organization and/or ideology behind a terrorist act. The 9/11 attacks on the World Trade Center and Pentagon are examples of this. Attacking the World Trade Center symbolizes that the terrorists can threaten the economic foundation of America and its capitalist ideals, and attacking the Pentagon symbolizes that America's great and prided military strength is yet vulnerable at its very core to the terrorists' power.

Perpetrated for a political goal: Something all terrorist attacks have in common is their perpetration for a political purpose. This is often the key difference between an act of terrorism and a hate crime or lone-wolf "madman" attack. Terrorism is a political tactic, not unlike letter writing or protesting, that is used by activists when they believe no other means will affect the kind of change they desire. The change is desired so badly that failure is seen as a worse outcome than the deaths of civilians. This is often where the interrelationship between terrorism and religion occurs. When a political struggle is integrated into the framework of a religious or "cosmic" struggle, such as over the control of an ancestral homeland or holy site such as Palestine/Israel and Jerusalem, failing in the political goal (nationalism) becomes equated with spiritual failure which, for the highly committed, is worse than their own death or the deaths of innocent civilians.

Deliberate targeting of non-combatants: It is commonly held that the distinctive nature of terrorism lies in its intentional and specific selection of civilians as direct targets. Much of the time, the victims of terrorism are targeted not because they are threats, but because they are specific "symbols, tools, animals or corrupt beings" that tie into a specific view of the world that the terrorist possesses. Their suffering accomplishes the terrorists' goals of instilling fear, getting a message out to an audience, or otherwise accomplishing their political end. This definition excludes attacks on military targets, but pertains regardless of whether the attackers made an attempt to reduce civilian casualties.

Counter-Terrorism Measures— The Types[3]

Through increasing global consensus and mutually supportive State Practice, the countries have been able to develop few modes of countering terrorism, as are outlined hereinunder:

Target-hardening: To place concrete barriers sufficiently distanced outside buildings to prevent truck bombing, aircraft cockpits being kept locked during flights, removal of waste bins from rail stations in Britain after 7/7, etc.

Pre-emptive neutralization: Capturing, killing, or disabling suspected terrorists before they can mount an attack, interrogation of known or suspected terrorists to obtain information about specific plots, targets, the identity of other terrorists, and whether the interrogation subjects himself is guilty of terrorist involvement, sleep deprivation, drugs etc. Such methods may lead captives to offer false information in an attempt to stop the treatment, or due to the confusion brought on by it.

Domestic intelligence and surveillance: Interception of communications, tracing of persons etc. New technology has, however, expanded the range of such operations. Domestic intelligence is often directed at specific groups, defined on the basis of origin or religion, which is a source of political controversy. Mass surveillance of an entire population raises objections on civil liberties grounds.

Military intervention: Terrorism has often been used to justify military intervention in countries where terrorists are said to be based. That was the main stated justification for the U.S. invasion of Afghanistan. It was also a stated justification for the second Russian invasion of Chechnya.

Non-military intervention: The human security paradigm outlines a non-military approach which aims to address the enduring underlying inequalities which fuel terrorist activity. Causal factors need to be delineated and measures implemented which allow equal access to resources and sustainability for all peoples. Such activities empower citizens providing "freedom from fear" and "freedom from want". This can take many forms including the provision of clean drinking water, education, vaccination programs, provision of food and shelter and protection from violence, military or otherwise. Successful human security campaigns have been characterized by the participation of a diverse group of actors including Governments, NGOs, and citizens.

Counter-Terrorism Measures and Human Rights Violations—Issues Raised[4]

However justified the purpose and necessity of the counter-terrorism measures may seem to be, it is undoubted that there are often questions, and justified ones, raised at the means which are used in the process. The challenges on their Human Rights conformity are largely on the following grounds:

- Curbing of Civil Liberties.
- Infringement of Privacy.
- Unlawful and Indefinite Detention (e.g., US Detentions in the Guantanamo Bay).
- Torture and other forms of Cruel, Inhuman, Degrading Treatments.

Counter-Terrorism Measures— Need for Human Rights Observance

> Terrorism is a threat to the most fundamental human rights. Finding common approaches to countering terrorism serves the cause of human rights. Some have suggested that it is not possible to effectively eliminate terrorism while respecting human rights. This suggestion is fundamentally flawed. The only long-term guarantor of security is through ensuring respect for human rights and humanitarian law. The essence of human rights is that human life and dignity must not be compromised and that certain acts, whether carried out by State or non-State actors, are never justified no matter what the ends.
>
> —Mary Robinson[5]

Such gross Human Rights violations as have been mentioned aggravate rather than counter the terrorist threat. Human Rights advocates argue for the crucial role of Human Rights protection as an intrinsic part to fight against terrorism. This suggests that respecting Human Rights may indeed help us to incur security. Amnesty International included a section on confronting terrorism in the recommendations in the Madrid Agenda arising from the Madrid Summit on Democracy and Terrorism (Madrid 8-11 March 2005):[6]

> Democratic principles and values are essential tools in the fight against terrorism. Any successful strategy for dealing with terrorism requires terrorists to be isolated. Consequently, the preference must be to treat terrorism

as criminal acts to be handled through existing systems of law enforcement and with full respect for Human Rights and the rule of law. We recommend: (1) taking effective measures to make impunity impossible either for acts of terrorism or for the abuse of Human Rights in counter-terrorism measures; (2) the incorporation of Human Rights laws in all anti-terrorism programmes and policies of national governments as well as international bodies.

Terrorism and the UN— A Human Rights Paradigm

While condemning terrorism unequivocally and recognizing the duty of States to protect those living within their jurisdictions from terrorism in the aftermath of the 9/11, the Office of the High Commissioner for Human Rights has placed a priority on the question of protecting Human Rights in the context of counter-terrorism measures.[7] The Secretary-General, the High Commissioner for Human Rights, and others in the UN system have emphasized that Human Rights norms must be rigorously respected, even in states of emergency. As then UN Secretary-General Kofi Annan stated at a special meeting of the Security Council's Counter-Terrorism Committee with international, regional, and sub-regional organizations, on 6 March 2003,[8] "Our responses to terrorism, as well as our efforts to thwart it and prevent it, should uphold the Human Rights that terrorists aim to destroy. Respect for Human Rights, fundamental freedoms and the rule of law are essential tools in the effort to combat terrorism—not privileges to be sacrificed at a time of tension."

Security Council

One inference that might be taken from Security Council Resolutions[9] about counter-terrorism measures and their need to comply with Human Rights arises from general statements that counter-terrorism is an aim that should be achieved in accordance with the Charter of the United Nations and international law. This implies that such measures must themselves be compliant with the principles of the Charter and international Human Rights law. In that regard, members of the United Nations have undertaken, under Article 55(c)[10] and through the Preamble[11] to the UN Charter, to observe Human Rights and fundamental freedoms for all without distinction as to race, language or religion.

On 28 September 2001, the Security Council adopted Resolution 1373[12] under Chapter VII of the UN Charter, obligating States to implement more effective counter-terrorism measures at the national level and Resolution 1377[13] to increase international cooperation in the struggle against terrorism. The Resolution created the Counter-Terrorism Committee (CTC) to monitor action on this issue and to receive reports from States on measures taken. Late High Commissioner Mr. Vieira de Mello, speaking to the CTC in October 2002, stated his conviction that "the best—the only—strategy to isolate and defeat terrorism is by respecting Human Rights, fostering social justice, enhancing democracy and upholding the primacy of the rule of law."[14] Since then, the CTC and the UN Human Rights Committee have exchanged briefings on their working methods and areas of concern.

In Resolution 1456,[15] the Security Council declared that "States must ensure that any measure taken to combat terrorism comply with all their obligations under international law, and should adopt such measures in accordance with international law, in particular international Human Rights, refugee, and humanitarian law." This was the express proclamation of the Security Council regarding the fact that compliance of Human Rights is an essential prerequisite to all counter-terrorism measures. Human Rights law has thus sought to strike a fair balance between legitimate national security concerns and the protection of fundamental freedoms.

General Assembly

Since December 1972, the UN General Assembly has adopted a series of Resolutions concerning terrorism.[16] Within the first set of Resolutions on terrorism, the last decade has seen the Assembly adopt and affirm a *Declaration* on Measures to Eliminate International Terrorism, first adopted in early December 1994 under its Resolution 49/60,[17] which pronounced that terrorism constitutes a grave violation of the purpose and principles of the United Nations. The Declaration was reaffirmed in the following two years, with a Declaration to Supplement the 1994 Declaration on Measures to Eliminate International Terrorism adopted in 1996.[18] Both sets of Resolutions contain various statements about the need, when implementing counter-terrorist measures, to comply with international Human Rights standards. A common phrasing of this idea was seen early on in Resolution 50/186 of 1995:[19]

> Mindful of the need to protect human rights of and guarantees for the individual in accordance with the relevant international human rights principles and instruments, particularly the right to life,
>
> Reaffirming that all measures to counter terrorism must be in strict conformity with international human rights standards,
>
> Calls upon States to take all necessary and effective measures in accordance with international standards of human rights to prevent, combat and eliminate all acts of terrorism wherever and by whomever committed.

A slightly less robust expression of these ideas was seen following the events of September 11, although still requiring measures to be taken consistently with Human Rights standards. That should not, however, be taken as a signal that the General Assembly was minded to turn a blind eye to adverse impacts of counter-terrorism upon Human Rights. Indeed, the issue became the subject of annual resolutions on that subject alone, entitled "Protection of Human Rights and Fundamental Freedoms While Countering Terrorism". The first operative paragraph of these resolutions affirm:[20]

> ...that States must ensure that any measure taken to combat terrorism complies with their obligations under international law, in particular international human rights, refugee and humanitarian law....

The Human Rights Committee and Commission

Threats to national security may, under very specific conditions, lead to a state of emergency under which certain rights are subject to derogation (suspension). However, certain rights are never subject to derogation. The question of states of emergency and derogation is addressed in Article 4 of the ICCPR. In July 2001, the UN Human Rights Committee adopted General Comment No. 29, concerning ICCPR Article 4, in which it clarified the scope of non-derogable rights and identified elements which cannot be subject to lawful derogation. Thus, whatever be the nature of the potential threat, derogation from the basic Human Rights like the right not to be subjected to torture cannot be justified. They have acquired the stature of a *jus cogens*, somewhat similar to the *Basic Structure* in the Indian Constitution.

The OHCHR action on the issue of Human Rights and terrorism is guided in part by General Assembly Resolution 58/187[21] and Commission on Human Rights Resolution 2003/68 ("Protection of Human Rights and fundamental freedoms while countering terrorism").

These Resolutions call on the High Commissioner's office to:

(a) examine the question of the protection of Human Rights and fundamental freedoms while countering terrorism, taking into account reliable information from all sources;

(b) make general recommendations concerning the obligation of States to promote and protect Human Rights and fundamental freedoms while taking actions to counter terrorism; and

(c) provide assistance and advice to States, upon their request, on the protection of Human Rights and fundamental freedoms while countering terrorism, as well as to relevant United Nations bodies. The issue of Human Rights and terrorism is also addressed in General Assembly resolution 58/174 (2003)[22] and Commission on Human Rights resolution 2003/37 ("Human Rights and terrorism").

The Report of the Commission's Special Rapporteur on the Promotion and Protection of Human Rights in June 2005[23] also addressed the matter. Although the original mandate of the Special Rapporteur was to consider the impact of terrorism on Human Rights, she commented in her 2004 report that a State's over-reaction to terrorism can itself also impact upon Human Rights. Rapporteur Kalliopi Koufa's mandate[24] was therefore extended to develop a draft of principles and guidelines concerning Human Rights and terrorism (which are to be discussed further in this part of the paper). Of note at this point, the first-stated principle under the heading "Duties of States Regarding Terrorist Acts and Human Rights" reads:[25]

> All States have a duty to promote and protect human rights of all persons under their political or military control in accordance with all human rights and humanitarian law norms.

The UNOHCHR implements the findings of the Secretary-General's Policy Working Group on Terrorism, in particular its sub-group on Human Rights and Terrorism. Based on a Policy Working Group recommendation, the Office published in 2003 the Digest of Jurisprudence of the UN and Regional Organizations on the Protection of Human Rights while Countering Terrorism.[26] The Digest makes several important contributions, for example by clarifying the concept of non-derogable rights under both the United Nations and regional Human Rights systems. It addresses the core principles of *necessity* and *proportionality*, which are fundamental to lawful counter-terrorism measures. Through excerpts from findings of the UN and regional Human Rights bodies, the Digest shows concerns that have been expressed over practices which are in use or under consideration by States today, such as the use of military tribunals to try civilians, and detention practices which disregard recognized international standards.[27]

Compliance with Human Rights— A Dilemma of Approaches

Now that with the sustained efforts of the UN through its different organs it is perceivable that there has to be adherence to the basic norms of Human Rights and humanitarian values even while countering a menace as severe as terrorism, the question that emerges is that whether the compliance has to be *absolute*, or can there be *limitations* imposed upon the free enjoyment of those rights by the terrorists?

The ICCPR adopts a reasonably absolute approach to rights limitations. Unless a limitation upon a particular right is expressly contained within the Covenant, any limitation upon the right is not permissible outside a state of emergency, the scope, ambit and application of which is again categorically mentioned in A/4 itself. The Inter-American Commission on Human Rights (IACHR) Report on Terrorism and Human Rights describes this common feature of international Human Rights treaties as follows:[28]

> ...through mechanisms such as derogations and restriction clauses, International Human Rights law recognizes and provides for means by which the restriction or suspension of certain rights may be necessary in exceptional circumstances to protect Human Rights and democracy.

Many domestic Human Rights instruments adopt a more general approach to the limitation of rights. Examples can be seen in the Canadian Charter of Rights and Freedoms 1982 and the New Zealand Bill of Rights Act 1990, both of which express that the rights and freedoms set out within those instruments may be "subject only to such reasonable limits prescribed by law as can be demonstrably justified in a free and democratic society". The Supreme Court of Canada[29] has held that expression to require that: *(a) any limitation is in pursuit of a sufficiently important objective to warrant overriding a constitutionally protected right or freedom; and (b) the limitation is reasonable and proportional, having regard to the importance of the right and of the objective.*

Drawbacks of the Absolute Approach— Need for Flexibility

One of the problems with absolute approaches is that such approaches are unable to cope with change. Thus, absolute rules tend to be an exception rather than the norm. Although this can be problematic for those seeking certainty, the benefit of reasonably fluid rules is that they are able to react to the changing needs of society. The qualification to this is that where rules seek to be fluid, they must also achieve an appropriate level of certainty to enable society to regulate its conduct.[30]

On another level, one must recognize that the "social contract" imports both rights and responsibilities upon members of any society. From a liberal democratic perspective, one's rights are to be balanced against the rights of others and the needs of society as a whole. The freedom of expression, for example, does not include the right to incite racial hatred, nor the ability to defame others. This is, in part, recognized within the Preamble to the ICCPR.[31]

Interface between Counter-Terrorism and Human Rights—International Guidelines

International Commission of Jurists

At its Biennial Conference in August 2004, the International Commission of Jurists was instrumental in the adoption of the Berlin Declaration on Upholding Human Rights and the Rule of Law in Combating Terrorism[32] that recognizes the need to combat terrorism and the duty of States to protect those within their jurisdiction. It also expresses that contemporary Human Rights law allows States a reasonably wide margin of flexibility to combat terrorism without contravening the essence of rights.

Council of Europe

In July 2002, the Committee of Ministers to the Council of Europe adopted Guidelines on Human Rights and the Fight against Terrorism.[33] Five of the more specific guidelines warrant mention. The first reflects the idea that counter-terrorism is an important objective in a free and democratic society. Article I accordingly talks of a positive obligation upon States to protect individuals within their territory from the scourges of terrorism. The second and third Articles are directly relevant to the question of compliance with Human Rights. Article II prohibits the arbitrary limitation of rights, and Article III requires limiting measures to be *lawful, precise, necessary* and *proportional*. Further guidance on possible derogations is found in Article XV, concerning derogations during situations of war or states of emergency threatening the life of a nation. Finally, Article XVI underlines that States may never act in breach of peremptory norms of international law. In 2005, the Council issued additional guidelines on the protection of victims of terrorist attacks.[34]

Inter-American Commission of Human Rights

A Report of the Inter-American Commission on Human Rights (IACHR) on Terrorism and Human Rights was issued in late 2002,[35] shortly after the adoption of the Inter-American Convention against Terrorism.[36] Interestingly, Article 15 of the latter Convention specifically requires all States parties to comply with Human Rights standards:

> The measures carried out by the states parties under this Convention shall take place with full respect for the rule of law, Human Rights, and Fundamental Freedoms.

The IACHR report undertakes a Right-based approach, focusing upon the scope and potential limitation of particular rights.[37] It also emphasizes the general need for any limitation to comply with the doctrines of necessity, proportionality and nondiscrimination.[38] As one of its annexes, the report resolves:[39]

1. To reiterate that the fight against terrorism must be waged with full respect for the law, Human Rights, and democratic institutions, so as to preserve the rule of law, freedoms, and democratic values in the hemisphere.
2. To reaffirm the duty of the member states to ensure that all measures taken to combat terrorism are in keeping with obligations under international law.

Thus, it can be seen that rather than imposing absolute and non-derogable restrictions on the operation of the Human Rights in cases specific to counter-terrorism as the treaties do, the Guidelines of the various international bodies have taken the more pragmatic qualified approach in aiming to strike a balance between the rights and necessities.

However, never since the adoption of the Treaties and Guidelines have come a question before the ICCPR Human

Rights Committee where despite the Covenant's jurisprudence aiming for an absolute approach, a country comes up with the defense that it had adopted the qualified approach as ordained by the different Guidelines of the International Bodies, more so in view of the fact that Human Rights Committee has never formally applied the "margin of appreciation doctrine",[40] a doctrine which is utilized by the European Court of Human Rights and defined as the notion that each society is entitled to a certain latitude in resolving the inherent conflicts between individual rights and national interests, or among different moral convictions.

Necessity and Proportionality— How to Ascertain?

Since counter-terrorism is a sufficiently important objective to warrant it, in principle, measures need to be taken which might place limits upon rights and freedoms (so long as the means by which such measures are implemented are appropriate and the objectives of such means are clear).[41] This is a position that can be arrived at without too many difficulties. Proportionality calls for a more detailed approach. Most importantly, it ultimately requires a balancing exercise, on a case-by-case basis. Recognizing these difficulties, this paper offers an understanding on the manner in which this balancing exercise is to be undertaken.

The Supreme Court of Canada has identified that,[42] in establishing that the means of achieving an important objective are reasonable and demonstrably justified, this involves a form of proportionality test involving three components. To begin, it said, *the measures must be carefully designed to achieve the objective and rationally connected to that objective*. Next, *the means should impair the right in question as little as reasonably possible*. Lastly, *there must be proportionality between the effects of the limiting measure and the importance of the objective*.

Thus... A Final Prescription[43]

After elaborately analyzing the prevalent practices and international opinions and guidelines focusing on the point of Human Rights observance of the counter-terrorism measures, it is submitted that such measures should conform to the broad prescription as given hereinunder:

1. **Counter-Terrorist Measures must Comply with Human Rights Standards:** Measures implemented to counter-terrorism must comply with applicable international Human Rights treaties and with relevant customary law norms of international Human Rights law. It must at this stage be determined whether:

(a) The counter-terrorist measure impacts upon a right that is a peremptory norm of customary international law. If so, the counter-terrorist measure cannot impose a limitation upon it.

(b) The counter-terrorist measure impacts upon a right that is not derogable under an applicable Human Rights treaty. This will normally mean that the counter-terrorist measure cannot impose any limitations upon the right, although this depends upon the particular expression of the right.

(c) The counter-terrorist measure impacts upon a right that is only derogable during a state of emergency threatening the life of the nation. In that case, the State must determine whether such an emergency exists, within the meaning of the applicable Human Rights treaty. If so, the State must:

(i) lodge a proclamation of derogation (in accordance with the requirements of the particular treaty);

(ii) continually review its circumstances to ensure that the derogation lasts only as long as the state of emergency exists; and

(iii) ensure that the derogation is proportionate.

(d) The counter-terrorist measure impacts upon a right that is neither peremptory nor derogable only in states of emergency. If so, the State must ensure that:

(i) the limitation is within the permissible range of limits provided within the treaty or customary definition of the right; and

(ii) the limitation is proportionate.

2. **The Objective of the Counter-Terrorist Measure must be Sufficiently Important:** In principle, the objective of counter-terrorism is one that is pressing and substantial in a free and democratic society and one that may therefore justify the limitation of derogable Human Rights. Notwithstanding the importance of counter-terrorism *per se*, it is the particular objective of the legislative provision or counter-terrorist policy/measure in question that must be assessed. It will be pertinent in this regard to identify how the measure or provision links with:

(a) the countering of an actual threat of terrorism against the State;

(b) the countering of a potential threat of terrorism against the State;

(c) its contribution to the international framework on counter-terrorism; and

(d) its contribution to other national interests.

3. **The Counter-Terrorist Measure must be Established by Proper Means:** Counter-terrorist measures seeking to impose limitations upon rights and freedoms must be prescribed by law, requiring such prescriptions to be adequately accessible and formulated with sufficient precision so that citizens may regulate their conduct. Prescriptions may not confer an unfettered discretion, they must not be arbitrarily applied, and they must be confined to counter-terrorism in their application. Linked to the latter notion, any prescription must also respect the principle of non-discrimination and equality before the law. Finally, the prescription must seek to effect a "limitation" upon rights, rather than an exclusion of them, which would impair the essence of the right or freedom being affected.

4. **The Counter-Terrorist Measure must be Rationally Connected to its Objective:** Any legislative or other counter-terrorist measure must be drafted and implemented in such a way that it is rationally connected to the achievement of the objective being pursued, requiring the counter-terrorist measure being examined to logically further the objective of

countering terrorism. It will also be relevant to identify the effectiveness of the counter-terrorist measure.

5. The Impairment of Rights must be as Little as Reasonably Possible: The limiting measure must impair the right or freedom as little as reasonably possible, and thereby be compatible with the objective of maintaining and promoting Human Rights. A degree of judicial deference might be appropriate, such that if the particular Human Rights limitation is trivial, then an examination of available alternatives might not be warranted. One must otherwise ensure that:

(a) the legislation or measure is the least intrusive means of achieving the counter-terrorist objective; and

(b) the legislation is interpreted (or policy/discretion applied) in favor of rights.

6. The Factors to be Balanced must be Properly Identified: Prior to determining the substantive issue of proportionality, the following factors must be clearly identified:

As to the counter-terrorist measure:

(a) What is the importance of the objective being pursued by the counter-terrorist provision or measure?

(b) How effective is the counter-terrorist measure in achieving its objective?

As to the Human Rights impact of the counter-terrorist measure:

(a) What is the importance of, or the degree of protection provided by, the right or freedom affected?

(b) What are the effects of the limiting provision (or measure) upon the right or freedom?

7. The Factors must be Balanced to Achieve Proportionality: Assuming that limitation of the right is permissible in the abstract [step 1]; and the counter-terrorism measure has been established by proper means [step 3]; and the proposed impairment of the right is as little as reasonably possible [step 5]; then the substantive issue of proportionality between counter-terrorism and the unlimited enjoyment of

Human Rights can be determined by answering the following question:

Having regard to the importance of the right or freedom, is the effect of the measure or provision upon the right proportional to the importance of the objective, and the effectiveness, of the legislative provision or measure?

Summary and Conclusion

The era of Global *Jihadism*, together with the threat of unconventional terrorism and the need for universal and effective implementation of the international framework on counter-terrorism, has brought with it public pressure for adequate security laws and a consequent proliferation of counter-terrorist legislation and policies. The manner in which some counterterrorist legislation and policies have developed has in turn seen a growing concern from both non-governmental and intergovernmental agencies about the need to ensure compliance with Human Rights when seeking to combat terrorism. The aim of this paper has been to assess the various international and regional directions and guidelines on the subject and draw from these a workable set of considerations to be taken into account when attempting to determine the balance to be struck between counter-terrorism and Human Rights. Of course, this exercise is merely illustrative in nature, but the policy prescription as has been envisaged may be instrumental in addressing the issues involving non-compliance of Human Rights and Fair Procedure Standards while countering terrorism, and in the process may act as a tool for social engineering of the apparently conflicting rights and interests, when it comes to tackling a menace as prolific in nature and content as terrorism.

Notes

1. *See* http://en.wikipedia.org/wiki/Terrorism, (last visited on 8th Sept 2006).
2. *Ibid.*
3. *Ibid.*
4. *See* generally, Ganor, Boaz, *et al*, "Legal and Policy Issues in Establishing an International Framework for Human Rights

Compliance When Countering Terrorism" at http://www.ict.org.il/Articles/researchdet.cfm?researchid=5, (last visited on 8th Sept 2006).

5. Mary Robinson, *Terrorism and Human Rights* (Press Release, United Nations Office of the High Commissioner for Human Rights, 20 March 2002).
6. "Amnesty International, Counter-terrorism and Criminal Law in the EU", www.amesty.org/library/Index/ENGIOR610132005, (last visited on 8th Sept 2006).
7. *See* http://ohchr.org/english/issues/terrorism/index.htm, (last visited on 8th Sept 2006).
8. *Ibid.*
9. Under Article 24 of the Charter of the United Nations, the Security Council is charged with the maintenance of international peace and security, paragraph 1 providing that: "In order to ensure prompt and effective action by the United Nations, its Members confer on the Security Council primary responsibility for the maintenance of international peace and security, and agree that in carrying out its duties under this responsibility the Security Council acts on their behalf".
10. Article 55. With a view to the creation of conditions of stability and well-being which are necessary for peaceful and friendly relations among nations based on respect for the principle of equal rights and self-determination of peoples, the United Nations shall promote: (c) Universal respect for, and observance of, Human Rights and fundamental freedoms for all without distinction as to race, sex, language, or religion. See Article 55(c), Charter of the United Nations, 1945.
11. "We the Peoples of The United Nations Determined to reaffirm faith in fundamental human rights, in the dignity and worth of the human person, in the equal rights of men and women and of nations large and small..." See Preamble, *ibid.*
12. SC Res. 1373, UN SCOR, 4385th Mtg, UN Doc S/Res/1373 (2001).
13. SC Res. 1377, UN SCOR, 4389th Mtg, UN Doc S/Res/1377 (2001).
14. See *Supra* 7.
15. UN SCOR, 4668th Mtg, UN Doc S/Res/1456 (2003).
16. The first resolution of the General Assembly concerning itself solely with the issue of terrorism was adopted on 18 December 1972 against the background of the disruption of the 1972 Olympic Games at Munich: GA Res 3034 (XXVII), UN GAOR, 27th Sess, 2114th Plen Mtg, UN Doc A/Res/XXVII/3034 (1972).

Its very title illustrates the view that terrorism is a matter affecting security and the enjoyment of rights: "Measures to prevent international terrorism which endangers or takes innocent lives or jeopardizes fundamental freedoms, and study of the underlying causes of those forms of terrorism and acts of violence which lie in misery, frustration, grievance and despair and which cause some people to sacrifice lives, including their own, in an attempt to effect radical changes". The same title was used to name eight subsequent resolutions of the General Assembly, from 1976 to 1989: GA Res 31/102, UN GAOR, 31st Sess, 99th Plen Mtg, UN Doc A/Res/31/102 (1976); GA Res 32/147, UN GAOR, 32nd Sess, 105th Plen Mtg, UN Doc A/Res/32/147 (1977); GA Res 34/145, UN GAOR, 34th Sess, 105th Plen Mtg, UN Doc A/Res/34/145 (1979); GA Res 36/109, UN GAOR, 36th Sess, 92nd Plen Mtg, UN Doc A/Res/36/109 (1981); GA Res 38/130, UN GAOR, 38th Sess, 101st Plen Mtg, A/Res/38/130 (1983); GA Res 40/61, UN GAOR, 40th Sess, 108th Plen Mtg, UN Doc A/Res/40/61 (1985); GA Res 42/159, UN GAOR, 42nd Sess, 94th Plen Mtg, UN Doc A/Res/42/159 (1987); and GA Res 44/29, UN GAOR, 44th Sess, 72nd Plen Mtg, UN Doc A/Res/44/29 (1989). The second series of General Assembly resolutions began in late December 1993, with the Assembly adopting resolution 48/122, entitled 'Terrorism and Human Rights': GA Res 48/122, UN GAOR, 48th Sess, 85th Plen Mtg, UN Doc A/Res/48/122 (1993). Echoing many of the expressions of concern contained in the Declarations on measures to eliminate terrorism, the preamble to this later resolution spoke of the serious concern of the General Assembly at the gross violations of Human Rights perpetrated by terrorist groups. Resolutions between 1995 and 2005 did the same, adding that terrorism creates an environment that destroys the right of people to live in freedom from fear: GA Res 50/186, UN GAOR, 50th Sess, 99th Plen Mtg, UN Doc A/Res/50/ 186 (1995), preambular paras 3, 4, 5 and 11, and operative para 2; GA Res 52/133, UN GAOR, 52nd Sess, 70th Plen Mtg, UN Doc A/ Res/52/133 (1997), preambular paras 6, 7, 8 and 10, and operative para 3; GA Res 54/164, UN GAOR, 54th Sess, 83rd Plen Mtg, UN Doc A/Res/54/164 (1999), preambular paras 7, 8, 9 and 12, and operative para 3; GA Res 56/160, UN GAOR, 56th Sess, 88th Plen Mtg, UN Doc A/Res/56/160 (2001), preambular paras 11, 12 and 13; GA Res 58/174, UN GAOR, 58th Sess, 77th Plen Mtg, UN Doc A/Res/58/174 (2003), preambular paras 12, 13 and 14; and GA Res 59/195, UN GAOR, 59th Sess, 74th Plen Mtg, UN Doc A/Res/59/ 195 (2004), preambular paras 12 and 13. The preamble to the Assembly's resolution 56/160 added (para 24): "Noting the growing consciousness within the international community of the negative effects of terrorism in all its forms and manifestations on the full enjoyment of human rights and fundamental freedoms and on the establishment of the rule of law and domestic freedoms as enshrined in the Charter of the United Nations and the International Covenants on Human Rights". See *Supra* 4.

17. GA Res 49/60, UN GAOR, 49th Sess, 84th Plen Mtg, UN Doc A/Res/49/60 (1994).
18. GA Res 51/210, UN GAOR, 51st Sess, 88th Plen Mtg, UN Doc A/Res/51/210 (1996).
19. GA Res 50/186, UN GAOR, 50th Sess, 99th Plen Mtg, UN Doc A/Res/50/186 (1995).
20. GA Res 57/219, UN GAOR, 57th Sess, 77th Plen Mtg, UN Doc A/Res/57/219 (2002); GA Res 58/187, UN GAOR, 58th Sess, 77th Plen Mtg, UN Doc A/Res/8/187 (2003); and GA Res 59/191, UN GAOR, 59th Sess, 74th Plen Mtg, UN Doc A/Res/59/191 (2004).
21. GA Res 58/187, UN GAOR, 58th Sess, 77th Plen Mtg, UN Doc A/Res/8/187 (2003).
22. *Ibid.*
23. Kalliopi Koufa (as Special Rapporteur to the Commission on Human Rights Sub-Commission on the Promotion and Protection of Human Rights), *Specific Human Rights Issues: New Priorities, in Particular Terrorism and Counter-Terrorism. A Preliminary Framework Draft of Principles and Guidelines Concerning Human Rights and Terrorism*, UN Doc E/CN.4/Sub.2/2005/39 (22 June 2005).
24. This mandate was consequent to the request of the General Assembly for the Commission to do so (see GA Res 49/185, UN GAOR, 49th Sess, 94th Plen Mtg, UN Doc A/Res/49/185 (1994), para 6) and through the Commission's own decision to consider the issue: see C.H.R. Res. 1994/46, UN ESCOR, 50th Sess, 56th Mtg, UN Doc E/CN.4/Res/1994/46 (1994).
25. See *Supra* 23.
26. United Nations Office of the High Commissioner for Human Rights, Digest *of Jurisprudence of the UN and Regional Organizations on the Protection of Human Rights While Countering Terrorism*, September 2003.
27. *Ibid.* At page 3, the digest introduces the compilation by saying: "No one doubts that States have legitimate and urgent reasons to take all due measures to eliminate terrorism. Acts and strategies of terrorism aim at the destruction of human rights, democracy, and the rule of law. They destabilize governments and undermine civil society. Governments therefore have not only the right, but also the duty, to protect their nationals and others against terrorist

attacks and to bring the perpetrators of such acts to justice. The manner in which counter-terrorism efforts are conducted, however, can have a far-reaching effect on overall respect for human rights."

28. Inter-American Commission on Human Rights, *Report on Terrorism and Human Rights*, Doc OEA/Ser.L/V/II.116 (22 October 2002), preface.
29. *R v Oakes* [1986] 1 SCR 103, 138-39.
30. *Sunday Times v United Kingdom* (1978) 58 ILR 491, 524-27; *Silver v UK* [1983] 5 EHRR 347.
31. See Rousseau, Jean Jacques, *The Social Contract* (Wordsworth Editions, 1998) 14-17.
32. International Commission of Jurists, *Berlin Declaration on Upholding Human Rights and the Rule of Law in Combating Terrorism*, adopted 28 August 2004.
33. Council of Europe, *Guidelines on Human Rights and the Fight against Terrorism*, (Council of Europe Publishing, 2002). The Council's guidelines point to decisions of the European Court, in which it recognized this duty and the particular problems associated with the prevention and suppression of terrorism. See, for example, *Ireland v. the United Kingdom*, Eur. Ct. H.R., 18 January 1978, para 11; *Askoy v. Turkey*, Eur. Ct. H.R., 18 December 1996, paras 70 and 84; *Zana v. Turkey*, Eur. Ct. H.R., 25 November 1997, paras 59 and 60; *Incal v. Turkey,* Eur. Ct. H.R., 9 June 1998, para 58; *United Communist Party of Turkey and Others v. Turkey,* Eur. Ct. H.R., 20 November 1998, para 59; and *Brogan and Others v. the United Kingdom*, Eur. Ct. H.R., 29 November 1999, para 48. In *Klass and Others v. Germany*, Eur. Ct. H.R., 6 September 1978, para 59, for example, the Court said: "The Court agrees with the [European] Commission that some compromise between the requirements for defending democratic society and individual rights is inherent in the system of the Convention".
34. Council of Europe, *Guidelines on the Protection of Victims of Terrorist Acts* (adopted by the Committee of Ministers at Strasbourg on 2 March 2005).
35. Inter-American Commission on Human Rights, *Report on Terrorism and Human Rights*, Doc OEA/Ser.L/V/II.116 (22 October 2002).
36. Inter-American Convention against Terrorism, Opened for Signature 3 June 2002, OAS Treaty A-66 (2003) 42 ILM 19.
37. The report considers the right to life (part III.A), the right to personal liberty and security (part III.B), the right to humane

treatment (part III.C), rights to due process and a fair trial (part III.D), the freedom of expression (part III.E), non-discrimination (part III.F), refugee and asylum rights (part III.H), and other civil rights (part III.G).

38. *Ibid*, Paras 51 and 55.
39. OAS General Assembly Resolution 1906, *Human Rights and Terrorism*, 4th plen Sess, 4 June 2002, OAS Doc AG/Res 1906 (XXXII-O/02).
40. Benvenisti, Eyal, "Margin of Appreciation, Consensus, and Universal Standards" (1999) 31 *International Law and Politics*, 843-44.
41. See *Supra* 29.
42. *Ibid*.
43. See generally *Supra* 4.

16

Indigenous People's Rights and Protection Mechanisms: An Overview

Abdullah Al Faruque

1. Introduction

It is increasingly recognized that indigenous peoples should be accorded a set of special category of rights by virtue of their distinctive cultural, social and political traits that other people do not share. Although the history of different indigenous peoples may differ, they have common history of oppression, subordination and subjugation either by the dominant minority group, or majority people or colonizers.[1] Historically, indigenous people had been subjected to the unjust and inhuman dispossession from their land, deprived of their own culture, and their rights have been denied both by the national and international legal system. But gradually, the international community recognized protection and promotion of indigenous people's rights as an integral part of the international movement for Human Rights as a result of their long struggle for self-determination and growing awareness of their plight around the world. The emerging norm of indigenous people's rights is a direct response partly to their demand of separate identity as distinct units of human interaction and partly influenced by the development of universal framework of Human Rights.

The suffering of indigenous people is not a thing of past, it continues and remains a contemporary global problem.[2] For example, in many parts of the world, indigenous people are still subjected to involuntary transfers and relocations by the settlement of non-indigenous people in their habitat, they have been forced to artificial assimilation with the non-indigenous people, and their social and political institutions are being destructed by the imposition of legal and political system by the nation states. In today's world, deprivation of indigenous peoples from enjoying Human Rights has also occurred due to the economic and industrial development that has taken place without recognition of and respect for indigenous peoples' rights to lands, territories and resources.[3]

The present article sets out to focus on elaboration of indigenous rights as both universal and particular phenomena. It argues that traditional notions of Human Rights or other legal or regulatory mechanism are insufficient or inappropriate to vindicate their rights. At the outset, an attempt has been made to address the definitional problems associated with indigenous people. It also sheds lights on prevailing mechanisms and procedures for the protection and promotion of indigenous rights at national and international level. The article makes an attempt to evaluate the effectiveness of these protection mechanisms in the light of current practice of States and prevailing system of international law.

2. Defining Indigenous People

The question as to who are indigenous peoples and by which criteria they should be defined has generated a great deal of controversy. This reflects a lack of consensus within the international community as to the meaning of indigenous peoples with the result that there is as such currently no universal definition of what constitutes an indigenous people. The problem of defining indigenous peoples remains one of the unresolved issues that creates an obstacle to the effective implementation of indigenous peoples' rights. Benedict Kingsbury, a leading scholar on indigenous peoples, provides a combined list of following requirements and *indicia* for defining indigenous people:[4]

(1) Essential requirements:

(a) self-identification as a distinct ethnic group;
(b) historical experience of, or contingent vulnerability to, severe disruption, dislocation, or exploitation;
(c) long connection with the region; and
(d) the wish to retain a distinct identity;

(2) Relevant *indicia*:

(a) strong *indicia*

(i) non-dominance in the national (or regional) society (ordinarily required);
(ii) close cultural affinity with a particular area of land or territories (ordinarily required);
(iii) historic continuity (especially by descent) with prior occupants of lands in the region;

(b) other relevant *indicia*

(i) socio-economic and socio-cultural differences from the ambient population;
(ii) distinct objective characteristics: language, race, material or spiritual culture, etc.

At the international level, international organizations have attempted to clarify this definitional problem. A widely used and well-known definition of indigenous people has been given by Jose Martinez Cobo, Special Rapporteur of the United Nations, which is also popularly known as the 'Cobo definition'. According to 'Cobo's' definition, indigenous peoples are:

> Indigenous communities, peoples and nations are those which, having a historical continuity with pre-invasion and pre-colonial societies that developed on their territories, consider themselves distinct from other sectors of the societies now prevailing in those territories, or parts of them. They form at present non-dominant sectors of society and are determined to preserve, develop and transmit to future generations their ancestral territories, and their ethnic identity, as the basis of their continued existence as peoples, in

accordance with their own cultural patters, social institutions and legal systems.[5]

The Cobo definition is well-accepted and is considered as the most comprehensive. According to one commentator, it is broad enough to encompass aboriginal populations throughout the world because it takes into account the common traits found in most indigenous populations, instead of focusing on the peculiarities of each indigenous group. By stressing an indigenous population's need for cultural protection and their ties to their territory as original occupiers of the land, the Cobo Report's definition succeeds in distinguishing them other ethnic and religious minorities.[6]

Other international institutions have also attempted to define indigenous peoples. The World Bank for example has adopted a functional approach to the definition of indigenous peoples, rejecting the criteria-based approach of historical continuity and colonialism. Rather, it has taken a functional view of "indigenous peoples" as groups with a social and cultural identity distinct from the dominant society that makes them vulnerable to being disadvantaged in the development process.

From the above definitions, it is clear that indigenous peoples can be defined as a group of peoples who share common characteristics and cultural and social world views that distinguish them from other population groups.

3. Conceptualizing Indigenous Peoples' Rights

The wording of the United Nations' Charter of 1945 and the Universal Declaration of Human Rights (UDHR) of 1948 only recognized individual rights rather than the rights of any particular group or community rights. This Human Rights approach was concerned only with the universal applicability of the most elementary Human Rights of individuals and in fact, the UDHR and UN Charter were silent on the question of indigenous peoples. It can nevertheless be fairly argued that the universal framework of individual rights has also embraced indigenous peoples. Gradually, the international community realized and recognized the need for the Human Rights as well as specific rights of indigenous peoples by virtue of which they can exist as collective human entities and preserve their separate identities.

The UN had started to make valiant efforts to elaborate Human Rights norms for indigenous peoples in the late 1980s. The UN Human Rights Commission of the Economic and Social Council approved in 1982 the establishment of the UN Working Group on Indigenous Populations. The establishment of the Working Group on Indigenous Populations was a direct response to the increased attention being focused on the plight of indigenous peoples throughout the world. The Working Group is an organ of the Sub-Commission on Prevention of Discrimination and Protection of Minorities, which comprised individuals who act in the capacity of independent Human Rights experts rather than government representatives. In 1985, the Working Group was mandated to draft a declaration on the rights of indigenous peoples. The Draft Declaration on the Rights of Indigenous Peoples was completed in 1992.[7] Prepared on the basis of generally applicable Human Rights principles, the draft is a manifestation of the long movement for the protection of indigenous peoples' rights worldwide, and is seen as a consensual nexus of opinion on the subject among relevant actors. The Draft Declaration was approved in August 1994 by the Sub-Commission. According to Dr. Erica-Irene A. Daes, a distinguished commentator on indigenous peoples' rights, the draft recognizes three important attributes to indigenous peoples, e.g. legal personality, territorial security and international responsibility, which distinguishes it from all other Human Rights instruments.

The Draft Declaration was finally approved with slight modifications and adopted by the General Assembly of the United Nations in October, 2007, which is widely seen as major step forward towards the protection of indigenous people, brought to an end nearly 25 years of contentious negotiations over the issue.[8] The Preamble of the Declaration states that indigenous peoples are equal in dignity and rights to all other peoples; proclaims that all doctrines, policies and practices based on superiority of peoples on the basis of national origin, religious, ethnic or cultural differences are racist and socially unjust; recognizes the urgent need to respect and promote the rights and characteristics of indigenous peoples; and emphasizes that indigenous peoples have the right freely to determine their relationship with states in a spirit of coexistence, mutual benefit and full respect.[9]

The International Labor Organization (ILO) has played a prominent role in formulating and elaborating indigenous peoples' rights. The ILO Convention on the Indigenous and Tribal Peoples adopted in 1957 (Convention No. 107) remains the international community's first attempt to address comprehensively and specifically the needs of indigenous and tribal peoples.[10] But due to dissatisfaction and widespread criticism of assimilationist approach of the Convention, the ILO adopted another but very comprehensive treaty on indigenous peoples in 1989 (ILO Convention No. 169). The preamble to Convention No. 169 recognizes "the aspiration of these indigenous peoples to exercise control over their own institutions, ways of life and economic development and to maintain and develop their identities, languages and religions, within the framework of the States in which they live." The Convention puts emphasis on the "improvement of the conditions of life and work and levels of health and education of indigenous peoples," and mandates "special projects...to promote such improvement." It acknowledges that special programmes, devised to ensure the social welfare and development of indigenous peoples, are to be established in cooperation with the indigenous peoples concerned.

According to Article 2, governments must develop "with the participation of the peoples concerned, a coordinated and systematic action to protect the rights of these peoples" and promote "the full realisation of the social, economic and cultural rights of these peoples with respect for their social and cultural identity, their customs and traditions and their institutions." Article 4 mandates that "special measures shall be adopted as appropriate for safeguarding the persons, institutions, property, labour, cultures and environment of the peoples concerned." However, the present treaty has been subjected to criticism for leaving in too much residual state authority over indigenous peoples. It has also failed to recognize firmly the right of indigenous "peoples" to self-determination.

4. Elaboration of Indigenous Peoples' Rights

Among the strategies for the survival and international legal protection of indigenous peoples, Human Rights discourse is considered to be the most important one for empowering them and to enable them to express their legitimate demands.[11] The necessity for special regime of indigenous rights can be explained by the fact that they require special legal protection and institutions to protect them within nation state and international community. Moral and ethical aspects of Human Rights discourse dictates that indigenous people should be portrayed as groups of human beings with fundamental Human Rights as well as special kind of rights as remedial measures for historical reasons. The moral responsibility on the part of non-indigenous citizens for giving both universal as well as special category of rights to indigenous peoples rests on two arguments: firstly, colonization created the absolute and relative poverty of indigenous communities, while simultaneously creating the wealth enjoyed by non-indigenous citizens. Secondly, the concept of indigenous rights is only possible within a colonial context, because indigeneity as a category is only possible when one group of people is to be distinguished from another group who arrived later.[12] The existing norms of indigenous rights merely establish the benchmarks for ensuring their minimum range of choices to which indigenous peoples are entitled in remedial-constitutive settings in the governing institutional order.[13]

Heightened awareness about environmental degradation and destruction of the land and ecosystem of the indigenous people and increased publicity focusing on the continuing disrespect for environment of indigenous peoples' habitat has provided further ground for elaborating indigenous peoples' rights norm. As a result, indigenous peoples are also protected by international environmental law and environmental protection has become a part of agenda for indigenous people's rights.[14] The contemporary demand for a special regime of Human Rights for indigenous people has also been conceptually supported by the emergence of concept of third generation rights which is based on human solidarity. Commenting on the implication of third generation rights on indigenous people, Richard Falk observed: "To stress the place of indigenous peoples in the emerging conception of the "rights of peoples" is to insist that the plight of indigenous peoples, with their history of persecution, degradation, genocide and ethnocide, be placed on the normative agenda".[15] The third generation rights encompass a number of collective rights such as the right to reasonable environment, economic development, international peace and security, the common heritage of mankind, communications and humanitarian assistance.[16] In this regard, indigenous people's claim for third generation rights is closely related to fundamental issues of land rights, self-government, control of natural resources, environmental protection, and the development assistance, which are necessarily collective in nature and arise from the fact that indigenous people can be collectively referred to as community or group. The indigenous peoples are therefore entitled to seek and assert their rights under the umbrella of third generation rights as a group or community. For instance, the African Charter of Human and Peoples' Rights of 1981 defines peoples to include an ethnic community or a community that identifies itself as such because of common interests and the Charter approaches people in the context of the right to self-determination. Under Article 20 of the Charter, the right to self-determination is guaranteed to all peoples.[17]

The philosophical justification of recognizing rights of indigenous people can be attributed to at least two factors: firstly, indigenous peoples' rights are pre-existing rights in the sense that they are not derived from the legal systems of the states, but arise *sui generis* from the historical conditions of indigenous peoples as distinct societies with the aspiration to survive as such."[18] In other words, indigenous peoples enjoyed nationhood prior to their subjugation of colonial powers or settlers and their statehood and sovereignty enjoyed under a nation state predate the modern nation states which now assert sovereignty over them.

Secondly, they should be given some preferential treatment either as compensation for historical suffering or a disproportionately disadvantaged present condition.[19] This preferential treatment has been described as 'restorative paradigm', which suggests that despite variations in the specific political and historical circumstances surrounding them, nearly all indigenous groups share a common set of problems and their claims to land, group equality, culture, and development stem from the right to reparations for the historical injustices against them.[20] The restorative rights should be given to them as a direct consequence of European colonial expansion, by which indigenous people have been deprived of their independence, and their land and their right to choose their role in the modern state.[21] An important dimension of the restorative paradigm is that the indigenous people, who have been persecuted, should be acknowledged as a group and should be provided with appropriate compensation for the injustice and oppression inflicted upon them.[22]

Closely related to the above justificatory assumption, there are two competing claims regarding assertion of indigenous peoples' rights: firstly, whether their rights can be addressed exclusively within the framework of international Human Rights law; secondly, whether a new legal category of rights should be created for them. Advocates of the former claim that indigenous peoples' problem and suffering can be addressed by conscientious application of universal Human Rights standards. On the other hand, protagonists of latter view hold that general Human Rights norms can hardly resolve their problems as many atrocities and injustice have been committed towards indigenous people living in countries where Human Rights are well protected. Rather, it has been contended that general Human Rights norm remains a conceptual obstacle to realization of indigenous people's aspiration. Therefore, a distinct programme for the rights of indigenous people going beyond universal Human Rights norms is essential.[23] The global movement of indigenous peoples' rights indicates that the latter view is more plausible. However, the balanced approached is that indigenous people should be afforded both universal Human Rights and special category of rights to enable them to survive with their distinct cultures and way of life.

In international Human Rights discourse, apart from basic civil, political and social, economic and cultural rights under universal Human Rights instruments, indigenous peoples are entitled to the following category of distinct rights or group rights:

Right to Self-determination: The right to self-determination as an irreducible minimum encompasses the right of all ethnic and indigenous communities to continue to exist.[24] The right to self-determination refers to political, economic and social self-determination, which are all necessary for the both internal autonomy and external sovereignty. While most states are willing to concede some degree of control over indigenous affairs, such as the power to administer special programmes designed by the state, states will not generally recognize self-determination claims involving secession.[25] Therefore, instead of independence, the prevailing trend is towards granting the right to autonomy to the indigenous people in matters relating to their own internal and local affairs, including education, information, culture, religion, health, housing, social welfare, traditional and other economic activities, land and resources administration and the environment.[26] For indigenous people, the right to self-determination is currently understood to be the internal autonomy in terms of their right to existence as a separate entity. The Declaration of Indigenous Peoples Rights of 2007 recognizes self-determination as one of the fundamental rights and expressed it in following terms: "Indigenous people have the right of self-determination. By virtue of that right they freely determine their political status and freely pursue their economic, social and cultural development."[27] Then, Articles 4 and 5 of the Declaration elaborate the right of self-determination in the sense of the right to autonomy, or self-government in matters relating to their internal and local affairs, and right to maintain their distinct political, legal, cultural, economic and social institutions.[28]

The right to self-determination for indigenous communities signifies them to continue to exist as distinct units of human interaction in larger societies.[29] According to James Anaya, a leading commentator on indigenous people, the provisions relating to right to self determination under the two covenants on Human Rights cover all aspects of the indigenous group's survival as a distinct culture and it requires states to act affirmatively to protect the cultural matrix of indigenous groups and not simply to refrain from coercing assimilation or abandonment of cultural practices.[30] Richard Falk defines contours of the right to self-determination in the following way:

First, there would be some response to needs for internal self-determination, using the term 'self' in an existential, not in a legalistic or statist way. That means some appropriate form of autonomy that allows for the protection and self-control over life in all its dimensions.

Second, some dimension of external self-determination in terms of capacity on the part of indigenous peoples to be able to form networks of solidarity with other indigenous groups and with organizations representing indigenous peoples on an international and trans-national level.[31] Thus, external aspect of self-determination in relation to indigenous people's rights should be interpreted to their right to make collaboration and network building with other indigenous groups, not in terms of secession from the State.

Rights to Lands and Livelihood: Indigenous people are still deprived of their land and access to life-sustaining resources in many countries. Governments are often reluctant to formally recognize indigenous rights to land.[32] Land has deep cultural and spiritual meaning in most indigenous societies and in their social organization. An important dimension in affirming indigenous rights is the exercise of a measure of control over their lands, territories and resources by them through their own institutions. Therefore, the indigenous people's right to land in the form of control and decision-making concerning development, use of natural resources, management and conservation is considered an essential aspect of their exercise of internal self-determination.[33] The land rights should be interpreted in the broader sense to include their right to demarcation, ownership, development, control, and use of their lands by traditional methods. The importance of lands and resources to the survival of indigenous cultures is also widely acknowledged in the Declaration. Article 25 of the Declaration provides:

> Indigenous peoples have the right to maintain and strengthen their distinctive spiritual relationship with their traditionally owned or otherwise occupied and used lands, territories, waters and coastal seas and other resources and to uphold their responsibilities to future generations in this regard.[34]

Right to Legal and International Personality: Since indigenous people have to live in the State and State may deny their rights, it is essential that they should be attributed with international personality under national and international legal framework, so that they can present their claims and grievances in arenas outside the national legal system. The Declaration is silent on this issue. However, it recognizes that indigenous peoples have the collective right to determine their own citizenship in accordance with their customs and traditions, while indigenous citizenship does not impair the right of indigenous individuals to obtain citizenship of the States in which they live.[35] The recognition of indigenous people's citizenship of and their entitlement of State Citizenship can enable them to espouse their claim in international organizations and fora.

Right to Cultural Integrity: A central aspect of self-determination of indigenous people is that they should be entitled to maintain and develop their distinct cultural identity. Cultural rights include respect and protection of cultural and religious integrity, preservation of sacred sites, respect their spirituality, language, and their traditional ways of life.

Cultural right is core of many other rights. Article 27 of the ICCPR couched the right to cultural integrity in universal language as it affords the cultural rights to the persons belonging to "ethnic, religious or linguistic minorities...to enjoy their own culture, to profess and practice their own religion, and to use their own language."[36] Articles 11, 12 and 13 of the Declaration are particularly concerned with cultural rights of indigenous peoples. According to Article 13 of the Declaration,

> Indigenous peoples have the right to revitalize, use, develop and transmit to future generations their histories, languages, oral traditions, philosophies, writing systems and literatures, and to designate and retain their own names for communities, places and persons.[37]

Right to Compensation: Right to compensation has been asserted as one of the distinctive rights of indigenous people.[38] However, it appears to be the most controversial of rights. The emerging norm relating to right to compensation suggests that this right should only be extended to consequences of future actions of the government or state agency or donor agency, rather than for past or historical injustice committed against them. The right to compensation should be specially claimed against State as well as non-state groups like armed forces, multinational corporations for past abuse and injustice committed against them.[39] Under Article 28 of the Declaration, indigenous people have the right to restoration of the lands, territories and resources which they have traditionally owned or otherwise occupied or used but have been confiscated or occupied or used without their free and prior consent. But where restoration is not possible, they have the right to just and fair compensation for such lands.[40]

Right to Participation in Decision-making Processes: Right to participation of the indigenous people in development projects and decision-making process is an evolving human right.[41] The right to participation requires that indigenous people should be consulted by the government, donor agencies and multinational companies if any development project or exploration of mineral is carried out in their lands which may have negative effect on their survival.[42] The right to participation of indigenous people in decision-making processes of resource development and other development projects has been implicitly recognized in the Declaration. Several Articles of the Declaration deal with this important right. Article 17 provides that States shall in consultation and cooperation with indigenous peoples take specific measures to protect indigenous children from economic exploitation and from performing any work that is likely to be hazardous or to interfere with the child's education. Article 18 recognizes that indigenous peoples have the right to participate in decision-making in matters which would affect their rights and right to maintain and develop their own indigenous decision-making institutions. Article 19 categorically states that indigenous peoples will be consulted before adopting and implementing legislative or administrative measures by the State that may affect them.

Right "not to be Subject to Genocide": As indigenous peoples had been subjected to genocide committed by colonizers and settlers or non-indigenous groups, the international community reached a consensus that they should not be subjected to genocide or ethnocide. Articles 7 and 8 of the Declaration provide that indigenous peoples have the collective and individual right 'not to be subject to genocide or forced assimilation including the prevention of and redress for any action with the effect of dispossessing them from their lands, territories or resources.[43]

Right to Protection of Indigenous Knowledge: The indigenous people around the world maintain their own knowledge system covering a wide range of fields including cultural, religious practices, health and agricultural practices. Given the fact that they are most vulnerable segment of any society, the Declaration especially recognizes the right to protection of indigenous knowledge. According to Article 31:

> Indigenous peoples have the right to maintain, control, protect and develop their cultural heritage, traditional knowledge and traditional cultural expressions, as well

as the manifestations of their sciences, technologies and cultures, including human and genetic resources, seeds, medicines, knowledge of the properties of fauna and flora, oral traditions, literatures, designs, sports and traditional games and visual and performing arts. They also have the right to maintain, control, protect and develop their intellectual property over such cultural heritage, traditional knowledge, and traditional cultural expressions.

5. Implementation of Indigenous Rights: Mechanisms and Procedures

The implementation of indigenous peoples' rights requires appropriate set of procedures, and mechanisms, and these should be defined and elaborated in national and international legal framework. The prevailing mechanisms of implementation of indigenous people rights at the national level consists of negotiated agreement or treaty, constitutional and legislative measures, the proactive role of the judiciary, and role of media and civil society.

5.1. Implementation mechanism at national level

5.1.1. Negotiated Agreement: Negotiated agreement between the indigenous people and the State authority in the framework of national and international law remains one of the most important means of implementation of indigenous people's rights. Historically, negotiated agreement concluded between indigenous people and state as a framework of securing their rights has been regarded as an effective instrument to establish the rights of indigenous peoples.[44]

The States generally confer some positive rights through negotiated agreement in the form of affirmative action on indigenous people taking into consideration past injustices committed against them.

History of negotiation to recognize the indigenous people's rights is old. For example, negotiation with a view to concluding peace and friendship treaties with Indian nations began in Canada in the 1640s. Land surrender treaties first were entered into in 1790. Although Canada never ceased to exercise sovereignty over these territories in which indigenous people lived, it allocated certain rights to native Indian people through treaties. Recent such example is negotiated agreement called the Nunavut Agreement (creating a new territory in northern Canada) for indigenous community called 'Inuit'. In Canada, treaty as negotiated settlement of land claims remains as a positive and practical measure for achieving desirable goals with respect to indigenous people relationship to lands and resources.[45] In New Zealand, the Treaty of Waitangi entered between the Maori of New Zealand and Great Britain is another example of such negotiated settlement. Recent example of negotiated settlement also includes Chittagong Hill Tracts treaty between tribal group of peoples and government of Bangladesh in 1997.[46]

Negotiated agreement provides an opportunity for the parties to accommodate diverse issues and perspectives pertaining to indigenous people's rights and their legitimate demands to be considered. An open negotiation process, which pays full regard to problems and respect to the indigenous peoples' rights, can create peaceful atmosphere and act as a confidence-building measure, particularly when violent situations are prevailing. A negotiated settlement of disputes can also create a better understanding between indigenous people and dominant groups, which can ultimately contribute to lasting political and legal solution of the conflict.

5.1.2. Legal and Constitutional Reform: Legislative and constitutional measures and reforms are considered as a valuable tool of promoting and protecting the rights of indigenous people. The constitutional and legislative measure are frequently used as means for adopting affirmative action policies and programmes, which are particularly beneficial to the indigenous groups. The legislative and constitutional mechanism is also important for promoting international Human Rights norm relating to indigenous peoples as these norms can only be implemented in national level through their incorporation in laws and constitution.

Over the last few decades, many countries have either reformed their constitutions, laws or adopted new legislation for conferring rights on indigenous people in the form of affirmative action as well as implementing international norms. For example, the new constitution of Argentina of 1994 directs the Congress of Argentina, *inter alia*, to guarantee respect for the cultural identity of indigenous people, to recognize the juridical personality of indigenous communities, and to secure their ancestral land rights.[47] In Colombia, the 1991 Constitution drafted with significant indigenous input constitutes a major breakthrough in conferring rights to indigenous people. It recognizes and protects the ethnic and cultural diversity of the Colombia nation.[48] It affords indigenous communities a high degree of political and administrative autonomy;[49] guarantees the respect for their institutions of self-government; recognizes their collective property rights and native languages and dialectics.[50] The 1988 Constitution of Brazil prescribed that the Indians shall have permanent possession of land, and has the rights to the exclusive usufruct of the natural resources and of all useful things that traditionally occupied by them.[51] The Constitution of the Federal Republic of Brazil of 1988 lays the foundations for indigenous land rights regime: recognizing rights of Indians to their own forms of social organization, customs, language, beliefs and traditions, and original rights over the lands they traditionally occupy.

Article 231 of the Constitution of Brazil provides:

1. Lands traditionally occupied by Indians are those inhabited by them permanently; those used for their productive activities; those indispensable for the preservation of the environmental resources necessary for their well being; and those lands necessary for their physical and cultural reproduction, according to their uses, customs and traditions.
2. Indians are entitled to the permanent ownership of the lands traditionally occupied by them including the exclusive fruition or enjoyment of existing soil resources, rivers and lakes.[52]

The Russian Constitution expressly accords Human Rights to indigenous people under international law. It states: “The

Russian Federation shall guarantee the rights of indigenous ethnic minorities in accordance with universally acknowledged principles and rules of international law and the international treaties of the Russian Federation."[53]

The Government of Bangladesh passed several legislation in 1989 for the granting limited autonomy and self-government of the tribal people in the Chittagong Hill Tracts, which set up three local elected and autonomous government councils with adequate power for the tribal people to run their own affairs and preserve their socio-cultural heritage and separate identity. In Canada, indigenous rights are protected at the level of the Canadian Constitution. The 1982 Constitution Act has included Section 25 of the Canadian Charter of Rights and Freedoms,[54] which stipulated that:

> Guarantees in this Charter of certain rights and freedoms shall not be construed so as to abrogate or derogate from any aboriginal, treaty or other rights or freedoms that pertain to the aboriginal peoples of Canada including (a) any rights or freedoms recognised by the Royal Proclamation of October 7, 1763; and (b) any rights or freedoms that now exist by way of land claims agreements or may be so acquired.

In Venezuela, Article 77 of the Constitution of 1961 establishes the principle of special protection for the indigenous peoples in order to facilitate their inclusion in the life of the nation.[55] Nicaragua's Political Constitution adopted by the Sandinista government in the mid-1980s recognized the communal property and cultural rights of the indigenous peoples of the Atlantic Coast.[56]

It is evident that constitutional and legislative measures are recognized as important means of protecting and promotion of indigenous peoples' right in many parts of the world and they offer special developmental programme to the cause of indigenous people.

5.1.3. Role of Judiciary: Domestic courts can play an important role in implementation of indigenous rights through enforcement of their rights, and progressive interpretation of national laws, constitution and international legal norms. The domestic courts can indirectly implement international norms by using them to guide judicial interpretation of domestic rules. This indirect implementation is particularly necessary in those countries, which do not have treaty arrangement or adequate legal provisions for protection of indigenous people. For example, Australia did not enter into treaties with its indigenous people and aboriginal lands were acquired on the basis of *terra nullius* doctrine. In Australia, aboriginal peoples were subjected to English common laws which did not recognize the aboriginals' proprietary interest in their land. But in 1992, the High Court of Australia in the case of *Mabo v. Queensland* discussed the legal and other effects of the doctrine of *terra nullius* and annulled the doctrine. Justice Brennan held: "unjust and discriminatory doctrine of that kind can no longer be accepted."[57] Justice Brennan was of the opinion that common law in its present formulation should be interpreted in conformity with contemporary values embraced by Australian society and also in light of contemporary international law."[58] Following the decision, the Australian Government entered into extensive negotiations with aboriginal leaders, which finally led to the adoption of the Native Title Act in 1993 which creates a framework by which indigenous peoples may secure possessory rights in lands and compensation for lost lands.[59]

6. Implementation Procedures at the International Level

At the international level, variety of complaints and monitoring procedures exist to promote and implement indigenous people's rights. There are special complaint procedures in ILO and UNO to monitor and supervise the implementation of indigenous rights as well as general complaint and monitoring procedures under international and regional instruments on general Human Rights.

6.1. Monitoring and complaint procedures under ILO Conventions

Currently, there are two distinct types of complaint procedures under ILO Conventions. First kind of complaints procedure exists under Convention relating to Indigenous people. The second kind of complaints procedures exist under the other existing ILO conventions, which are of general application. The later types of complaint procedure are designed in accordance with the ILO's central focus on labor issues and they facilitate communication among labor unions, employer's organizations, and governments. However, neither types of complaint procedures can be invoked directly by the indigenous peoples themselves. But they can be invoked indirectly by the labor unions and employee organizations to redress for the violation of indigenous people' rights. The states, which are parties to the International Labour Organization Convention No. 107, are subject to the periodic reporting requirements and supervisory mechanisms under it. The periodic government reports on the implementation of ratified conventions are reviewed by the ILO Committee of experts on the Applications of Conventions and Recommendations. However, only few reports have been submitted to the committee about indigenous people rights. The ILO supervisory bodies sometimes interpret government obligations under Convention No. 107. Although indigenous people are not entitled to send complaint directly under the Convention No. 107, NGOs and other organizations can send complaints on behalf of them.

6.2. Complaints to the U.N. working group on indigenous populations

A five member-working group on indigenous peoples established under the mandate of U.N. Economic and Social Council, has been entrusted to review developments concerning indigenous peoples. The Working Group is a fact-finding and standard-setting body, whose members come from a racially and culturally diverse group of individuals and serve in their individual capacities.

The group receives written reports from governments, inter-governmental institutions, indigenous peoples' representatives, and non-governmental organizations regarding implementation of indigenous people rights and violation of their rights. The group also hears from the government, inter-governmental institutions, indigenous peoples' representatives,

NGOs representatives at its annual public sessions. This open and public deliberation and consideration of reports about indigenous peoples' problems and violation of their rights have persuasive impact upon the governments, who are responsible for such abuse or violations. In this regard, the working group is able to exert some pressure upon the governments to redress the wrongs committed against indigenous people. However, efficacy of the working group is limited to merely giving opinions as it is not currently equipped to investigate the abuse or violation. As such, the ability of the Working Group insofar as concerning implementation of indigenous people's rights is only a persuasive one. It has been rightly commented: "whatever effect these communications may have is usually limited to the value of their utterance in an official public forum of the United Nations."[60]

6.3. The U.N. Human Rights Committee

Apart from specific complaint procedures on indigenous peoples, violation of indigenous peoples' rights can also be redressed under general complaint procedures under international Human Rights instruments. For example, Article 14 of the Convention on the Elimination of All Forms of Racial Discrimination authorizes the Committee on the Elimination of Racial Discrimination (CERD) to receive complaints, or "communications," from individuals or group of individuals" claiming to be victims of violations of rights specified in the Convention. Another complaint procedure mechanism is the Human Rights Committee under the Optional Protocol to the Covenant on Civil and Political Rights. The Human Rights Committee is entitled to hear "communications" from "individuals" subject to their jurisdiction who claim to be victims of violations of rights included in the Covenant.[61] In the broader jurisdiction of the Committees, violation of indigenous people's rights can also be addressed and investigated and remedied. However, only a few communications are received by these Committees regarding indigenous people's rights and these are resolved by the Committee. One significant case resolved by the Human Rights Committee is the *Lubicon Lake Band case*, where the

Committee resolved that Canada's denial of the indigenous *Lubicon Lake Band*'s right to dispose freely of its natural wealth and resources constituted a violation of Article 27 of the International Covenant on Civil, and Political Rights, which stipulates that "in those States in which ethnic, religious or linguistic minorities exist, persons belonging to such minorities shall not be denied the right, in community with other members of their groups, to enjoy their own culture, to profess and practice their own religion, or to use their own language.[62] The Committee on the Elimination of Racial Discrimination (CERD) decided on 18 March 1999 that the *Native Title Amendment Act* of 1998 discriminates against indigenous title holders by validating past acts, extinguishing native title, upgrading primary production and restricting the right to negotiate."[63] The lack of effective participation by indigenous communities in the formulation of the amendment was also thought by CERD to breach Articles 1(4) and 2(2) of that treaty.[64]

7. Effectiveness of Implementation Mechanisms

Like universal Human Rights norms, the ultimate protection of indigenous rights depends upon their effective implementation at national level. Since indigenous people live in the territory of a Nation State, it is at the national level that indigenous people can enjoy their full rights. Although many countries have adopted legal and constitutional reforms in order to protect indigenous peoples' rights, their implementation are largely dependent upon the political willingness of the governments.

At the national level, the main barriers to the implementation of their rights are three fold: firstly, the traditional international law principle of state sovereignty remains a stumbling block to the realization of their rights. Their right to self-determination is essentially limited to internal autonomy, and is defined in 'statist' form in international instruments and soft law, which exclude them from asserting the external aspect of self-determination in terms of the right to have a separate State. Secondly, the implementation of indigenous peoples' right is impeded by the international law principle of the territorial integrity of States and with non-intervention with States' internal affairs, which can effectively preclude international community and organizations to prevent the violation of their rights.[65] Thirdly, Indigenous peoples claims to Human Rights and special rights are also challenged by the juridical concept of a unified 'nationality' administered by government. They may be forbidden to bear their self-identification.[66]

Despite the legal reform or formal legal title to the land, indigenous people cannot effectively enjoy their rights due to lack of supporting regulations. Many countries have not ratified the ILO conventions. Even the States which have ratified the ILO Conventions, may not have any implementing legislation. Furthermore, even having legislation and legal framework, indigenous people may still be deprived of exercising their rights by discriminatory laws and the application of these laws by the Courts. The States may disregard or violate the treaty concluded with indigenous people and neglect to implement the treaty through relevant laws and regulation and institutional and infrastructure support. In case of violation of negotiated agreement or treaty, indigenous people may be left without compensation and remedied by the Court sponsored by the State.

At the international level, the implementation mechanisms are also fraught with conceptual difficulties of state sovereignty so far as their enforcement is concerned. Due to the traditional international legal principle of state sovereignty, the States cannot be compelled to implement them. Most of the mechanisms are not equipped with punitive measures for the violation of rights of indigenous peoples' rights, and their effectiveness is limited to persuasion of the State authority to adhere to the existing laws and instruments.

8. Conclusion

The violation of indigenous people's rights as a collective one is unique in many respects and therefore, requires innovative remedies which differ from traditional ones. The national and international legal framework on protection of indigenous people's rights must accommodate the innovative measures and remedies for the protection of indigenous people's rights.

While elaboration of their rights at the international level is an important step in recognition of their collective identity, much should be done at the level of protection through making provisions at both the national and international level. Although there is a clearly discernible trend toward legal recognition of their rights, legal protection of their rights suffers from many drawbacks of the domestic and international legal order. Legal mechanisms are still evolving in view of the fact that indigenous rights discourse is a relatively new phenomena in Human Rights jurisprudence. In this regard, the Declaration of Indigenous Peoples' Rights, 2007 represents a broad consensus of international community regarding the necessity of recognition of universal Human Rights for the indigenous people as well as formulation of special category of rights for the indigenous peoples reflecting their special needs and an urgency of remediation of past injustices committed against them. The international community should reach further consensus to adopt a legally binding Convention in order to fully realize the aspirations, needs and rights of indigenous peoples around the world.

Notes

1. C J Iorns, 'Indigenous Peoples and Self-Determination: Challenging State Sovereignty', (1992) 24 *Case Western Reserve Journal of International Law,* 199.
2. See, J P Kastrup, 'The Internationalisation of Human Rights from the Environmental and Human Rights Perspective', (1997) 32 *Texas International Law Journal,* 96-122 at 106. Describing the suffering on Indian peoples in Latin America, the author observes: "Ever since white men set foot in the Americas, there has been a continuous destruction of indigenous societies accompanied by sporadic attempts to repair the sometimes acknowledged crime. Indigenous people have been taken away from their territories, slaughtered, or imprisoned in reservations." See also, A Fabra, 'Indigenous Peoples, Environmental Degradation, and Human Rights: a Case Study', in: A E Boyle and M R Anderson, *Human Rights Approaches to Environmental Protection,* (Oxford: Clarendon Press, 1996) 245-263. (Discussing the negative impacts

of oil development operations in the rain forest on Amazonian indigenous people of Ecuador.)

3. For example, hydroelectric project has been carried out without the consent of the indigenous people of Chittagong Hill tracts of Bangladesh, see, R C K Roy, *Land Rights of the Indigenous Peoples of the Chittagong Hill Tracts, Bangladesh*, (Norwegian Agency for Development Corporation (NORAD), (1996).
4. Benedict Kingsbury, 'Indigenous Peoples in International Law: A Constructivist Approach to the Asian Controversy', 92 *The American Journal of International Law* (1998), p. 418.
5. 'UN Sub-Commission on Prevention of Discrimination and Protection of Minorities (1986), Study of the Problem of Discrimination against Indigenous Populations', UN Doc. E/CN.4/Sub.2/1986/7/Add. 4, para. 379 (José Martinez Cobo, Special Rapporteur).
6. Raidza Torres, "The Rights of Indigenous Populations: The Emerging International Norm", 16 *Yale Journal of International Law* (1991), pp. 127-29.
7. Discrimination against Indigenous Peoples: Report of the Working Group on Indigenous Populations on Its Tenth Session, U.N. ESCOR Commission on Human Rights, 10th Sess., Annex 1, at para. 8, U.N.Doc.E/CN.4/Sub.2/1992/33.
8. United Nations Declaration on the Rights of Indigenous Peoples, 2007, General Assembly Resolution A/Res./61/295; 2 October, 2007 (Sixty-first session agenda item 68).
9. *Ibid.*
10. Convention (No. 107) Concerning the Protection and Integration of Indigenous and other Tribal and Semi-Tribal Populations in Independent Countries, adopted in June 26, 1957, 328 U.N. T.S. 247.
11. R A Williams, 'Encounters on the Frontiers of International Human Rights Law: Redefining the Terms of Indigenous People's Survival in the World', *Duke Law Journal*, (1990) p. 664, at 701.
12. S Curry, 'Indigenous Rights', in: Tom Campbell, Jeffrey Goldsworthy, and Adreinne Stone, (eds), *Protecting Human Rights: Instruments and Institutions*, (Oxford: Oxford University Press, 2003), 311.
13. S J Anaya, 'The Native Hawaiian People and International Human Rights Law: Toward A Remedy For Past and Continuing Wrongs', (1994). 28 *Georgia Law Review* 309, at 342.
14. See, J P Kastrup, *op. cit.* above n. 2, at 106.

15. R Falk, 'The Rights of Peoples (In particular Indigenous Peoples)', in: J Crawford (ed), *The Rights of Peoples,* (Oxford: Clarendon Press, 1988), 24.
16. S P Marks, 'Emerging Human Rights: A New Generation for the 1980s?' (1981), 33 *Rutgers Law Review* 435.
17. The African Charter on Human and Peoples Rights also known as the Banjul Charter on Human and Peoples rights, was adopted by the 18th Assembly of Heads of State and Government of the Organisation of African Unity, held in Nairobi in June 1981. It came into force on October 21, 1986. See, R N Kiwanuka, 'The Meaning of "People" In the African Charter on Human and Peoples' Rights', (1988), 82 *American Journal of International Law* 80.
18. See, Remarks by H R Berman on: 'Are Indigenous Populations Entitled to international Juridical Personality?' *American Society of International Law Proceedings of 79th Annual Meeting*, (April, 25-27, 1985), New York, 190.
19. F H Naqvi, 'People's Rights or Victim's Rights: Re-examining the Conceptualisation of Indigenous Rights in International Law', (1996), 71 *Indiana Law Journal* 674.
20. R Torres, 'The Rights of Indigenous Populations: The Emerging International Norm', (1991) 16 *Yale Journal of International Law* 127, 133.
21. A Lawrey, 'Contemporary Efforts to Guarantee Indigenous Rights Under International Law', (1990), 23 *Vanderbilt Journal of Transnational Law* 703, 762.
22. C Weisbrod, 'Minorities and Diversities: The "Remarkable Experiment" of the League of Nations,' (1993), 8 *Connecticut Journal of International Law* 359, 376.
23. B Kingsbury, 'Reconciling Five Competing Conceptual Structures of Indigenous Peoples' Claims in International and Comparative Law', in: P Alston (ed), *Peoples' Rights*, (Oxford: Oxford University Press, 2001), 71-72, 102.
24. F H Naqvi, *op. cit* n. 19, at 726.
25. R Torres, *op. cit.* n. 20, at 162.
26. See also, A Lawrey, *op. cit.* n. 21, at 765-66.
27. Article 3 of the Declaration.
28. Articles 4 & 5 of the Declaration.
29. S J Anaya, 'The Rights of Indigenous Peoples and International Law in Historical and Contemporary Perspective', (1989), *Harvard Indian Law Symposium* 191, 219.

30. S J Anaya, 'Indigenous Rights Norms in Contemporary International Law', (1991), 8 *Arizona Journal of International and Comparative Law* 1.
31. R Falk, *op. cit.* n. 15, at 34--35.
32. B Ganz, 'Indigenous Peoples and Land Tenure: An Issue of Human Rights and Environmental Protection', (1996), 9 *Georgetown International Environmental Law Review* 173.
33. Mrs. Erica-Irene A. Daes, Human Rights of Indigenous Peoples, Second progress report, prepared by Mrs. Erica-Irene A. Daes, Special Rapporteur, Sub-Commission on Prevention of Discrimination and Protection of Minorities, Fifty-first session, Item 7 of the provisional agenda, E/CN.4/Sub.2/1999/18. p. 11, at 21.
34. Article 25 of the Declaration.
35. Article 33 of the Declaration.
36. S J Anaya, 'The Native Hawaiian People and International Human Rights Law: Toward A Remedy For Past and Continuing Wrongs', (1994), 28 *Georgia Law Review* 309, 343.
37. See, Declaration, *op. cit.*
38. G Nettheim, 'Peoples' and 'Populations'-Indigenous Peoples and the Rights of Peoples, in: J Crawford (ed), *The Rights of Peoples*, (Oxford: Clarendon Press, 1988), 116.
39. See, contrary view regarding right to compensation: "Compensation for past harms is a weak basis for rights because compensation demands that those harmed get back either what they should have had all along, or something of equal value. Compensation in this sense is a material one, having regard to the value of lost resources, but will not be of much use in securing intangibles such as lost nation, or cultural rights that must be enjoyed in a much different context." S Curry, op. cit. above n. 9, at 313, See also, A C Crehan, 'Compensating for Historical Injustice: Three Important Issues', (1999), 1 *Australian Journal of Professional and Applied Ethics* 2.
40. See, Declaration, *op. cit.*
41. See details on the rights of indigenous people to participation in relation to resource development, G Triggs, 'The Rights of Indigenous Peoples to Participate in Resource Development: An International Legal Perspective', in: D N Zillman, A R Lucas and G (Rock) Pring, (eds), *Human Rights in Natural Resources Development: Public Participation in the Sustainable Development of Mining and Energy Resources,* (Oxford: Oxford University Press, 2002) 123-54.

42. See, G Triggs, 'Australia's Indigenous Peoples and International Law: Validity of the Native Title Amendment Act 1998,' (1999) 23 *Melbourne University Law Review* 394.
43. See, Declaration, *op. cit.*
44. S J Anaya, *Indigenous Peoples in International Law*, (New York: Oxford University Press, 1996), 130.
45. Mrs. Erica-Irene A. Daes, *op. cit* n. 33, at 23-24.
46. See I H Kawharu, (ed), *Waitangi: Maori and Pakeaha Perspective of the Treaty of Waitangi,* (Oxford: Oxford University Press, 1989); J Merritt & T Fence, 'The Nunavut Land Claims Settlement: Emerging Issues in Law and Public Administration,' (1990), 15 *Queens Law Journal* 255.
47. Constitution of Argentina-sanctioned by the National Constitutional Convention convened by law 24.309, 1994.
48. Political Constitution of Colombia, Gaceta Constitutional No. 127 of 10 October 1991, reprinted in IV Constitutions of the Countries of the World (Gisbert H. Flanz., Peter B. Heller & Marcia W. Coward trans., 1995).
49. *Ibid*, Arts. 246, 286, 321, 329.
50. *Ibid*, Arts. 10, 68, 246, 330.
51. Art. 198, Brazilian Constitution of 1988, cited in: M Pallemaerts, 'Development, Conservation, and Indigenous Rights in Brazil' (1986), 8 *Human Rights Quarterly* 374.
52. See, A P Blaustein & G H Flanz (eds), *Constitutions of the Countries of the World*, (1998).
53. Constitution of the Russian Federation Art. 69, (1993) (Vladimir V. Belykov & Walter J. Raymond Trans. 1993).
54. Canadian Constitution (Constitution Act, 1982) Schedule B (Canadian Charter of Rights and Freedoms), See L C Green, 'Aboriginal Peoples, International Law and the Canadian Charter of Rights and Freedoms', (1983), 61 *Canadian Bar Review* 339.
55. R Kuppe, 'The Indigenous Peoples of Venezuela and the National Law', (1987), 2 *Law and Anthropology* 113.
56. Arts. 80, 180 of the Political Constitution of the Republic of Nicaragua, No. 19, 1986, as amended July 4, 1995, reprinted in XIII Constitutions of the Countries of the World (G H Flanz (ed), Anna I. Velleve Torres trans., 1998).
57. (1992) 175 C.L.R. 1 At 25 (per Brennan, J.).
58. Id. At 42 (per Brennan, J.).
59. Native Title Act of 1993 (Commonwealth), No. 110 of 1993. For a discussion of principles emerging from the *Mabo* decision, see M Hunt, 'Mineral Development and Indigenous People—The

Implications of the *Mabo* Case', (1993), 11 *Journal of Energy and Natural Resources Law* 155.

60. S J Anaya, *op. cit.* n. 45, at 159.
61. *Ibid.* pp. 162-63.
62. See, Communication 167/1984 (*Ominayak and Lubicon lake Bank v. Canada)*, UN Doc. CCPR/C/38/D/167/1984, Annex II (Decision of 28 March 1990), especially paras. 32.1 and 32.2.
63. CERD, Findings on the Native Title Amendment Act 1998, UN Doc ERD/C/54/Misc.40/Rev.2 (18 March 1999) (7).
64. *Ibid*, 8.
65. C J Iorns, *op. cit.* n. 1, at 236.
66. R Falk, *op. cit.* n. 15, at 18.

17

Rights of Women under International Law

Sadiq A.J. Syed

I. Introduction

The crusade for women's rights and empowerment has a long history and can be found in most of the ancient texts, scriptures and legal documents around the world. It gained momentum with the establishment of the United Nations Organization in 1945. The members of the UN through the UN Charter preamble declared their faith "in fundamental human rights, in the dignity and worth of the human person, in the equal rights of men and women and of nations large and small...." Within a year of its existence the UN had appointed the Commission on the Status of Women, in 1946, which meets annually to make recommendations and reports promoting equal rights for women and men in political, economic, civil, social and educational fields.

Ever since its inception, the UN has been instrumental in establishing common standards for measuring and accomplishing women's rights and gender equality through the adoption of international laws and treaties. For example, it ensured that the Universal Declaration on Human Rights included provisions on gender equality. The Universal Declaration of Human Rights adopted on December 10, 1948 became the guiding document for the nations and helped in incorporating the principles into the national Constitutions.

The concept and recognition of women's rights further attained global recognition with the raising voices of the women's movement the world over. The movement has been a major force in contributing to the evolutionary process of women's all round development in general and protection of women from violence and sexual abuse in particular. The spearheading of the women's movement throughout the world towards the protection of women and their empowerment resulted in a landmark initiative by the UN in 1972 to commemorate 1975 as "International Women's Year" and also the beginning of the observance of the UN Decade for Women. The UN over the years adopted series of Conventions, Declarations and other documents including the Convention on the Elimination of All Forms of Discrimination Against Women (also known as Women's Convention or CEDAW)[1] and its Optional Protocols, the Convention on the Rights of the Child (CRC) and its two-Optional Protocols etc., calling upon the States Parties to ratify[2] and incorporate these provisions into their national laws. By adopting international laws and treaties on women's rights, the UN has helped set a common standard for measuring how societies advance equality between men and women.

The CEDAW, adopted by the UN in 1979, is often described as an international bill of rights for women. CEDAW comprises a preamble and 30 Articles, and defines what constitutes discrimination against women and sets up an agenda for national action to end such discrimination. The CEDAW was also supplemented by an Optional Protocol which among others gives a right to the individual to submit a complaint to the CEDAW Committee.

According to the Convention, discrimination against women is "...any distinction, exclusion or restriction made on the basis of sex which has the effect or purpose of impairing or nullifying the recognition, enjoyment or exercise by women, irrespective of their marital status, on a basis of equality of men and women, of human rights and fundamental freedoms in the political, economic, social, cultural, civil or any other field."

Further the UN Decade was culminated with the adoption of the "Forward Looking Strategies" document at the UN Conference held in Nairobi in 1985 served as a blueprint for women's advancement and its 372 paragraphs deal with the entire spectrum of women's role in society. The Nairobi Conference was followed by the "Beijing Conference" (Fourth World Conference on Women), which adopted the 'Platform of Action Document'. In December 1993, the UN adopted the Declaration on the Elimination of Violence against Women, which defined what constitutes violence against women and also outlined the actions governments and communities should take to prevent such acts. Earlier, in June 1993, the World Conference on Human Rights in Vienna, Austria, reaffirmed that "women's rights are also human rights". The Conference in its landmark initiative also provided for the appointment of a Special Rapporteur on Violence against Women. These landmark initiatives by the UN substantially contributed in prioritizing action by the States Parties through legislative and other initiatives. Quite apart from these, one of the significant developments in the recent times is the adoption by the UN Security Council of Resolution 1325,[3] advocating for the "protection of women during armed conflict, and calls for an end to impunity for gender-based abuses during and after conflict, the integration of a gender perspective in peace-making and peace-keeping, and the participation of women in all levels of decision-making and issues related to prevention management and resolution of conflict. It calls for action from a wide range of stakeholders, including governments, the UN Security Council, UN Secretary-General and all parties to armed conflict."

The following section outlines the significant contributions by the UN and international community towards the protection and empowerment of women in various fields.

II. Women's Right to Health Care

Enjoyment of the human right to health is vital to all aspects of a person's life and well being. Article 25 of the Universal Declaration of Human Rights states:

> Everyone has the right to a standard of living adequate for the health and well-being of himself and his family, including food, clothing, housing and medical care and necessary social services, and the right to security in the event of unemployment, sickness, disability, widowhood, old age or other lack of livelihood in circumstances beyond his control.

Article 12 of the Convention on the Elimination of All Forms of Discrimination Against Women, 1979, the International Covenant on Economic, Social, and Cultural Rights, 1966, the International Covenant on Civil and Political Rights 1966, World Medical Association Declaration of Helsinki 1964 (revised in 1975) etc., also contain provisions mandating the States parties to take effective measures to provide health care facilities accessible to all. The World Health Organization (WHO), which was established with a specific mandate to secure health care for all also takes up programmes and provides financial and technical assistance in addressing specific issues concerning health care also focusing on women. Further, the international community while considering the increasing number of maternal deaths around the world especially in Asia endorsed the reduction of maternal mortality as a key development goal for countries. The consensus documents emanating from international conferences such as the World Summit for Children 1990, the International Conference on Population and Development 1994 and the Fourth World Conference on Women 1995, and their respective five-year follow-up evaluations of progress 1999 and 2000, the Millennium Declaration 2000 and the United Nations General Assembly Special Session on Children 2002[4] strongly advocate for providing basic and qualitative health care facilities.

Women's right to health and reproduction

The struggle for reproductive choice, which is central to the existence of a right to reproduce, has been debated both locally and internationally. The Convention on the Elimination of All Forms of Discrimination against Women (CEDAW) serves as the landmark Human Rights treaty that affirms the reproductive rights of women and targets culture and tradition as influential forces shaping gender roles and family relations. Quite apart from this, the International Conference on Population and Development (ICPD) Programme of Action advocates Governments at all levels "to institute systems of monitoring and evaluation of user-centered services with a view to detecting, preventing and controlling abuses by family-planning managers and providers and to ensure a continuing improvement in the quality of services". Further, the Beijing Platform for Action urges Governments to ensure that all health services and workers conform to Human Rights and to ethical, professional and gender-sensitive standards in the delivery of women's health services. Moreover, recognizing that confidentiality and accessibility of information are critical to the realization of women's reproductive rights, the Platform for Action directs Governments to "redesign health information, services and training for health workers so that they are gender-sensitive and reflect the user's...right to privacy and confidentiality".[5] Besides, the Beijing Conference also called upon the nations to enact legislative provisions to protect women from marital rape.

Thus international Human Rights law mandates that women should be given the full right to control their sexual and reproductive health, free from discrimination or coercion, and be given access to information about sexual and reproductive health care and safe reproductive technology.

Women's rights to maternity benefits

Reduction of maternal mortality has been endorsed as a key development goal by countries and is included in consensus documents emanating from international conferences such as the World Summit for Children 1990, the International Conference on Population and Development 1994 and the Fourth World Conference on Women in 1995, and their respective five-year follow-up evaluations of progress 1999 and 2000, the Millennium Declaration 2000 and the United Nations General Assembly Special Session on Children 2002.

The UN estimates every year 600,000 women die worldwide due to pregnancy and childbirth related complications. Out of them, 98 per cent of these deaths occur in developing countries. According to a recent study,[6] the estimated number of maternal deaths in 2000 for the world was 529,000. These deaths were almost equally divided between Africa (251,000) and Asia (253,000), with about four per cent (22,000) occurring in Latin America and the Caribbean, and less than one per cent (2,500) in the more developed regions of the world. In terms of the Maternal Mortality Ratio (MMR), the world figure is estimated to be 400 per 100,000 live births. By region, the MMR was highest in Africa (830), followed by Asia (330), Oceania (240), Latin America and the Caribbean (190), and the developed countries (20). The country with the highest estimated number of maternal deaths is India (136,000), followed by Nigeria (37,000), Pakistan (26,000), Democratic Republic of Congo and Ethiopia (24,000 each), the United Republic of Tanzania (21,000), Afghanistan (20,000), Bangladesh (16,000), Angola, China, Kenya (11,000 each), Indonesia and Uganda (10,000 each).

These 13 countries account for 67 per cent of all maternal deaths. To overcome this the four UN agencies, UNFPA, UNICEF, the World Health Organization (WHO) and the World Bank by joining national Governments declared that reducing maternal mortality is an integral part of upholding women's Human Rights.

Protection to women from HIV/AIDS

Women are fighting both a virus and systemic discrimination in trying to overcome the threat of HIV/AIDS. Across the world, they face a number of circumstances which increase their risk of HIV infection in gender-specific ways. Many women are exposed to sexual violence and coerced sex inside and outside marriage, including through harmful traditional practices such as genital mutilation, early marriage, and wife inheritance. The number of people living with HIV/AIDS in 2003 was estimated by UNAIDS to be 35.7 million adults (of whom 17 million were women) and 2.1 million children.[7] In Sub-Saharan Africa 57% of adults living with the virus are women, and two-thirds of young HIV-positive people are women and girls. Women as a proportion of all adults living with HIV/AIDS rose from 43 per cent in 1998 to 48 per cent in 2003, and the proportion continues to grow worldwide, 60 per cent of new HIV transmissions are to women, and 52 per cent to young adults.[8]

Sexual rights embrace Human Rights that are already recognized in national laws, international Human Rights documents and other consensus documents. These include the right of all persons—free of coercion, discrimination and violence—to the highest attainable standard of health in relation to sexuality, including access to sexual and reproductive health care services; to seek, receive and impart information in relation to sexuality; to have access to sexuality education; and other related rights.[9] For sexual rights, as with all rights, the responsible exercise of Human Rights requires that all persons respect the rights of others. In reality, women frequently are deprived of the realization of many or most of these rights. The Declaration of Commitment agreed at the 2001 UN General Assembly Special Session on HIV/AIDS took a small step forward by calling on governments to take action to "empower women to have control over and decide freely and responsibly on matters related to their sexuality to increase their ability to protect themselves from HIV infection."[10]

The United Nations Commission on Human Rights, in its Resolutions, has declared that the term 'or other status' in the various international Human Rights instruments should be interpreted to cover health status, including HIV/AIDS. It also further confirmed that discrimination on the basis of HIV/AIDS status (actual or presumed) is prohibited by existing Human Rights standards.[11] Quite apart from this the UNAIDS and the Office of the United Nations High Commissioner for Human Rights (OHCHR) convened an International Consultation on HIV/AIDS and Human Rights in Geneva in 1996. This meeting adopted the *International Guidelines on HIV/AIDS and Human Rights*[12] which were also endorsed by the UN Commission on Human Rights in 1997. In 2002, following a further consultation, a revised *Guideline 6: Access to prevention, treatment, care and support* was adopted, providing up-to-date policy guidance based on current international law and best practice at country level.[13]

III. Women's Right to Education

Education is one of the most important means of empowering women with the knowledge, skills and self-confidence necessary to participate fully in the development process. More than 60 years ago, the Universal Declaration of Human Rights asserted, "everyone has the right to education". In 1990, governments meeting at the World Conference on Education for All in Jomtien, Thailand, committed themselves to the goal of universal access to basic education. Despite notable efforts by countries around the globe that have appreciably expanded access to basic education, there are approximately 960 million illiterate adults in the world, of whom two-thirds are women. The recent decades witnessed added emphasis by the UN and national governments on the right to education and its recognition as a prerequisite for promoting peace, development and good governance.

IV. Women's Right to Employment

Economic empowerment of women is central to considerations of personal independence and self-esteem. To this end employment and entrepreneur opportunities would go a long way in making a woman self-reliant. To end discrimination against women in the field of employment and to realize their right to work, women should be given the right to employment opportunities, the free choice of profession, job security, equal remuneration, the right to compensation in respect of domestic work, the right to protection of health and safe working conditions, especially in safeguarding the function of reproduction and special protection in times of pregnancy from work that may be harmful.

Over the years gender mainstreaming is widely advocated at all levels as a strategy to ensuring gender equality and women empowerment. In July 1997, the United Nations Economic and Social Council (ECOSOC) defined the concept of gender mainstreaming as follows:

> Mainstreaming a gender perspective is the process of assessing the implications for women and men of any planned action, including legislation, policies or programmes, in any area and at all levels. It is a strategy for making the concerns and experiences of women as well as of men an integral part of the design, implementation, monitoring and evaluation of policies and programmes in all political, economic and societal spheres, so that women and men benefit equally, and inequality is not perpetuated. The ultimate goal of mainstreaming is to achieve gender equality.

The economic empowerment of women and providing of suitable working conditions including her protection from all forms of discrimination and harassment has become a matter of concern and priority at the national and international levels. This is very much reflected in the Convention on the Elimination of All Forms of Discrimination against Women (CEDAW), Beijing Declaration and other documents.

The overarching objective of the ILO has been re-phrased as the promotion of opportunities for women and men to obtain decent and productive work in conditions of freedom, equity, security and human dignity. Decent work is the converging focus of the four strategic objectives, namely rights at work, employment, social protection and social dialogue. Decent work is an organizing concept for the ILO in order to provide an overall framework for action in economic and social development.

V. Registration of Marriages

The registration of marriage and consent to marriage has been widely recognized amongst all societies and religions including the international community for a long time. As early as 1962, the United Nations adopted the Convention on Consent to Marriage, Minimum Age for Marriage and Registration of Marriages and called upon the States Parties to take legislative and other measures to achieve the objectives. It is needless to emphasize that the registration of marriages will not only contribute significantly towards women's independence and decision making but also facilitate in prevention of child and bigamous marriages.

VI. Protection of Women from Violence

Women are increasingly subjected to various forms of violence over the years and were denied access to justice due to various reasons. It is in this context the United Nations adopted specific Conventions and Declarations aimed at prevention and protection of women from all forms of violence. In December 1993, the UN adopted the Declaration on the Elimination of Violence against Women,[14] which defines violence against women as:

> any act of gender-based violence that results in, or is likely to result in, physical, sexual or psychological harm or suffering to women, including threats of such acts, coercion or arbitrary deprivation of liberty, whether occurring in public or in private life.[15]

According to this Declaration violence against women shall be understood to encompass, but not be limited to, the following:[16]

(a) Physical, sexual and psychological violence occurring in the family, including battering, sexual abuse of female children in the household, dowry related violence, marital rape, female genital mutilation and other traditional practices harmful to women, non-spousal violence, and violence related to exploitation;

(b) Physical, sexual and psychological violence occurring within the general community, including rape, sexual abuse, sexual harassment, and intimidation at work, in educational institutions and elsewhere, trafficking in women and forced prostitution;

(c) Physical, sexual and psychological violence perpetuated or condoned by the State, wherever it occurs.

The Committee on the Elimination of Discrimination against Women recognized that violence directed against a woman because she is a woman, including "acts that inflict physical, mental or sexual harm or suffering", represents a form of discrimination that seriously inhibits the ability of women to enjoy Human Rights and freedoms.[17] Accordingly, it has called up on the States parties to take effective measures to combat all kinds of violence against women.

Protection from domestic violence

Not even an hour passes without a steady stream of women file into the Crime Against Women Cells, Police Stations, Legal Aid Centers and other counseling centers. All have a similar story to tell. They are victims of domestic violence—perhaps the most prolific and insidious form of violence against women, the world experiences today.[18]

Many a time the cases of domestic violence and marital rape go unreported due to the predominance of patriarchy, customary practices, ignorance of laws, threat to life, loss of face and in majority of cases women want to keep the issue private.

The United Nations model legislation on 'domestic violence' defines domestic violence as:[19]

> All acts of gender-based physical, psychological and abuse by a family member against women in the family, ranging from simple assaults to aggravated physical battery, kidnapping, threats, intimidation, coercion, stalking, humiliating verbal abuse, forcible or unlawful entry, arson, destruction of property, sexual violence, marital rape, dowry or related violence, female genital mutilation, violence related to exploitation through prostitution, violence against household workers and attempts to commit such acts shall be termed "domestic violence".

Domestic violence against women has become a global issue with the increase in the number of cases. The first ever international recognition of domestic violence was by the United Nations in 1993 with the adoption of the Declaration of Violence against Women. The Declaration defined violence as physical, sexual and psychological both in public and private life. This Declaration was unprecedented, the first of its kind. It sets the standards and outlines the basic rights of women. Further delegates from 180 countries reached agreement on June 10, 2000 during the Beijing + 5 Conference at New York and called upon the Governments for the prosecution of all forms of domestic violence including marital rape. Keeping in view the need nearly 45 countries have enacted specific legislations and provisions to combat domestic violence.

VII. Accountability for Women's Rights: Conventional Mechanisms to Monitor and Protect Women's Rights

One of the outstanding developments at the international level towards the monitoring and implementation of commitments under the UN Charter and Treaties is the setting-up of Conventional and extra-Conventional mechanisms to monitor the implementation. In this context, the UN has set-up Charter based bodies, Treaty monitoring bodies, Special Rapporteurs etc.

There came to exist in the recent times Conventional mechanisms popularly known as "Human Rights Treaty-Monitoring Bodies" to review and monitor Human Rights violations such as:

- *Human Rights Committee:* monitors the implementation of the International Covenant on Civil and Political Rights.
- *Committee on Economic, Social and Cultural Rights:* monitors the implementation of the International Covenant on Economic, Social and Cultural rights.
- *Committee on the Elimination of Discrimination against Women:* monitors the implementation of the Convention on the Elimination of All Forms of Discrimination Against Women.
- *Committee on the Rights of the Child:* monitors the implementation of the Convention on the Rights of the Child.
- *Committee Against Torture:* monitors the implementation of the Convention against Torture and Other Cruel, Inhuman or Degrading Treatment or Punishment.

Individual complaints procedure

Apart from the Charter based and Treaty-Monitoring bodies there exist "Extra-Conventional Mechanisms" in the form of Special Rapporteurs, Special Representatives, Special Envoys and Independent Experts, Working Groups—thematic or country (Urgent Actions) for the promotion and effective monitoring of the implementation of women's rights standards.

Some Treaties also provide for individual complaints procedures. The Optional Protocol to the International Covenant on Civil and Political Rights, the Optional Protocol to the Convention on the Elimination of All Forms of Discrimination Against Women, Article 22 of the Convention against Torture, and Article 14 of the International Convention on the Elimination of All Forms of Racial Discrimination all provide for an individual complaints procedure.

Besides, the Commission on the Status of Women is the principal technical body of the United Nations towards the development of substantive policy guidance with regard to the advancement of women. The Commission presently consists of 45 government experts elected by the Economic and Social Council for a period of four years.

VIII. Women's Right to Information and Technology

The role of Information and Communication Technologies (ICT) as a tool for development has attracted the sustained attention of the United Nations over recent years. While there is recognition of the potential of ICT as a tool for the promotion of gender equality and the empowerment of women, a "gender divide" has also been identified, reflected in the lower numbers of women accessing and using ICT compared with men. ICT can be a powerful catalyst for political and social empowerment of women, and the promotion of gender equality.[20]

The success of Beijing Conference held in China in 1995 can be mainly attributed to the information and communication technologies principally the internet. The Beijing Declaration and Platform for Action adopted at the Fourth World Conference on Women in 1995 drew attention to the emerging global communications network and its impact on public policies, as well as the attitudes and behavior of individuals. It called for the empowerment of women through enhancing their skills, knowledge, access to and use of information technologies. It also included a strategic objective: "Increase the participation and access of women to expression and decision-making in and through the media and new technologies of communication".

In 2000, the Economic and Social Council adopted a Ministerial Declaration on the role of information technology in the context of a knowledge based economy. In 2001, the Secretary-General established a high level Information and Communication Technologies Task Force to provide overall leadership to the United Nations on the formulation of strategies to put ICT at the service of development.[21]

The United Nations Commission on Science and Technology identified significant gender differences in levels of access to, control of and advantages accruing from a wide range of technological developments. It concluded that "the information revolution appeared to be by-passing women; that information society literature was silent on gender issues, and that neither research nor practical projects in the information technology field had addressed the specific circumstances of women".[22]

Based on knowledge and experience that had emerged in the previous five years, the twenty-third special session of the General Assembly, held in June 2000 to review progress in implementation of the Platform for Action, recognized that ICT had created new opportunities for women and contributed to knowledge sharing, networking and electronic commerce activities.[23]

IX. Conclusion

In the light of the above it may be stated that the initiatives by the United Nations joined by the national Governments and organizations contributed significantly towards the protection and empowerment of women in various fields. Yet, there are disturbing trends of gender discrimination, sexual and gender based violence, lack of opportunities and participation of women in education, employment and decision-making reported on a large scale from across the globe. It is hoped that with increased commitment, participation and accountability by the States Parties, institutions and individuals the UN and the international community will accomplish the objective of promoting global peace, security and gender justice.

Notes

1. As of 16 June 2006, CEDAW has 183 States Parties to it.
2. Ratification defines the international act whereby a State indicates its consent to be bound to a treaty if the Parties intended to show their consent by such an act.
3. Adopted by the Security Council at its 4213th meeting, on 31 October 2000.
4. *See*, *Maternal Mortality in 2000: Estimates Developed by WHO*, UNICEF and UNFPA, p. 2.
5. *See*, para 106, Beijing Platform of Action.
6. *Maternal Mortality in 2000: Estimates Developed by WHO*, UNICEF and UNFPA, p. 2.
7. Amnesty International, *ACT 77/084/2004*, 24 November 2004.
8. Source, ILO, *ILOAIDS Brief*, December 2004.
9. World Health Organization, Draft working definition of sexual rights. WHO, Geneva, 2002.
10. United Nations, Declaration of Commitment on HIV/AIDS, Document A/S-26/L.2, New York, 2001, para. 59. Available at: http://www.un.org/ga/aids/coverage/FinalDeclarationHIVAIDS.html
11. United Nations Commission on Human Rights, *Resolutions 1999/49, 2001/51, 2002/47*.
12. Office of the High Commissioner for Human Rights (OHCHR), UNAIDS. International Guidelines on HIV/AIDS and Human Rights. Geneva, 1998.
13. Amnesty International, "AI Index: Act 77/084/2004", 24 November 2004.
14. Resolution adopted by the General Assembly on the report of the Third Committee (A/48/629), Resolution 48/104.
15. *Ibid.*, Article 1.
16. *Ibid.*, Article 2.

17. Committee on the Elimination of Discrimination against Women, General Recommendation No. 19, Eleventh-Session, (1992), para. 6.
18. Sadiq A.J. Syed, *Women in India: Legal and Human Rights,* Women's Studies and Development Centre, University of Delhi (2001).
19. Article 11, A Framework for Model Legislation on Domestic Violence, Commission on Human Rights, 52nd Session, Item 9(a) of the Provisional Agenda.
20. Women Watch, *Women 2000 and Beyond,* DAW, September 2005.
21. *Ibid.*
22. United Nations Commission on Science and Technology, Gender Working Group, 1995.
23. *Ibid.*

18

Legal Control of Domestic Violence in India in Perspective of International Human Rights Instruments

Debasree Lahiri

I. Introduction

Domestic violence is being recognized globally as a major issue for women's Human Rights. In recent years, domestic violence is being increasingly recognized also as a social and public health concern.[1] It primarily affects women and operates to diminish women's autonomy and sense of self-worth. Domestic violence usually involves the infliction of bodily injury accompanied by verbal threats and harassment, emotional abuse or the destruction of property as means of coercion, control, revenge or punishment, on a person whom the abuser is involved in an intimate relationship. She may also begin to believe that her inability to avoid abuse in an intimate relationship demonstrates that she is a failure and deserves or is powerless to escape the abuse.[2] There are various reasons for its occurrence:

(i) Cultural systems legitimize violence, legal authorities fail to protect women, economic structures subordinate women, and political systems marginalize women's needs;

(ii) Marital violence was more prevalent in those societies where patriarchal systems were strong, where women have few options outside of marriage (e.g. divorce restrictions and low access to economic resources); and where violence is an accepted means for conflict-resolution;

(iii) Violence against women is a reflection of the power relationships between spouses;

(iv) Violence against women is linked to a women's lower self-esteem, severe depressive symptoms with minimal personal resources, and little institutional support;

(v) Society encourages husbands to exercise their rights to dominate and control wives.[3]

Human Rights Watch's investigations found, unfortunately, that law enforcement officials frequently reinforce the batterers' attempts to demean and control his victim. The police and judicial authorities often dismiss domestic violence as a "private" matter rather than a widespread scourge that demands urgent State action. The forms of violence that women experience in the home, including rape, murder, assault and battery, are condemned by the criminal laws of virtually all countries. However, when committed against a woman in an intimate relationship, these attacks are more often tolerated as the norms than prosecuted as crimes, even when laws exist on the books that specifically condemn domestic violence. In many places, those who commit domestic violence are prosecuted less vigorously and punished more leniently than perpetrators of similarly violent crimes against strangers.[4]

At every step of the process to obtain legal protection from domestic assault, women face barriers that prevent them from prosecuting their batterers and make a mockery of the justice system. Legislatures pass laws that exempt marital rape from criminal sanction; police refuse to arrest men who beat their wives, and in some cases even intimidate women into withdrawing complaints of spousal abuse; prosecutors fail to charge men with domestic assault; Court clerks turn away women who seek restraining or protection orders; and judges accept "honor" and "heat of passion" defenses that allow wife-murder based upon "legitimate provocation", usually adultery.[5]

On this background, the paper wishes to identify international Human Rights laws specifically addressing this burning issue and endeavor to implement those laws in the Indian context to make the homes safest place for the women.

II. International Legal Protection on Domestic Violence

Although domestic violence by definition is committed by private individuals (although some State agents also abuse their wives, girlfriends or children), States nonetheless are bound by numerous international laws and norms that oblige them to protect women's lives and physical security. Where States routinely fail to prosecute domestic violence against women because of the sex and status of the victim, in contrast to their efforts to prosecute other criminal violence, they deny women equal protection of law.

Under international law, governments are obliged to guarantee equality before the law for all its citizens, without regard to sex. The *Universal Declaration of Human Rights, 1948* states that "all human beings are born free and equal in dignity and rights", and it declares that everyone is entitled, without distinction of any kind, to the various rights articulated in the Declaration. The *International Covenant on Civil and Political Rights (ICCPR)* and the *International Covenant on Economic, Social and Cultural Rights (ICESCR)* were adopted by the UN General Assembly in 1966, and they were drafted and adopted as legally binding international treaties meant to ensure protection of the rights proclaimed in the Universal Declaration.

The ICCPR prohibits sex discrimination in three different Articles. Article 2(1) of the ICCPR states that, "Each State Party...undertakes to respect and to ensure to all individuals within its territory and subject to its jurisdiction the rights recognized in the present Covenant, without distinction of any kind, such as...sex".

Article 3 of the ICCPR provides for the right of men and women to the enjoyment of all civil and political rights.

Article 26 further guarantees that, "All persons are equal before the law and are entitled without any discrimination to equal protection of the law. In this respect, the law shall prohibit any discrimination and guarantee to all persons equal and effective protection against discrimination on any grounds such as...sex."

In addition to ICCPR, the *Convention on the Elimination of all Forms of Discrimination Against Women (CEDAW)* also prohibits sex discrimination by requiring State Parties "to pursue a policy of eliminating discrimination...[and] to ensure that public authorities and institutions shall act in conformity with this obligation".[6] Almost all regional treaties contain similar prohibition.[7]

Where States respond to evidence of murder, rape or assault of women by their intimate partners with inaction, they send the message that such attacks are justified or at a minimum fail to take steps necessary to protect their female citizen's rights to physical integrity, and in extreme cases, to life. The *International Covenant on Civil and Political Rights (ICCPR)* contains several prohibitions against violence that implicate domestic violence. Article 6(1) provides that "Every human being has the inherent right to life. This right shall be protected by law. No one shall be arbitrarily deprived of life". Article 7 states that "No one shall be subjected to torture or to cruel, inhuman or degrading treatment". Article 9(1) guarantees that "Everyone has the right to...security of person". While the ICCPR does not explicitly refer to private violence, including domestic violence, the broad language in the above provisions clearly can encompass such abuse. State Parties are obliged to combat domestic violence by virtue of having undertaken "to respect and to ensure" the rights recognized in the Covenant.[8]

The international recognition of the status and the problems of women all over the world resulted in the U.N. declaring 1975 as the International Women's year and the period between 1975 and 1985 as *Women's Decade.*[9] The issue of wife abuse was recognized as problematic at the 1975 Mexico-International Women's year World Conference. At the second and third World Conferences on Women in Copenhagen (1980) and Nairobi (1985), domestic violence was recognized as an offence to human dignity and an obstacle to equality.[10]

The *Convention Against Torture and Other Cruel, Inhuman or Degrading Treatment or Punishment, 1984* defines torture as "an act by which severe pain or suffering, whether physical or mental, is intentionally inflicted on a person" for a purpose such as obtaining information or a confession, punishment, intimidation, or coercion, "or for any reason based on discrimination of any kind". Domestic violence is a violation of woman's rights to bodily integrity, to liberty, and often right to life itself. Therefore, domestic violence is a form of torture and should be dealt in line with other Human Rights instruments.

The recognition of violence against women, and especially domestic violence, as a Human Rights violation is first articulated in *Vienna Declaration and Programme of Action* adopted at the *1993 United Nations World Conference of Human Rights*. Although CEDAW does not explicitly address violence against women, it recognizes that discrimination is a root cause of violence against women and that the denial of equal right to women reinforces and perpetuates violence against women. The *UN Convention on the Elimination of Violence Against Women, 1993*, is the first Protocol to specifically focus on the full continuum of violence experienced by women. It defines violence against women as"...any form of gender based violence, that results in or is likely to result in, physical, sexual or psychological harm or suffering to women, including threats of such acts, coercion or arbitrary deprivations of liberty, whether occurring in public or private life". This encompasses, *inter alia*, "...physical, sexual or psychological violence occurring in the family and in the general community, including battering, sexual abuse of children, dowry-related violence, rape, female genital mutilation and other traditional practices harmful to women, non-spousal violence, violence related to exploitation, sexual harassment, and intimidation at work, in educational institutions and elsewhere, trafficking in women, forced prostitution, and violence perpetrated or condoned by the state".

In June 2000, the UN General Assembly reviewed the implementation of the *Beijing Platform (Beijing +5)* and reaffirmed governments commitment to work for the realization of women's rights. The new document (Women 2000/Beijing +5 Outcome Document) reaffirms the 150 page platform for Action at the landmark 1995 UN Women's Conference and moves forward with together measures to combat domestic violence and trafficking of women. The Outcome Document calls for prosecution of all forms of domestic violence, now including marital rape.

International law applies to the actions of State responsibility and has developed to recognize that States are "obligated to investigate every situation involving a violation of the rights protected by [international law]". The *Committee on the Elimination of Discrimination Against Women in 1992* affirmed Government accountability for the routine non-prosecution of domestic assault. In another significant step towards enhancing State accountability for gender-based violence, the United Nations Commission on Human Rights appointed the first Special Rapporteur on Violence against Women in 1994. The Special Rapporteur is tasked to carry out and follow up on missions, undertaken either separately or jointly with other Special Rapporteurs or Working Groups, on all forms of violence against women and to recommend ways of eliminating such violence. The Special Rapporteur's first report set forth the international legal framework condemning domestic violence and detailed actions that were currently being pursued by Governments to reduce the occurrence of domestic assault. In recent years, women's Human Rights groups are pressurizing Governments to implement CEDAW, and take positive measures to end legal, social and economic gender inequality.

III. Adaptation of International Human Rights Law in India

During UN Decade for Women, the Government of India constituted a *Committee on the Status of Women* by resolution for education and social welfare on 22nd September 1971. The Committee was entrusted with the task of making a comprehensive examination of all questions relating to the rights and status of women in India and to provide useful guidelines for the formulation of social policies. The Status of Women Committee had eminent women like Phulrenu Guha, M.P. and Vina Majumdar, academician as members. The report of the Committee, '*Towards Equality*', was published in 1974 that blew apart the myth that post-Independence Indian Women were gradually "progressing". Faced with stark facts on the abysmal status of the mass of Indian women, who suffered from poverty, illiteracy and ill health as well as discrimination in both the domestic and the public spheres, middle class women in the metros began to campaign against the worst manifestations of sexism and patriarchy.

India has ratified international Conventions such as the *Convention on the Elimination of All Forms of Discrimination Against Women (CEDAW), in June 1993*. The domestic Courts are under an obligation to give due regard to the international conventions *United Nations Charter* and the *Universal Declaration of Human Rights, 1948, CEDAW etc.* and norms for construing domestic laws when there is no inconsistency between them. As a party to the *Convention on the Elimination of All Forms of Racial Discrimination* since 1948 and the *International Covenant on Civil and Political Rights* since 1979, India has been committed for many years to ensuring civil and political rights to all its citizens without discrimination of any kind.

Recognizing its international commitments towards the rights of women and urged on by a dynamic women's movement, successive Governments have unveiled policies of empowerment for women which have sought to address the full range of women's Human Rights. As a result, there are many positive aspects of women's empowerment which have taken place in recent years in India. This includes political representation of women at the lowest levels of government, increases in life expectancy amongst women and education.[11]

Following the *Fourth UN World Conference on Women in Beijing in 1995*, the Government of India promised several measures to ensure the advancement of women's rights in India. The Department of Women and Child Development began work on a national policy on women which would seek to bridge the gap between the equal *de jure* status and unequal *de facto* position of women in the country. In January 2000, while hearing India's first periodic report, the *Committee on the Elimination of Discrimination Against Women (CEDAW)* recommended that a national plan of action be developed to address in a holistic manner the issue of gender-based violence, in line with the Committee's General Recommendation 19. In January 2001 the Prime Minister of India announced that 2001 would be the *Year of Women's Empowerment* and that a national policy on women's empowerment would soon be unveiled. The policy reportedly included a plan to ensure that all laws deemed discriminatory to women be reviewed and suitably amended by 2003. It also included plans to establish an effective machinery to monitor the delivery of justice to women in a context of rising crimes against women and suggested requesting State Governments to set up district committees to monitor and expedite disposal of cases of atrocities against women.[12]

The recently passed the *Protection of Women from Domestic Violence Act, 2005* provides immediate relief to women in emergency situations of violence in the home. In this Act, the definition of "Domestic violence" has been made wide enough to encompass in its scope all types of violence resorted to within the precincts of a home. For designing a comprehensive definition, *the UN framework for model legislation on domestic violence, Convention on the Elimination of All Forms of Discrimination Against Women (CEDAW) 1979, Declaration on the Elimination of Violence against Women (A/RES/48/104, 20 December, 1993), Beijing Declaration and Platform for Action* were resorted to. Under Section 3 of the Act, four types of domestic violence have been proposed i.e., physical abuse, sexual abuse, verbal and emotional abuse and economic abuse. For the first time in India a law has recognized the need to 'protect' women from domestic violence that is emotional or economic in nature. This is possible only by taking inspiration from international Human Rights laws.

IV. Concluding Remarks

Within the burgeoning discourse on Human Rights, domestic violence against women is increasingly viewed as a serious violation of Human Rights. It exists in every country and culture in epidemic proportion, and is disproportionately committed against women. The irony is that international Human Rights instruments and many domestic laws prohibit and condemn such violence. And still, it occurs. In reality, the societal responses to domestic violence, to date, primarily focus on crisis intervention after the harm has occurred. What is needed is a comprehensive strategy that addresses the prevention of domestic violence. The biggest challenge is to unwrap the silence that covers domestic violence. Sadly, even today some women themselves don't question their husbands' violence against them. In India most systems are still so woefully patriarchal that there is no room for an egalitarian concept like respect for a woman. It is no use fighting for safe streets if women feel threatened in the place where they ought to feel the safest. A society that cannot provide its women enough security to live fearlessly within their own homes can only pretend a dangerous world.

Notes

1. Panda, Pradeep Kumar, (2003); *Right Based Strategies in the Prevention of Domestic Violence*, Working Paper series (344) by Centre for Development Studies, Kerala, p. 39.
2. Human Rights Watch Women's Rights Project, (1995); *The Human Rights Watch Global Report On Women's Human Rights*, published by Oxford University Press, New Delhi, p. 341.
3. *Supra* note 1.
4. *Supra* note 2, p. 142.
5. *Ibid.*
6. CEDAW, Article 2.
7. African Charter on Human and Peoples Rights, Articles 2, 3; American Convention on Human Rights, Articles 1, 24; and European Convention for the Protection of Human Rights and Fundamental Freedoms, Article 14.

8. *Supra* note 2, p. 344.
9. Shamla, S.K; "Indian Women: Problems and Challenges", in Ruhela, Dr. Sarya (Ed.) (1999); *Understanding The Indian Women Today— Problems And Challenges,* Indian Publishers, New Delhi, p. 24.
10. Krishna, S. Sri and Kumar S. Anil, "The Impact of Poverty on Violation of Women Human Rights" in Bhumali, Anil (Ed.) (2005); *Poverty and Human Rights of Women,* Serial Publications, New Delhi, p. 204.
11. Mukherjee, Isita (2002); *Violence Against Women—A Popular Intervention,* Vyas Prakashan, Kolkata, p. 61.
12. *Ibid.*, p. 62.

19

Cataclysmic Indian Dialectics of Collective Rights

Naorem Sanajaoba

Introduction

Globalization has brought the sovereign States economically closer to each other, while the political devolution of imperial States into building block Nation States remains as the ongoing process and the Multinational Corporations (MNCs) attempt to capture as much space as they could from the sovereign jurisdictions. Human Rights standard setting and benchmarking had preceded the globalization era and the Cold War confrontations. The world has achieved tangible Human Rights perceptions and consciousness thereby censuring rogue States and failed States, while sparing the soft States for their eventual self-corrections. India which is neither a rogue State like the USA,[1] nor one among the crowd of failed third world States passes through a rigorous test in advancing the post-modernist structuralism on the one hand, and also in holding into seize incompatible pluralistic historical legacies, particularly in the After Acquired Non-Self Governing Territory (AANSGT).[2]

Consequentially, collective national rights and Human Rights of the citizens in AANSGT[3] like the States of Manipur, Nagaland, Tripura and the other North-Eastern States (NES) at the far east of the mainland India have been subjected to military repression for more than half a century after the

British imperialists abandoned the occupied territories. State violence and reciprocal non-State violence provide the cataclysmic text and the cycle of violence that preempt peaceful resolutions of deep national contradictions[4] through either UN or international community sponsored dialogues on the one hand or, by way of holding plebiscites of the people in the region for suitable choice of their own international political and economic status, as it has been invariably conduced across the continents.

The Cataclysm

The plural State that India has been, had passed through the partition phobia of the 1947 vintage at the loss of a million lives in the most barbaric Hindu-Muslim bi-ethnic mobilization, has to undergo the nation building test with a loss of thousands of Sikh lives in 1984 in just three days and another thousand Muslim lives in 2002 Gujarat strife. Kashmiris claim that they lost several thousands of Kashmiri lives due to Indian military repression against the freedom fighters otherwise labeled as terrorists by the Indian administration.

Similarly, the north-eastern States that came to the Indian fold not so long ago in the mid-20th century make more or less similar pathetic claims as a result of State repression. East Pakistan, the present Bangladesh,[5] had witnessed in 1971 another loss of a couple of million lives during the liberation war; the Indian army played the decisive role in the partition of Pakistan. The Indian sub-continent obviously presents a clear testimony of sustained group violence or, armed conflicts[6] between the State and the non-state actors (NSAs) or the national liberation movements on a grand scale. Peasants' rights are also not fully addressed as Indian peasants commit suicide time and again. The glorified iniquitous globalization also marches upon the corpses of the Indian peasants and the debate goes on.

Besides the restive Kashmir State and seven NES, Maoist communist revolutionaries[7] (Communist Party Maoists—naxalites), unlike the official communist revisionist parties which prop up the Congress government from falling down because of want of numbers, contest the State administration in as many as thirteen additional States including Andhra Pradesh, Bihar, Chhattisgarh, Jharkhand, Madhya Pradesh, Maharashtra, Orissa, Uttar Pradesh and West Bengal, among others—as reported by the home ministry—while trying to liberate the Indian poor from capitalist exploitation and imperialist globalization. The encounters occupy the social space with the State torture machine geared up to meet the economic revolutionaries.

The Indian State simply finds its State repression counterproductive and faces clash of economies rather than what the American perceives of clash of civilizations in the non-Christian world. Unlike the USA which as the self-proclaimed Human Rights world leader, evades the binding obligations of the International Covenant on Economic, and Social Cultural Rights 1966, (ICESCR) India[8] which is a party to the ICESCR has binding international obligations towards the economic rights of the poor and the underprivileged. The professedly natural alliance that binds both India and the USA can hardly explain their parallel and divergent commitment towards economic obligations to the people.

Ethnic pluralism, multiple historical legacies and late territorial acquisitions characterize Indian human biomass and multinational entity. Indian State does not take cognizance of existence of indigenous population groups[9] as such in the context of the international peoples' Declarations[10] and profound contemporary concern of the indigenous issues. By default, the scheduled castes and tribes could be conceived as indigenous surrogates. The ethnic fissures and embedded racism create ethnic seductions and tremors that could lead to local or widespread cataclysm among the population groups.

Gender equality is undoubtedly a luxurious slogan of the power elites and the intellectuals, notwithstanding the failure of both the civil society and the State to wipe out gender inequality and religiously glorified male chauvinism. India comprises two nations—India of the vast poor people and India of the few rich people. The gender divide and subjugation of the national minorities render the official nationhood shaky.

The Indian Muslims who constitute nearly ten per cent of the entire population fail to get barely two per cent of membership of the national defense forces, possibly due to a deep-rooted mistrust of national minorities for one invented reason or another. The racial divide deeply runs in between the mainland India and the 40 million strong people of the NES. In spite of the utopian official propaganda, apartheid divides the NES people from the mainland dominant people. Mainland India routinely ridicules the NES people[11] of the AANSGT as Chinkis [Chinese particularly after the defeat of India in Indo-Chinese war in 1962]. The racial divide is very very natural.

The sporadic and intermittent populations or ethnic cataclysms that occur in mainland India are overshadowed by the half a century old engagement between the State forces and the national liberation guerrillas[12] of the NSAs. The parties involved in the State repression as well as the counter violence let loose by the NSAs have not reached out at or even outsourced a fair, just and durable political solution[13] and the political crises remain as festering wounds.

Poverty of Philosophy

The endemic social cataclysms could be officially attributed to cosmetic and rationalized reasons of State that could hardly be contested by a rational discourse of one kind or another and the State's argument holds the fort as long as the State defines its own existentialist, metaphorical truth or untruth whatever. Indian State since its inception in 1947 and access to republican status in 1950 by virtue of landlord-feudal-cattiest-racialist dominated constitution-making process, has been legitimizing asymmetrical hegemonic rule of the hegemonic mainland population group over the peripheral and after-acquired territorial population groups, particularly in the seven NES of the Indian State.

The embedded hegemony dictates the hegemonic interest under the cloak of legitimacy and unequal constitutionalism that inherently suffers from the basic premises of unequal nationalities *viz.*, the ruling nationality and the subject races in the peripheral States. The official constitutionalism, based on egalitarian values like socialism, secularism, among others is negated by the hegemonic constitution slim in practice. The hierarchical Indian civil society poses a monstrous evil and terror to Indian womanhood, Indian peasantry, national minorities and the subject race of the later occupied AANSGT in the NE region. The cataclysm happens to be the favorite child of the inherently unequal Indian civil society, which even the dignified Human Rights NGOs dare not fight out; the NGOs fight out the symptoms of the hidden terror within the unequal Indian civil society.

No other demonstration would be as loud and clear than the post-1991 Indian capitalism, officially adopted by the Union Government in direct and blatant negation of the State policy of socialism, as enshrined in the Preamble of the Constitution. Secularism is in the preamble while not more than two per cent of Indian Muslims could be recruited into defense forces. The north-easterners and the NES had been denied equal State representation in the Council of States and the union cabinet, although quislings could be occasionally recruited in key positions based on their proportionate loyalty to neo-colonialism and hegemonic rule.

The original sin that denied the principle of equality of nationalities and nations in the constitution-making process has been accepted by Indian States as virtue that transcends any opposition whatsoever from any rational discourse, and even the Indian leftist fails to contest the national inequalities because of their hidden racial philosophy and hackneyed hegemonic preeminence. The imperialism that the Indian State nurtured with sufficient labor and ingenuity had been virtually instrumental in resurrection of the festering wounds and inevitable historical uprisings addressed to the hegemonic Indian State as well as the mainland hegemonic people who retain the Indian State as their permanent hostage.

Even the National Human Rights Commission and national institutions failed to rise above the deeply entrenched hegemonic philosophy and institutions. The battle line has not, therefore, been drawn exclusively between the Indian State and the contesting NSAs or liberation groups, but more explicitly between the hegemonic, neo-colonial, imperial philosophy impregnably shrouded by a far-fetched patriotic cloak and the democratic philosophy of equalities of nations and nationalities that would hit hard upon all the conceptualized hegemonic philosophy.

It would be appropriate to cite the Indian Supreme Court judgment in 1997[14] on the humanity's most black law—the Armed Forces Special Powers Act (AFSPA), 1958,[15] Section 4[a] which permits any low level army officer to shoot to death any suspected citizen in the NES for more than half a century. Normally, at the drop of a hat when any mainland Indian citizen faces Human Rights discomfort, the Supreme Court admits and hears the case in a day or two under the Public Interest Litigation (PIL).

The Supreme Court did not take up a 1982 PIL case challenging the black law for a long 15 years until in the year 1997, when the UN Human Rights Committee grilled the Indian representative at the UN and he assured the Committee of triggering off the Supreme Court mechanism. The Supreme Court, with its racialist logic, invented all racial justification to uphold the black law. They call it judicial logic and the NES jurists call the 1997 judgment apartheid verdict.

Justice Jeevan Reddy in 2005 recommended for the repeal of the black AFSPA, in 1958. The United Nations Convention on the Elimination of All Forms of Racial Discrimination [CERD][16] also made the case in 2007 March for the repeal of the same statute. The critical conclusions of the UN Human Rights Committee in 1991[17] onwards about the same black statute, compounded by the global juristic tirade against such extrajudicial execution law isolate the Supreme Court's explicitly racialist and genocidal verdict as pariah. The Supreme Court has glorified and justified extrajudicial execution of the people of the AANSGT with its own shrouded reasons.

The cataclysmic apex Court juridical logic reinforces the otherwise racialist Indian mainstream philosophy. Somebody had rightly said that capitalist USA should never appoint a Marxian judge in the Supreme Court and in similar vein, Cuba should never appoint a capitalist judge in her bench *mutatis mutandi*, Indian hegemony would never make an exception to the isotopic hegemonic law. He is at first a first blood hegemony *a la* Nazi judge and then, a judge with bequeathed colonial common law traditions. Before the world fought the noble Nazis, it had to fight out the Nazi gospel and preaching. Under these given conditions, universally endorsed Human Rights standards have to be the first casualty and the rest is masterpiece of rhetoric and political metaphors—the metaphors that sabotage and hijack justice from within thereby leaving the civil society to respond naturally, presumably under the social contract theory that justifies the ultimate revolt.

The national institutions do the inbreeding of the cataclysms and the cycle continues in the best tradition of the chicken or the egg: which comes out first—the State repression or the NSA counter-violence. The cataclysm exists in one form or another—constitutional, juridical, institutional and whatever. The phenomena sustain because of the poverty of Indian political, legal, constitutional and national, hegemonic philosophy. Behind this very mistaken theory lies the great Indian empire instinct.

Sustained Casualty

The de-hegemonic evangelism which would launch a frontal assault on the philosophy of cataclysm and hegemony would be prejudicial one way or another, unless one records and re-affirms the widely approved benchmark of Human Rights standard setting and principles of good governance in equal measure either in the context of liberal democracy or a left-of-the-centre system.

No other fundamental Human Rights could ever be exercised until and unless the people in the AANSGT or, dependent territories or, colonial areas are first allowed to exercise their inalienable right to self-determination. In the nation-building process of Indian Republic of 1950, peripheral areas in the Indo-Myanmar region have been acquired by the administration without holding popular plebiscites and taking the people into confidence by way of officially assessing their consent to be taken over and governed.

Princely States of early Hindustan or Mughal Empire found the least difficulty in joining the dominion or later day republic. The federating process happened to be smooth and nostalgic; however, resistance occurred in the case of AANSGT in the north-eastern region of India. The questions remain hitherto unresolved albeit suppressed under tedious statecraft.

The historical imperative of properly addressing the national questions has to confront the Indian nation-building process in acquired territories. *Firstly*, the Government of India with its excellent reasons contests the national liberation movements in the NES as separatist forces that undermine the territorial integrity of the country. *Secondly*, the national liberation authorities in the region contest the above stance as a colonial pretence of the imperialist India and resist the Indian defense forces by way of guerrilla resistance.

The West as usual had never seen human causes beyond their western interests only and had never tried to play a peace broker in places where both Marxist rule and hydrocarbons are found missing. They love the Arab oil as long as the subterranean stocks are not exhausted. This is again a demonstration of poverty of the Western philosophy. The international community simply ignores the conflicts and eludes responsibility.

As the *sine qua non* of the individuals and people willing to exercise their fundamental individual Human Rights have been victims of a poverty of philosophy, the fundamental human freedoms queue at the end of the traffic jam. The much talked about conflict-resolution of the epoch has given stress to democratic and people friendly mechanisms. One of the most efficient and peace conducive instrumentalities, among others, is the resort to plebiscite on the political status of people or, the status plebiscites.

International law and international relations had been consistently favorable to the resort to the peaceful, democratic method in the course of conflict-resolutions.[18] Henry Kissinger armed with his unprecedented Vietnam statecraft, in his diplomacy had categorically stated that guerrillas could not be given a decisive defeat even by the USA. If conflict-resolution is taken seriously by the parties in conflict, plebiscite could be instrumental.

The contemporary State practices about resorting to plebiscite as a credible, democratic mechanism of peaceful conflict-resolution of chronic national issues of vital importance give evidence to the strong possibility of reaching out to durable and fair solutions across the five continents. In the past, during the epoch of the League of Nations too, as many as fifty-two plebiscites had been conducted. Judicial settlement of disputes and armed conflicts might have been chosen ways of advancing international relations, yet the plebiscite had never been made a second choice by several rational actors in international relations. The applied science of international law and relations demonstrate the success story of plebiscites. Proven cases testify the mechanism as reliable and democratic.

The Indian system has very closely followed British system for historical reasons. Among others, reference may be made of Good Friday Agreement in April 1998 in order to resolve nearly a century-old British-Northern Ireland armed conflicts with the USA as a guarantor. Indian decision makers could look towards Scottish example in spite of drawing inspiration from the statecraft of Idi Amin or President Milosevic *et. al.* Poverty of philosophy or enhanced imperial thought may block the creativity of the rulers and their conscience.

The USA, which India looks up to as the natural democratic ally, also did not hold up the conducting of a series of plebiscites in its commonwealth of Puerto Rico in 1967, 1991, 1993 and in 1998. A fifth Puerto Rico status plebiscite has not been ruled out.

The people freely express their wishes about their political and economic status and no democratic government of significance would stall the people from exercising their inalienable right to express wishes freely.

The Puerto Rico[19] case which has been on the American political agenda since 1950 until today would emulate Indian leadership who had far too long had the hand in armed hostilities. Canada too followed suit in allowing Francophone Quebec to conduct plebiscites in 1980 and for the second time in 1995. Even the Canadian Supreme Court in 1998 juridically endorsed plebiscite in Quebec, and the Indian Supreme Court could take similar positions in spite of taking the assumed stance of political hardliner. The Government of India could also seek Supreme Court's advisory opinion on the subject in order to terminate the hostilities in the NES, among others.

Successful plebiscites had been performed in Montenegrin in Europe in 2006 and in East Timor (Timor Leste) in Asia in 1999. In Africa, even after the lapse of the MINURSO mandate of the UN, the Western Saharan plebiscite has been merely deferred. In India, plebiscite had never been an ordinary folk tale. The Government of India had performed plebiscite in Junagadh on 20 February, 1948 in order to ascertain the peoples' choice of either acceding to Indian dominion or Pakistan and also one more referendum in associate State of Sikkim after Indian military occupation in 1975.

However, the Kashmir plebiscite as UN Security Council had resolved to conduct in 1951 could not be held by India[20] and Pakistan. The select plebiscites substantially demonstrate the successful and peaceful resolution of deep conflicts which rational actors resort to with honest convictions. However, war mongers would not pay heed to peaceful methods of conflict resolutions, of which the plebiscite is the most democratic device so far.

A RATIONAL DISCOURSE

[In lieu of a conclusion]

International Human Rights and humanitarian laws have been codified and complied by a large number of States in the comity of nations, notwithstanding certain reservations, Declarations and selective non-compliance of international obligations by a couple of States or in extreme cases by the rogue States, which selectively comply with general international law at their convenience.

The international community has set the benchmarks, deviation from which is considered exceptional and immoral.

A rational discourse, however, has made the world worthy of dignified living and security of communities and individuals. The Indian State has its own legitimate responsibility and enormous contributions to the common human causes. However, it could correct the clearly defined fault-lines and address to issues of enormous Human Rights significance like those cited above.

The dialectics of conflict resolution advances by breaking up the conventional and imperial mindsets of the decision makers and explores new ways of breaking up the impasse. In the process, the international actors have to honor their treaty obligations—particularly of the 1966 Covenants. India, unlike other southern States, had been a NAM (Non-Aligned Movement) leader and incidentally India had strongly espoused the global decolonization since 1960s by way of seconding the Soviet proposal of UN General Assembly Resolution No. 1514 of 1960.

India's global decolonization agenda would be fruitful if it would also implement its own resolution in regard to the AANSGT of the country, by resorting to peaceful and democratic methods like plebiscite and leaving aside its half a century old brutal State repression in the NES. India is under binding treaty obligations to report to the UN Human Rights Committee, its concern over other under-addressed collective Human Rights, at the time of its submission of the fourth report, which was long overdue in 2001.

Notes

1. See books by Noam Chomsky about American enterprises in sovereign countries.
2. The UN General Assembly Resolution No. 66[1] dated, 13.12.1946, 74 NSGT [Non-Self Governing Territories] had been recognized. After 1955, several other territories administered by Spain and Portugal had been added as AA-NSGT [After Acquired-NSGT].

   Subsequently determined NSGT in addition to the 74 NSGT of 1946 had been—Cocos Islands, Comoro, New Hebrides, British Ocean

   Indian territory, Cape Verde, Guinea-Bissau, Sao Tome, Sao Joao, Angola, Mozambique, Goa dependencies, Macau, East Timor,

Equatorial Guinea Ifni, Western Sahara, Southern Rhodesia.

James Crawford, *The Creation of States in International Law*, Oxford, 1979, Ch. 14, pp. 356-86. As many as 7 Associate States emerged in 1977.

Even today UN recognizes 16 NSGT for subsequent self-determination and UNPO lists another 40 more nations. However, two dozen AANSGT are being left out by the UN due to lack of international pressure.

The NSGT would bear the following criteria: geographically separate, ethnically distinct, politically subjugated [see NE region of India], not being a tiny enclave, absence of full measure of government, right of self-determination had not been exercised even once. See Literature on Right of the People to Self-determination in international law.

Contemporary international law has accepted progressive interpretation of the laws and rules by the International Court of Justice, exercise of procedural discretion of the UN general assembly in extending the list of the AANSGT in the context of Article 73 of the UN Charter, 1945.

3. R.M. Lahiri, The Annexation of Assam, Firma, 1975; PDM, Annexation of Manipur, 1949, Imphal, 1995; See Nicholas Mansergh, *Transfer of Power*, 1942-47, all volumes.

   Army occupation of Sikkim, Indian protectorate in 1975 and rigged referendum for annexation to India, see M.K. Dhar, *Open Secrets-India's Intelligence Unveiled*, Manas, New Dlehi, 2005, pp. 192, 222, 232. Leaders including Prime Minister Morarji Desai criticized Indian annexation of Sikkim.

4. N. Sanajaoba's works:

   Right of Oppressed Nations [And Peoples], Omsons, New Delhi, 1996;

   Human Rights in the New Millennium, Manas, New Delhi, 2000, chapters 8 and 10 on Indigenous Peoples;

   Human Rights Current Issues, Omsons, New Delhi, 2004, chapters 8 and 9 on National questions;

   Current Legal Essays, Akansha, New Delhi, 2007, chapters 5 to 8 on Ethnic conflicts, Federal issues, Negotiations etc., among others.

5. Bangladesh—the erstwhile East Pakistan in 1971 had been an inalienable part of Pakistan. However, the Government of India in 1971 had recognized East Pakistan or Bangladesh thereafter as a Non-Self Governing Territory at the United Nations Security Council-SCOR, 1606th meeting, 4 December, 1971, para 185,

cited in *op. cit.* James Crawford, p. 116. Arguments had been advanced from different perceptions as well.

Cf. "Secession of Bangladesh in Ingrid Detter", *The Law of War*, Cambridge University Press, 2000, p. 431; Malcom N. Shaw, *International Law*, CUP, 1997, p. 141; *Sunday Magazine*, 18-24 September, 1988, p. 35. Indira Gandhi and RAW, trained refugees to become Mukti Bahini.

See M.K. Dhar, *Open Secrets op. cit*, p. 138, among others about Indian initiative to create Bangladesh. The author had been India's top secret service official to run the show and create events.

6. See "Indian Invasion of Goa" in Malcom N. Shaw, *op. cit.*, p. 795; James Crawford, *op. cit.*, p. 112-13, 319, 370, 435, among others. Apart from million lives lost during partition, and ongoing war casualties in Kashmir from 1947-48 till date, massacres took place in Hyderabad in 1948. Sunderlal report submitted to the prime minister had recorded the killing of 27 to 40 thousand civilians during Indian police action in Hyderabad and Nehru wrote to his home minister Sradar Patel about the massacre of 'possibly some thousands of Muslims by the Hindus', see "Of a Massacre Untold", in *Front Line*, March 16, 2001, p. 113-15. The human cataclysm in India had been unprecedented. Media by and large does the cover up against professional ethics even today.
7. Fifty-five districts had been affected by Maoist revolutionary violence and BRGF [Backward Regions Garnt Fund] had been organized in as many as 250 districts as response to Maoist revolutions, see *Frontline*, "Naxal Terror" cover story, September 21, 2007, p. 24. In India's adjoining sovereign State of Nepal, as many as 13,000 Maoists cadres lost lives till 2006 in their struggle to abolish any form of monarchy and authoritarianism.
8. Naorem Sanajaoba, International Dimensions of Human Rights and International Obligations of India, in 40 *J.I.L.I.* [1998], Human Rights special issue, pp. 87-113.
9. *Op. cit.* N. Sanajaoba, *Human Rights in the New Millennium*, pp. 106-16
10. The UN Human Rights Council has in June 2006, adopted the Draft Declaration on the Rights of the Indigenous Peoples.
11. Barring Lower Assam, the rest of the seven States are the homeland of the Mongolian and Austric peoples since historical times. Abundant literature is available about the people of the NE region. See, among others, N. Sanajaoba (ed.), *Manipur Past and Present* Volume I, II, III, IV, 1988 to 2005, Mittal Publications, New Delhi. [Search Naorem Sanajaoba in Google that makes about 800 plus entries on the author.]

12. Home pages of the NLMs; ULFA home page claims "To liberate Assam [a land of 78, 529 square kms], through armed national liberation struggles from clutches of the illegal occupation of India and to establish a sovereign Independent Assam".

    The PLA [RPF] of Manipur State in India in its memorandum dated 21 Spetember, 1999 addressed to the UN Secretary General, had appealed the UN , "The Revolutionary Peoples Front [RPF] beseeches and petitions all the appropriate UN authorities to allow the indigenous Manipur people to exercise their inalienable right to self-determination, independence and sovereignty". The 171-pages memorandum in its annex incorporates 10 official, historical maps which did not include Manipur in India.

    The NSCN home page: since 1980, the NSCN, later on bifurcated into two outfits demands independence of Nagaland State of India and both the wings desire to create greater Nagaland including large parts of Burma, Manipur, Assam, Arunachal Pradesh and present Nagaland State. Talks with Government of India had started since 1997 and the talks continue *ad infinitum*. The liberation movements continue in Tripura, Meghalaya, Arunachal Pradesh, among others.

13. *Op. cit.* N. Sanajaoba, *Current Legal Essays*,—ch. 7, "Structure of Negotiation between Metropolitan Power and National Liberation Authority", pp. 187-227.

    Cf. Law Department, Gauhati University, A REPORT-open forum-GOI-ULTRA NEGOTIATION, 22 January 2005, circulated to NGOs, government officials and media.

14. Naga Peoples Movement for Human Rights vs. Union of India, 27.11.1997, in 1997 [III] GLT [SC] 50. The Supreme Court judgment had been criticized by PUDR, PUCL, Amnesty International, all the NGOs in the region and by academics.

15. Justice Jeevan Reddy report, 2005 recommended the repeal of the black law.

    Cf. All India peoples Tribunal comprising Justice Rajinder Sachar, Professor Naorem Sanajaoba, Justice Vinod Shankar Dave, and two more members conducted public hearing and recommended on 20 February, 2005 the repeal of the draconian law, see *Assam Tribune* 21 February, 2005.

    Cf. N. Sanajaoba, "Revisiting Justice Reddy Report on Armed Forces Special Powers Act, 1958", in *Gauhati University Journal of Law*, VI, 2006, pp. 9-42.; see *Asian Centre for Human Rights*, New Delhi, The AFSPA, 2005 [www.achrweb.org]; Amnesty International, A Briefing on the Armed Forces [Special Powers] Act, 1958, 2005, among others.

16. 70th session 19 February-9 March, 2007 of the UN CERD urged upon Government of India to repeal AFSPA, 158, UN Human Rights Council took up the same position on 27 March, 2007. In August, 2007, Administrative Reforms Commission of the Government of India also urged the government to repeal the *black law*; reportedly the Indian army, the second largest in the world expressed that without the *black law*, their hands are tied before the liberation guerrillas. The admission of the AFSPA discussion in the UN CERD in 2007 itself gives sufficient evidence that there are strong racial undertones in the essence of the *black law*, as it had been discriminatory against the NE region peoples since 1958.
17. See UN, yearbook of the UN Human Rights Committee 1983-84, volume II, India Initial report, pp. 341-52; UN official Records of the Human Rights Committee 1990/91,volume II, India, pp. 137-50, 381-86; UN, Official Records of the Human Rights Committee, 1990/91,volume I, India discussion of the second report, pp. 147-68; Critical observations etc. See UN, Human Rights Committee, CCPR/C/79 Add.81, 4 August 1997, India, Concluding observations, among other reports of the UN.
18. *Supra* f.n. 4, works of Naorem Sanajaoba; Records—Special Lectures of Naorem Sanajaoba-8 February, 1976, Regional Medical College forum, 'Is revolution necessary for social change?' His other lectures on South Asia, UN decolonisation, East Timor, Minurso's mandate, Microstates, NSGT in general, NSGT in South Asia, Palestine, Chechenya, Montenegro and Purto Rico, 2007, among others [cited in Acknowledgement, *op. cit.* Current Legal Essays].
19. Puerto Rico plebiscites had been held in 1967, 1991, 1993 and 1998 for the determination of its political status either full independence from the USA or, commonwealth status or, American statehood. [Wikipedia, the free encyclopedia].

    After President Jimmy Carter had supported the plebiscites of Puerto Ricans, in August, 1979, the USA Congress had passed a joint politics resolution backing self-dètermination the island nation of the USA. [Source, SPAN, July, 1980, USIS, New Delhi, p. 6.]

    In Canada, the Supreme Court, in 'Reference re-Secession', 20 August, 1998 made the decision about Quebec:

    "...The other provinces and the federal government would have no basis to deny the right of the Government of Quebec to pursue secession should a clear majority of the people of Quebec choose that goal, so long as in doing so, Quebec respects the rights of others."

[Source—Canada's portal—Quick guide]. Scottish referendum, plebiscites in Quebec and Puerto Rico could emulate the South Asian regimes in honestly resolving national questions as old as more than half a century, particularly in Assam, Manipur, Nagaland just to cite a few, as military solution had been found counterproductive.

20. Pakistan factor had confused the plebiscite issue of the Kashmiris. The three Indo-Pak wars since 1948 have not succeeded in giving a lasting Kashmir solution; consequently, both the countries paid a heavy price in remaining as underdeveloped economies. Recently, Government of India had shifted towards developmental issues while hinting at a dialogue process. See Shreedhar, "UPA's Strategy on J&K", in *World Focus*, Dec., 2004, pp. 15-16.; Cf. features on Kashmir by A.G. Noorani, in *Frontline* issues, July 31, 1998, among others. Nearly every periodical in India carries features on Kashmir issues almost religiously till 2007.

20

Protecting Human Rights in the European Union: The Charter of Fundamental Rights Perspective

Md. Jahid Hossain Bhuiyan

Introduction

The text of the founding treaties of the European Communities,[1] in their original form, did not contain specific provision guaranteeing fundamental Human Rights.[2] This caused considerable unease in the constitutional Courts of some Member States, especially in Germany which incorporated Human Rights provisions in its Constitution.[3] Nonetheless, it is possible to say that the Treaty of Rome incorporated certain provisions which paved the way to protect basic Human Rights. Thus, the Treaty affirms willingness of the organization to preserve and strengthen peace and liberty,[4] to improve living and working conditions and to abolish discrimination based on nationality among citizens of the Member States.[5] It also guaranteed equal pay for equal work for male and female workers.[6] In order to strengthen the respect for Human Rights/Fundamental Rights some proposals have been made.[7]

The European Court of Justice (ECJ) enjoys the credit for gradually developing a system of guarantees for Fundamental Rights and strengthening the Human Rights doctrine within the European Union (EU).[8] In the landmark *Stauder* case, in 1969, the Court held that "the fundamental human rights enshrined in the general principles of Community law and protected by the Court".[9] Witte has stated that the ECJ created its Community doctrine of Fundamental Rights in order to protect the supremacy of EC law over the national law of the Member States. He adds, however, that the Court's activism must also be seen as a straightforward response to the Community's growing capacity to affect Fundamental Rights to an extent unforeseen at the time the European Communities were created.[10]

In the judgment *Internationale Handelsgesellschaft* in 1970, the Court acknowledged that respect for Fundamental Rights formed an integral part of the general principles of Community law whose observance is the prime obligation of the Community. The Court also said that constitutional traditions common to the Member States inspire Fundamental Rights as general principles.[11] Later, in the *Nold* case the Court reinforced this, and also asserted that for the protection of Fundamental Rights, the international Human Rights treaties which Member States had ratified were also relevant.[12] In *Rutili*, the Court explicitly referred to the European Convention on Human Rights (ECHR).[13] In *Wachauf*, the Court expressed the view that the requirements of securing the protection of Fundamental Rights in the Community legal order are also binding on the Member States when they implement Community laws.[14] In the *ERT* judgment of June 18, 1991, the ECJ held that the Community law obliges the Member States to respect for Fundamental Rights.[15]

It should be borne in mind that though the ECJ referred to the ECHR in numerous judgments it for the first time referred to the caselaw of the European Commission or European Court of Human Rights in 1996.[16]

In fact, the Court through its judgments has played a significant role to secure judicial protection of Community rights across the European Union by setting standards. In such situations, the individual Member States are only required to comply with the minimum standards laid down when they are implementing Community law.[17] But many Member States have not restricted themselves to the standards of protection required by EC law. They apply higher standards of protection than those mentioned in EC law. However, the expansion of the EU's activities and competences, particularly in the third pillar areas, has added a new dimension to the ECJ's jurisdiction, particularly in areas which is also covered by the ECHR.[18]

The issue of the protection of Fundamental Rights came to the fore in Treaty text in the Preamble to the Single European Act (SEA) in 1986.[19] It is noted that throughout the years, the European Parliament (EP) has played a crucial role in promoting and protecting Human Rights within the Community.[20] For instance, in 1989, the EP proposed the adoption of a Declaration of Fundamental Rights as part of a 'Constitution' for the EU. In fact, the parliament is under an obligation to respect for Human Rights in the exercise of its advisory, supervisory, and budgetary powers under the Union and Communities Treaties.[21]

The Maastricht Treaty, establishing the European Union (EU), declared respect for Human Rights as explicit preconditions for accession of new members to the EU, among the Union's guiding principles.[22] Though TEU is not a Human Rights instrument, it speaks of Human Rights in the economic and social spheres.[23] The Treaty says: "The Union shall respect fundamental rights, as guaranteed by the European Convention for the Protection of Human Rights and Fundamental Freedoms...and as they result from the constitutional traditions common to the Member States, as general principles of Community law".[24]

The next development is the treaty amending the TEU, Treaty of Amsterdam, which was signed in October 1997 and came into force on May 1, 1999. New Article 6(1) of the Treaty states: "The Union is founded on the principles of liberty, democracy, respect for human rights and fundamental freedoms, and the rule of law, principles which are common to the Member States".[25] Article 7 of the TEU and Article 309(2) of the Treaty establishing European Community (TEC) authorize the Council to take measures against Member States which have violated the principles of Article 6. The Treaty of

Amsterdam also incorporated provisions to strengthen the Community's legal basis for the protection of Human Rights. For instance, it authorizes the Community to act against discrimination based on sex, racial or ethnic origin, religion or belief, disability, age or sexual orientation.[26]

The object of this paper is to trace the origins of the Charter of Fundamental Rights of the European Union. The paper will further consider some of the issues surrounding the Charter. It will also examine the legal status of the Charter. It will further examine whether the Charter and the European Convention on Human Rights are complementary or competing. This paper will state Human Rights standards in the Charter. It will also examine the Human Rights that will be most commonly invoked in competition law cases.

The Issues

Whether the EU needs a Bill of Rights

Member States of the European Union have ratified European, especially European Convention on Human Rights (ECHR),[27] and international Human Rights instruments.[28] The ECJ has also generally upheld ECHR rights. So, the question raises whether the EU needs a Bill of Rights. One author observed that the prime advantage of adopting a Human Rights instrument would be in its symbolism—the visible commitment of the Community to Human Rights.[29] On the other hand, Witte said: "there is no glaring human rights deficit in the legal orders of the Member States, which the ECJ should set out to remedy".[30] It may be inferred from his statement that he did not find any justification to adopt a written catalogue of rights. It is true that the situation of Human Rights in the EU is better than any other region of the world. The members of the EU are party to the European Convention on Human Rights, 1950 which came into force in 1953. The Convention has enormous contribution to develop Human Rights in Europe. But in order to strengthen more Fundamental Rights/Human Rights within the EU, adoption of a written catalogue of rights is required.

The debate on how to strengthen the respect for Human Rights within the Community started in the early 1970s. In 1973, the European Parliament invited the Commission to submit a report on how the Commission intends to protect Fundamental Rights contained in the Constitutions of Member States.[31] The Commission in its report to the Parliament, *inter alia,* stated that a written catalogue of Fundamental Rights would improve the protection of Fundamental Rights within the Community. In 1976, the Commission supported for adopting a catalogue of Fundamental Rights. But the Commission emphasized the development of economic and fundamental social rights. The Commission's report in 1976 did not satisfy the European Parliament. And the European Parliament wanted the Commission to follow-up its study. Within the Community, it becomes burning issue that the Commission should commit itself to a written catalogue of guaranteed Fundamental Rights either in the form of a Community Bill of Rights or by accession of the Community to the ECHR. The result was the 1979 Memorandum on Accession of the Communities to the European Convention for the Protection of Human Rights and Fundamental Rights.[32] The Commission in its Memorandum stated that absence of a written catalogue of Fundamental Rights is, *inter alia*, responsible for affecting the legal order of the Community. The Commission felt it necessary to create a special Bill of Rights for the EU to cover up the lackings of a written catalogue. But the Commission rejected the idea for the time being.[33]

From the above discussion it is clear that before the adoption of the Charter of Fundamental Rights, the EU's institutions also felt the necessity of adopting a separate catalogue of Fundamental Rights/Bill of Rights for the EU.

One of the principal advantages of adopting a special Bill of Rights for the EU lies in the opportunity to consider the advances in Human Rights protection since the adoption of the European Convention on Human Rights in 1950. Another principal advantage is that it can be adapted fully to the particular characteristics and requirements for the European Community. In addition, it would strengthen the position of individuals in relation to the Union and its institutions as well as in relation to Member States acting within the scope of Community law. Adopting a Bill of Rights would ensure the visibility and transparency of the rights of the citizens.[34]

However, some scholars expressed the view that Bill of Rights for the EU is not necessary. O'Learey seems to be of the view that additional differences in the Fundamental Rights standards guaranteed by the European Court of Justice and the Court of Human Rights will take place through the adoption of a Bill of Rights.[35]

Sometimes, it is contended that the adoption of a separate catalogue of Fundamental Rights for the EU would protect Fundamental Rights within the Community. And this could be done either in conjunction with, or as an alternative to, accession to the ECHR.[36] As regards this opinion, Toth says:

> In many ways, this would probably be the worst possible scenario. It would mean establishing a dual system of human rights protection in Europe, one for the Community and one for the other States; a splitting up of the present single set of rights, which would undermine the authority of the Convention.[37]

Should the EU accede to the ECHR?

Although in the mid-1970s, the Commission was in favor of adopting a catalogue of Fundamental Rights,[38] in 1979 it was reluctant to adopt such catalogue and floated the idea that the European Community should accede to the ECHR in order to strengthen the respect for Human Rights.[39] The Commission renewed the proposal in 1990 and argued, "there is a conspicuous gap in the Community legal system" that could be covered up by an accession of the Community to the ECHR.[40] On April 26, 1995, the Council of the European Union requested the ECJ to give its opinion on whether accession of the European Community to the ECHR was consistent with the Treaty establishing the European Community. In its Opinion in 1996,[41] the ECJ said that accession of the Community to the ECHR was not compatible with the Treaty establishing the European Community because, at the time when the Opinion was sought, no specific arrangements had been made concerning the way in which the Community would become subject to the machinery of judicial control established by the Commission. The Court said the Treaty did not give any general power to the Community institutions to make rules on Human Rights or to conclude international conventions in this field.[42] It was suggested that Article 308 (former Article 235)[43] of the Treaty could be used as the legal basis for accession. The Court found that Article 308 (former Article 235) does not give the legal basis for accession.

However, the Opinion acknowledged that "respect for human rights is...a condition of the lawfulness of Community acts",[44] a view affirmed by ECJ in caselaw time and again over the decades, even before the incorporation of Human Rights provision in the Treaties.[45] The Court stated that an accession could take place only by way of Treaty amendment.[46] According to Lenaerts, this was a "thinly veiled appeal to the Community legal order's constituent power to assume its responsibilities by amending the "constitutional character" of that legal order".[47] Jacobs says, it does not mean that the Court opposed to accession by the Community or by the Union. He also adds that the President and other members of the Court have expressed themselves personally in favor of accession of the Community to the ECHR.[48]

The Opinion of the Court has been criticized by several scholars. Craig and Burca observed:

> The Court of Justice may be attempting to act as another European Human Rights Court, when its primary purpose and function were originally quite different, and when another Court has specifically been entrusted by the Member States of the Council of Europe with that jurisdiction and role. Related to this concern is the view that the Community and its institutions should in fact subject to the ECHR system, including to the jurisdiction of the Strasbourg institutions, but the ECJ has for the moment blocked this by ruling that the Community lacks competence to accede, and the Member States are

> unwilling to make the amendments necessary to facilitate accession.[49]

Weile and Fries say:

> The suspicion is, therefore, despite strenuous denials by certain members of the Court, that it was the 'institutional implications' that caused most trouble and that principal among these was the institutional implication which would submit the Court of Justice, like its constitutional brethren in the Member States, to scrutiny by the Strasbourg Court.[50]

Burrows states that it is a disappointing decision since, in practice, Treaty amendment is not an easy task and, the Member States and the Community institutions failed to reach into conclusion on how to ensure protection of Human Rights in the Community.[51] Tridimas says that the view of the Court is not wholly convincing. As to the competency, the Commission and several Member States argued that protection of Fundamental Rights within the Community is a component of all Community policies or, as the Commission put it, a transverse objective forming an integral part of the Community's objectives. The ECJ did not pay attention of that argument which, it submitted, is not unmeritorious. The Court held that the competence of the Community and the powers of the institutions are not similar.[52] According to Butterman: "in Opinion 2/94 the Court fails to distinguish between respect for human rights as an *objective* of the European Community and respect for human rights as a *condition* for the lawfulness of Community action".[53] She also adds that the failure to distinguish between these two issues ignores the special character of Human Rights as an expression of a vision of humanity which vests the deepest values in the individual which, hence, may not be compromised by anyone.

But Arnull supported the Opinion and said that accession is not necessary. He wrote: "The House of Lords Select Committee on the European Communities has examined the question of accession on two occasions, once in 1980[54] again in 1992.[55] On both occasions the Committee opposed accession on the basis that any benefits would be marginal and that the

Community had more pressing tasks. That seems to me to be even more true today."[56]

Though the ECJ in its Opinion 2/94 acknowledges respect for Human Rights as a condition of the lawfulness of Community acts it also took the position that accession of the Community to the ECHR could not take place without Treaty amendment. This opinion of the Court created an obstacle to accession of the Community to the ECHR as it is well known that Treaty amendment is a long and complex task. Thus the accession of the EU to the ECHR became uncertain.

However, accession of the Community to the ECHR would have different advantages. Accession to the ECHR, including submission of the Community institutions to the jurisdiction of European Court of Human Rights, would make uniform interpretation of Human Rights jurisprudence in Europe.[57] If the accession takes place, the European Court of Justice would be accountable to the European Court of Human Rights like the superior Courts of ECHR States are accountable to it.[58] Justice urged EU accession to the ECHR in order "to ensure the best possible protection of human rights within the Union".[59] Accession would be a strong political signal for coherence between the Union and the "greater Europe".[60] Siskova offers the following advantages of accession: the accession will formalize the status of the Convention in the Community legal order; the accession will to a great extent strengthen the protections of the rights and freedoms of the individuals and their legal certainty, the accession will define precisely the limits of the responsibility of the EC/EU institutions for their actions which interfere in the areas dealing with the Human Rights; the accession will exclude the divergent interpretations of Human Rights terms from the ECJ and ECHR; the accession will increase the democratic legitimacy of EC/EU and of its actions; the accession will develop Human Rights in the whole of Europe without the dividing lines. The respect for Human Rights will become the basis for the future construction of Europe.[61]

Amongst scholars also there are divergent views concerning accession to the Convention. For instance, Toth says, *inter alia*, that if the accession takes place the ECJ would become subject to the control machinery established by the Convention, and in particular, to the jurisdiction of the ECHR in respect of Human Rights. This might be contrary to the existing rules which provides that the ECJ alone to be the final interpreter of Community law.[62]

Notwithstanding the divergent opinions as regards the EU accession to the ECHR, the EU should accede to the ECHR. It will play an important role to protect the rights of the individuals. At present EU is not touchable by the Court of Human Rights. In other words, activities of the EU are not subject to examination by the European Court of Human Rights and individuals do not have opportunity to bring actions against the EU institutions before the European Court of Human Rights. So in order to fill up this gap, the EU should accede to the ECHR. Thus Human Rights situation within the EU will improve significantly. The ECHR being a 'living document' is developed all the time by the Court of Human Rights in the light of contemporary standards.[63] And accession to the ECHR would not undermine the autonomy of the Community legal order.[64]

Origins of the Charter of Fundamental Rights of the European Union

In 1996 the European Court of Justice expressed the view that "as Community law now stands, the Community has no competence to accede to the European Convention for the Protection of Human Rights and Fundamental Rights".[65] Certain Member States which took a negative attitude to accession were extremely happy owing to this view.[66] However, the discussion on how to protect Fundamental Rights within the EU has not been set aside. During the tenure of the German Presidency of the EU, the German Government launched an idea of drafting a Charter of Fundamental Rights for the EU.[67] At the Cologne European Council, the EU Heads of State or Government agreed on June 3 and 4, 1999 to set up a body with the task of drafting a charter "in order to make their overriding importance and relevance more visible to the Union citizens". At the Cologne Council, it was further agreed that this body should prepare a draft document in advance of the European Council at the end of the year 2000, under the French Presidency.[68] On October 15 and 16, 1999, the Heads of State and Government at the Tampere European Council agreed on the precise composition[69] and working method[70] of the Body charged with the task of drafting the Charter of Fundamental Rights.[71] Inclusion of representatives from applicant countries on this Convention was not felt necessary by the Council, only an "open dialogue" with the Heads of State or Governments was foreseen.[72] But the Council granted access to the Convention's meeting rooms to the person who so intended. Such person was also able to obtain documents produced by it.[73]

The Body *i.e.*, the Convention has enjoyed liberty in defining its aims, setting criteria as to the rights to be included, formulating the rights to be included, drafting the necessary restrictions, and answering open questions.[74] It is noted that German Government nominated Roman Herzog, their former President, to the Convention. His subsequent selection as the President of the Convention dashed the hopes of some EU Member States that the Convention and the Charter would be low-key affair.[75] The Convention finalized its work on October 2, 2000[76] and the draft of the Charter was approved at the informal *European Council Session* in Biarritz on October 13 and 14. The European Parliament and the European Commission respectively approved the Charter on November 14, 2000 and December 6, 2000.[77] On December 7, 2000, at the European Council meeting in Nice, the President of the European Parliament, Mrs. Nicole Fontaine, the President of the European Commission, Mr. Romano Prodi and the President of the Council of Ministers, Mr. Hubert Vedrine signed and proclaimed the EU Charter of Fundamental Rights.[78] The Charter was signed in five minutes, in the presence of the Heads of State and Government, and the President of the EC as well as the President of the EP were not allowed time to deliver the speeches they had prepared for the occasion.[79]

The Legal Status of the Charter

At Cologne, no decision was taken as to the incorporation of the proposed Charter into the Treaties.[80] Apparently, all the Member States did not unanimously support the idea of incorporating the Charter into the Treaties.[81] However, in his speech to the body, Roman Herzog on December 17, 1999 expressed the view that "we are going to draft a text that will not immediately binding as European law or Community law. Despite this, we should constantly keep the objective in mind that the Charter which we are drafting must one day, in the not too distant future, become legally binding...we should therefore proceed as if we had to submit a legally binding list..."[82] Due to the strong opposition of certain Member States "the Charter of Fundamental Rights was not adopted as a legally binding instrument *per se* in Nice".[83] Jacobs and White state, "The waters have been...clouded by the solemn proclamation of the Charter" because "This document has no legally binding force and there remains intriguing questions about its impact on the protection of fundamental rights within the European Union".[84] Kyriaku says unless the Charter is incorporated into the Treaty, it is not binding.[85] The Charter as a political Declaration is not completely deprived of any practical significance. As Douglass-Scott says, "in spite of its non-binding status and history of wrangling, the Charter already does have some legal, even constitutional effect".[86] Eeckhout states that "As the Charter is primarily aimed at strengthening the protection of fundamental rights as regards policies and acts carried out by the EU institutions, the solemn proclamation already expresses some level of voluntary commitment which may produce some type of legal effect".[87] Wiener observes that the Charter has no legal standing but national constitutions of Member States, the ECHR, the UDHR, and the TEU legally protect the rights contained in the Charter.[88]

Though the Charter is not legally binding, "[i]n practice...the legal effect of the solemn proclamation will tend to be similar to that of its insertion into the Treaties on which the Union is founded".[89] Groussot observes, "a good half of the

Charter is already *de facto* binding. Indeed, it might be said that the Charter represents a codification *de facto* of the general principles. Those general principles constitute legal binding norms and justiciable".[90] Liisberg says that the Charter is non-binding "soft law" instrument in the Community legal order.[91] Tesauro states that though the Member States representatives who were gathered in Cologne and then in Nice did not intend that the Charter should be legally binding that the Charter will soon become a standard of Constitutions' legality which both the EU and national institutions are due to respect, as well as the citizens of the EU.[92] Weatherill says that the Charter "is currently non-binding, but it carries with it a claim to a central role in any more ambitious constitutional re-shaping of the Union. After all it is not politically easy to resist the claims of a 'Charter of Fundamental Rights'."[93] McBridge is of the opinion that the Charter is not legally binding. But it does not necessarily mean that the provisions contained in the Charter will not be implemented nor that, like the UDHR, its provisions will not ultimately lead to instruments with more legal force.[94] Eeckhout states that although the Charter is not legally binding the Courts can use it as confirmation rather than legal basis of their rulings on the issue relating to Fundamental Rights.[95] Looking at the practical use of the Charter, it can be concluded that it "has legal bite even if it is formally not binding".[96]

Some commentators expressed that incorporation of the Charter in the EU Constitution will determine the legal status of the Charter. If the Charter is incorporated in the Constitution it will undoubtedly become the centerpiece of European Human Rights discourse.[97] However, "Draft Treaty Establishing a Constitution for Europe" incorporated the provisions of the Charter of Fundamental Rights of the European Union. On July 18, 2003 the final text of the complete draft Constitution was submitted to the President of the European Council in Rome.[98] On October 29, 2004 Heads of State and Government signed finally perfected texts of the EU Constitution in all official languages. But the EU

Constitution has not yet come into force because of non-ratification by all EU Member States.

Though it is not legally binding, a number of Advocates General at the ECJ have refereed to specific provisions of the Charter, using it as a source for identifying Community Fundamental Rights.[99] The Court of First Instance invoked the provisions of the Charter as legal authority.[100] In its judgment, the European Court of Human Rights also referred to the Charter.[101]

The other institutions of the EU also followed the emerging practice of referring to the Charter as a legal authority. The Council of Ministers' decision setting up Eurojust with a view to reinforce the fight against serious crime[102] acknowledges the role of the Charter as an instrument codifying the Fundamental Rights recognized by Article 6(2) of the Treaty of Amsterdam,[103] while in its decision on the terms of reference of hearing officers in one set of competition proceedings, the European Commission expressly referred to it.[104]

Considering the growing tendency of referring to the Charter as a legal authority, Gucht comments that: "The Charter will in the future form a basic 'Bill of Rights' that has a formal legal status and is in principle a full part of the EU's binding legal framework. The clauses of the Charter will be formally implemented in the Union and many of them will be enforceable by the people."[105]

The foregoing discussion reveals that national Constitutions of Member States protect the rights contained in the Charter. Besides, EU Member States have ratified international and European Human Rights instruments which also protect the rights proclaimed in the Charter. A number of Advocate-Generals at the ECJ, the Court of First Instance, the European Court of Human Rights, the Council of Ministers and the European Commission also referred to the provisions of the Charter as legal authority. But unfortunately the EU Constitution which incorporated the provisions of the Charter has not yet come into force. As the EU Constitution has not yet come into force, the provisions of the Charter is not legally binding but citizens of the EU can enjoy the taste of the rights proclaimed in the Charter by resorting to their national constitutions as well as international and European Human Rights instruments.

The Charter and the ECHR: Complementary or Competing?

We have already stated that different international Human Rights instruments coexist in EU Member States. Coexistence plays an important role in protecting individual rights. But the coexistence of the European Convention on Human Rights and the Charter of Fundamental Rights raises certain issues. It should be borne in mind that as the EU is not a contracting party of the ECHR, the EU and its institutions are not bound by the ECHR. But the case-law of the European Court of Human Rights[106] reveals that in order to implement an obligation under the Union law, the Member State may be required to adopt a measure at national level which may adversely affect a right guaranteed in the ECHR. And such measure may fall within the scrutiny of the Court of Justice. The requirements of that case law and EU law indicate that the concurrent existence of the ECHR and the Charter is risky and it will bring case-law divergence between the ECJ and the European Court of Human Rights system.

The makers of the Charter made their instruments as a part of Community with the ECHR. The object behind it is to avoid case-law divergence. The words used in Articles 52(3) and 53 of the Charter clearly refer that rights taken from the ECHR have the same meaning and same scope in the Charter as the corresponding rights guaranteed by the ECHR, providing the possibility of Union law's affording more extensive protection than the ECHR. That is entirely compatible with the Convention.[107] One author noted that reference to the case law was not included in Article 52(3) of the Charter. The reason behind it is that the European Court of Human Rights cannot set the standard for the interpretation of the Charter.[108]

Some commentators are of the opinion that the phraseology used in Articles 52(3) and 53 of the Charter has not eradicated the risk of divergent interpretations of Fundamental Rights between the European Court of Justice and the European Court of Human Rights.[109] So, in order to avoid such risk, the EU should accede to the ECHR. The Draft Constitution also proposes that the EU should accede to the Convention.[110] In entrusting one institution—the European Court of Human Rights—interpretations of Convention rights incorporated in the Charter, accession would totally eradicate the risk of divergence between the ECHR and the Charter. EU institutions will be able through accession to take part fully in Strasbourg proceedings in which Union law is at issue, thus avoiding Member States carrying sole responsibility under the Convention and perhaps being unable to give Strasbourg judgments the effect they require in Union law. Accession would bring equality between Member States and the Union concerning the external review available under the ECHR.[111]

The European Court of Human Rights is a specialized Court which is responsible under Article 19 of the EUCFR for ensuring the observance of the engagements undertaken by the High Contracting Parties in the Convention and the Protocols thereto. The Court is competent enough to deal with Human Rights issues and to examine compatibility of EU law with Human Rights provisions. If there is any contradiction between the provisions of EU law and the ECHR, the Court of Human Rights shall uphold the provisions of the ECHR. And in the arena of Human Rights, Court of Human Rights shall be the responsible Court and the ECJ shall not interfere with the activities of the European Court of Human Rights.

It is clear that the Charter and the ECHR are complementary and not competing.

Human Rights Standards in the Charter

The provisions of the Charter are based on the Fundamental Rights and freedoms recognized by the national Constitutions of the Member States and international Human Rights instruments. The English version of the Charter contains fewer than 3,500 words. Seventy-five per cent of the Charter consists of transcriptions of the ECHR and its Protocols.[112] The Charter "is elegantly conceived, beautifully drafted, and a mastery combination of pastiche, compromise and studies ambiguity".[113] The Charter is divided into seven chapters on dignity, freedoms, equality, solidarity, citizenship, justice and general provisions. The main objective of the Charter was to make the rights more visible and explicit for citizens of the EU.

Apart from the provisions at the end of the document, the Articles are grouped around six fundamental values. Chapter I—*Dignity* contains 5 Articles: Human Dignity,[114] Right to life,[115] Right to the integration of the person,[116] Prohibition of torture and inhuman or degrading treatment or punishment,[117] Prohibition of slavery and forced labour.[118] Chapter II—*Freedom* embraces 14 Articles: Right to liberty and security,[119] Respect for private and family life,[120] Protection of personal data,[121] Right to marry and right to found a family,[122] Freedom of thought, conscience and religion,[123] Freedom of expression and information,[124] Freedom of assembly and of association,[125] Freedom of the arts and sciences,[126] Right to education,[127] Freedom to choose an occupation and right to engage in work,[128] Freedom to conduct a business,[129] Right to Property,[130] Right to asylum,[131] Protection in the event of removal, expulsion or extradition.[132] Chapter III—*Equality* has 7 Articles: Equality before the law,[133] Non-discrimination,[134] Cultural, religious and linguistic diversity,[135] Equality between men and women,[136] The rights of the child,[137] The rights of the elderly,[138] Integration of persons with disabilities.[139] Chapter IV—*Solidarity* contains 12 Articles: Worker's right to information and consultation within the undertaking,[140] Right of collective bargaining and action,[141] Right of access to placement services,[142] Protection in the event of unjustified dismissal,[143] Fair and just working conditions,[144] Prohibition of child labour and protection of young people at work,[145] Family and professional life,[146] Social security and social assistance,[147] Health care,[148] Access to services of general economic interest,[149] Environmental Protection,[150] Consumer Protection.[151] Chapter V—*Citizen's Rights* comprises 8 Articles: Right to vote and to stand as a candidate at elections to the European Parliament,[152] Right to vote and to stand as a candidate at municipal elections,[153] Right to good administration,[154] Right of access to documents,[155] Ombudsman,[156] Right to petition,[157] Freedom of movement and of residence,[158] Diplomatic and consular protection.[159] Chapter VI—*Justice* consists of 4 Articles: Right to an effective remedy and to a fair trial,[160] Presumption of innocence and right of defense,[161] Principles of legality and proportionality of criminal offences and penalties,[162] The Right not to be tried or punished twice in criminal proceedings for the same criminal offence.[163] Chapter VII—*General Provisions* deal with the scope of the Chapter,[164] The scope of guaranteed rights,[165] The level of protection,[166] and The protection of abuses of rights.[167]

The above mentioned provisions of the Charter show that the Charter contains international standards of Human Rights provisions.

Human Rights and Competition Law Cases

I. Respect for Private and Family Law, Protection of Personal Data (Articles 7 and 8 of the Charter).

Article 7 says:

Everyone has the right to respect for his or her private and family life, home and communications.

Article 8 states:

Everyone has the right to the protection of personal data concerning him or her.

Such data must be processed fairly for specified purposes and on the basis of the consent of the person concerned or some other legitimate basis laid down by law. Everyone has the right of access to data which has been collected concerning him or her, and the right to have it rectified.

Compliance with these rules shall be subject to control by an independent authority.

The Commission is empowered to undertake such inspections as are necessary to detect any agreement, decision or concerted practice prohibited by Article 81 of the Treaty or any abuse of a dominant position prohibited by Article 82 of the Treaty.[168] The Commission in conducting such inspections are empowered to enter any premises, land and means of transport of undertakings and associations of undertakings; to examine the books and other records related to the business, irrespective of the medium on which they are stored; to take or obtain in any form copies of or extracts from such books or records; to seal any business premises and books or records for the period and to the extent necessary for the inspection; to ask any representative or member of staff of the undertaking or association of undertakings for explanations on facts or documents relating to the subject-matter and purpose of the inspection and to record the answers.[169] If a reasonable suspicion exists that books or other records related to the business and to the subject-matter of the inspection, which may be relevant to prove a serious violation of Article 81 or Article 82 of the Treaty, are being kept in any other premises, land and means of transport, including the homes of directors, managers and other members of staff of the undertakings and associations of undertakings concerned, the Commission can conduct an inspection in such other premises, land and means of transport.[170]

So when the European Commission exercises the above-mentioned powers, the defense mentioned in Articles 7 and 8 may be invoked.

II. The Right to an effective remedy and to a fair trial and presumption of innocence and right of defense (Articles 47 and 48 of the Charter).

Article 47 provides:

Everyone, whose rights and freedoms guaranteed by the law of the Union are violated, has the right to an effective remedy before a tribunal in compliance with the conditions laid down in this Article.

Everyone is entitled to a fair and public hearing within a reasonable time by an independent and impartial tribunal previously established by law. Everyone shall have the possibility of being advised, defended and represented.

Legal aid shall be made available to those who lack sufficient resources insofar as such aid is necessary to ensure effective access to justice.

Article 48 declares:

1. Everyone who has been charged shall be presumed innocent until proved guilty according to law.
2. Respect for the rights of the defense of anyone who has been charged shall be guaranteed.

The above-stated defense may be invoked when a Commission, acting on a complaint or on its initiative, in its decision finds that a company has abused its dominant position by starting legal proceedings. This defense may also be invoked when the undertaking accused does not have sufficient access to the file of the European Commission which is essential to conduct their defense.

III. Principles of legality and proportionality of criminal offences and penalties (Article 49 of the Charter).

Article 49 says:

1. No one shall be held guilty of any criminal offence on account of any act or omission which did not constitute a criminal offence under national law or international law at the time when it was committed. Nor shall a heavier penalty be imposed than that which was applicable at the time the criminal offence was committed. If, subsequent to the commission of a criminal offence, the law provides for a lighter penalty, that penalty shall be applicable.

2. This Article shall not prejudice the trial and punishment of any person for any act or omission which, at the time when it was committed, was criminal according to the general principles recognised by the community of nations.

3. The severity of penalties must not be disproportionate to the criminal offence.

4. This defense may be invoked when the European Commission applies new laws imposing fine on an undertaking on account of an act which did not impose fine at the time when it was committed. This defense may also be invoked when the European Commission imposes a heavier fine than the one that was applicable at the time when the act was committed.

IV. Right not to be tried or punished twice in criminal proceedings for the same criminal offence (Article 50 of the Charter).

Article 50 states:

No one shall be liable to be tried or punished again in criminal proceedings for an offence for which he or she has already been finally acquitted or convicted within the Union in accordance with the law.

This defense may be invoked when the European Commission initiates a second prosecution after a conclusion of first prosecution by the national competition authority. This defense may also be invoked when several national competition authorities initiate prosecutions for the same infringements. Council Regulation (EC) No 1/2003 tries to solve this situation. As it says that where competition authorities of two or more Member States have received a complaint or are acting on their own initiative under Article 81 or Article 82 of the Treaty against the same agreement, decision of an association or practice, the fact that one authority is dealing with the case shall be sufficient grounds for the others to suspend the proceedings before them or to reject the complaint. The Commission may likewise reject a complaint on the ground that a competition authority of a Member State is dealing with the case. It also says that where a competition authority of a Member State or the Commission has received a complaint against an agreement, decision of an association or practice which has already been dealt with by another competition authority, it may reject it.[171] Article 50 of the Charter may be invoked as a defense in competition law cases as the language of Article 13 of the Council Regulation is not strong.

Conclusion

At the time of inception the European Communities did not give specific attention to protect Fundamental Rights. The European Court of Justice is the pioneer for the development and recognition of the importance of Fundamental Rights, and its protection within the European Union. The ECJ has protected Fundamental Rights within the European Union as part of the unwritten general principles of Community law.

In December 2000, the EU Charter of Fundamental Rights was proclaimed at the Nice European Council. It "can be seen as the remarkable product of a revolutionary process".[172] The Charter is important not just as milestone in EU Constitution-building but as a feature of incorporation of Human Rights in the Constitutions of the different countries of the world.[173] Though the Charter is not legally-non-binding, it has already had a significant impact. A number of Advocate-General of the ECJ, judgments of the Court of First Instance and the European Court of Human Rights have referred to specific provisions of the Charter. Case law would continue to evolve smoothly and the Charter would gradually be used in politics as a standard for democracy and Fundamental Rights.[174] For noteworthy progress to the promotion and protection of Human Rights all EU Member States should ratify the EU Constitution. Thus it will be possible to invoke Human Rights in competition law cases.

In 1996, the ECJ expressed the view that the Community has no competence to accede to the Convention. But the Community accession to the Convention is important to avoid divergent interpretation of akin provisions of the ECHR and the Charter and thus to securing the effectiveness of the Strasbourg system.[175] In order to remove this obstacle, the Draft Constitution proposes that the EU shall seek accession to the Convention. If the accession takes place, the protection of Human Rights in the EU will be strengthen.

The impact of the Charter as a legally binding instrument cannot be neglected and should be secured in a coherent, legally convincing manner.[176] The Charter should be applauded because it strengthens EU law and because it is apt to respond to the challenge of modern times.[177] In this way, the Charter will undoubtedly play unprecedented role in promoting and protecting Fundamental Rights/Human Rights within the European Union, and set example for others to follow.

Notes

1. The Treaty of Paris establishing the European Coal and Steel Community, April 18, 1951; the Treaty of Rome establishing the European Economic Community, March 25, 1957 and the Treaty of Rome establishing the European Atomic Energy Community, March 25, 1957. For the Text of these treaties, *see* Bieber, Ronald (ed.), *Constitutional Law of the European Union*, Baden, 1996, pp. 81, 282.
2. In this context, Devuyst says: "This is not entirely surprising. First, the EEC Treaty contained mainly economic provisions...Second, the six original Member States were also party to the Council of Europe's European Convention for the Protection of Human Rights and Fundamental Freedoms of 1950. There seemed no need to duplicate the Council of Europe's advanced protection mechanisms that had entered into force in 1953." Devuyst, Youri, *The European Union at the Crossroads*, Brussels, 2003, pp. 98-99.
3. Schermers, Henry G., *Judicial Protection in the European Communities*, Deventer, 1979, at p. 32.
4. Preamble. Jaeckel states that the reference to liberty with the use of the terms "preserve" and "strengthen" means not only a commitment to the traditional defensive function of Fundamental Rights but also effective and comprehensive protection of these rights. Jaeckel, Liv, "The Duty to Protect Fundamental Rights in the European Community", *European Law Review*, 28 (2003), at p. 509.
5. Article 7. For details about discrimination on grounds of nationality, *see* Kapteyn, P.J.G. and Themaat, P. VerLoren van, *Introduction to the Law of the European Communities*, London, 1998, pp. 163-74.
6. Article 119. And later Directive 75/117/EEC (OJL 45, 1975, at p. 19) on 'equal pay for equal work'. For landmark Court judgment on this subject, *see* Bermann, George, A. et al., *Cases and Material on European Communities Law*, Minnesota, 1993, pp. 1158-92. *See* also Ellis, Evelyn, "The Recent Jurisprudence of the Court of Justice in the Field of Sex Equality", *Common Market Law Review*, 37 (2000), 1403; Barnard, Catherine, "Gender Equality in the EU: A Balance Sheet" in Alston, Philip (ed.), *The EU and Human Rights*, Oxford, 1993, pp. 215-79. For details, *see* Verwilghen, Michel (ed.) *Equality in Law between Men and Women in the European Community*, Louvain-La-Neuve, 1987.
7. The terms Fundamental Rights and Human Rights will be synonymous in this paper. Within the EU, Human Rights are

in most cases referred as Fundamental Rights. But there is no major conceptual difference. However, the difference between fundamental (human) rights (not incorporated in the Treaties) and fundamental (economic) freedoms (incorporated in the Treaties) is relevant. Some scholars consider that the economic freedom to be Human Rights, but that is not the generally accepted view. *See* Bogdany, A. von, "The European Union as a Human Rights Organizations?", *Common Market Law Review*, 37 (2003), 1326.

8. Ward, Ian, *A Critical Introduction to European Law*, London, 1996, at p. 139. However, during the initial period, the ECJ was not very keen to take into account Fundamental Rights. In *Stork*, in which a coal wholesaler complained of a decision of the High Authority governing the sale of coal, the Court refused to consider the argument that the decision breached basic rights which were protected under German law. According to the Court, "the High Authority is not empowered to examine a ground of complaint which maintains that, when it adopted its decision, it infringed principles of German constitutional law". Case 1/58, *Stork* v *High Authority* (1959) ECR 17. Similarly, in *Geitling*, the Court not only rejected the relevance of a Fundamental Rights in German constitutional law, but also dismissed the suggestion that Community law might of itself protect such a right. Cases 36, 37, 38, and 40/59, *Geitling* v *High Authority* (1960) ECR 423.
9. Case 29/69, *Stauder* v *City of Ulm* (1969) ECR 419, at p. 425.
10. Witte, Bruno de, "The Past and Future Role of the European Court of Justice in the Protection of Human Rights" in Alston, Philip (ed.), *The EU and Human Rights*, *Supra* note 6, at p. 866.
11. Case 11/70, *Internationale Handelsgesellschaft mbH* v *Einfuhr- and Vorratsstelle fur Getreide und Futtermittel* (1970) ECR 1125. As regards the constitutional traditions of Member States, Meehan pointed out that: "This source, however, was problematic. Even with the six countries at the time of the decision in 1970, the constitutional traditions were very different. Although it can undoubtedly be said that these countries shared certain common values, their expression in the various legal orders could be quite different. This made it very problematic to clearly define individual rights at the Community level." Meehan, Michael, "(Un)Chartered Waters: The Legal Background to Fundamental Rights Protection in the EU" in Feus, Kim (ed.), *An EU Charter of Fundamental Rights: Text and Commentaries*, London, 2000, at p. 85.
12. Case 4/73, *Nold* v *Commission* (1974) ECR 491. The *Nold* judgment of 1974 followed by 11 days France's ratification of the European Convention on Human Rights (ECHR), the last (then) Member State to do so. It is beyond doubt that May 1974 was

important for the ECHR and the Court of Justice jointly as well as severally. Guild, Elspeth and Lesieur, Guillaume, *The European Court of Justice on the European Convention on Human Rights*, London, 1998, at p. XVII.

13. Case 36/75, *Rutili* v *Minister for the Interior* (1975) ECR 1219.
14. Case 5/88, *Wachauf* v *The State* (1989) ECR 2609.
15. Case C-260/89, *Elliniki Radiophonia Tileorassi AE & Panellinia Omospondia Syllogon Prossopikou* v *Dimotiki Etairia Pliroforissis & Sotirios Kouvelas & Nicolaos Avdellas et al.* (1991) ECR I-2925.
16. Case C-13/94, *P* v *S and Cornwall County Council* (1996) ECR I-2143.
17. Case C-299/95, *Kremzow* v *Austrian Republic* (1997) ECR I-2629.
18. For a good overview of third pillar rights, *see* Peers, Steve, "Human Rights and the Third Pillar" in Alston, Philip (ed.), *The EU and Human Rights*, *Supra* note 6, pp. 167-86.
19. The SEA refers in its preamble to "the fundamental rights recognized in the constitutions and laws of the Member States, in the Convention for Protection of Human Rights and Fundamental Freedoms and the Social Charter, notably freedom, equality and social justice".
20. *See* Rack, Reinhard and Lausegger, Stefan, "The Role of the European Parliament: Past and Future" in Alston, Philip (ed.), *The EU and Human Rights*, *Supra* note 6, pp. 801-37.
21. Bradley, Kieran St C., "Reflections on the Human Rights Role of the European Parliament" in Alston, Philip (ed.), *The EU and Human Rights*, *Supra* note 6, at p. 845.
22. For Human Rights conditionality for accession of new members to the EU, *see* Nowak, Manfred, "Human Rights 'Conditionality' in Relation to Entry to, and Full Participation in, the EU" in Alston, Philip (ed.), *The EU and Human Rights*, *Supra* note 6, pp. 687-98.
23. *See* Kardos-Kaponyi, Elisabeth, *The Charter of Fundamental Rights of the European Union*, at p. 142, available at http://www.lib.bke.hu/ gt/2001-1-2/Kardos-Kaponyi.pdf> (last visited on 10.06.2004).
24. Ex Article F(2). The following general principles have been referred by the Courts: the protection of legitimate expectation, the right to be heard, freedom of trade union activity, legal certainty, equal treatment, proportionality, non-discrimination and good administration. Mathijsen, P.S.R.F., *A Guide to European Union Law*, London, 1999, at p. 137.

25. Nowak says that Article 6(1) is widely regarded as confirmation of the Copenhagen political criteria. They are, however, not identical. For instance, Copenhagen speaks of the protection of minorities but this issue was not mentioned in the Treaty's Human Rights provision, which applies to all Member States, i.e., even to those countries which do not recognize minorities, such as France. Nowak, *Supra* note 22, at p. 692. Even France has not signed the Council of Europe's Framework Convention for the Protection of National Minorities. Sadurski, Wojciech, "Charter and Enlargement" *European Law Journal*, 8(2002) at p. 344.
26. New Article 13. *See* also Bell, Mark, "The New Article 13 EC Treaty: A Sound Basis for European Anti-Discrimination Law?", *Maastricht Journal of European and Comparative Law*, 6 (1999), 5; Flynn, Leo, "The Implications of Article 13 EC—After Amsterdam, Will Some Forms of Discrimination be More Equal than Others?", *Common Market Law Review*, 36 (1999), 1127; Gearty, Conor, A., "The Internal and External 'Other' in the Union Legal Order: Racism, Religious Intolerance and Xenophobia in Europe" in Alston, Philip (ed.), *The EU and Human Rights*, *Supra* note 6, pp. 327-58; Ellis, Evelyn, "The Principle of Non-Discrimination in the Post-Nice Era" in Arnull, Anthony and Wincott, Daniel (eds.), *Accountability and Legitimacy in the European Union*, Oxford, 2002, pp. 291-305.
27. All Member States of the Council of Europe had ratified the ECHR on November 4, 2000. Under the Dayton Peace Agreements the Convention has even become applicable in a State which has not ratified it. Polakiewicz, Jorg, "The Status of the Convention in National Law" in Blackburn, Robert and Polakiewicz, Jorg (eds.), *Fundamental Rights in Europe*, Oxford, 2001, at p. 36. It is noted that the United Kingdom Government was the first Member State which ratify the Convention. But at the beginning the United Kingdom Government was unhappy about the amount of adverse publicity generated by actions against it in Strasbourg. Higgins, Rosalyn, "The European Convention on Human Rights" in Meron, Theodor (ed.), *Human Rights in International Law*, Oxford, 1984, at p. 504. However, at present, Human Rights Act 1998 incorporates the ECHR into the domestic law of the UK. For details, *see* Blackburn, Robert, "The United Kingdom" in Blackburn, Robert and Polakiewicz, Jorg (eds.), *Fundamental Rights in Europe*, *ibid*, pp. 935-1008.
28. These include the following (a) European and (b) International instruments:

    (a) European Social Charter, 1961; European Convention for the Prevention of Torture and Inhuman or Degrading Treatment or

Punishment, 1987; European Convention on the Exercise of Children's Rights, 1996; Convention for the Protection of Human Rights and dignity of the human being with regard to the application of biology and medicine: Convention on Human Rights and Biomedicine, 1997.

(b) Slavery Convention, 1926; International Labour Organisation Convention No. 29 on Forced or Compulsory Labour, 1930; International Labour Organisation Convention No. 87 Concerning Freedom of Association and Protection of the Right to Organise, 1948; Universal Declaration of Human Rights, 1948; Geneva Convention Relative to the Protection of Civilian Persons in time of War, 1949; Geneva Convention Relative to the Treatment of Prisoners of War, 1949; United Nations Convention Relating to the Status of Refugees, 1951; Convention on the Abolition of Slavery, the Slave Trade and Institutions and Practices similar to Slavery, 1956; International Labour Organisation Convention on Discrimination (Employment and Occupation), 1958; Covenant against Discrimination in Education (UNESCO), 1960; International Covenant on Civil and Political Rights (ICCPR), 1966; International Covenant on Economic, Social and Cultural Rights (ICESCR), 1966; International Convention on the Elimination of All Forms of Racial Discrimination (ICERD), 1966; Convention on the Elimination of All Forms of Discrimination against Women (CEDAW), 1979; United Nations Convention against Torture and Other Cruel, Inhuman or Degrading Treatment or Punishment (CAT), 1984; United Nations Declaration against Torture, 1984, United Nations Convention on the Rights of the Child (CRC), 1989.

29. Weiler, J.H.H., "European Citizenship and Human Rights" in Winter, Jan, A., et al (ed.), *Reforming the Treaty on European Union—The Legal Debate*, London, 1996, at p. 79.
30. *Supra* note 10, at p. 873.
31. OJC 26 of 30.4.1973.
32. Bulletin of the EC–S 2/1979.
33. *Ibid.*
34. *See* Lindfelt, Mats, *A Bill of Rights for the European Union*, Institute for Human Rights, Abo Akademi University, available at http://www.abo.fi/instut/imr/norfa/mats_billofrights.pdf (last visited on 05.02.2007).
35. O'Leary, Siofra, "Accession by the European Community to the European Convention on Human Rights—The Opinion of the ECJ", *European Human Rights Law Review*, 4(1996) at p. 375.
36. There is option as well, as proposed by Lenearts. In accordance with this proposal, the Fundamental Rights guaranteed in the

ECHR would be included in the Constitution of the Community. When Community institutions or Member States act outside the scope of Community law, the ECHR control machinery in relation to the Member States as it has always done. In acting within the scope of Community law, the normal mechanisms of judicial protection offered by national judiciaries and/or the Court of Justice will ensure that the Fundamental Rights contained in the ECHR as part of the Community Constitution is being observed. If a fundamental right was interpreted by the Court of Human Rights and the issue is raised before the ECJ, then the ECJ is not entitled to adopt different interpretation *i.e.*, the ECJ will be bound, on the basis of the Community Constitution, to adopt the interpretation of the Court of Human Rights. Lenearts, Koen, "Fundamental Rights to be included in a Community Catalogue", *European Law Review*, 16 (1991), pp. 377-81.

37. Toth, A.G., "The European Union and Human Rights: the Way Forward", *Common Market Law Review*, 34 (1997), at p. 501.
38. *See* EC Commission Report, "The Protection of Fundamental Rights as Community Law is Created and Developed", EC Bull. Suppl. 5/76.
39. *See Supra* note 32.
40. Commission Communication SEC (90) 2087 of November 19, 1990.
41. Opinion 2/94, (1996), ECR I-1759.
42. *Ibid*, para 27.
43. Article 235 says: "If action by the Community should prove necessary to attain, in the course of the operation of the common market, one of the objectives of the Community and this Treaty has not provided the necessary powers, the Council shall, acting unanimously on a proposal from the Commission and after consulting the European Parliament, take the appropriate measures".
44. *Supra* note 41, para 34.
45. e.g., Joined Cases 60 and 61/84, *Cinetheque SA* v *Federation Nationale de Cinemas Francais* (1985), ECR 2605, para 26.
46. *Supra* note 41, para 35.
47. Lenaerts, Koen, "Fundamental Rights in the European Union", *European Law Review*, 25 (2000), at p. 575.
48. Jacobs, F.G., "The EU Charter of Fundamental Rights" in Arnull, Anthony and Wincott, Daniel (eds.), *Accountability and Legitimacy in the European Union*, *Supra* note 26, at p. 289.
49. Craig, Paul and Burca, Grainne de, *EU Law: Text, Cases, and Materials*, Oxford, 1998, pp. 337-38.

50. Weiler, J.H.H. and Fries, Sybilla C., "A Human Rights Policy for the European Community and Union: The Question of Competences" in Alston, Philip (ed.) *The EU and Human Rights*, *Supra* note 6, at p. 150.
51. Burrows, Noreen, "Question of Community Accession to the European Convention Determined", *European Law Review*, 22 (1997), at p. 61.
52. Tridimas, Takis, *The General Principles of the EC Law*, Oxford, 1999, at p. 242.
53. Bulterman, Miele, *Human Rights in the Treaty Relations of the European Community*, Antwerpen, 2001, at p. 88.
54. House of Lords Select Committee on the European Communities, *Human Rights* (Session 1979-80, 1st Report, HL Paper 362).
55. House of Lords Select Committee on the European Communities, *Human Rights Re-examined* (Session 1992-93, 3rd Report, HL Paper 10).
56. Arnull, A.M., "Opinion 2/94 and its Implications for the Future Constitutions of the Union" in *The Human Rights Opinion of the ECJ and Its Constitutional Implications*, University of Cambridge, CELS Occasional Paper No. 1, June 1996, at p. 7.
57. Kokott, Juliane and Hoffmeister, Frank, "Opinion 2/94, Accession of the Community to the European Convention for the Protection of Human Rights and Fundamental Freedoms", *American Journal of International Law*, 90 (1996), at p. 667. But Spielmann says, "divergent interpretation should not necessarily be ruled out. A dissenting or merely separate voice from Luxembourg could indeed be a valuable input, especially as the Strasbourg Court is accustomed to separate opinions coming from its own members. Moreover, in systems where the Convention is self-executing, divergent interpretation of domestic Courts is possible and frequent, and sometimes local Courts go even far beyond the minimum standards set by the European Court of Human Rights". Spielmann, Dean, "Human Rights Case Law in the Strasbourg and Luxembourg Courts: Conflicts, Inconsistencies, and Complementaries" in Alston, Philip (ed.), *The EU and Human Rights*, *Supra* note 6, at p. 779. In *Loizidou* v *Turkey*, the International Court of Justice and European Court of Human Rights expressed different views on Turkey's restrictive acceptance of the jurisprudence of the Court in each case, available at http://www.cyprus.com.cy (last visited on 09.01.2007).
58. Cooper, Jonathan and Pillay, Roisin, "Through the Looking Glass: Making Visible Rights Real" in Feus, Kim (ed.), *An EU Charter of Fundamental Rights: Text and Commentaries*, *Supra* note 11, at p. 117. Russell-Johnston States that if the European Union

proceeds with creating a parallel system for the protection of Human Rights, with the Luxembourg Court as the last instance of appeal, for the very same rights protected by the Convention, will inevitably weaken and undermine the broader mechanisms with the Strasbourg Court at its core. Russell-Johnston, Lord, "Contribution to the Federal Trust Publication on the EU Charter of Fundamental Rights" in Feus, Kim (ed.), *An EU Charter of Fundamental Rights: Text and Commentaries*, *Supra* note 11, at p. 54.

59. *See* "House of Lords Select Committee on the European Union", *The Future Status of the EU Charter of Fundamental Rights* (Session 2002-03, 6th Report, HL Paper 48), at p. 29.
60. *Ibid.*
61. Sislova, Nadia, *The outline of Some Current Issues of the Human Rights Protection at EU Level*, available at http://www.ecsanet.org/ecsaworld6/contributions/others/Siskova.doc (last visited on 15.01.2007).
62. *Supra* note 37, at p. 503.
63. Goldsmith, Lord, "Consolidation of Fundamental Rights at EU Level—The British Perspective" in Feus, Kim (ed.), *An EU Charter of Fundamental Rights: Text and Commentaries*, *Supra* note 11, at p. 35.
64. Betten, Lammy and Grief, Nicholas, *EU Law and Human Rights*, London, 1998, at p. 114.
65. *Supra* note 41.
66. Before the ECJ, France, Spain and the United Kingdom pleaded that they oppose accession to the ECHR. The position of Denmark, Portugal and the Netherlands appeared to be undecided, assessing the political effect of accession as positive. But these countries had reservation as to the legal and political side of accession and indicated that the outcome of negotiations would determine their position.
67. *See* Scappucci, Gioia, "Road Taken towards a Charter of Fundamental Rights for the EU Unveiled", *EU Focus: Essential Developments in EU Law and Policy Biecester*, 64 (2000), at p. 2.
68. Conclusions of the European Council in Cologne, June 3 and 4, 1999, Annex IV.
69. The task of drafting the Charter was entrusted by the European Council to an *ad hoc* Body known as "the Convention". It was composed by:

Members—

Heads of State or Government of Member States: Fifteen representatives of the Heads of State or Government of Member States.

Commission: One representative of the President of the European Commission.

European Parliament: Sixteen members of the European Parliament to be designated by itself.

National Parliaments: Thirty members of national Parliaments (two from each national Parliament) to be designated by national Parliaments themselves. Members of the Body may be replaced by alternates in the event of being unable to attend meetings of the Body.

Chairperson and Vice-Chairpersons of the Body: The Chairperson of the Body shall be elected by the Body. A member of the European Parliament, a member of a national Parliament, and the representative of the President of the European Council if not elected to the Chair, shall act as Vice-Chairpersons of the Body. The member of the European Parliament acting as Vice-Chairperson shall be elected by the members of the European Parliament serving on the Body. The member of a national Parliament acting as Vice-Chairperson shall be elected by the members of national Parliaments serving on the Body.

Observers: Two representatives of the Court of Justice of the European Communities to be designated by the Court. Two representatives of the Council of Europe, including one from the European Court of Human Rights.

Bodies of the European Union to be invited to give their views: The Economic and Social Committee. The Committee of the Regions the Ombudsman.

Exchange of views with the applicant States: An appropriate exchange of views should be held by the Body or by the Chairperson with the applicant States.

Other bodies, social groups or experts to be invited to give their views: Other bodies, social groups and experts may be invited by the Body to give their views.

Secretariat: The General Secretariat of the Council shall provide the Body with secretariat services. To ensure proper coordination, close contacts will be established with the General Secretariat of the European Parliament, with the Commission and, to the extent necessary, with the secretariats of the national Parliaments. Available at: http://www.europarl.europa.eu/summits/tam_en.htm (last visited on 27.01.2007).

The Convention was chaired by Mr Roman Herzog, former President of the Federal Republic of Germany and of the German Constitutional Court.

The Convention Bureau was made up of:

Mr Pedro Bacelar de Vasconcelos and Mr Guy Braibant—on behalf of the representatives of the Heads of State and Government.

Mr Gunnar Jannson—on behalf of the representatives of the national parliaments.

Mr Inigo Mendez de Vigo—on behalf of the representatives of the European Parliament.

Mr António Vitorino—representing the President of the Commission. Aavailable at: http://www.europarl.europa.eu/charter/composition_en.htm (last visited on 27.01.2007).

Pernice says that the composition of the Convention entrusted with the task of drafting the Charter of Fundamental Rights shows a majority—about 75%—of Parliamentarians. Undoubtedly, this is a new development in the history of the EU, specially, when we take into view the significance of the document drafted. Pernice, Ingolf, *The Charter of Fundamental Rights of the European Union*, available at http://www.fes.or.kr/Publications/pub/Grundrechtscharter2001full-text.htm (last visited on 27.01.2007).

70. Working methods:

Preparation: The Chairperson of the Body shall, in close concentration with the Vice-Chairpersons, propose a work plan for the Body and perform other appropriate preparatory work.

Transparency of the proceedings: In principle, hearings held by the Body and documents submitted at such hearings should be public.

Working groups: The Body may establish *ad hoc* working groups, which shall be open to all members of the Body.

Drafting: On the basis of the work plan agreed by the Body, a Drafting Committee composed of the Chairperson, the Vice-Chairpersons and the representative of the Commission and assisted by the General Secretariat of the Council, shall elaborate a preliminary Draft Charter, taking account of drafting proposals submitted by any member of the Body. Each of the three Vice-Chairpersons shall regularly consult with the respective component part of the Body from which he or she emanates.

Elaboration of the Draft Charter by the Body: When the Chairperson, in close concentration with the Vice-Chairpersons, deems that the text of the draft Charter elaborated by the Body can eventually be subscribed to by all the parties, it shall be forwarded to the European Council through the normal preparatory procedure." Available at http://www.europarl.europa.eu/summits/tam_en.htm (last visited on 27.01.2007).

71. Conclusions of the European Council in Tampere, October 15 and 16, 1999.
72. Clauwaert, Stefan, "The EU Charter of Fundamental Rights: Its Treatment of Social and Trade Union Rights. A Chronological Overview", *European Trade Union Yearbook*, 2000, at p. 48.
73. Vitorino, Antonio, "The Charter of Fundamental Rights of the European Union: The point of view of the European Union", *European Trade Union Yearbook*, 2000, at p. 25.
74. Editorial Comments: "Towards an EU Charter of Fundamental Rights?", *Maastricht Journal of European and Comparative Law*, 7 (2000) at p. 111.
75. Alhadeff, Giampiero and Summer, Suzanne, "A Clarion Voice for Human Rights", *European Trade Union Yearbook*, 2000, at p. 37.
76. Beres, Socialist Member of EP said: "The fact that 62 people from different and sometimes rival circles were able to drawn up this common text and adopt it by consensus is a sign of the Union's political health". Speeches of the Parliament meeting, October 4, 2000.
77. *See* Regan, Eugene, *The Charter of Fundamental Rights*, Dublin, 2002, available at http://ww.iiea.com/futeuro/er_tcofr.pdf (last visited on 15.06.2004).
78. For the text of the Charter, *See* http://www.europarl.eu.int/comparl/libe/elsj/charter/default_en.htm (last visited on 27.01.2007).
79. Editorial Comments: "The EU Charter of Fundamental Rights still under Discussion", *Common Market Law Review*, 38 (2001) at p. 1.
80. In absence of such decision, the Convention charged with the task of drafting the Charter of Fundamental Rights did not know whether the text it was preparing would remain a political Declaration or would turn into a legally binding document. Paciotti, Elena, "The Charter of Fundamental Rights: An ID Card for the European Union", *The International Spectator*, 36 (2002) at p. 33.
81. The EP Draft Report on the Treaty of Nice and the future of the European Union States "six governments—Denmark, Finland, Ireland, the Netherlands, Sweden, and the United Kingdom—rejected the idea of incorporating the Charter into the Treaties and also the compromise advocated by Parliament, which called for a reference to the Charter to be included in Article 6(2) of the EU

Treaty. The refusal to allow such a reference was paradoxical since the article in question mentions the European Convention for the Protection of Human Rights and Fundamental Freedoms, to which the IGC also refused to accede." Committee on Constitutional Affairs, March 22, 2001, doc. PE 294. 755.

82. http://db.consilium.eu.int/df (last visited on 07.06.2004).

83. Griller, Stefan, "Primacy of Community Law: A Hidden Agenda of the Charter of Fundamental Rights" in Melissas, Dimitris and Pernice, Ingolf (eds.), *Perspectives of the Nice Treaty and the Intergovernmental Conference in 2004*, available at http://www.ecln.net/elements/constitutional_debate/perspective2004/part1/1_05.html (last visited on 06.06.2004). The UK was the leading opponent of incorporating the Charter into the Treaties. But other Member States, including Ireland, the Netherlands and Sweden, supported view taken by the UK. *See* Goldsmith, Lord, "A Charter of Rights, Freedoms and Principles", *Common Market Law Review*, 38 (2001) at p. 1214; Betten, Lammy, "Human Rights—Current Development: European Community Law", *International and Comparative Law Quarterly*, 50 (2001) at p. 690; Smith, Jeremy, "EU Charter of Fundamental Rights—A Local Government Perspective", in Feus, Kim (ed.), *An EU Charter of Fundamental Rights: Text and Commentaries*, *Supra* note 11, at p. 70. The Government of the UK expressed the view that the Charter should make existing rights more visible and more accessible to promote rights and responsibilities at all levels across the EU, identifying and complementing contemporary instruments relating to Fundamental Rights. *See* Miller, Vaughne, *Human Rights in the EU: The Charter of Fundamental Rights*, Research Paper 00/32, March 20, 2000, International Affairs and Defense Section, House of Commons Library, available at http://www.parliament.uk/commons/lib/research/rp2000/rp00-032.pdf (last visited on 24.02.2007).

84. Jacobs and White, *European Convention on Human Rights*, edited by Overy, Clare and White, Robin C.A., Oxford, 2002, at p. 446.

85. Kyriakou, Tania, "The Impact of the Fundamental Rights on the EU System of Protection of Rights: Much Ado about Nothing?", *Web Journal of Current Legal Issues Ltd*, 5(2001), available at http://webjcli.ncl.ac.uk/2001/issue5/kyriakou5.html (last visited on 07.01.2007).

86. Douglas-Scott, "The Charter of Fundamental Rights as a Constitutional Document", *European Human Rights Law Review*, 1 (2004) at p. 40.

87. Eeckhout, Piet, "The Charter of Fundamental Rights and the Federal Questions", *Common Market Law Review*, 39 (2002) at p. 947.
88. Wiener, Antje, "The Constitutional Significance of the Charter of Fundamental Rights", *German Law Journal*, 2 (2001), available at http://germanlawjournal.com/print.php?id=113 (last visited on 04.01.2007).
89. Lenaerts, Koen and Smitjer, E. De, "A 'Bill of Rights' for the European Union", *Common Market Law Review*, 38 (2001), pp. 298-99.
90. Groussot, Xavier, "A Third Step in the Process of EU Constitutionalization: A Binding Charter of Fundamental Rights?", *Europarattslig Tidskrift*, 6 (2003) at p. 538. Groussot also compares the Fundamental Rights case law of the ECJ with the corresponding provisions incorporated both in the Charter of Fundamental Rights and the European Convention on Human Rights. *Ibid*, pp. 539-42.
91. Liisberg, Jonas Bering, "Does the EU Charter of Fundamental Rights Threaten the Supremacy of Community Law? Article 53 of the Charter: A Fountain of Law or just an Inkblot?" Joen Monnet Working Paper 4/01, at p. 7.
92. Tesauro, Giuseppe, "Some Thoughts on the Charter of Fundamental Rights", available at http://www.ecln.net/rome2002/tesauro.pdf (last visited on 23.02.2007).
93. Weatherill, Stephen, *Cases and Material on EU Law*, Oxford, 2003, at p. 23.
94. McBride, Jeremy, "Protecting Fundamental Rights in Europe: A Legal Analysis" in Arnull, Anthony and Wincott, Daniel (eds.), *Accountability and Legitimacy in the European Union*, *Supra* note 26, at p. 265.
95. Eeckhout, Piet, "The Proposed EU Charter of Fundamental Rights: Some Reflections on its Effects in the Legal Systems of the EU and of its Member States" in Feus, Kim (ed.), *An EU Charter of Fundamental Rights: Text and Commentaries*, *Supra* note 11, at p. 104.
96. Menendez, Agustin Jose, "Chartering Europe: Legal Status and Policy Implications of the Charter of Fundamental Rights of the European Union", *Journal of Common Market Studies*, 40 (2002) at p. 476.
97. Wilkins, Richard G. and Reed, Marya, "The Impact of the Charter of Fundamental Rights and the Proposed EU Constitution on the Domestic Policies of EU Member States", available at

http://www.spuc.org.uk/papers/EUCharterandConstitution.pdf(last visited on 26.06.2004).

98. *See* CONV 850/03.

99. *See* Case C-337/98, *Netherlands* v *Parliament and Council*; Case C-224/98, *Marie-Nathalie D'Hoop contre Rijksdienst voor arbeidsvoorziening*; Case C-313/99, *Mulligan* v *Attorney General*; Case C-413/99 *Baumbast* v *Secretary of State for the Home Department*; Case C-340/99, *TNT* v *Poste Italiane*; Case C-270/99P *Z* v *European Parliament*; Joint Cases C-122 and 125/99, *D* v *Council*; Case C-353/99P *Council* v *Hautala*; Case 309/99, *Wouters* v *Netherlands Orde van Advocaten*; C-459/99, *Mouvement contre le racisme, l'antisemitisme et la xenophobie ASBL* v *Belgium*; Case C-173, *R* v *Secretary of State for Trade and Industry ex parte BECTU*; C-49/00, *Commission des Commautes europeenes contre Republique italienne*; Case C-131/00, *Ingemar Nilsson* v *Lansstyrelsen I Norrbottens lan*; Case C-60/00, *Mary Carpenter* v *Secretary of State for the Home Department*; Case C-224/00, *Commission des Communautes europeenes contre Republique italienne*; Case C-112/00, *Eugen Schmidberger Internationale Transporte Planzuge* v *Austria*; Case C-466/00 *Kaba* v *Secretary of State for the Home Department*; Case C-50/00P, *Union de Pequenos Agricoltores* v *Council*; Joint Cases C-20/00 and 64/00, *Booker Aquaculture* v *The Scottish Ministers*; Case C-491/01, *R* v *Secretary of State for Health ex parte: British American Tobacco (Investments) Ltd* v *Imperial Tobacco Ltd*; Case C-126/01, *Ministre de l'economie, des finances et de l'industrie* v *GEMO SA*.

100. Judgments of January 30, 2002, in Case T-54/99, *Max-mobil Telecommunications Service GmbH* v *Commission*, in Case T-177/01, *Jego-Quere* v *Commission*.

101. *See Goodwin* v *United Kingdom*, judgment of July 7, 2002, Reports 1996-II, para 100.

102. Council Decision 2002/187/JHA of 28/2/2002; OJ, L 63, 6/3/2002, at p. 1.

103. *See* Preamble.

104. "The Commission must ensure that right (of the parties concerned and of third parties to be heard before a final decision affecting their interests is taken) is guaranteed in its competition proceedings, having regard in particular to the Charter of Fundamental Rights."

105. Gucht, Karel De, "The Charter of Fundamental Rights", Lecture held on February 17, 2004 in the framework of the Vrije Universiteit Brussel, Institute for European Studies' lecture series on "The Convention in Perspective".

106. *Matthews* v *United Kingdom* (1999), 28 EHRR 361. *See* also *Cantoni* v *France* No. 17862/91, Judgment of November 15, 1996.
107. *See* Article 53 of the ECHR.
108. *See* Lindfelt, Mats, "The Implications of the Proposed EU Charter of Fundamental Rights—A Political Declaration or Legally Binding Instrument?", Institute for Human Rights, Abo Akademi University, at p. 58, available at http://www.abo.fi/instut/imr/norfa/mats2_implications.pdf (last visited on 13.01. 2007).
109. *See* Arnull, Anthony, "From Charter to Constitution and Beyond: Fundamental Rights in the New European Union", *Public Law*, 2003, at p. 786; Drzemczewski, Pierre, "The Council of Europe's Position with Respect to the EU Charter of Fundamental Rights", *Human Rights Law Journal*, 22 (2001) at p. 28.
110. Part I, Article 7 of the Draft Constitution (Fundamental Rights) para 2 says: "The Union shall seek accession to the European Convention for the Protection of Human Rights and Fundamental Freedoms. Such accession shall not affect the Union's competences as defined in the Constitution."
111. Fischbach, March, "The European Convention on Human Rights and the European Charter of Fundamental Rights—Complementary or Competing?", available at http://www.coe.int/T/e/com/files/events/2002-09-Symposium-Judges/Fischbach.asp#TopOfPage (last visited on 03.02.2007).
112. Roos, Nico, "Fundamental Rights, European Identity and Law as a Way to Survive", available at http://www.rechten.unimaas.nl/ozic/LegalIntegration/paper%20Roos%20Fundamental%20rigths.pdf (last visited on 21.05.2004).
113. McCrudden, Christopher, "The Future Status of the EU Charter of Fundamental Rights", UNCES On-line Reflection Papers, No. 1, February 2002, available at http://www.uaces.org/RP-1-CM.pdf (last visited on 29.07.2004).
114. Article 1. *See* also Part II, Article II-1 of the Draft Constitution.
115. Article 2. *See* also Part II, Article II-2 of the Draft Constitution.
116. Article 3. *See* also Part II, Article II-3 of the Draft Constitution.
117. Article 4. *See* also Part II, Article II-4 of the Draft Constitution.
118. Article 5. *See* also Part II, Article II-5 of the Draft Constitution.
119. Article 6. *See* also Part II, Article II-6 of the Draft Constitution.
120. Article 7. *See* also Part II, Article II-7 of the Draft Constitution.
121. Article 8. *See* also Part II, Article II-8 of the Draft Constitution.
122. Article 9. *See* also Part II, Article II-9 of the Draft Constitution.

123. Article 10. *See* also Part II, Article II-10 of the Draft Constitution.
124. Article 11. *See* also Part II, Article II-11 of the Draft Constitution.
125. Article 12. *See* also Part II, Article II-12 of the Draft Constitution.
126. Article 13. *See* also Part II, Article II-13 of the Draft Constitution.
127. Article 14. *See* also Part II, Article II-14 of the Draft Constitution.
128. Article 15. *See* also Part II, Article II-15 of the Draft Constitution.
129. Article 16. *See* also Part II, Article II-16 of the Draft Constitution.
130. Article 17. *See* also Part II, Article II-17 of the Draft Constitution.
131. Article 18. *See* also Part II, Article II-18 of the Draft Constitution.
132. Article 19. *See* also Part II, Article II-19 of the Draft Constitution.
133. Article 20. *See* also Part II, Article II-20 of the Draft Constitution.
134. Article 21. *See* also Part II, Article II-21 of the Draft Constitution.
135. Article 22. *See* also Part II, Article II-22 of the Draft Constitution.
136. Article 23. *See* also Part II, Article II-23 of the Draft Constitution.
137. Article 24. *See* also Part II, Article II-24 of the Draft Constitution.
138. Article 25. *See* also Part II, Article II-25 of the Draft Constitution.
139. Article 26. *See* also Part II, Article II-26 of the Draft Constitution.
140. Article 27. *See* also Part II, Article II-27 of the Draft Constitution.
141. Article 28. *See* also Part II, Article II-28 of the Draft Constitution.
142. Article 29. *See* also Part II, Article II-29 of the Draft Constitution.
143. Article 30. *See* also Part II, Article II-30 of the Draft Constitution.
144. Article 31. *See* also Part II, Article II-31 of the Draft Constitution.
145. Article 32. *See* also Part II, Article II-32 of the Draft Constitution.
146. Article 33. *See* also Part II, Article II-33 of the Draft Constitution.
147. Article 34. *See* also Part II, Article II-34 of the Draft Constitution.
148. Article 35. *See* also Part II, Article II-35 of the Draft Constitution.
149. Article 36. *See* also Part II, Article II-36 of the Draft Constitution.
150. Article 37. *See* also Part II, Article II-37 of the Draft Constitution.
151. Article 38. *See* also Part II, Article II-38 of the Draft Constitution.
152. Article 39. *See* also Part II, Article II-39 of the Draft Constitution.
153. Article 40. *See* also Part II, Article II-40 of the Draft Constitution.
154. Article 41. *See* also Part II, Article II-41 of the Draft Constitution.
155. Article 42. *See* also Part II, Article II-42 of the Draft Constitution.
156. Article 43. *See* also Part II, Article II-43 of the Draft Constitution.
157. Article 44. *See* also Part II, Article II-44 of the Draft Constitution.
158. Article 45. *See* also Part II, Article II-45 of the Draft Constitution.
159. Article 46. *See* also Part II, Article II-46 of the Draft Constitution.
160. Article 47. *See* also Part II, Article II-47 of the Draft Constitution.

161. Article 48. *See* also Part II, Article II-48 of the Draft Constitution.
162. Article 49. *See* also Part II, Article II-49 of the Draft Constitution.
163. Article 50. *See* also Part II, Article II-50 of the Draft Constitution.
164. Article 51. *See* also Part II, Article II-51 of the Draft Constitution.
165. Article 52. *See* also Part II, Article II-52 of the Draft Constitution.
166. Article 53. *See* also Part II, Article II-53 of the Draft Constitution.
167. Article 54. *See* also Part II, Article II-54 of the Draft Constitution.
168. Point 24 of Council Regulation (EC) No 1/2003.
169. Article 20, *Ibid. See* also Article 13 of Council Regulation (EC) No. 139/2004.
170. Article 21, Council Regulation (EC) No. 1/2003.
171. Article 13.
172. Brand, Michiel, "Towards the Definitive Status of the Charter of Fundamental Rights of the European Union: Political Document or Legally Binding Text?", *German Law Journal*, 4 (2003), available at http://www.germanlawjournal.com/pdf/Vol04No04/PDF_Vol_04_No_04_395-409_Legal_Culture_Brand.pdf (last visited on 18.01.2007).
173. Parmar, Sejal, "International Human Rights and the EU Charter", *Maastricht Journal of European and Comparative Law*, 8 (2001) at p. 370.
174. Rochere, Jacqueline Dutheil de la, "The Charter of Fundamental Rights and Beyond", *Cambridge Yearbook of European Legal Studies*, 4 (2001) at p. 145.
175. Venice Commission, Draft Opinion on Implications of a Legally-Binding EU Charter of Fundamental Rights on Human Rights in Europe, Opinion No. 256/2003, Strasbourg, available at http://www.venice.coe.int/docs/2003/CDL%282003%29092-e.html (last visited on 13.06.2004).
176. Weber, Albrecht, "The European Charter of Fundamental Rights", *German Yearbook of International Law*, 43 (2000) at p. 105.
177. McInerney, Siobhan, "The Charter of Fundamental Rights of the European Union and the Case of Race Discrimination", *European Law Review*, 27(2002) at p. 483.

Contributors

K.V.K. Santhy is Assistant Professor of Criminal Law in NALSAR University of Law, Justice City, Hyderabad, India. She has participated in national seminars. She has to her credit several articles published in journals of great repute. Her main research interests are in the areas of criminal law, Human Rights, and environmental law.

M. Abdul Hannan is Associate Professor at the Department of Law and Justice, Rajshahi University, Bangladesh. He has written some 30 research articles published in different recognized academic journals in Bangladesh, India, Pakistan, Australia and UK. He is a member of Commonwealth Legal Education (CLEA), London, and Commonwealth of Learning (COL), Vancouver, Canada. He has participated in a good number of seminars in Bangladesh, India, UK France and Germany.

Sairam Bhat is Assistant Professor of Law, National Law School of India University, India. He is co-author of *Environmental Law: Handbook for Law Practitioners*. He has written more than 10 articles. He served as Adjunct Faculty at Golden Gate University, California, USA. He has also presented papers at various national and international conferences. His areas of interest are environmental law, law of contract and Human Rights.

Swarupama Chaturvedi is Lecturer at National Law School of India University, Bangalore, India. She has published a book entitled *New World Economy: Changing Dimensions of the Common Clauses* and many research papers in different national and international journals. Her areas of interest are constitutional law, Human Rights and taxation.

V.P. Tiwari teaches law at National Law University, India. He has written articles on environmental law. His research interests are Human Rights, constitutional law, gender justice and females' rights.

Rajarshi Sen is student of National Law University, India. His research interests are Human Rights, trade law, and intellectual property rights.

Nirmal Kanti Chakrabarti is Reader at the Department of Law, Calcutta University, India. He has authored many books. He has contributed over 50 research papers and articles in reputed national and international journals. He has presented papers in Japan and Korea. His research interests include criminal justice, environmental law, and Human Rights.

Anuradha Saibaba Rajesh is Lecturer at National Law School of India University, India. She is the faculty coordinator of the research center National Institute of Human Rights established by NHRC, India. She is co-author of the book, *Justice for Children,* on the implementation of the Juvenile Justice Act 2000 & 2006 in India. She has published several articles on Human Rights issues. Her areas of interest are Human Rights, international law, refugee rights, child rights, transitional justice, and international criminal and humanitarian laws.

Sadiq A.J. Syed is a Human Rights Officer with the United Nations Mission in Sudan. He headed the legal unit of National Commission for Women (NCW), Government of India. He also served as an Assistant Research Professor with the Indian Law Institute, India. He has authored and co-authored various research publications. The Human Rights research, field studies and investigations interest him.

V. Seshaiah Shasthri is Associate Professor and Assistant Dean (Academic Affairs) Faculty of Law, Chairman, Center for Human Rights Education, Research and Studies (CHEARS), and Chairman for Distance Education Programs, National Law University, Mandore Jodhpur. He has widely participated in and presented research papers at over 75 national and international conferences.

A.S. Dalal is Professor, Nirma Institute of Law, Nirma University of Law and Technology, Ahmedabad, Gujarat. He was Professor and Dean at the Faculty of Law, National Law University, India. He was Member of Faculty of Law, M.D. University, Rohtak and Chairman, Distance Education Programs, National Law University. He has published almost 30 research papers. He has organized many seminars and conferences. His research interests include commercial law, intellectual property rights, and criminal law.

Subhram Rajkhowa is Director of the Centre for Refugee Law Studies and Research, Department of Law, Guahati University, India. He is Professor at the Indian Institute of Human Rights. He has authored several books. He has written more than 50 articles. He has participated in many international seminars. His areas of interest include Human Rights, humanitarian law, and refugee law.

Stuti Deka is Lecturer in Department of Law, Guahati University, India. She is author of *Juridical Thoughts on Constitutional and Administrative Law* and *Constitutionalism* (in press). She has published a number of legal articles in various journals. Her areas of interest are constitutional law and administrative law.

Dipa Dube is Assistant Professor at the Rajiv Gandhi School of Intellectual Property Law, IIT Kharagpur, India. She is author of *Rape Laws in India, Crimes Against Women, Halsbury Annotated Statutes of India* (in press) and co-editor of *Criminal Justice India Series—West Bengal 2001, Criminal Justice India Series—Karnataka 2001*, and *Criminal Justice India Series—Uttar Pradesh 2001*. She has contributed around 12-15 articles in different national and international journals as well as books. Her main research interests are criminal justice, gender and law.

J.L. Kaul is Professor at the Faculty of Law, University of Delhi, India. He is President, All India Law Teachers Congress. He was awarded fellowship by Institute of Public and International Law, Greece, and also Hague External Fellowship. He is editor of *Human Rights: Issues and Perspectives.* He has published articles on globalization, Human Rights, and social justice. He has specialized in international law, international economic law, and Human Rights.

Anju Vali Tikoo is Lecturer at the Faculty of Law, University of Delhi, India. She is visiting Faculty of Jamia Millia Islamia, LNJP National Institute for Criminology and Forensic Sciences (Ministry of Home Affairs, Government of India). She has published several articles and book reviews. Her main research interests are public health laws, criminal law, and consumer law.

Nimushakavi Vasanthi is Associate Professor at the NALSAR University of Law, India. She is author of Constitutional Policy and Environmental Jurisprudence in India. She has written several articles. As part of the Criminal Justice Project at NALSAR she has coordinated many workshops on Human Rights education for person with disabilities. Her research interests include Human Rights, environmental law, and constitutional law.

Shameek Sen is Faculty Member at the West Bengal National University of Juridical Sciences, India. He is author of *The WTO Agreements and the Right to Health: A Third World Perspective*. He has presented papers in seminars. His chief research interests include international law, constitutional law, Human Rights, health law and media law.

Abdullah Al Faruque is Associate Professor and Chairman at the Department of Law, University of Chittagong, Bangladesh. He has written more than 35 articles published at home and abroad. He has participated in various international conferences, seminars and workshops. His main research interests are petroleum law, Human Rights, environmental law, and public international law.

Debasree Lahiri is UGC Junior Research Fellow at the Department of Law, Calcutta University, India. She has published articles on domestic violence, and offence. Her area of research is domestic violence.

Naorem Sanajaoba is Professor at the Department of Law, Guahati University, India. He has authored and edited about 25 books. He has 800 plus insertions in Google. His areas of interest are critical legal philosophy, jurisprudence, Human Rights, international humanitarian law, and administrative law.

Md. Jahid Hossain Bhuiyan teaches law in the Department of Law, ASA University Bangladesh (ASAUB), Dhaka, Bangladesh. He was coordinator of the Department of Law, Uttara University from 2005-06. He was also teacher at the Department of Law and Justice, Bangladesh University of Business and Technology. During his studies in Belgium he gained experience in legal practice with the lawyers of European countries. He has to his credit articles published in reputed journal of Australia, Bangladesh and India. He is co-editor of *International Humanitarian Law—An Anthology* (edited with Louise Dowsald-Beck and Azizur Rahman Chowdhury) (published by LexisNexis Butterworths in 2009). He is co-editor of his forthcoming co-edited book entitled *An Introduction to International Human Rights Law* to be published by BRILL (Martinus Nijhoff Publuishers), Netherlands in 2010. He is co-editor of his forthcoming co-edited book entitled *Compendium of International Humanitarian Law* to be published by LexisNexis in April 2009.

